The Real Genesis Creation Story

A Credible Translation and Explanation at Last

J. Gene White

Sunnybrooke Publications
ST. LOUIS, MO 63301
http://www.sunnybrookepub.com

Promoting the search for truth in a world of confusion

ISBN 978-1-4675-6870-8
First Edition

Scripture quotations marked "LHEIB" are taken from The Lexham Hebrew-English Interlinear Bible, Copyright © 2004 by Logos Research Systems Inc., Bellingham, WA. All rights reserved.

Scripture quotations marked "ESV" are taken from the Holy Bible, English Standard Version, Copyright © 2001 by Crossway Bibles, a division of Good News Publishers. The "ESV" and "English Standard Version" are registered trademarks. Used by permission. All rights reserved.

Scripture quotations marked "NKJV" are taken from the Holy Bible, New King James Version, Copyright © 1982 by Thomas Nelson, Inc. The "NKJV" and "New King James Version" are registered trademarks. Used by permission. All rights reserved.

Scripture quotations marked "NASB" are taken from the Holy Bible, New American Standard Bible, Copyright © 1960, 1962, 1963, 1968, 1971, 1972, 1973, 1975, 1977, 1995 by The Lockman Foundation. The "New American Standard Bible" is a registered trademark. Used by permission. All rights reserved.

Scripture quotations marked "NIV" are taken from the Holy Bible, New International Version, Copyright © 1973, 1978, 1984 by the International Bible Society. The "NIV" and "New International Version" are registered trademarks. Used by permission of Zondervan. All rights reserved.

Scripture quotations marked "NLT" are taken from the Holy Bible, New Living Translation, Copyright © 1996, 2004. The "New Living Translation" is a registered trademark. Used by permission of Tyndale House Publishers, Inc., Wheaton, Illinois 60189. All rights reserved.

Scripture quotations marked "The Message" are taken from The Message, Copyright © 1993, 1994, 1995, 1996, 2000, 2001, 2002. Used by permission of the NavPress Publishing Group. All rights reserved.

The following Bible translations referenced herein are public domain within the United States: William Tyndale's Pentateuch (1530), Myles Coverdale's Bible (1535), Noah Webster's Translation (1833), John Darby's Translation (1890), Robert Young's Literal Translation (1898), Douay-Rheims Bible (1899), American Standard Version (1901), World English Bible and King James Bible.

Table of Contents

Acknowledgements

I am deeply indebted to my wife, Karen, for her support during this entire project. She acted as a sounding board for many of my thoughts. By carefully reading the manuscript and then questioning my intent, she helped clarify several complex subjects. Her tender spirit and candid comments also infused civility into the discussion of several thorny issues.

I wish to thank Justin Watkins and Rhonda Barfield for editing and proofreading the initial manuscript and Jill Calkins for final proofreading. Appreciation is extended to the following individuals (in alphabetical order) for reviewing portions and in some cases the entire manuscript. Dr. Pat Campbell, a dedicated student of biblical origins, was especially helpful in pointing out errors and deficiencies in the original version of Chapters 2, 5, and 6. The assistance of these individuals does not necessarily indicate endorsement of the material presented herein.

Dr. Robert D. Bergen, Professor of Old Testament and Biblical Languages, Hannibal LaGrange College, Hannibal, MO.

Dr. Pat Campbell, Senior Pastor, Ridgecrest Baptist Church, St. Charles, MO

Dr. Gordon H. Johnston, Assistant Professor of Old Testament Studies, Dallas Theological Seminary.

Ben Merold, Senior Minister, Harvester Christian Church, St. Charles, MO

Rev. Jeff Spaulding, Senior Pastor, Faith United Methodist Church, St. Charles, MO

Dr. Roger C. Wiens, Physics, Space & Atmospheric Sciences Group at the Los Alamos National Laboratory.

Dr. Wilbur G. Williams, Professor of Biblical Literature and Archaeology, Indiana Wesleyan University.

Dr. Abraham Winitzer, Visiting Assistant Professor, Department of Theology, Notre Dame University.

Preface

Sometimes major events are accompanied by great fanfare, while at other times they come quietly in the night. In 2004, Logos Bible Software partially released their Hebrew-English interlinear version of the Old Testament (the full release followed several months later). Logos commissioned Professor Christo van der Merwe and his team of Hebrew scholars at the University of Stellenbosch in South Africa to translate the Old Testament. The end resultant of their labor is a highly consistent, crystal clear, interlinear translation in an electronic format for the personal computer.

Hebrew-English interlinear Bibles (the Old Testament Hebrew text with each corresponding English word underneath) have been around for a long time, and about every serious Bible student has one on his shelf. However, the print is often small and the text is difficult to follow. Although readable, the student has no way of knowing how a specific Hebrew word relates to the rest of scripture. In other words, is he looking at the *ad hoc* translation of a word or a consistent translation followed throughout the Old Testament? *The Lexham Hebrew-English Interlinear Bible* solves this problem by allowing the Bible student to rapidly and exhaustively search the Old Testament. For a given Hebrew word, every single occurrence can be quickly identified to permit viewing the exact spelling, root, and verse context. The Lexham Bible brings the study of the Old Testament into the twenty-first century.

Other software products that have markedly improved Bible study are electronic concordances that permit searching for English words of interest. Although *Strong's Exhaustive Concordance of the Bible* has been around since 1890, its use is tedious and time consuming. Software search programs represent a significant improvement. Although electronic word search programs lack the detail and thoroughness of the Lexham Bible, they are an important tool in the arsenal of the serious Bible student. One leading Internet program is the Blue Letter Bible at http://www.eliyah.com/lexicon.html. This powerful lexicon permits searching for English words, Strong's numbers, and word and number combinations. With the click of a mouse, one can view multiple English translations and a Hebrew or Greek lexicon. In addition, e-Sword, a free downloadable electronic version of Strong's Concordance, is available at http://www.e-sword.net/downloads.html.

Several websites offer multiple English translations of the Bible for viewing. Two useful sites are Bible Gateway at http://www.biblegateway.com/ and Bible Study Tools at http://www.biblestudytools.com/.

A number of biblical texts, courtesy of many dedicated individuals, are freely available on the Internet. These include several modern English Bible translations, a number of targums, and three Septuagint translations (Brenton, Pietersma and the Orthodox Study Bible). Some of the old English Bible translations available include Wycliffe's Bible of 1384, Tyndale's Pentateuch of 1530, the Coverdale Bible of 1535, The Bishop's Bible of 1568, The Geneva Bible of 1587, The Webster Bible of 1833, the Darby Translation of 1890, Young's Literal Translation of 1898, and the Douay-Rheims Version of 1899. All these have come on the scene with little fanfare, yet were invaluable in my study of Genesis.

In addition to the Internet, I referred to a number of books about systematic theology, creation, origins, grammar, and science related to Genesis Chapters 1 and 2.

I mention these resources to emphasize the number of aids available for studying the Bible. One fact became quite clear during 6,000 plus hours of research and writing; the Bible has been poked, prodded, and examined more closely than any other book in the history of man. I have found it to be truthful and trustworthy.

This book reflects the work of many people, and in a sense I stand on their shoulders. I am humbled by their efforts. Their contribution has been invaluable. Without *The Lexham Hebrew-English Interlinear Bible,* I would have never gained the insight necessary to understand Genesis. The development of a credible translation, explanation, and defense of the Bible creation story would have been impossible.

J. Gene White
G.White@sunnybrookepub.com

Be diligent to present yourself approved to God,
a worker who does not need to be ashamed, rightly
dividing the word of truth. (2 Timothy 2:15) NKJV

Chapter 1

The Battle over Biblical Creation

Charles B. Templeton, a close friend and contemporary of Billy Graham, was a rising star in the Christian evangelical world in the 1940s. Templeton's talent and enthusiasm for the gospel put him on an accelerated track to become a national religious figure. But before this could occur, he was convinced of the need for a good religious education. Although lacking the proper academic qualifications, Templeton was admitted to Princeton Theological Seminary as a "special student" at the age of thirty-three. While attending seminary, he became acutely aware of scientific evidence supporting an old age for the Earth, Darwinian evolution, and related theological issues. After completing seminary in 1951, he continued to wrestle with the apparent clash of science and the Bible. Finally, Templeton's doubts prevailed and in 1957 he abandoned his promising ministry for secular pursuits.

Near the end of his productive life in 1996, at the onset of Alzheimer's, Templeton wrote *Farewell to God: My Reasons for Rejecting the Christian Faith*. His basis for rejecting God began with the perceived conflict between scripture and science. He chose to trust the physicist, anthropologist, geneticist, and geologist rather than the theologian.[1] As Templeton said in his own words, "Whom should you believe, the Christian church or your own common sense?"[2] He was unable to reconcile evolution, with the apparent support of science, and the Bible.

Without question, Templeton made the wrong decision. He failed to separate the evidence of science from the inferences of science. He failed to consider the huge influence philosophical naturalism has on scientific thought. He did not understand that the real battle over origins is between the Bible and philosophical naturalism, rather than the Bible and science. He was never exposed to a significant critical analysis of evolutionary ideas. He fell short of realizing that thorny problems, including those of a biblical nature, can often be resolved with additional data and a new perspective. Based on a combination of incorrect scientific theory and errant theology, Templeton made a life changing mistake. Had better theory and theology been available, his decision might have been different.

Templeton was not an average preacher—he was a great preacher. He had a brilliant mind and could captivate audiences with the powerful, clear message of the gospel. His leadership abilities were extraordinary and, had he remained in the ministry, he might have eclipsed Billy Graham as a national figure. After leaving the ministry, Templeton began a successful career in news and broadcasting. He wrote a total of twelve books, with several being best sellers in Canada. One book was adapted for a movie. Using fame and fortune as a measuring stick, Templeton's achievements easily put him in the top one percent of the population.

Templeton died on June 7, 2001, due to a combination of failing health and Alzheimer's. He had a successful career and was eulogized by several newspapers and news services. Yet Templeton's death was tragic in many respects. Tragic in the sense his mind was destroyed by Alzheimer's and his Godly faith by philosophical naturalism. Tragic because he abandoned God based on a combination of errant theology and incorrect scientific theory about origins.

As illustrated by Templeton's life, what we think about origins, and specifically biblical creation, is important. As thinking people grow and mature, in one way or another, questions about "beginnings" are answered, whether through concentrated study or in sound bites and disconnected bits of information. This most likely occurs during the teenage years, but may also happen in college or later in life. The resulting answer affects our view of the Bible, moral values, science, and evolution. Everyone struggles in developing a worldview and, once established, it tends to set the course for the remainder of life.

Many consider Templeton's leaving the ministry an anomaly, while in reality it denotes a systemic problem. How many promising Bible students, ministers, educators, and Christian leaders must lose their faith because of a perceived conflict between the Bible and scientific evidence? Templeton's life is proof that the Genesis creation story is a significant issue for Christianity in the twenty-first century.

Division in the Ranks

Biblical origins are a significant issue for the church today. Although Christians readily accept God as creator of the heavens and Earth, explanations of the Genesis account vary widely. Bible believers are deeply divided over how to interpret Genesis Chapters 1 and 2. National surveys of American adults by Gallup, CBS News, Newsweek, and Pew Research have repeatedly tabulated this division. Approximately 44–50% of Americans more than 18 years old say they believe in traditional young-Earth creation, while 30–38% accept theistic evolution. About 12–14% believe in naturalistic evolution and 10% have no opinion. Due to the wording of these surveys, respondents are forced into a limited number of categories. The actual diversity of belief is much greater than indicated.

The debate regarding origins can be framed in several ways. Evolutionists often frame the debate between (1) science and faith, (2) science and religion, or (3) science and the Bible. Framing the debate in this manner is biased from inception. By inference, anything opposed to science must be false. Creationists more fairly frame the debate between creation and evolution. The conflict can be explained as a struggle between philosophical naturalism and the Bible. In a strict scientific sense, the issues can be viewed in terms of intelligent cause and natural cause.

For Christians, at this time, the most significant debate is not between creation and evolution, but between *creation* and *creation*. In other words, which interpretation of the biblical creation account is correct? Does the Bible give a creation account that is credible in light of the solid evidence amassed by twenty-first century science? Without a credible story of origins, the church cannot have a strong, unified front against the attacks of philosophical naturalism. Without a plausible explanation of Genesis, the Bible will continue to be attacked as false rather than truthful and trustworthy.

God as a powerful, intelligent, knowledgeable creator should be fully capable of inspiring an origins account that does not conflict with solid physical evidence. General revelation (the world about us) and special revelation (the Bible) should be capable of harmonizing with each other where they intersect. Skeptics and unbelievers have long criticized the biblical creation account for conflicting with scientific evidence, especially in regard to time.

Before Christians can hope to win the creation versus evolution debate, they must resolve the *creation* versus *creation* debate among themselves. Division concerning this issue has widened and deepened during the past two hundred years. At present, Bible believers are splintered in regard to interpreting the Genesis creation account with no resolution in sight.

Four leading ideas, with a biblical focus, have emerged to explain Genesis: (1) traditional young-Earth creation theology, (2) gap theology, (3) day-age theology, and (4) literary interpretations. A careful analysis of these different views helps shed light on their strengths and weaknesses. However, before beginning, the following statements represent the accepted fundamentals of this book and, although they may be occasionally referenced in succeeding chapters, they may not be discussed in detail. The foundational basics of this book are:

(1) God is creator of the heavens and Earth. (We can argue about the translation and explanation of Genesis using the Hebrew text of the Bible as our authority, in addition to relevant scientific evidence.)

(2) Noah's flood is a separate issue from the creation account and not discussed. (I believe there is a credible explanation for Noah's flood that respects the biblical account, yet harmonizes with scientific knowledge.)

(3) Scientific evidence in support of significant time is fully admissible. (Evidence supporting an old age for the heavens, Earth, and its biosphere are discussed in Chapter 4.)

(4) Natural cause has not demonstrated the ability to create design information, complex functional systems, mathematically improbable structures, and fine-tuned arrangements. The undirected laws of chemistry and physics are not a significant constructive mechanism, even given millions of years.

(5) God will not falsify evidence, lie, mislead, or deceive.

(6) We have a reliable copy of the Hebrew text of Genesis Chapters 1 and 2 that God inspired Moses to write.

Traditional Young-Earth Creation Theology

Traditional young-Earth creation theology is the oldest and most well-known explanation of biblical origins. The universe, Earth, and its biosphere (all biological life and their ecosystems) were created in six 24-hour days in the recent past around 4,000 BC. Young-Earth theology proposes that the Sun, Moon, and stars were created on the fourth day of the Genesis account. Adam and Eve were created on the sixth day. *The Genesis Record* by Henry Morris allows extending the creation date back to around 10,000 BC.[3] *Refuting Compromise* by Jonathan Sarfati, PhD, defends traditional young-Earth creation theology and points out this belief was the primary teaching of the church until 1800.[4]

Young-Earth creation theology has been the traditional belief of the church for more than two thousand years. This theology is supported by a host of Bible translations and commentaries. At the other extreme, most scientists and academics regard this theology as anti-intellectual because of its conflict with scientific evidence in regard to time. Rejection of this belief in Christian academia is quite common. For example, in 2004, the Institute for Creation Research conducted a survey of Christian colleges to identify what they teach about origins. Of 649 Protestant Christian colleges in the United States sent a questionnaire, 140 stated they teach only traditional young-Earth creation theology. Of that number, the great majority are small Bible colleges and seminaries.

Strengths:

(1) In orthodox English translations, the obvious first impression reading of Genesis 1:3–31 is that the heavens, Earth, and its biosphere (all biological life and their ecosystems) were created in six 24-hour days. The simple, straightforward language of the Genesis 1:3–31 clearly teaches the events took place in six days.

(2) The Hebrew word translated "day" in Genesis is *yom* (Strong's 03117). When *yom* is used in the context of six consecutive, numerically increasing, numbered days—bounded by evening and morning—they are literal 24-hour days.

(3) In Exodus 20:8–11, 31:12–17, and Deut. 5:12–15 the Sabbath is codified in

the Ten Commandments as a day of rest after six days of work, and uses the Genesis account as an example. The work days in Genesis are viewed as six literal days followed by a day of rest.

(4) An acceptance of the genealogies of the Old Testament, including Genesis Chapters 5 and 11, support a recent creation date for the Earth and universe. Anglican Archbishop James Ussher (1581–1656) calculated a widely accepted creation date of 4004 BC.

(5) Three ring radiohalos (discussed in Chapter 4) allegedly support Earth's recent creation.

(6) Proponents of this theology steadfastly believe in the inspiration and inerrancy of the Bible. The Bible is our only religious authority and the clear teaching of scripture must not be compromised.

(7) Leaders of this view clearly recognize the importance of the creation account and its influence on accepting the remainder of the Bible as true. They understand the significance of biblical origins.

Objections:

(1) Genesis 1:1 and 1:2 are not easily integrated into the rigid six-day time frame of Genesis 1:3–31. These two verses are problematic, and their removal from the creation account would be advantageous.

(2) Genesis 1:1, 1:2, and 1:3 are viewed as having little or no chronological significance.

(3) Within the six-day chronicle of Genesis 1:3–31, no mention is made of God creating the Earth.

(4) When God speaks in the alleged command verses of Genesis 1:3, 6, 9, 11, 14, 20, and 24, no good explanation is given for the absent dynamic verbs "create, make, form, plant, grow, and build."

(5) No good explanation is given for alleged repetitive "creative actions" on the second, fourth, fifth, and sixth days in Genesis 1:6–7, 14–17, 20–21, 24–25.

(6) Hypothetically, God made a temporary light to provide illumination until He created the Sun on the fourth day. The temporary light was then removed. No scripture directly supports this idea.

(7) Creation of the Sun on the fourth day is completely out of order. Logically, the Sun would have been created first to provide light and a large mass around which our planet could orbit.

(8) Within the last two hundred years scientists have discovered significant evidence (discussed in Chapter 4) supporting an old age for the heavens, Earth, and its biosphere—much older than a 4004 BC creation date. Evidence of significant time has accumulated to the point it will never be overturned.

(9) Apparent age (the idea that some things are quite young, although God created things with an appearance of age) cannot legitimately be used to explain away evidence of significant time. This argument makes God a great deceiver.

(10) Supporters of this theology do not acknowledge the addition, mistranslation, and poor translation of key words in Genesis Chapters 1 and 2 found in orthodox English Bibles.

Gap Theology

Gap theology was among the first alternate explanations to young-Earth creation theology and was developed because of the conflict between scientific evidence and orthodox translations of the Bible in regard to time. Thomas Chalmers (1780–1847), founder of the Free Church of Scotland, brought gap theology into prominence through his preaching.[5] *Earth's Earliest Ages,* first published in 1884 by George H. Pember, defends gap theology. The Scofield Reference Bible, published in 1917, promotes this theology in its explanatory notes of Genesis. *Without Form and Void,* published in 1970, by Arthur C. Custance promotes gap theology through an in-depth analysis of the word "was" in Genesis 1:2.

Gap theology proposes that millions of years occurred between Genesis 1:1 and 1:2. During this time, dinosaurs and other prehistoric animals lived, hydrocarbon reserves were formed, the fossil record was laid down, sediment layers were built, and geologic change occurred. According to Donald G. Barnhouse, the Earth was then ruined by God when Lucifer rebelled. Genesis 1:2 is translated to say, "And the earth became without form and empty."[6] Earth was subsequently reformed and re-populated during the six-day Genesis chronicle.

Gap theology is a knee-jerk reaction by theologians who failed to consider the full implications of their idea. To begin with, the translation of Genesis 1:2 is flawed. Secondly, although allowing significant time to occur between Genesis 1:1 and 1:2 may be reasonable, gap theology creates a new problem by proposing the complete destruction of Earth's surface and biosphere within the recent geologic past. Scientific evidence does not support the complete destruction and reconstruction of Earth 6,000 years ago.

Strengths:

(1) Genesis 1:1 and 1:2 are viewed as being outside the rigid six-day time frame of Genesis 1:3–31.

(2) Time is undefined between Genesis 1:1 and 1:2, and significant time (millions of years) is allowed to harmonize with scientific evidence in support of significant time.

(3) Genesis 1:1, 1:2, and 1:3 occur in a chronological sequence.

(4) This theology permits accepting the six days described in Genesis 1:3–31 as six 24-hour days.

(5) God is creator of the heavens and Earth. Natural cause (evolution) is not a significant constructive mechanism.

Objections:

(1) Gap theology requires the mistranslation of "was" as "became" to indicate change in Genesis 1:2. The Hebrew verb *hâyâh* (היתה), a stative state-of-being verb, is interpreted to indicate action.

(2) This theology relies on mistranslation of the Hebrew words *tôhûw* and *bôhûw* in Genesis 1:2. These two rhyming words have essentially the same meaning and should be translated "vacant and empty" to indicate the absence of life on Earth. Proponents of gap theology translate this expression as "without form and empty" or "ruin and desolation."

(3) This theology requires the Hebrew word *malé* in Genesis 1:22 and 1:28 be translated "refill" rather than "fill" to indicate God's desire for the Earth to be populated.

(4) The creation of light on the first day and creation of the Sun, Moon, and stars on the fourth day are not satisfactorily explained.

(5) The recent formation of Earth's continents and oceans is not supported by scientific evidence (dividing of the land from water on the third day).

(6) Supporters of this theology do not acknowledge the addition, mistranslation, and poor translation of key words in Genesis Chapters 1 and 2.

(7) Geology and paleontology do not support an event within the recent past that destroyed the Earth's surface to make it "without form and void." Scientific evidence does not support the complete annihilation and then reappearance of all life on Earth within the recent geologic past.

Day-Age Theology

Day-age theology is a second idea developed to force orthodox translations of the Bible to agree with scientific evidence in regard to time. Prior to 1800, Thomas Burnet, William Whiston, and Hermann Venema separately proposed that the six days of Genesis were long periods of time. In the 1800s, Professor Tayler Lewis of the Reformed Church of America advocated long ages in *The Six Days of Creation*. Donald MacDonald, a minister of the Free Church of Scotland, advocated the same in *Creation and the Fall: A Defence and Exposition of the First Three Chapters of Genesis*. Princeton theologians Charles Hodge, Archibald A. Hodge, and Benjamin Warfield supported a day-age approach.[7]

Day-age theology proposes that each day of the creation account was millions or billions of years long and the days may have overlapped. The recent book, *A Matter of Days* by Hugh Ross, PhD, discusses day-age theology and its connection with time, natural cause, and evolution. Accepting each day as millions of years relegates significant portions of the Genesis creation story to a metaphorical explanation. This idea is a brute-force, frontal assault on the clear language of six days described in Genesis 1:3–31. Rather than being an interpretation, this theology is more of an outright rejection of the biblical language.

Strengths:

(1) This theology allows for millions of years to occur to harmonize with scientific evidence in support of significant time.

(2) The seventh day does not close with the expression, "And the evening and the morning were the seventh day." Supporters of this theology believe God did not end the seventh day and is currently resting. Accordingly, if the seventh day can be thousands of years long, then the six work days can be millions and billions of years long.

(3) An analysis of family lineages in the Old and New Testament reveals that the genealogies in Genesis Chapters 5 and 11 do not require a direct father-to-son relationship. Gaps in the Genesis genealogies permit extending the appearance of man on Earth backward in time.

Objections:

(1) Day-age theology does not provide a satisfactory explanation for treating the six days described in Genesis 1:3–31 as long epochs of time. Significant time is forced into the text.

(2) The Hebrew word translated "day" in Genesis is *yom* (Strong's 03117). When *yom* is used in the context of six consecutive, numerically increasing, numbered days—bounded by evening and morning—they are literal 24-hour days. Context does not allow *yom* to be interpreted as millions of years.

(3) The Hebrew word *yom* (Strong's 03117) occurs 2,287 times in the Old Testament and is translated "day" 2,008 times, "time" 64 times, and "daily" 44 times in addition to other miscellaneous words in the KJV.[8]

(4) The overlap of days is not supported by the language of the six-day Genesis chronicle.

(5) Supporters say the Earth was covered by clouds for millions of years during the first three creation days. The Sun, Moon, and stars were incapable of being observed during this time. This is not a credible explanation.

(6) No satisfactory explanation is given for creation of the Sun, Moon, and stars on the fourth day. Many stars are older than our solar system. Logically, the Sun and its attendant light would have been created before the Earth. The events of this day are completely out of sequence.

(7) Trees and plants are created on the third day and marine life is created on the fifth day. According to the geological record, marine life appeared before land based trees and plants. Simply saying that each day is millions of years long does not correct this sequence problem.

(8) Some proponents of this theology accept naturalistic evolution as a significant constructive mechanism. Galaxies, stars, planets, and our solar system evolved following the Big Bang strictly due to natural cause.

(9) Supporters of this theology do not acknowledge the addition, mistranslation, and poor translation of key words in orthodox English translations of Genesis Chapters 1 and 2.

Literary Interpretations

The literary interpretation of Genesis 1:3–31 is a third idea developed to make orthodox translations of the Bible agree with scientific evidence in regard to time. One literary interpretation, analogical days, as explained by Dr. C. John Collins, "are God's workdays, their length is neither specified nor important, and not everything in the account needs to be taken as historically sequential."[9] Collins explains his idea in *Genesis 1–4: A Linguistic, Literary and Theological Commentary*. Another closely related literary interpretation is the framework view championed by Meredith G. Kline, described as "a literary framework for us to understand the work of creation, without committing anyone to see the days as either sequential or normal."[10] Both the analogical day position and framework view treat the six-day Genesis chronicle as significantly metaphorical.

Literary interpretations of Genesis Chapter 1 essentially place the six-day chronicle outside scientific examination. The creation account becomes an imaginative tale with little or no historical basis. While this approach may eliminate any conflict with scientific evidence, acceptance comes at the expense of scripture. Such an interpretation leads one to question God's knowledge of origins and His ability to inspire the writing of a credible account.

Literary interpretations are a subtle, yet aggressive assault on the clear language of six days described in Genesis 1:3–31. Literary interpretations are quite similar to day-age theology, which proposes the days are millions of years long and overlapping. As an additional feature, literary interpretations allow the sequence of days to be rearranged. The highly structured, clear language of six, literal, sequential days is completely dismissed.

On the positive side, Collins' discussion of Genesis contributes to a better understanding of some portions of the creation story. For example, Genesis 1:1–2 lie outside the rigid six-day time frame. The initial creation of the heavens and Earth in Genesis 1:1, and the description of Earth in Genesis 1:2 occur in chronological order, followed by Genesis 1:3. Genesis 2:5 applies to a land that was dry and barren where the garden was to be planted rather than the entire Earth.

Strengths:

(1) Genesis 1:1 and 1:2 are outside the rigid six-day time frame as described in Genesis 1:3–31.[11]

(2) Genesis 1:1, 1:2, and 1:3 occur in a chronological order.[12]

(3) The six days of Genesis 1:3–31 are rearranged to solve sequence problems based on scientific evidence. For example, the existence of plants on the third day for millions of years before creation of the Sun and Moon on the fourth day is a sequence problem.

(4) Genesis 2:4–25 is viewed as a detailed account of the sixth day given in Genesis 1:24–31.

(5) Genesis 2:5 is interpreted as applying to a land that was dry and barren where the garden was to be planted, rather than the entire Earth.[13]

(6) Literary interpretations allow for millions of years to harmonize with scientific evidence in support of significant time.

Objections:

(1) Literary interpretations do not provide a satisfactory explanation for treating the six days described in Genesis 1:3–31 as long epochs of time. Acceptance is at the expense of a straightforward reading of scripture.

(2) When *yom* is used in the context of six consecutive, numerically increasing, numbered days—bounded by evening and morning—they are literal 24-hour days. Context does not suggest a metaphorical explanation.

(3) The credibility of Genesis 1:3–31 as an accurate story of origins is destroyed by allowing the six days to be millions of years, the days to overlap and the order of days to be rearranged.

(4) Supporters of a literary interpretation do not acknowledge the addition, mistranslation, and poor translation of key words in orthodox English translations of Genesis Chapters 1 and 2.

Each of the above four theologies has its strengths and weaknesses. Traditional young-Earth creation theology accepts a straightforward reading of orthodox translations of Genesis Chapter 1, although it strongly conflicts with scientific evidence regarding time. Gap theology allows for significant time, but is not supported by the Hebrew text or science. Day-age theology and literary interpretations allow for significant time, but at the expense of scripture. Words used to describe the six 24-hour days are essentially irrelevant. Rather than being an interpretation, the Genesis story is essentially dismissed as a credible historical account. One common theme among all four approaches is the afore mentioned failure to recognize the addition, mistranslation, and poor translation of key words in orthodox English translations of Genesis Chapters 1 and 2.

In addition to the above, belief that the Genesis creation story is a compilation of pagan mythology is quite popular in some religious circles. Some individuals think the creation account represents a collection of Sumerian, Egyptian, Babylonian, Assyrian, and Canaanite stories. Poetical and metaphorical expressions in Job, Psalms, Proverbs, and Isaiah are given to support the argument that the Bible is full of incorrect scientific information. Common themes and words in scripture are tenuously connected to pagan mythology and used by critics to attack the Bible as untrue.

The reasoning of critics is similar to taking present-day factual events and then discounting their credibility by connecting common words and themes with those found in fictional works. For example, with this type of logic the account of man's walk on the Moon can be accused of being false because of its connection to hundreds of science fiction books, short stories, and movies. Bible believers can reject this type of fallacious reasoning.

Genesis and the remainder of the Old Testament were written by righteous men who rejected the spurious beliefs of the surrounding cultures. The Bible clearly states that the Hebrews repeatedly worshipped idols, adopted false religions, embraced pagan practices, and married outside their faith in disobedience to God. The nation of Israel repeatedly violated the Ten Commandments and turned away from God. Scripture plainly documents their unfaithfulness. So while it is true that many Israelites were influenced by the false beliefs of the people around them, this does not require the Genesis creation story to be an amalgamation of Egyptian and Babylonian beliefs. A remnant, although small in number at times, was always faithful and rejected the pagan ideas and practices of their contemporaries.

A number of other explanations related to the above, ranging from heretical to bizarre, have been developed in an attempt to reconcile scripture and scientific evidence. One or two ideas combine elements of all four approaches, and all alternate proposals rely heavily on metaphorical or mythological explanations of the biblical text. In general, developers have abandoned the language of Genesis in favor of their own private interpretations.

Theistic Evolution

Evolution with a religious flavor, known as theistic evolution, has emerged as a fifth explanation of origins. Descriptions of this belief vary among individuals depending on their knowledge of the Bible, science, evolution, design theory, and philosophy. A layman's definition may vary significantly from that of the scientist.

Theistic evolution is the belief that God, or some cosmic deity, used natural cause as his primary mechanism to create the universe and all therein. *Significant time is directly equated with naturalistic evolution.* Some proponents believe God started things in the beginning and occasionally stepped in to jump-start natural processes when they stalled out. Typically, God's role in creating is minimized and natural cause is maximized. A prevalent theme among adherents is the belief that humans evolved from lower animals according to Darwinian or neo-Darwinian theory.

For some, theistic evolution is an attempt to combine philosophical naturalism with faith in God as taught in the Bible—two antithetical viewpoints. Philosophical naturalism is a belief that the quest for knowledge is limited to explanations that are natural, mechanistic, and material. In regard to origins, natural cause and significant time have resulted in all life, Earth, our solar system, and the universe. Philosophical naturalism can be summarized as, "Nature is all there is and all basic truths are truths of nature."[14] Philosophical naturalists reject all theistic influence—there is no omnipotent, creator God. Philosophical naturalism requires natural cause to be a powerful constructive mechanism.

One of reasons for the rise of theistic evolution is the conflict between young-

Earth creation theology and scientific evidence in support of significant time. Although many Christian leaders say the Bible and scientific evidence do not conflict, they have failed to explain areas where they *appear* to conflict. Proponents typically state that the Bible is not a scientific book (which is true); however, they have failed to explain biblical statements that *appear* to conflict with scientific evidence. Biblical leaders claim that we have made the Bible say things it doesn't in regard to origins, yet they have failed to clarify what scripture *truly says.*

It appears that theistic evolutionists want to believe in God, yet desire respect from other scientists who accept evolution as a scientific fact. Theistic evolutionists attempt to straddle the fence between believing in God and philosophical naturalism. However, as William Dembski points out, the Darwinist establishment despises theistic evolution.[15] From a Darwinist perspective, naturalistic evolution provides an all-encompassing explanation of origins and is fully capable of creating all that we observe in nature and the universe at large. Biblical-based belief in God is not allowed a single fragmentary scrap of credibility.

The limitations of natural cause should be addressed before stating that God used evolution as His method of creating the universe and all therein. Proponents of natural cause as an all-encompassing explanation of origins often say, "Evolution is a fact." However, when we accurately evaluate natural cause, this statement loses essentially all its force. Natural cause over time as a *destructive mechanism* is fully capable of wearing away, deteriorating, and randomizing—a fact. Natural cause over time as a *weak constructive mechanism* is capable of building simple structures represented by snowflakes, mineral crystals, concretions, freeze-thaw rock circles, sand dune formations, caves, dried mud crack patterns, eroded structures, sand particles, salt grains, rocks, and basic molecules—a fact. Natural cause over time as an alleged *powerful constructive mechanism* has not demonstrated the ability to create design information, complex functional systems, mathematically improbable structures, and fine-tuned arrangements observed in nature and the universe at large—also a fact. Random, naturally directed, purposeless, mechanistic change is severely limited as constructive mechanisms. Although we can correctly say evolution happens, the limited changes observed do not support naturalistic evolution as an all-encompassing explanation of origins.

If God wanted to use evolution as His creative mechanism, is it possible? If God wanted to get things started and then remove himself completely from any further involvement, could natural cause create the universe and all therein? The answer is best given in the form of an illustration. When a new automobile is completed and rolls off the assembly line, the resultant vehicle is one hundred percent the product of human achievement. Engineers have selected and combined a multitude of metals and non-metals to create the structures and systems that represent an automobile. By the controlled application of the laws of chemistry and physics on selected materials, skilled technicians have made a complex, fine-tuned, functional machine. Generically speaking, intelligent cause has built a non-natural, extra-natural, and in fact supernatural product completely beyond the ability of natural cause.

So if engineers wanted to use evolution (natural cause) as their mechanism to build an automobile, is it possible? Absolutely not! Suppose engineers jump start the process by collecting iron, copper, and aluminum ore in a pile, combined with silica sand and several gallons of crude oil—all the requisite raw materials. At that point, if all they did was observe and wait, we would not have a single automobile, even given billions of years. Undirected change cannot produce a machine of this nature. And if engineers assist in the developmental process in any way, then whatever is accomplished is due to intelligent cause rather than natural cause. Likewise, God could not have used natural cause throughout time as His constructive mechanism. When uncontrolled and unsequenced, the laws of chemistry and physics are incapable of building anything of significance. Evolution is not false because it is godless, atheistic, amoral, cruel, slow, wasteful, and uncaring, as stated by some, but because natural cause is not a significant constructive mechanism.

One prominent believer in theistic evolution is Dr. Francis S. Collins, head of the Human Genome Project and author of *The Language of God*. In his book, Collins defines six basic points of theistic evolution, paraphrased as follows.[16]

(1) The universe came into being out of nothingness approximately 14 billion years ago. (No mention is made of God.)

(2) The universe appears to have been precisely fine-tuned for life despite the extremely small probability. (God is not referenced as the cause.)

(3) Life originated on Earth, although the precise mechanism is unknown. (No appeal is made to God, and no plausible natural mechanism is identified.)

(4) Once life arose and biological evolution got underway, no special supernatural intervention was required. (Collins never says where God was required.) The process of random change and natural selection resulted in the development of Earth's many diverse and complex species throughout long periods of time. (In a leap of faith, Collins appeals to these limited mechanisms.)

(5) Humans are a result of the biological evolution process and share a common ancestry with the great apes. (God is not identified as man's creator.)

(6) Humans are unique in ways that defy an evolutionary explanation. Our spiritual nature is shown by the existence of Moral Law—the knowledge of right and wrong—and the search for God that characterizes all human cultures throughout history. (No appeal is made to the Bible as the basis for our belief in God or as an ethical, moral, or religious authority.)

Evolutionists typically frame the debate regarding origins as between science and faith, between science and religion, or between science and the Bible. By implication, any position in opposition to science is false. According to their view, science deals in facts and biblical belief is strictly faith-based. The two exist in completely separate realms.

Science can be defined as a rational search for dependable knowledge about the world in which we live based on physical evidence and its logical inferences. Science as a truth-seeking process does not have an inherent position about origins. One meaningful way to frame the origins debate is between natural cause and intelligent cause, with scientific evidence as the arbitrator. These two competing ideas can be evaluated based on (1) the amount of specifically supportive evidence, (2) the amount of discrediting evidence, (3) failed or successful experiments, (4) the ability or inability to plausibly explain important phenomena within the realm of applicable theory, and (5) failed or successful predictions.

Theistic evolutionists often accept natural cause as a total explanation of origins, yet claim to believe in God. They typically consider the Genesis story and related verses as myth. Their belief requires ignoring the severe limitations of natural cause to create design information, complex functional systems, mathematically improbable structures, and fine-tuned arrangements. Advocates of theistic evolution readily appeal to natural metaphysical cause, which they believe is somehow more logical and satisfying than appealing to intelligent cause. Collins condemns "God of the gaps" type thinking[17] although he apparently has no issue with appeals to unknown phenomena and natural metaphysical cause to fill in the gaps.

Theistic evolutionists may be people of faith; however, the god they believe in has little relation to the God of the Bible. Their god is distant and uncaring, lacking the desire, power, or intelligence to create anything. He is a fuzzy, ill-defined, universal, cosmic kind of god. In fact, he may be nonexistent and simply a product of wishful thinking.

Intelligent Design

Intelligent design (ID) has emerged as a sixth way of explaining origins and is a scientific alternative to evolution. Intelligent design proposes that some phenomena in nature are best explained as the result of intelligent cause rather than natural cause.[18] The search for intelligent directed action encompasses cosmology, the origin of life, and the development of Earth's many species.[19]

Opponents of intelligent design attempt to connect it with creationism, the Bible, and religious belief. By making this connection, they attempt to discredit intelligent design as a legitimate scientific enterprise. Intelligent design is not creationism and is not based on the Bible. One primary distinction between the two is that creationists start with the Bible and then attempt to reconcile scientific evidence with their belief. In contrast, ID starts with scientific evidence and then draws certain inferences from that information. A second important difference is that the Bible clearly identifies God as the sole creator of the universe. In comparison, ID has no requirement to identify a specific designer.

We should realize that *all theories of origin* have profound philosophical and religious implications. All ideas of origin can be interpreted within a framework of either natural cause or intelligent cause. Ideas of natural cause can be construed to support atheism, philosophical naturalism, and secular humanism. In a similar vein, ideas of intelligent cause can be accused of promoting religion and belief in God. From a scientific perspective, acceptance or rejection of a theory should be based on the data and not its philosophical and religious implications.

Design theory in support of the concept of intelligent design is based on: (1) Dependable knowledge about the physical world in the form of verified empirical data (2) Acceptance of the severe limitations of natural cause as a constructive mechanism. (3) Human design as an aid to identify generic design in nature.[20]

(1) Dependable knowledge – The first leg of design theory is founded on dependable knowledge about the physical world based on observation, measurement, and experimentation. Design theory relies on the evidence of empirical science. Design theory rests on a comprehensive understanding of nature and the universe at large—both its capabilities and limitations. Scientific research and increasing scientific knowledge are the foundation on which design theory is built.

(2) Limitations of natural cause – The second leg of design theory is based on accepting the severe limitations of natural cause as a constructive mechanism. Purposeless change as a destructive mechanism can wear away, deteriorate, and randomize. Mechanistic change can build simple structures such as snowflakes, mineral crystals, rocks, and basic molecules. Naturally directed change (i.e., random beneficial mutations in a species genome acted on by natural selection) has not shown itself to be a powerful constructive mechanism. Natural cause has not demonstrated the ability to build design information, complex functional structures, systems with numerous fine-tuned variables, and mathematically improbable objects. The severe limitations of natural cause compel the consideration of design theory.

(3) Applied science – A third leg of design theory is based on understanding *human design* as an aid to recognizing *generic design* in the world about us. Beginning with the industrial revolution two centuries ago, human design has made dramatic advances and is responsible for the explosion of technical products beneficial to mankind. By a careful analysis of human design, its phenomena, characteristics, categories, and traits can be identified, which in turn helps us recognize generic design found in nature (e.g., the eye, ear and thyroid system). In contrast to natural cause, humans can create design information, complex functional systems, mathematically improbable structures, and fine-tuned arrangements. Human design has identifiable features separate from natural cause.

In regard to the biblical account of creation, views vary significantly among scientists who are proponents of intelligent design. Some supporters of ID are not Bible believers at all, and accept other philosophies or religions to explain intelligent cause. Leading ID proponents who believe in God overwhelmingly accept an old age for the universe, Earth, and its biosphere, based on scientific evidence. Significant time is explained in the Genesis story by some of the theologies mentioned.

Christians must realize that intelligent design is primarily a scientific idea rather than a theological enterprise. Intelligent design poses a serious challenge to philosophical naturalism and ancillary evolutionary thinking, and most Bible believers view the movement as positive. However, ID cannot help Bible believers with their errant theology. The church is at war with philosophical naturalism and must fight its own battles. An important part of winning this war is the development of credible, biblically based, and scientifically sound origins theology.

On the Horns of a Dilemma

Young-Earth creation, gap theology, day-age theology, and literary interpretations all have major biblical and scientific issues, and give a small indication of the absolutely chaotic condition of current biblical-based origins belief. Proponents attempt to force the evidence to fit their respective ideas. When carefully analyzed, these four different explanations of Genesis Chapters 1 and 2 are analogous to driving a square peg into a round hole—the pieces do not fit.

At this point, the rational a truth-seeker finds himself on the horns of a dilemma. If he accepts traditional young-Earth creation theology, he is impaled by the horn of science. To deny firm scientific evidence is to commit intellectual suicide. However, if he accepts scientific evidence, then he is impaled on the other horn by dishonoring the biblical text. To deny the words of Genesis, is to deny God's knowledge of origins and His ability to inspire a credible written account.

All present explanations of the creation account either conflict with scientific evidence in regard to significant time or violate the clear language of orthodox Bible translations. They fail to respect the language of the biblical text. Currently, no one has developed a credible explanation. A number of evangelical theologians and Hebrew scholars reject traditional young-Earth creation theology, yet not a single one has constructed a plausible alternative. Because a good explanation is lacking, Christian laymen have adopted a number of different beliefs. Most accept one of the four theologies mentioned, while others have created their own private theological mixture. A few have adopted theistic evolution.

A sampling of available material illustrates the diversity of belief about the Genesis creation account and the intractable problem it presents. For example, Bible Study Fellowship International, headquartered in San Antonio, Texas, is a fifty-year-old organization that promotes serious Bible study among laymen. Class members in more than 1,000 study groups meet weekly. The BSF study materials for Genesis briefly discuss several different ideas, which include evolution, intelligent design, theistic evolution, gap theory, literal six-day creation, and day-age theology. The twenty-four-page lesson series fails to resolve any of the problems with Genesis. Students are left without a credible solution, although perhaps slightly more informed about the different explanations.

On a much higher academic level, in 2000, the 28th General Assembly of the Presbyterian Church in America (PCA) received a 44,000-word report by the Creation Study Committee about the interpretation of Genesis. The thirteen-member committee consisted of professors, academics, and theologians. In the report, strengths and objections for a number of interpretations are discussed, including calendar-day, gap, day-age, and analogical days theology. They concluded that Genesis Chapters 1 to 3 are the inerrant word of God and are historical and true. Adam and Eve were real human beings and not a product of evolution from a lower life form. No consensus could be reached about the nature and duration of the creation days. They presented "a unanimous report with the understanding that the members hold to different exegetical viewpoints."[21] They recommended that the General Assembly of the PCA affirm acceptance of the different ideas covered in the report as long as the creation account is treated as historical.[22]

Books by leading academics, theologians, and teachers represent a third category of discourse to address the Genesis problem. Books by Dr. Bruce K. Waltke, Dr. Allen P. Ross, Dr. James M. Boice, Dr. C. John Collins, Dr. John H. Sailhamer, Dr. Meredith G. Kline, and Dr. John MacArthur represent some of the current diverse ideas about biblical origins. One of the better books on the subject, first published in French in 1979, is *In the Beginning: The Opening Chapters of Genesis* by Dr. Henri Blocher, a French professor of systematic theology. Blocher describes the four major theological viewpoints as: (1) A literal interpretation typically known as young-Earth creation theology. (2) A reconstruction interpretation usually known as gap theology. (3) The concordist interpretation commonly known as day-age theology. (4) The literary interpretation represented by framework theology. He discusses biblical and scientific issues applicable to each of the four approaches, both pro and con. Although Blocher offers no solution to the Genesis problem, he advances the cause by clearly delineating most of the major issues in an objective fashion. Blocher accepts an old created Earth, yet rejects biological evolution. He rejects a common ancestry of man and apes due to evolution, although admits hominids have walked our planet for tens of thousands of years.[23] Considering when it was written, Blocher's book is remarkably thorough and insightful.

Within Christian circles, a "big tent" approach has emerged as an interim solution. As long as the Genesis story is considered historical, interpretations can vary widely. Unfortunately, every idea thus far proposed is about as invalid as the next. While Christians may find unity in a "big tent" approach, no idea has emerged that solves the apparent conflict between the Bible and scientific evidence in regard to time, *while respecting the biblical text*. Christians lack a credible response to atheists, philosophical naturalists, secular humanists, and biblical skeptics.

Lack of a credible explanation for Genesis has had a profound negative affect on Christian colleges and universities. Bible colleges and theological seminaries can essentially ignore scientific evidence, and teach biblical origins as they desire. On the other hand, Christian colleges that offer degrees in medicine, engineering, biology, archaeology, astronomy, anthropology, and other sciences are forced to confront the apparent clash of Genesis with scientific evidence in regard to time. In many cases, science professors who teach at Christian colleges reject the Genesis creation account and completely embrace natural cause as an explanation of origins. For example, Baylor University, the largest Baptist college in the United States, at their Department of Biology website proudly makes the following statement:

> Evolution, a foundational principle of modern biology, is supported by overwhelming scientific evidence and is accepted by the vast majority of scientists. Because it is fundamental to the understanding of modern biology, the faculty in the Biology Department at Baylor University, Waco, TX, teach evolution throughout the biology curriculum. We are in accordance with the American Association for Advancement of Science's statement on evolution. We are a science department, so we do not teach alternative hypotheses or philosophically deduced theories that cannot be tested rigorously.[24]

The Baylor Biology Department teaches naturalistic evolution and, in conjunction with the Department of Anthropology, promotes the evolution of humans from an animal ancestor.[25] In general, their science departments are openly hostile to any consideration of intelligent design. From their perspective, evolution is a fact and alternate explanations need not be explored. All Christian colleges, regardless of their denominational affiliation, are headed in the same direction as Baylor. Without a credible biblical explanation of origins, apostasy is only a matter of time and administration turnover. Ideas have consequences.

Intelligent, talented, educated, and motivated Christians of sound judgment want a credible solution to the Genesis problem. Lack of a solution will continue the erosion of church leadership from the loss of capable people who require credible answers about biblical-based origins theology. Failure to find a solution will allow philosophical naturalism and its workhorse, naturalistic evolution, to maintain their domination of intellectual high ground within higher religious education, the church, and personal Christian belief.

Most pastors and religious leaders knowledgeable about the complexities of biblical origins typically address the problem by avoiding it. They are smart enough to recognize the lack of a plausible solution. Publicly, they may give lip service to one of the above theologies. Privately, they admit that no credible solution exists when considering both the Bible and scientific evidence in regard to time. This is reflected in the absence of preaching about the Genesis creation account from the church pulpit and in church literature targeting adults. And so, the truth-seeker is left to fend for himself in a world hostile to biblical belief.

Solution to a Dilemma

At this juncture in my personal study, I felt trapped. After more than two hundred years, the brightest theological minds had failed to come up with a good solution to the Genesis problem. There appeared to be no plausible explanation, but on further reflection I felt there should be one. God, as described in the Bible, is intelligent, knowledgeable, wise, and powerful—fully capable of orchestrating the creation story and inspiring Moses to accurately record it. Based on my understanding of God, He is competent for such a task.

God does not falsify evidence, lie, mislead, or deceive; however, man is not bound by any such limitations. Humanity's misdeeds are capable of filling volumes. I suspected the problem had to be with man and not God. Men have copied the original Hebrew text that Moses wrote and passed those copies down through the centuries. Using textual criticism, men have compiled various Hebrew manuscripts into a standardized version. In addition, men have translated the Hebrew text into English. This led me to question if men had tinkered with the text of Genesis. This questioning was reinforced by a critical study of the language of Genesis Chapters 1 and 2 found in English translations.

As a starting point, I decided to verify translation of the Hebrew text of Genesis Chapters 1 and 2 into English. From my professional training and experience, going back to the original source of information is important in strong conflicts of this nature—secondary knowledge is always suspect. My first major purchase was software containing *The Lexham Hebrew-English Interlinear Bible* by Logos Research Systems of Bellingham, Washington. This Bible is based on the *Biblia Hebraica Stuttgartensia*, an edition of the Masoretic text accepted by Hebrew scholars.

The digital format of the Lexham version gives a crisp, clear, word-for-word translation from the Old Testament Hebrew text. The powerful Boolean search capability permits studying Hebrew words of interest and allows checking for consistent translation and usage—an absolute necessity based on my investigative approach. I was able to perform exhaustive word studies in a matter of minutes that would normally take weeks or months. The Lexham Bible allows serious students to examine in detail the transformation of the Old Testament into English through the eyes of skilled Hebrew scholars.

To begin with, I cleared the creation story and all associated verses off the table. I then began verifying the story one word at a time. Each word was copied from the Hebrew Bible without any interpretative framework in mind; however, every word was rigorously checked to ensure its translation was legitimately supported elsewhere in the Old Testament. There was no attempt to connect verses, develop a rational flow of events, or integrate science and scripture. Early on, Genesis 1:2 to be exact, I realized something was amiss with orthodox English translations. After completing the first two chapters, smoothing out the wording, and making some adjustments, a different creation story emerged. Based on my knowledge of science, I quickly developed an explanatory framework. When correctly translated, the Genesis creation story easily harmonized with scientific evidence in regard to time. I found that approximately ninety-eight percent of the words in orthodox translations of Genesis Chapters 1 and 2 are satisfactorily translated, but the remaining two percent seriously distort the original story. The mistranslated words are quite subtle yet have a significant impact on one's understanding of the account. At that point, my personal Bible study expanded rapidly and writing this book became inevitable.

Based on my findings, a shocking deception unfolded. Young-Earth creation theology has been embedded into all orthodox translations of the Old Testament. This influence extends beyond Genesis into other verses related to the creation story. Rules of Hebrew grammar have been fabricated and key words have been intentionally mistranslated to support this errant theology. This deception has been ongoing for more than two thousand years and is deeply ingrained within biblical theology and scholarship.

Hebrew scholars and theologians are naturally skeptical that an error of this magnitude could exist. However, when the Hebrew text is carefully examined, the evidence is undeniable. Chapters 5 and 6 and Appendix B substantiate this trail of deceptive information.

Bible scholars are further skeptical that a scientific professional could discover a solution to the creation problem, and although improbable, it is not impossible. In this regard, the majority of books written within the past thirty years in an attempt to resolve both the theological and scientific issues of Genesis have been authored by scientists, engineers, physicians, and lawyers, all speaking partially outside their professional specialties.

It is interesting to note that several individuals have made significant contributions to the advancement of science, technology, and religion outside their areas of formal training. Thomas Young (1773–1829), a physician and physicist best known for Young's modulus, made an important contribution to deciphering the Rosetta Stone. Two bicycle mechanics, Orville and Wilbur Wright, bested the most brilliant scientific minds of the time and built the first successful airplane. Henry M. Morris, a PhD in hydraulic engineering, completely revitalized young-Earth creation theology in America. Bill Gates, a college dropout (not because of a lack of intelligence or drive), started the Microsoft Corporation with little formal scientific or business training and became one of the wealthiest people in America. Phillip Johnson, a law professor, essentially started the modern intelligent design movement by writing *Darwin on Trial*.

I realize that advancements within specialized areas of knowledge normally come from formally trained professionals (in this case Hebrew and theology), but this is not an absolute requirement. The search for truth cannot be restricted to a select group of people. In respect to biblical origins, I believe it is easier for an individual with a science background to cross over into theology than for the reverse to occur. Information found in the Bible about the creation story is quite limited, while related science is broad and covers many specialized disciplines including biology, genetics, chemistry, physics, geology, archaeology, paleontology, anthropology, and astronomy. Hebrew scholars and theologians whose knowledge is primarily confined to scripture become quickly entangled and overwhelmed by the scientific complexities involved. They find it difficult to distinguish between fact, theory, hypothesis, conjecture, and speculation, when commingled together in science publications. (Scientists often struggle with this issue when reading outside their specialty.) Typically, scientific articles about origins, driven by a firm belief in philosophical naturalism, commingle fact and conjecture with little pretense of a difference.

In defense of my work, keep in mind it is based on books written by skilled Hebrew scholars. For example, numerous Hebrew scholars have compiled and edited the *Biblia Hebraica Stuttgartensia*, the basis of today's Hebrew text. *The Lexham Hebrew-English Interlinear Bible* is a conservative translation by nine Hebrew scholars and used as the basis for my translation. I sometimes refer to *A Hebrew and English Lexicon of the Old Testament* written by the Hebrew scholars Francis Brown, S. R. Driver, and Charles A. Briggs. *Strong's Exhaustive Concordance of the Bible* written by James Strong, a Hebrew scholar, is often referenced in my book. Most of my word studies are based on the well-accepted King James Version. Most Bible versions referenced in my book have been translated by teams of Hebrew scholars. The basis of my work rests firmly on a foundation of Hebrew language professionals.

My approach to understanding Genesis focuses on identifying words that have been poorly or illegitimately translated from the Hebrew Bible. The unique translation of words applicable only to Genesis, and unsupported by usage elsewhere in the Old Testament, is forbidden. Obviously created homographs (words spelled the same but with a different meaning) are disallowed. Special rules of grammar that apply to the creation story are likewise rejected. The KJV is used as the prime reference when analyzing Hebrew words and their frequency of translation into English. I fully discuss the rationale for my translation in Chapters 5 and 6 and Appendix B of this book. Confirmation of my work lies well within the capability of any serious Bible student.

And you shall know the truth, and the truth shall make you free. (John 8:32) NKJV

Chapter 2

Exemplar Creation: The Original Story

According to traditional young-Earth creation theology, God created the Earth around 4004 BC by speaking it into existence. Initially the Earth was without form and void (a mixed up ball of water and dirt). During six literal days, the Earth was totally transformed. In the first three days, God created light, formed the sky, separated land from water, and created plants to cover the Earth. On the fourth day, the Sun, Moon, and stars were spoken into existence. On the fifth and sixth days, God created marine life, flying creatures, and land-dwelling animals. Lastly, man was created in the image and likeness of God.

While this theology has been taught for hundreds of years, in the twenty-first century we are faced with addressing the truthfulness of the traditional biblical creation narrative. Is the Genesis story really true, especially in regard to time? If not true, then what does the Bible say about origins? In light of the controversy regarding this issue, we must be absolutely sure we correctly understand the text that God inspired Moses to write.

The *exemplar* translation of Genesis Chapters 1 and 2 is a careful rendering of the Hebrew text based on the *Biblia Hebraica* (Hebrew Bible). God-inspired scripture is treated with respect. The word *exemplar* means "original" in Latin, and refers to the original Genesis creation story recorded by Moses in the Pentateuch. The primary focus of *exemplar* creation is a credible translation and explanation of the creation account, with a secondary objective of harmonizing special and general revelation. Special revelation is God's word, the Bible, while general revelation is God's creation, the physical world.

As mentioned, words in the *exemplar* translation of Genesis Chapters 1 and 2 are about two percent different from orthodox translations such as the English Standard Version (a conservative, word-for-word translation). The changes are quite subtle, yet permit a significantly different explanation of the creation story while respecting the clear language of the inspired text. *Exemplar* creation revolutionizes one's understanding of the creation account.

The most significant error in orthodox translations of the creation account is acceptance of the "jussive/command" verb. Few people, except biblical Hebrew scholars, have ever heard of this little-known verb classification. Outside Genesis Chapter 1, "jussive/command" verbs have essentially no significance in the Old Testament. In addition, outside biblical Hebrew grammar this verb classification is not linguistically relevant.

In the English language, sentences may be classified as imperative, declarative, interrogative, or exclamatory. Imperative statements are commands while declarative statements give information or describe something. In English, "jussive/command" verbs are not a part of either imperative or declarative sentences.

Furthermore, in English verbs may be generally classified as either stative or dynamic. Stative verbs express a *state or condition*. Dynamic verbs indicate *action or change.* Dynamic verbs are typically used in imperative sentences. When a command is given, some type of action is normally expected or desired. Although dynamic verbs are used in imperative sentences, "jussive/command" verbs are not—nor are they needed.

However, in biblical Hebrew some verses are claimed to contain "jussive/command" verbs capable of turning a declarative sentence into a command. Allegedly, "jussive/command" verbs have the power to totally change the meaning of a verse. This is a major issue—significantly exceeding all others—in correctly understanding and translating Genesis Chapter 1. The "jussive/command" verb explanation has seriously distorted the Genesis creation account for more than twenty-two hundred years.

The critical difference between the *exemplar* translation and orthodox translations of the creation story is rejection of the "jussive/command" verb. Seven key verses in Genesis 1:3, 6, 9, 11, 14, 20, and 24 start with the expression, "And God said," and are traditionally explained as commands. The word "let" in these verses indicates the presence of a jussive verb. By fiat command, God created the Earth and all therein during six days. *Exemplar* creation rejects this embellished explanation and the alleged "jussive/command" verbs on which it is based.

A careful analysis reveals that the "jussive/command" verb is a myth and reflects a rule of biblical Hebrew grammar fabricated to support traditional young-Earth creation theology. Hebrew verbs in the Bible are categorized as perfect, imperfect, imperative, infinitive, or participle. Another category, the jussive verb, has been added. Allegedly, jussive verbs are only used in commands. The seven key verses identified above are claimed to contain "jussive/command" verbs that make them commands. Based on a careful examination of the Hebrew text of Genesis Chapter 1, these seven alleged commands are nothing more than declarative statements. During the six-day Genesis chronicle, God simply describes significant features about the Earth and heavens. Chapters 5 and 6, and Appendix B discuss Genesis 1:3, 6, 9, 11, 14, 20, and 24 and their ten alleged "jussive/command" verbs in detail.

Bible scholars contend that context is king when interpreting scripture. In regard to Genesis Chapter 1, what is the context? Can context be determined by the language used, or are we strictly at the mercy of centuries old tradition and theological presumption? Careful analysis of the language supports God as describing, identifying, distinguishing, approving, and blessing. The absence of dynamic verbs following the phrase, "And God said," strongly discredits the notion that God is commanding anything to be created in Genesis 1:3, 6, 9, 11, 14, 20, and 24.

The clear language of the biblical text must be given priority over any presumed context based on theology. The command interpretation of Genesis Chapter 1 is driven by more than twenty-two hundred years of errant theology and reliance on the "jussive/command" verb—rather than the words of scripture.

Other important changes in the exemplar translation apply to key words whose mistranslation has been forced into the text to support the "jussive/command" explanation. For example, in Genesis 1:2, the illegitimate term "without form" is replaced by "vacant" as a correct translation. In Genesis 1:9, the illegitimate phrase "let the waters be gathered together" is replaced by "the waters wait" as a correct rendering. In Genesis 1:10, "the gathering together of the waters" is replaced by "the collection of waters" as a more credible translation. In Genesis 1:20, the illegitimate expression "Let the waters bring forth abundantly the moving creature" is replaced by "The waters swarm *with* swarms of living creatures." These corrections and others support God as making declarative statements rather than commands.

Exemplar creation addresses the critical issue of harmonizing scripture and scientific evidence supporting an old heaven and Earth. Three important features of *exemplar* creation are: (1) Acceptance of the Genesis story as a God-inspired account that is truthful and trustworthy. (2) A careful translation of Hebrew words, supported by their use throughout the Old Testament. (3) The harmonization of special revelation and general revelation. God's word and His work should not conflict. The real Genesis story allows for significant time.

General revelation is not the Bible's enemy. Knowledge of general revelation helps us understand past events related to the heavens and Earth. Scientific knowledge about galaxies, stars, our solar system, and Earth is invaluable in fleshing out details regarding the Genesis creation account. I have no issue with appealing to firm scientific evidence that has accumulated throughout the centuries. On the other hand, I do not appeal to questionable scientific theories driven by philosophical naturalism and a firm belief in natural cause as an all-encompassing explanation of origins. Natural cause, in the form of random, naturally directed, purposeless, mechanistic change, is severely limited as a constructive mechanism.

In the remainder of this chapter, the *exemplar* translation of Genesis Chapters 1 and 2 is given followed by commentary. Words printed in italics in the *exemplar* translation are not in the Hebrew text and are added for grammatical and explanatory purposes, similar to the King James Version. All added words with a significant effect on verse meaning are in italics. Accuracy from the Hebrew text is favored over style, and some verses may be slightly repetitive or awkward due to an emphasis on literal translation. (Before continuing, reading the *exemplar* translation in Appendix A is recommended. Appendix C provides a side-by-side comparison with the ESV.)

The *Exemplar* Translation — Genesis Chapter One

Genesis 1:1 In the beginning, God created the heavens and the Earth.

Genesis 1:1 is an absolute statement acknowledging God as creator, when His actions initiated physical reality as we know it. As an omnipotent being, He created our universe. The following verses in the Old and New Testament are linked with this verse and attribute God as creator of the heavens and Earth.

(1) Psalm 33:6 By the word of the LORD the heavens were made, And all the host of them by the breath of His mouth. (NKJV)

(2) Psalm 102:23 Of old You laid the foundation of the earth, And the heavens are the work of Your hands. (NKJV)

(3) Nehemiah 9:6 You alone are the LORD; You have made heaven, the heaven of heavens, with all their host, the earth and everything on it, the seas and all that is in them. (NKJV)

(4) Isaiah 42:5 Thus says God the Lord, Who created the heavens and stretched them out, Who spread forth the earth and that which comes from it. (NKJV)

(5) Isaiah 45:18 For thus says the Lord, Who created the heavens, Who is God, Who formed the earth and made it, Who has established it, Who did not create it in vain, Who formed it to be inhabited. (NKJV)

(6) Jeremiah 10:12 He has made the earth by His power, He has established the world by His wisdom, And has stretched out the heavens at His discretion. (NKJV)

(7) John 1:1–3 In the beginning was the Word, and the Word was with God, and the Word was God. He was in the beginning with God. All things were made through Him, and without Him nothing was made that was made. (NKJV)

(8) Acts 4:24 So when they heard that, they raised their voice to God with one accord and said: "Lord, You are God, who made heaven and earth and the sea, and all that is in them." (NKJV)

(9) Colossians 1:16 For by Him all things were created that are in heaven and that are on earth, visible and invisible, whether thrones or dominions or principalities or powers. All things were created through Him and for Him. (NKJV)

(10) Ephesians 3:9 And to make all see what is the fellowship of the mystery, which from the beginning of the ages has been hidden in God who created all things through Jesus Christ. (NKJV)

(11) Hebrews 1:10 And: "You, LORD, in the beginning laid the foundation of the earth, And the heavens are the work of Your hands." (NKJV)

(12) Revelation 4:11 Thou are worthy, O Lord, to receive glory and honor and power, for You created all things, and by Your will they exist and were created. (NKJV)

(13) Revelation 10:6 And swore by Him who lives forever and ever, who created heaven and the things that are in it, the earth and the things that are in it, and
the sea and the things that are in it. (NKJV)

(14) Revelation 14:7 Saying with a loud voice, "Fear God and give glory to
Him, for the hour of His judgment has come; and worship Him who made heav-
en and earth, the sea and springs of water." (NKJV)

Genesis 1:1 clearly says that God created the heavens and Earth (the total universe). He existed from before the beginning and made them both; however, scripture does not give any details how this was accomplished. The exact time, sequence,
and method God used to create the heavens and Earth are not revealed in the Bible,
and we can only speculate why this information was withheld. Perhaps it was due to
the limited ability of the Hebrew language to describe technical processes and procedures. Perhaps God knew man would be incapable of understanding the complex
physics of creation. Regardless, these details are unknown and man is left to his own
resources to fill in the missing information.

Evidence discovered by scientists indicates the universe is very old. The Earth is
theorized to be 4.6 billion years old, based on radiometric dating and isotope decay.
The heavens are older based on spectral redshift from distant galaxies.

Scientific evidence points to our planet being completely molten at some time in
the distant past. A molten condition permitted the formation of Earth into an almost
perfect sphere, with a smooth surface (almost as round and smooth as a billiard ball)
due to self-gravity. A molten state and significant time allowed differentiation of
elements and their compounds according to density into the crust, mantle, outer core,
and inner core.[1] The density of the Earth's core is about four times that of the crust.[2]
Density increases progressively from the outside skin to the center.

Earth's crust and interior are significantly different. The top eight elements in
Earth's relatively light crust are oxygen (in the form of oxides and other oxygen
compounds), silicon, aluminum, iron, calcium, sodium, magnesium, and potassium.[3]
Materials that make up the mantle and core are not firmly known, although they are
believed to be primarily iron or nickel. Seismic tomography has confirmed the existence of three distinct regions within the interior of the Earth.[4,5] Based on seismic
evidence, the outer core is believed to be molten while the inner core and mantle are
theorized to be solid.

Exemplar creation proposes that special and general revelation combined best
explain how the Earth came about. Genesis 1:1 boldly proclaims that our planet was
created by a powerful intelligence, rather than natural cause. God was directly responsible for initially forming the Earth as a molten ball. Once all the raw materials
were collected together and melted, self-gravity held the Earth in a spherical shape
and caused the internal density changes.

Scientists have discovered that Earth is one planet of eight (Pluto was demoted
from planet status) orbiting a star that is one among an estimated 400 billion visible

stars in the Milky Way Galaxy.[6,7] Our galaxy in turn is one of approximately 125 billion galaxies in the visible universe.[8] Earth is neither the center of our solar system nor the center of our galaxy, but is in the Orion Arm of the Milky Way, an estimated 27,700 light years from the center.[9] Earth is an infinitesimal dot in the cosmos, but to our knowledge is unique. The many conditions responsible for making our planet a habitat for life are extraordinary.

By clearly identifying God as the one who created the heavens and Earth, Genesis 1:1 rejects the pagan beliefs of early cultures. This verse stands in stark contrast to the polytheistic beliefs of the Egyptians, Sumerians, Babylonians, and Assyrians prevalent during the time of Abraham and Moses. These cultures worshiped many pagan gods and goddesses. For example, the *Amduat*, an ancient Egyptian religious book, lists 908 Egyptian gods and goddesses. All Egyptian books of the underworld combined list a total of around 2,500 deities.[10]

In the twenty-first century, Genesis 1:1 refutes philosophical naturalism as an explanation for the origin of the universe. Random, naturally directed, purposeless, mechanistic change does not have the ability to form galaxies, stars, solar systems, and planets. Natural cause is rejected as an all-encompassing explanation for the heavens and Earth.

Genesis 1:2A And the Earth was vacant and empty *of life*.

Genesis 1:2 describes the Earth sometime after its creation. Although Genesis 1:1 and 1:2 occur in chronological sequence, the time between them is undefined by scripture and could be one day or millions of years. Genesis 1:1 and 1:2 lie outside the rigid six-day structure given in Genesis 1:3–31. At this point, the Earth is vacant and empty. God has not yet created plants and animals.

Scientific evidence indicates that Earth was completely sterile after cooling during a period of several million years from being a red hot molten ball. Not a single microscopic organism existed on the entire globe. It contained no bacteria, mold spores, blue-green algae, protozoa, single-celled life, or multicellular life. Our planet's surface consisted exclusively of solidified igneous rock, minerals, elements, simple molecules, and water.

Exemplar creation proposes that special and general revelation combined best describe the absence of life on early Earth sometime after its formation. The words "vacant" and "empty" in Genesis 1:2 emphasize the complete absence of life. With an estimated initial surface temperature of 600° C, our planet was completely sterile after it cooled from its molten state. Earth was totally devoid of all biological life.

Genesis 1:2B And darkness *was* over the surface of the deep *waters*.

Evidence discovered by scientists indicates the Earth gained an enormous supply of surface water early in its history. The primary water source appears to be from materials out of which the Earth was made (rather than comets striking the Earth), now consisting of the mantle and core. Some mantle rock may still contain a small percentage of water.[11] The most plausible theory is that prior to solidification of the crust, prolonged outgassing of water vapor from molten material within the Earth provided water for its oceans.[12] The effects of heat, pressure, density, and gravity forced water out of molten rock to the surface. All water on Earth was initially in vapor form (steam). As our planet slowly cooled, water condensed out of the atmosphere into liquid form and covered its surface with one large ocean.

Planetary surface water is a rarity in our solar system, and Earth is unique because it has abundant water compared to other planets and moons. Earth's oceans, seas, lakes, and rivers presently contain an estimated 332,500,000 cubic miles of water.[13] As a smooth sphere, enough water exists to cover the Earth to a depth of approximately 1.69 miles. The only other significant surface water in the solar system is on Jupiter's moon, Europa, and Saturn's moon, Enceladus (both covered with ice). Surface water is hypothesized to have existed at one time on Mars due to visible erosion features.

Exemplar creation proposes that special and general revelation combined best describe the surface water on early Earth. Genesis 1:2 testifies to the existence of deep water covering the planet. This water was probably due to the release of moisture from molten material within the Earth. We can hypothesize that originally one large ocean covered the entire planet with no significant upraised land (some volcanic cones and upraised meteor impact craters may have existed).

The Genesis 1:2 description of darkness appears to be supported by other scripture. In Job 38:4–11, God metaphorically discusses the Earth's creation. In Job 38:8, the sea bursts from the womb and comes out (water escapes from the Earth's interior). In Job 38:9, the Earth is described as covered by a garment of clouds and swaddled with thick darkness. In Job 38:10, the appointed place for the sea is established by breaking up (God broke up Earth's crust, raised the continents, and created the ocean basins). In Job 38:11, the sea and its waves are held within set boundaries established by the land.

- Job 38:4 Where were *you* when *I* established *the* Earth? Tell *me*, if *you* know understanding.

- 38:8 And *who* covered *the* sea with doors, when it burst from *the* womb *and* came out?

- 38:9 When I made clouds *for its* garment and thick darkness *for its* swaddling band.

- 38:10 And broke up for my decreed *place*, and set bars and doors.

- 38:11 And *I* said, *"The sea may* come until here and not more, and against here *shall* your proud waves set."

The conditions on early Earth were radically different from today due to high temperatures, outgassing, and meteor impacts. As mentioned, estimates place the surface temperature of early Earth at 600° C. During roughly the first one billion years, our planet and the Moon were subject to extensive meteor bombardment.[14] Some meteors had the potential of creating impact craters 31 miles in diameter or more. Significant outgassing occurred in the form of water vapor and smoke because of Earth's molten state. Our planet's atmosphere was heavily polluted by both meteor impacts and planetary outgassing.

Exemplar creation proposes that special and general revelation combined best describe the surface conditions of early Earth. Genesis 1:2 says that darkness was over the surface of the deep waters. Meteor impacts threw immense quantities of debris into the atmosphere. Planetary outgassing added steam and smoke. As the planet cooled, water vapor condensed to form one large ocean. The prevailing hot conditions (imagine an ocean temperature of 200° F) kept a substantial amount of water vapor in the atmosphere. All effects combined created dark, continuous, heavy cloud cover over the entire globe. Conditions were probably similar to those found on Venus today, consisting of complete cloud cover, high temperatures, and crushing atmospheric pressure (discussed more fully in Chapter 7).

Genesis 1:2C And the Spirit of God hovered over the surface of the waters.

Scientists have discovered that Earth is fine-tuned for life. Our planet has a consistent, yet slightly elliptical orbit around the Sun. The Sun is not too large, not too small, and quite stable for a G2 yellow dwarf star. Earth's orbital distance from the Sun appears just right. Our planet is neither too close to be boiling hot, nor too distant to be freezing cold. A strong magnetic field generated within the Earth shields its surface from dangerous solar winds. An ozone layer high in the atmosphere protects life from intense ultraviolet radiation produced by the Sun. Our planet has no significant harmful gases or minerals distributed in its atmosphere and oceans. Earth's axial tilt creates a greater habitable zone for life and results in four seasons with more variable planetary weather. The Moon is just the right mass and distance to provide strong tidal action for mixing the ocean waters. Earth rotates at an optimum speed to moderate day and night temperatures.

Exploration has revealed that metals and minerals, vital to human technology, are conveniently concentrated at specific locations on Earth. Critical metals include copper, iron, nickel, titanium, aluminum, chromium, cadmium, lead, zinc, gold, silver, and uranium. Important mineral deposits include boron, fluorspar, graphite, bromine, sodium sulfate, soda ash, salt, and barite.[15] If these metals and minerals were spread uniformly throughout the Earth's crust, their mining and extraction would be prohibitive. They would probably be little more than scientific curiosities.

Clean air, soil, and water should not be taken for granted. The Earth's crust contains several harmful minerals and metals such as antimony, arsenic, barium, cadmium, chromium, copper, lead, mercury, selenium, thallium, and zinc. Fortunately, these are concentrated at specific locations, rather than being evenly distributed throughout the Earth's soil and water. As an added benefit, concentrated deposits permit the mining of these metals for technological uses.

Exemplar creation proposes that special and general revelation combined best explain the conditions on Earth favorable to life and human technology. Genesis 1:2 describes the Spirit of God continuously hovering over our planet. This verse subtly alludes to the active part God had in shaping Earth. God did not abandon our planet and leave it to evolve in some mindless fashion, but He was active in developing it according to His plan. The fine-tuned features that make Earth habitable for mankind and favorable to human technology are the result of God's creative hand. He is responsible for the clean air, soil, and water that make abundant life possible. Metal and mineral concentrations may be viewed as quasi-natural deposits orchestrated by God to aid man in the development of technology.

Between Genesis 1:2 and 1:3, God directed action and limited natural change shaped the Earth. As time passed, our planet continued to cool and its crust grew progressively thicker. Intense meteor bombardment began tapering off. We can hypothesize that because of the enormous amount of water vapor in the atmosphere, Earth was in the grip of a massive self-sustaining greenhouse effect that required God's intervention to stop (water vapor is a stronger greenhouse gas than carbon dioxide). Conditions slowly improved and eventually the Earth's surface cooled to a point where life was possible.

Between Genesis 1:2 and 1:3, when conditions were right, God began creating life. He first created small, one-celled organisms such as algae and placed them in Earth's single, vast ocean. As the planet continued to change and conditions became more favorable, God created additional marine life. The first major creation event recorded in the fossil record is the Cambrian explosion. During this period, God created complex animals with eyes, skeletons, hard outer shells, limbs, internal organs, spinal columns, and body symmetry. Earth's waters teemed with all kinds of complex marine life.

Between Genesis 1:2 and 1:3, God continued to work as He raised portions of the Earth's crust out of the water to create the continents. The original arrangement of the continents was different from today—they have drifted throughout time. Continents, whose edges are sharply defined by a continental shelf, may be considered unnatural features and the result of God's creative power.

Earth's raised continents appear to be unique when compared with Mercury, Mars, Venus, and the 18 spherical moons in our solar system. Venus and Mars have high and low areas, but appear to lack clearly defined continents bordered by a sharp edge as found on Earth. Further exploration may clarify this issue; however, at this time we may view Earth's original continents as being directly formed by God rather than natural cause. Earth's continents as observed today may be considered a combination of God-directed change and natural change. The continents were originally created by God, but have drifted and separated throughout time.

The raising of the continents appears to be supported by other scripture. Psalm 104 is commonly known as the "creation psalm." *The Treasury of David* by Charles Spurgeon views Psalm 104:5–9 as a metaphorical description of Earth's creation (not a description of Noah's flood). Psalm 104:6 describes the hills covered with water like a garment (meaning the entire planet was covered). God then rebukes the water in 104:7, raises the mountains in 104:8, and promises water will never again cover the Earth in 104:9. The raising of the mountains and lowering of the plains in Psalm 104:8 can be explained in reference to the time between Genesis 1:2 and 1:3 when God raised the continents out of the water and created the ocean basins. The *exemplar* translation given below may be compared with orthodox translations about this important piece of scripture.

- Psalm 104:5 *He* established *the* Earth over *its* foundation, not *to* be moved forever.

- 104:6 Like the garment *of the* deep, He covered over *the* hills *with* standing water.

- 104:7 From your rebuke *the water* fled, from *the* voice *of* your thunder *the water* ran away.

- 104:8 *The* mountains went up *and the* plains went down to the place established for them.

- 104:9 *Water shall* not pass *this* set boundary, *water shall* not again cover the Earth.

Between Genesis 1:2 and 1:3, God created plants and animals to fill the land, air, and water. Every single plant and animal species was created by God (they did not occur due to evolution). Earth's fossil record clearly indicates the sudden appearance of many biological species. As a part of His plan, God developed a complex system of dependent, symbiotic, and synergistic relationships between plants and plants, plants and animals, and animals and animals. Dinosaurs and the great prehistoric animals were eventually created, followed by many of the species familiar today. Some species became extinct due to catastrophic events, environmental changes, disease, predators, and other phenomena. When necessary, God restored Earth's livable conditions. At various intervals throughout time, God created new species to populate the planet.

Between Genesis 1:2 and 1:3, God directed the creation of oil and gas deposits beneath Earth's surface. Their existence, concentration, and location are often taken for granted, yet if hydrocarbon deposits were distributed throughout the air, soil, and water, Earth might not be habitable. For example, Titan, a moon of Saturn, has an atmosphere polluted by methane. Yet on Earth, essentially all oil, gas, and methane are safely tucked away hundreds and thousands of feet underground, in concentrations suitable for drilling and extraction. Our planet contains enough hydrocarbon stores to completely pollute its atmosphere, soil, and water. Earth's petroleum reserves may be considered quasi-natural deposits orchestrated by God for the future needs of humanity to aid in the expansion of technology and civilization.

Between Genesis 1:2 and 1:3, coal deposits were formed. Some of these deposits were created during long periods of time in peat bogs, marshes, and swamps. As plant material slowly accumulated, it turned into coal. Other coal was formed by local and regional water catastrophes. In some instances, flood waters stripped vegetation from the land, concentrated it in low-lying areas, and then covered it with sediments where it eventually turned into coal. Huge coal reserves were developed for the future energy needs of mankind, and they may be viewed as a combination of natural processes and God-directed action throughout time.

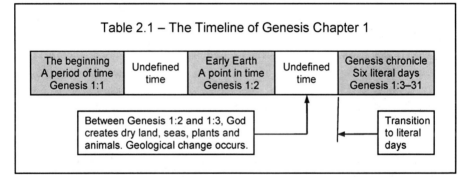

Table 2.1 – The Timeline of Genesis Chapter 1

The beginning A period of time Genesis 1:1	Undefined time	Early Earth A point in time Genesis 1:2	Undefined time	Genesis chronicle Six literal days Genesis 1:3–31

Between Genesis 1:2 and 1:3, God creates dry land, seas, plants and animals. Geological change occurs.

Transition to literal days

Between Genesis 1:2 and 1:3, limited undirected change occurred due to the laws of chemistry and physics within systems established by God. The planet cooled due to the laws of thermodynamics. Earth's continents randomly drifted. Meteor impacts, volcanoes, earthquakes, tsunamis, floods, erosion, sedimentation, uplifting, settling, glacial action, hurricanes, tornadoes, fires, and environmental change transformed Earth in a natural fashion. The fossil record was laid down during many local and regional catastrophic events. Valleys, canyons, and river channels were formed by the action of water.

Exemplar creation views Genesis 1:3 as a critical dividing line in the Genesis creation story. The events prior to this verse have a different time frame from those that follow. Genesis 1:1, 1:2, and 1:3 occur in chronological order and the length of time between them is undefined by scripture. The time could be one day or millions of years. Between Genesis 1:3 and 1:31, the six-day Genesis chronicle takes place, and time is rigidly defined in normal, 24-hour, sequential days. Table 2.1 illustrates the timeline of Genesis Chapter 1.

Exemplar creation views Genesis 1:3–31 (the six-day Genesis chronicle) as when God describes His completed work. Nothing is created in these verses. In addition, the description of His completed work has little relation to the sequence of creation. For example, a house is built starting with the foundation, floor, walls, and roof. A general sequence is then followed for installing the heating and air conditioning ducts, drain lines, water supply pipes, electrical wiring, windows, exterior doors, insulation, sheetrock, cabinets, interior trim, and carpeting. In describing the same house when completed, we might mention the date it was finished, its square footage, and that it has two stories, a detached garage, a brick veneer exterior, hardwood floors, and three baths. Items typically mentioned in describing a completed house are almost totally disconnected from the sequence of events that occur during construction. Likewise, Genesis 1:3–31 describes a completed Earth, and the description is totally disconnected from its method and sequence of creation.

A major point in the six-day Genesis chronicle concerns the description of Genesis 1:2, in contrast to the description given in Genesis 1:3–31. The Earth transitions from being dark, empty of life, and water covered in Genesis 1:2, to being full of light and life in Genesis 1:3–31. Logically, this transition took place during a long period of indefinite time between Genesis 1:2 and 1:3. God is clearly identified as responsible for this change.

The six-day chronicle in Genesis 1:3–31 emphasizes five major themes: (1) God describes a mature Earth, the result of a long series of God-directed changes (specific creative events) and limited natural change, all of which occurred prior to Genesis 1:3. (2) God describes a world full of light and life in contrast to a lifeless, dark, water covered world portrayed in Genesis 1:2. (3) God identifies by name five features of His creative work. (4) God approves His creation as "good" and "very good." (5) God is proclaimed as sole creator in contrast to the polytheistic beliefs of the Egyptians and subsequent cultures.

Genesis 1:3 And God said, "There is light, and light exists."
1:4 And God saw that the light *was* good. And God distinguished between the light and between the darkness.
1:5 And God called the light "day" and called the darkness "night." And evening was, and morning was—day one.

Genesis 1:3 begins day one of the six-day Genesis chronicle. In this verse God describes the existence of light coming from the Sun, created at some time during the beginning in Genesis 1:1. Often taken for granted, sunlight represents a unique phenomenon. It is completely unnatural and without it our solar system would be cold, dark, and lifeless.

In Genesis 1:4–5, God distinguishes between light and darkness. He identifies the light as "day" and darkness as "night." One cycle of light and darkness establish the basis for one full day. Through astronomy, scientists have come to understand how this cycle of light and darkness occurs. Earth rotates on its axis to produce day and night as one hemisphere is illuminated with light from the Sun while the other is covered in darkness.

God uses the terms "day" and "night" to identify alternating periods of light and darkness. This is the first of several events where God calls out (identifies) the common name of the feature being described.

> **Genesis 1:6 And God said, "There is an expanse in the middle of the water, and it exists to separate between water *above* from water *below*."**
> **1:7 And God *is the one who* made the expanse and separated between the waters under the expanse and between the waters over the expanse. And *it was so.***
> **1:8 And God called the expanse "sky." And evening was, and morning was—second day.**

Genesis 1:6 begins the second day of the six-day Genesis chronicle. In this verse God describes the existence of Earth's expanse, created prior to Genesis 1:3. Sometimes "expanse" is translated from Hebrew into English as "dome." As viewed from the surface of the Earth, an expanse of clear space stretches from horizon to horizon. Water vapor and clouds may be explained as the water above the expanse, and the oceans, seas, lakes, and rivers are the water below. God calls out (identifies) the common name of the expanse as "sky."

Genesis 1:6–7 narrates events structured in a style identical to the fourth, fifth, and sixth days. In verse six, a direct quotation by God describes the expanse as existing to separate water from water, and in verse seven He is identified as its maker. These verses represent a sequence of events starting with (1) creation of the expanse prior to Genesis 1:3, (2) the existence of an expanse in Genesis 1:6, and (3) identifying God as maker of the expanse in Genesis 1:7.

In Genesis 1:6, the words "create, make, form, plant, grow, and build" are not used. These action verbs are absent and nothing is happening. This verse describes what has already been created. It should be obvious that if God describes the expanse as present in Genesis 1:6, He cannot create it in Genesis 1:7, because it already exists. Genesis 1:6 and 1:7 are not repetitive actions.

Genesis 1:7 proclaims God as maker of the expanse, in contrast to the pagan gods of the time. After being slaves in Egypt for several hundred years, the Hebrew people were thoroughly familiar with the many gods of the Egyptians. When Moses wrote the Pentateuch, he rejected the polytheistic beliefs of the day. This rejection applied to the Egyptian gods, in addition to the Babylonian, Assyrian, Phoenician, and Canaanite gods they would become familiar with in the future. These cultures created gods of the Sun, Moon, sky, air, weather, water, ground, mountains, rivers, and other objects.

In the twenty-first century, Genesis 1:7 is a refutation of philosophical naturalism and ancillary ideas about how the Earth's sky was created by natural cause. God is identified as the one who selected nitrogen and oxygen as the major atmospheric gases. He kept harmful hydrocarbons out of the air. God fine-tuned the evaporation, condensation, and precipitation of water to permit a transparent atmosphere. The sky we observe today is a direct result of God's creative hand.

Earth and its sky contrast sharply with other planets in our solar system. Earth is the only one with a significant atmosphere that permits viewing the stars from its surface. Other planets such as Venus, Uranus, Saturn, and Jupiter have an atmosphere consisting of essentially non-transparent soup.

Genesis 1:9 And God said, "The waters under the sky wait in one place and the dry ground is seen." And *it* was so.
1:10   And God called the dry ground "land" and called the collection of waters "seas." And God saw that it *was* good.
1:11   And God said, "The land is sprouting sprouts: plants seeding seeds and the fruit trees making fruit—to which kind is in the seed—over the land." And *it* was so.
1:12   "And the land is growing sprouts: plants seeding seeds *according* to *their* kind, and the trees making fruit—in which seed is to kind." And God saw that *it was* good.
1:13   And evening was, and morning was—third day.

Genesis 1:9 begins the third day of the six-day Genesis chronicle. In this verse God describes Earth's waters waiting tranquilly in one place. Sometime prior to Genesis 1:3, God formed depressions in the Earth's crust to create ocean basins while raising its continents. The collected waters in this verse are the oceans, seas, and lakes of the world. In Genesis 1:10, God calls out (identifies) the common name of dry ground as "land" and the collected waters as "seas."

In Genesis 1:11–12, God appears to have repeated himself, albeit with some slight variation. On closer examination, the Hebrew words in these verses distinguish between *sprouting* and *growing* (bringing forth), and contrast two totally different plant phenomena. This perceived repetitive statement (or command) is actually a sophisticated observation of two distinct phases of plant maturation.

In Genesis 1:11, "sprouting" is the key word. God observes the land sprouting sprouts. When a seed is put into the soil, sprouting occurs first. Sprouting involves a series of complex mechanisms within the embryo of a seed, generally triggered when the correct temperature, moisture, and sunlight are sensed. Some seeds can sense very specific requirements before sprouting, such as the presence of friendly fungi or the absence of embryo inhibitors. When the right conditions are detected, hormones produced within the seed turn on DNA that creates specific proteins and enzymes. One of the critical enzymes produced, amylase, converts starch, stored in the endosperm of the seed, into sugar. Sugar is transported from the endosperm back to the embryo to fuel more growth. The endosperm contains all the stored energy for the seed during sprouting. When a seed sprouts, chlorophyll-rich green growth emerges and travels upwards toward the sunlight.

In Genesis 1:12, "growing" (bringing forth) is the key word. God observes the land growing sprouts—a different process than seed sprouting. A sprout switches from using internally stored nutrients in the seed to gathering them from its surroundings. A sprout sends out roots to take in moisture and minerals from the adjacent soil. The sprout uses energy from sunlight and photosynthesis to create the materials needed to continue plant growth. The sprout may die if the soil is extremely poor, moisture is lacking, or sunlight is inadequate.

In Genesis 1:11–12, God describes a mature land covered with vegetation, created between Genesis 1:2 and 1:3. His carefully designed process of sprouting, growth, and plant reproduction is working. Seeds spread over the land carrying the genetic code of the parent plant. As seeds are buried and sprout, they faithfully reproduce to continue the cycle of life. God observes the plant world functioning as designed and declares it good.

> **Genesis 1:14 And God said, "There are luminaries in the expanse of the heavens to distinguish between the day and between the night, and *they* are for a sign for appointed times and for days and years."**
> **1:15 "And luminaries exist in the expanse of the heavens to give light over the Earth." And *it* was so.**
> **1:16 And God *is the one who* made two great luminaries: the greater luminary to rule the day and the smaller luminary to rule the night and the stars.**
> **1:17 And God gave them in the expanse of the heavens to give light over the Earth.**
> **1:18 And to rule in the day and in the night and to distinguish between the light and between the darkness. And God saw that *it* was good.**
> **1:19 And evening was, and morning was—fourth day.**

Genesis 1:14–15 begin the fourth day of the six-day Genesis chronicle. In these two verses God describes two luminaries in the heavens (the Sun and Moon) created sometime during the beginning in Genesis 1:1. The greater and the smaller luminary are the main focus of Genesis 1:14–19. No statement is made about the *creation* of stars in these verses. Stars are only mentioned in Genesis 1:16 as being dominated by the smaller luminary during the night.

Genesis 1:16 is connected with two other verses in the Bible that discuss how luminaries rule in the heavens.

> • Psalm 136:8–9 The sun to rule over the day. . . The moon and stars to rule over the night, for his steadfast love endures forever. (ESV)

> • Jeremiah 31:35 Thus says the LORD, who gives the sun for light by day and the fixed order of the moon and the stars for light by night. (ESV)

In Genesis 1:14–16, the order of events is important. In verses 14 and 15, a direct quotation by God describes two luminaries in the heavens. In verse 16, He is identified as their maker. These verses represent a sequence of events starting with (1) the creation of these luminaries prior to Genesis 1:3, (2) the existence of luminaries in Genesis 1:14–15, and (3) identifying God as maker of these two great luminaries in Genesis 1:16.

In Genesis 1:14–15, the words "create, make, form, plant, grow, and build" are not used. These action verbs are absent and nothing is happening. These verses describe what has already been created. It should be obvious that if God describes the luminaries as present in Genesis 1:14–15, He cannot create them in Genesis 1:16—they already exist. Genesis 1:14–15 and 1:16 are not repetitive actions.

As mentioned in Genesis 1:14, heavenly luminaries determine times, days, and years. Earth's rotation and orbit around the Sun establish our days and years. The orbit of the Moon around the Earth is an additional method of marking time. Earth's orbital position about the Sun clearly marks the Winter Solstice, Spring Equinox, Summer Solstice, and Fall Equinox (the beginning days of the four seasons). The relationship of the Sun, Earth, and Moon determine the occurrence of eclipses.

Genesis 1:16 and 1:17 identify God, in contrast to the many pagan gods, as the *maker* and *giver* of the two great luminaries. The words written by Moses are a direct refutation of the polytheistic beliefs of the Egyptians. Moses spent the first forty years of his life living in Egypt among royalty and was no doubt thoroughly educated in regard to their religious practices. Genesis 1:16 rejects any belief the Israelites may have held regarding Re, the Egyptian sun god, and the other Egyptian gods of Amon-Re, Re-Harakhty, Sobek-Re, and Khunm-Re.[16] This verse also rejects belief in the Egyptian moon god, Thoth, as creator of the Moon.[17]

In the twenty-first century, Genesis 1:16 is a direct refutation of philosophical naturalism and the solar nebular hypothesis as an explanation for the origin of the Sun and Moon. By identifying God as creator, natural cause is rejected as an all-encompassing explanation for these objects. God is responsible for the origin, functional complexity, and fine-tuning of the Sun, which includes its size, stability, temperature, and distance from Earth. The Sun is a sophisticated fusion energy device built to run for millions of years, that appears to operate unattended and without need of repair or replenishment. God is responsible for the creation and fine-tuning of the Moon in regard to its size, mass, and orbital distance from Earth.

In Genesis 1:18, God describes the operation of the Sun and Moon in general terms and approves them as "good." When measured by the standards of twenty-first century science, this description is still relevant.

Genesis 1:20 And God said, "The waters swarm *with* swarms of living creatures, and fliers flying over the land and over the surface of the expanse of the sky."
1:21 And God *is the one who* created the great reptiles and every moving living creature with which the waters swarm, *according* to *their* kinds, and every winged flier *according* to *its* kind. And God saw that *it was* good.

1:22 And God blessed them saying, "Be fruitful and multiply and fill the waters in the seas and multiply the fliers on the land."
1:23 And evening was, and morning was—fifth day.

Genesis 1:20 begins the fifth day of the six-day Genesis chronicle. In this verse, God describes marine life and flying creatures He created between Genesis 1:2 and 1:3. The abundant life portrayed contrasts sharply with the lifeless, dark, water covered planet described in Genesis 1:2. Swarming marine creatures indicate the presence of giant schools of fish and other abundant life found in Earth's rivers, lakes, and seas. Winged fliers represent all creatures that can fly, including birds, bats, and insects. Both marine and flying creatures represent an intricate arrangement of elemental materials into extremely complex living machines that move, metabolize food, excrete waste, self-repair, reproduce, and respond to their environment. An enormous variety of creatures with different shapes, sizes, and capabilities have multiplied to fill the seas and skies of planet Earth.

In Genesis 1:20–21, the order of events is significant. In verse twenty, God describes the presence of marine life and flying creatures on Earth, and in verse twenty-one, He is identified as their creator. These verses represent a sequence of events starting with (1) the creation of marine life and flying creatures in the past between Genesis 1:2 and 1:3, (2) the existence of these creatures in Genesis 1:20, and (3) identifying God as creator of these creatures in Genesis 1:21.

As usual, notice that in Genesis 1:20, the words "create, make, form, plant, grow, and build" are not used. These action verbs are absent and nothing is happening. This verse describes what has already been created. If God describes marine life and winged fliers as present in Genesis 1:20, He cannot create them over again in Genesis 1:21—they already exist. Genesis 1:20 and 1:21 are not repetitive actions.

The word "create" is mentioned in Genesis 1:1 and then not again until the fifth day in Genesis 1:21. From Genesis 1:3 through 1:20, the word "create" is not used. The complete absence of this word discredits the idea that God commanded and created anything during this time. As explained by *exemplar* creation, during the six-day Genesis chronicle, God describes what was created prior to Genesis 1:3.

Genesis 1:21 proclaims God as the creator of all marine life and flying creatures on Earth, in direct refutation of the polytheistic beliefs prevalent in Egyptian culture during the time of Moses. These animals were not created by Amon, the Egyptian king of gods, or Sobek, the crocodile god.

In the twenty-first century, Genesis 1:21 is a refutation of philosophical naturalism fleshed out as chemical evolution and Darwinian evolution. According to these beliefs, microscopic life developed from non-life and then evolved into a multitude of species over time. These ideas are rejected, and God is identified as the creator of all marine life and flying creatures. He is the powerful intelligence who created the design information, complex functional systems, mathematically improbable structures, and fine-tuned arrangements found within these living creatures.

Genesis 1:21 mentions God as creator of the "great reptiles." The Hebrew word translated "reptiles" is used several times in the Old Testament to describe reptilian animals. This verse is unique because it mentions large animals previously unknown to science until the relatively recent discovery of their skeletal remains. Great marine reptiles include the lizard-like mosasaurs, measuring up to 50 feet long. Icthyosaurs had a fish-like body shape, and fossils have been measured up to 50 feet long. Plesiosaurs were marine reptiles resembling a turtle with an extremely long neck, small head, and no shell. Fossils up to 46 feet long have been found. Crocodiles, such as kronosaurus, were great amphibious reptiles up to 33 feet long. Pterosaurs, classified as flying reptiles, had wing spans up to 36 feet. Great reptiles mentioned in this verse, and their confirmation by science, support the historical accuracy of the Bible.

In Genesis 1:21, God approves Earth's marine life and flying creatures as good. The reproduction process God designed is working. DNA contained in their eggs is faithfully passing on genetic information from parent to offspring. Profuse animal reproduction is supported by a carefully balanced biosphere. The intricate dependent, symbiotic, and synergistic relationships among biological species is functioning as designed. In Genesis 1:22, God blesses the animals with the statement, "Be fruitful and multiply."

Genesis 1:24 And God said, "The land brings forth living creatures *according* to *their* kind: beasts and moving *things* and animals of the land, *according* to *their* kind." And *it* was so.
1:25 And God *is the one who* made the animals of the Earth *according* to *their* kind: the beasts *according* to *their* kind and every moving *thing* upon the ground *according* to *its* kind. And God saw that *it was* good.

Genesis 1:24 begins the sixth day of the six-day Genesis chronicle. God describes an Earth filled with land-dwelling beasts, moving things, and animals thriving on the bounty of the land.

Genesis 1:24–25 narrates events in a parallel style identical to the second, fourth, and fifth days. In verse 24, God describes a multitude of land-dwelling creatures, and in verse 25, God is identified as their maker. These verses represent a sequence of events starting with (1) the making of these creatures in the past between Genesis 1:2 and 1:3, (2) the existence of these land creatures in Genesis 1:24, and (3) identifying God as maker of these creatures in Genesis 1:25.

Notice that in Genesis 1:24, the words "create, make, form, plant, grow, and build" are not used. These action verbs are absent and nothing is happening. This verse describes what has already been created. If God describes the land creatures as present in Genesis 1:24, He cannot create them in Genesis 1:25—they already exist. Genesis 1:24 and 1:25 are not repetitive actions.

Genesis 1:25 identifies God, in contrast to the many heathen gods, as the maker of all land creatures. This is a direct rejection of false Egyptian religious beliefs about the origin of land animals. Cattle were not made by Hathor, the Egyptian cow goddess.[18]

In the twenty-first century, Genesis 1:25 refutes philosophical naturalism, a belief in conflict with the creation story for more than twenty-five hundred years. God is identified as the creator of all land creatures.

> **1:26 And God said, "Man, made in our image *and* after our likeness, has dominion on fish of the sea and on fliers in the sky and on beasts and on all the Earth and on all the moving *things* that move over the land."**
>
> **1:27 And God *is the one who* created man in His image, in God's image created him, male and female *God* created them.**
>
> **1:28 And God blessed them, and God said to them, "Be fruitful and multiply and fill the Earth and subdue it and have dominion on fish of the sea and on fliers in the sky and on all living *things* that move over the land."**

The sixth day continues in Genesis 1:26. God states that man is made in His image and likeness. Mankind has dominion over all marine life, flying creatures, and land animals. Man has intelligence and power. He is a self-aware, self-directed entity with free will. Man, created in the image of God and endowed with His characteristics, is capable of love and hate, mercy and wrath, patience and judgment, but in a reduced capacity. Man has the ability to be a designer, builder, and creator in his own right.

God purposefully created humans different from animals. As pointed out by John MacArthur, "Man's very posture, standing upright, distinguishes him from four-footed beasts and creeping things. The animals' natural posture directs their gaze downward toward the earth. Man, on the other hand, is naturally positioned to look upward, toward the heavens, where he can contemplate the glory of God displayed there."[19]

Genesis 1:26–27 follows the same parallel style found in Genesis 1:6–7, 14–16, 20–21, and 24–25 to introduce the sky, luminaries, marine creatures, fliers, and land animals. In verse 26, a direct quotation by God describes the existence of man and his domination over animals. In verse 27, God is clearly identified as man's creator.

The actual description of how God made man is recorded in Genesis 2:7. God formed man's body from the dust of the ground and gave him the breath of life. This event no doubt took place quite rapidly, within a fraction of one day. Other than animals for the garden, humans were the last creatures created by God—a relatively recent event in Earth's history. Scripture does not reveal any additional details about the creation of man.

Exemplar creation proposes that special and general revelation combined best explain the origin of humanity. God formed man from elements and molecules found in the Earth's crust. Man did not evolve from lower animals, but was a finished product of God's creative power. A significant difference exists between man and the nearest primate, both at the functional and molecular level. When examined in detail, natural cause cannot be used to plausibly explain the vast improvements between chimpanzees and humans and their alleged primate ancestor. Anatomically modern humans appear suddenly in the fossil-archaeological record (within the recent past), which sets the date for the Genesis story.

Attributing the creation of man and woman to God is a direct refutation of biological evolution, which theorizes humans are a product of random beneficial mutation and natural selection throughout millions of years. According to evolutionary theory, humans, chimpanzees, and gorillas slowly evolved from a common ancestor during a period of four million years or more. Scripture clearly contradicts this belief. The following verses in the Old and New Testament are linked with this verse and attribute God as creator of mankind.

(1) Genesis 5:1–2 This is the book of the generations of Adam. When God created man, he made him in the likeness of God. Male and female he created them, and he blessed them and named them Man when they were created. (ESV)

(2) Genesis 9:6 "Whoever sheds the blood of man, by man shall his blood be shed, for God made man in his own image." (ESV)

(3) Deuteronomy 4:32 For ask now of the days that are past . . . since the day that God created man on the earth, and ask from one end of heaven to the other, whether such a great thing as this has ever happened or was ever heard of. (ESV)

(4) Isaiah 45:12 I made the earth and created man on it; it was my hands that stretched out the heavens, and I commanded all their host. (ESV)

(5) Jeremiah 27:5 It is I who by my great power and my outstretched arm have made the earth, with the men and animals that are on the earth. (ESV)

(6) Malachi 2:10 Have we not all one Father? Has not one God created us? Why then are we faithless to one another, profaning the covenant of our fathers? (ESV)

(7) Matthew 19:4 He answered, "Have you not read that he who created them from the beginning made them male and female." (ESV)

(8) Mark 10:6 But from the beginning of *their* creation, He made them male and female. (ET)

(9) Luke 3:38 The son of Enos, the son of Seth, the son of Adam, the son of God. (ESV)

(10) Acts 17:28 In him we live and move and have our being; as even some of your own poets have said, "For we are indeed his offspring." (ESV)

(11) 1 Corinthians 11:9 Neither was man created for woman, but woman for man. (ESV)

(12) 1 Corinthians 15:45 Thus it is written, "The first man Adam became a living being;" the last Adam became a life-giving spirit. (ESV)

(13) Romans 9:20 But who are you, O man, to answer back to God? Will what is molded say to its molder, "Why have you made me like this?" (ESV)

(14) Colossians 3:10 And have put on the new self, which is being renewed in knowledge after the image of its creator. (ESV)

(15) 1 Timothy 2:13 For Adam was formed first, then Eve. (ESV)

(16) Hebrews 2:6–7 What is man, that you are mindful of him, or the son of man, that you care for him? You made him for a little while lower than the angels; you have crowned him with glory and honor. (ESV)

Genesis 1:28 records the *first command* given in the creation story (none of the previous verses are commands). Often viewed as a cultural mandate, God commands man and woman to: (1) multiply and fill the Earth, (2) subdue the land, and (3) have dominion over all living things.

God specifically made mankind with unique features that permit him to dominate animals. Man does not have the speed, strength, protective apparatus, or fighting equipment given most wild creatures. Man has no significant offensive features such as powerful muscles, strong claws, or sharp teeth. Humans lack the keen sense of smell, extraordinary hearing, and exceptional long range vision found in some animals. He is completely without a single strong defensive mechanism such as the hard shell of a turtle, the camouflage of a chameleon, the quills of a porcupine, or the scented spray of a skunk. On the other hand, man's phenomenal brain, five senses, full-color vision, exceptional language ability, fully functional opposable thumb, dexterous hands, and distinctive upright stature allow him to have superiority over the animal kingdom and fulfill God's mandate.

> **1:29 And God said, "Behold, *I have* given to you every plant seeding seed which is over the surface of all the land, and every tree in which fruit is seeding seed. For you, *they* are for food."**
> **1:30 "And to every animal of the land and to every flier in the sky and to every moving *thing* over the land, which is a living creature, *I have given* every green plant for food." And *it* was so.**
> **1:31 And God saw all that *He had* done, and behold *it was* very good. And evening was, and morning was—the sixth day.**

In Genesis 1:29, God says that seed-bearing plants and fruit trees have been given to man for food. Plants are a major part of man's food supply, which include leaves such as spinach and roots typified by carrots. Generally, seeds are the basis for the majority of man's food and include grains such as wheat, rice, corn, oats, rye, and barley. Also included are seed pods such as peas, lentils, and beans. Fruits include grapes, plums, lemons, apples, pears, peaches, oranges, and watermelons. God in His wisdom designed a variety of seeds, seed pods, and fruits edible by humans.

In Genesis 1:30, God says that green plants have been given to animals for food. Animals have a digestive system made to handle a greater variety of leaves, grasses, and seeds than man's. This verse subtly points out a fundamental issue of biological life: plants are the bottom of the food chain. Ultimately all animal life, whether herbivorous, omnivorous, or carnivorous, is dependent on plants for food.

Genesis 1:29–30 apply to the entire Earth. God gave seeds, fruit trees, and green plants to man and animals for food. We should not incorrectly infer these two verses apply strictly to the Garden of Eden.

The garden was a protected place from the violence, predator-prey relationships, and survival of the fittest that ruled the world outside. Based on this, we can hypothesize that animals in the garden were essentially harmless and primarily herbivorous. Birds fed on seeds, worms, and harmless insects. No saber tooth tigers, lions, hyenas, wolves, venomous snakes, or poisonous spiders lived in the garden.

Throughout the six-day Genesis chronicle, God repeatedly affirms pleasure in what He has created. In Genesis 1:4, light is proclaimed as "good." In Genesis 1:10, the collected waters and dry land are described as "good." In Genesis 1:12, sprouting sprouts and growing sprouts are called "good." In Genesis 1:18, the Sun and Moon are recognized as "good." In Genesis 1:21, swarms of marine life and flying creatures are labeled as "good." In Genesis 1:25, land animals, beasts, and moving things are identified as "good." In Genesis 1:28, man is blessed and commanded to multiply, fill the Earth, subdue, and have dominion over it. God is pleased with His handiwork and repeatedly calls it "good."

In Genesis 1:31, God looks on all He has done and shows His pleasure by summarizing it as "very good." The descriptions and pronouncements in Genesis 1:3–31 are in sharp contrast to Genesis 1:2, where the Earth is dark, empty of life, and covered with water.

The *Exemplar* Translation – Genesis Chapter Two

Genesis 2:1 And the heavens and Earth *were* finished, and all their multitude *of miscellaneous things*.
2:2 And on the seventh day God finished His work that *He had* done, and rested on the seventh day from all His work that *He had* done.
2:3 And God blessed the seventh day and sanctified it, because on it *God* rested from all work that He created to do.

Genesis 2:1 brings to a close the six-day Genesis chronicle. The description of things God did to the heavens and Earth is now complete.

Genesis 2:2 mentions God resting on the seventh day from "work that He created to do." Work He did regarding creation during the six-day period includes describing, identifying, distinguishing, approving, and blessing.

Was God really tired and in need of rest? Of course not! The creation story in Genesis Chapter 1 simply establishes a pattern of working six days and resting on the seventh, codified in the Ten Commandments. In Exodus 20:8–11 and Deut. 5:12–15, God instituted the requirement of working six days and resting on the Sabbath. As pointed out in Mark 2:27, the Sabbath was for man's benefit. God knew man needed a day of rest every week to refresh, renew, and restore himself.

Genesis 2:3 marks an end to the creation preamble. Genesis 1:1–2:3 historically and theologically set the stage for the creation account that follows. In general terms, God has been identified as creator of the heavens and Earth. God has been identified as the creator and maker of plants, animals, and mankind.

Keep in mind that originally the Old Testament was not divided into chapters and verses. Shortly before his death, Stephen Langton (1150–1228), Archbishop of Canterbury, England, divided the Bible into the chapter divisions we currently use. Although useful, chapter and verse divisions are a human development. Genesis Chapter 1 should end at the verse currently identified as Genesis 2:3.

Genesis 2:4 These accounts *that follow are about* the heavens and the Earth at their creation—in the days Yahweh God did *the* Earth and heavens.

Genesis 2:4 introduces the next section of scripture which includes all events that occur between Genesis 2:5–4:26, a span several years. Genesis Chapter 2 details the planting of the Garden of Eden, growing trees in the garden, forming man from the dust of the ground, forming animals for the garden, and building Eve from Adam's rib. Genesis Chapters 3 and 4 describe Satan's temptation of Eve, eating of the forbidden fruit, banishment from the garden, the murder of Abel, and the birth of Seth.

Genesis 2:4 starts by saying that an account will be given about the heavens and Earth at their creation. The specific account concerns the days when God did the Earth and heavens. Reversal of the term "heavens and Earth" to "Earth and heavens" implies a shift in emphasis.

The first half of Genesis 2:4 mentions the creation of "the heavens and the Earth." The heavens are mentioned first to emphasize the greatest of God's works. With an estimated 125 billion galaxies, each containing an estimated 400 billion stars, the creation of heaven was a magnificent feat. Following second in order is the Earth, a lesser creation and mentioned last.

The second half of Genesis 2:4 emphasizes the days that God did things to the "Earth and heavens." The order is now reversed. The Earth is mentioned first to emphasize its importance, and then the heavens. During this time, the majority of God's effort applied to the Earth and less was expended on the heavens. This is one of only two places in the Old Testament Hebrew text where the exact phrase "Earth and heavens" occurs.[20]

What did God do to the heavens on these days? Scripture is silent on any specific details. We can speculate that God did things in the heavens to intentionally leave signs in our solar system for modern man as evidence of His presence. The ice rings of Saturn may include such phenomenon. Currently no plausible natural explanation exists for Saturn's thin, uniform, multi-colored, distinctly separated, perfectly aligned, and concentric rings.

Genesis 2:5 And every bush of the field was not yet on the land, and every plant of the field *did* not yet grow, because Yahweh God had not caused rain over the land and there was no man to cultivate the ground *where the garden was to be*.

2:6 And mists rose up from the land and watered all the surface of the ground *where the garden was to be*.

2:7 And Yahweh God formed the man *of* dust from the ground and breathed in his nostrils the breath *of* life. And the man existed as a living creature.

2:8 And Yahweh God planted a garden from the east in Eden, and there *He* put the man whom *He had* formed.

2:9 And Yahweh God grew from the ground every tree *that was* desirable to the sight and good for food, and the tree of life in the middle of the garden and the tree of knowledge of good and evil.

Genesis 2:5 describes the ground chosen for the Garden of Eden before God began planting. We can infer from this verse that the climate at the location selected for the garden was hot and arid, similar to the present-day Arabian Desert. Little or no rain fell, and there were no bushes or plants.

Genesis 2:6 describes how mists rose from the land and watered the ground. This verse refers to an effect above the ground of the garden that was a substitute for rain. The Hebrew word translated "mist" is only mentioned one other place in the Bible, and its exact meaning is unclear. We can attribute God as being responsible for these mists. He produced a phenomenon to water the ground not normally found in this arid land.

Genesis 2:5–6 do not teach that rain never fell on the entire Earth until the flood of Noah. Such an effect would have required the suspension of Earth's hydrologic cycle, one of the most fundamentally important systems on the planet. The hydrologic cycle describes when water evaporates, condenses into clouds, and then returns to the ground as rain, sleet, and snow. Snowmelt and rain runoff find their way into springs, streams, rivers, lakes, seas, and oceans. If water in the higher elevations was not replenished, all springs, streams, and rivers would eventually dry up. If no rain fell for hundreds of years previous to Noah's flood, the absence of precipitation would have created serious environmental problems.

Genesis 2:7 describes in more detail how God created the first man. Adam was formed out of "dust from the ground." Scientists have confirmed that the ground

(Earth's crust) contains all the necessary elements to make the human body. The top ten elements and their use in the human body are listed in Table 2.2. Approximately 70% of body weight is water, composed of the elements oxygen and hydrogen. Other elements used in biological processes in decreasingly smaller amounts below those listed include magnesium, iron, zinc, copper, selenium, boron, iodine, chromium, and cobalt.[21]

Table 2.2 – Elements in the Human Body by Weight				
Rank	Element	Weight	Percent	Location and Use
1	Oxygen	43 kg	61.43	Water, amino acids, DNA, RNA
2	Carbon	16 kg	22.86	Amino acids, DNA, RNA, sugar molecules
3	Hydrogen	7.0 kg	10.00	Water, amino acids, DNA, RNA
4	Nitrogen	1.8 kg	2.57	Amino acids, DNA, RNA, ammonia
5	Calcium	1.0 kg	1.43	Bones, teeth
6	Phosphorus	780 g	1.11	Bones, DNA, RNA, ATP, phosphate molecules
7	Potassium	140 g	0.20	Brain, nerve, muscle function
8	Sulfur	140 g	0.20	L-cysteine metabolism, sulfate molecules
9	Sodium	100 g	0.14	Salt, cellular tissues, blood, sweat
10	Chlorine	95 g	0.14	Salt, cellular tissues, blood, sweat

Notes:
(1) Weights are based on a 70 kg (154.3 lb) person.
(2) Hydrogen and oxygen are found primarily as water in the body.
(3) Sodium and chlorine are found primarily as salt in the body.
Reference: Emsley, John (1998). *The Elements.*

The difference between man's physical body and a pile of dirt is: (1) the selection of the proper elements, (2) the selection of the proper amount of each element, and (3) the precise arrangement of those elemental materials. The *sequencing and placement* of selected atoms is what creates DNA, genes, chromosomes, amino acids, proteins, enzymes, and other molecules. During the creation of man, God rapidly assembled the required components while protecting them from deterioration. When all was complete, God breathed life into Adam, thus starting his bodily processes.

Genesis 2:8–9 describe the making of the Garden of Eden. God plants and grows a variety of fruit trees for man. Food is available and abundant. Two special trees are placed in the center of the garden—the tree of life and the tree of knowledge of good and evil. Adam is placed inside the garden as its first occupant.

God deliberately placed the tree of life and the tree of the knowledge of good and evil in the garden. Yahweh gave man free will, in addition to a means of expressing that will. Through these two trees, man could choose life or death. God granted mankind freedom of choice, with full power to obey or disobey.

Exemplar creation views the Garden of Eden as having firm boundaries. The garden was a secure place for Adam and Eve to grow and mature. Plants and animals were carefully selected to create a place of safety and harmony. There were no thorns or thistles. The garden was a carefully controlled, nurturing environment to ensure man survived in an otherwise hostile world. The garden offered protection from the predatory animals that lived outside where tooth and claw reigned. Beyond its protecting boundary, wild animals roamed the land and survival of the fittest was the rule. Food edible by man was scarce and life was hard.

> **Genesis 2:10 And a river went out from Eden to water the garden and from there diverged and became four branches.**
> **2:11   The name of the first is Pishon; it winds through all the land of Havilah, where there is gold.**
> **2:12 And the gold of that land is good; bdellium and onyx stone are there.**
> **2:13 And the name of the second river is the Gihon. It winds through all the land of Cush.**
> **2:14 And the name of the third river is the Tigris; it goes east of Asshur. And the fourth river is the Euphrates.**

These verses give the geographical location of the Garden of Eden with respect to four rivers. Contrary to some claims, the precise location of the Garden of Eden is unknown. Two of the rivers cannot be positively identified with existing rivers today. This does not invalidate the garden's existence, but only illustrates that information is sometimes lost due to the passing of time, although carefully documented.

> **Genesis 2:15 And Yahweh God took the man and put him in the Garden of Eden to cultivate and to keep it.**
> **2:16 And Yahweh God commanded over the man saying, "From every tree of the garden, you *may* eat-eat."**
> **2:17 "But from the tree of the knowledge of good and evil, *do* not eat from, because on the day you eat from it you *shall* die-die."**
> **2:18 And Yahweh God said, "*It is* not good *for* the man to be alone. For him *I shall* make as his counterpart a helper."**

God placed Adam in the Garden of Eden and gave him the responsibility of cultivating and caring for the garden as part of his training. God in His foreknowledge knew mankind would sin and be cast out. God looked beyond Adam's sin and equipped him to survive in a hostile world beyond the garden.

Genesis 2:16–17 constitute the *second command* given in the creation story (the first command is Genesis 1:28). Adam was commanded to "eat-eat" of the trees of the garden, but could not eat of the tree of knowledge of good and evil. If Adam ate from the forbidden tree, he would "die-die." In the Hebrew text, both eating and dying are emphasized through word repetition. Throughout the Old Testament, word repetition is often used for emphasis, although not readily evident in English translations.

Genesis 2:17 contains a stern warning that if Adam ate of the tree of the knowledge of good and evil he would die. In Hebrew culture, a future event could be considered as completed in the present when commanded by one in authority—in this case, God. The day Adam ate of the forbidden tree, he was condemned to die. His physical death was absolutely certain, although it occurred years later.

In Genesis 2:18, God recognizes that Adam should not live alone and purposes to make a helper for him. This is fulfilled in the creation of Eve in Genesis 2:21–22. However, before Eve was created, God formed the animals of the garden.

Genesis 2:19 And Yahweh God formed from the ground every animal of the field and every flier of the sky *that lived within the garden*. And *God* brought *them* to the man to see what he *would* call them and whatever the man called the living creature, that was its name.

2:20 And the man called names to all the beasts and to the fliers of the sky and to all animals of the field *that lived within the garden*. And for Adam *was* not found as his counterpart a helper.

Genesis 2:19 describes when God formed animals of the field and fliers of the sky for the garden. Notice that no marine life is mentioned. Since the garden was located on arid land, without any significant bodies of water, the lack of marine life is not unexpected. All animals were formed from the elements of the ground similar to man in Genesis 2:7. A number of land animals and fliers (estimated at no more than one hundred species) were created to populate the garden and complete this learning, nurturing environment.

Genesis 2:19–20 are often misunderstood. These verses refer only to animals created for the garden. There is no need to believe God created all animals on the entire Earth at this time and brought them to Adam for naming in one day. There is no need to require that Adam hold a marathon session to name more than ten thousand animals on his first day alive. Such belief represents a misunderstanding of the creation story.

Genesis 2:21 And Yahweh God caused a deep sleep to fall over the man and *during* sleep took from one of his ribs and closed up under the flesh.

2:22 And Yahweh God built—which *He* took *of* the rib from the man—into a woman, and brought her to the man.

2:23 And the man said, "This is now bone from my bones and flesh from my flesh; for this *shall* be called woman, because this *was* taken from man."

2:24 So over *this reason*, a man *will* leave his father and his mother and hold fast on his wife. And *they shall* be as one flesh.

2:25 And the two were naked, the man and *his* wife, and not ashamed.

Genesis 2:21–22 describe the building of Eve. With our current knowledge of biotechnology, this description appears completely plausible. God put Adam to sleep and removed genetic material from one of his ribs. Advances in biology point out that DNA from one person can theoretically be used to make another. Stem cells inside bone are ideally suited for cloning. Males have one X and one Y chromosome, while females have two X chromosomes. Conceptually, a woman can be made from a man, but not vice versa. God could have easily duplicated Adam's one X chromosome. Two X chromosomes and Adam's remaining 44 chromosomes provided the basic genetic material for making the first female. Eve was no doubt similar to Adam except for being female. She was his sexual complement and a true counterpart. God completed the job by closing up the incision in Adam's side.

Genesis 2:23–24 describe Adam's acceptance of Eve and acknowledgement of their common flesh. The first wedding ceremony in history is not defined in any detail; however, the requirements for leaving father and mother and becoming one flesh in marriage are emphasized. In marriage, the bond between child and parent is weakened and replaced by that between husband and wife. These verses stress a one man, one woman permanent bond and establish the pattern of marriage God intended for mankind. A man is to hold fast to his wife so tightly they can be considered one, which becomes physical reality in their offspring. Children receive half of their chromosomes from their father and half from their mother.

Genesis 2:25 describes Adam and Eve living in a state of innocence, naked and unashamed. The necessity of a warm climate is subtly pointed out since humans without clothing are quite limited to cold temperatures they can continuously endure. The general environment of the garden was selected for their comfort.

Summary

The vast majority of Earth's history occurs prior to Genesis 1:3, and unfortunately little information is given about this period. The exact time, sequence, and method God used to create the heavens and Earth are not revealed in scripture, and man is left to his own resources to fill in the details. A combination of special and general revelation helps us understand events during this era.

Genesis 1:1, 1:2, and 1:3 are in chronological order, although the time between each verse is undefined by scripture. The time could be one day or millions of years. Genesis 1:1 begins with a statement about God creating the heavens and Earth. In Genesis 1:2, Earth is described as empty of life, dark, and covered with deep water sometime after its creation. Between Genesis 1:2 and 1:3, God creates Earth's biosphere. Dinosaurs and other prehistoric animals are created, roam the land, and become extinct. Hydrocarbon reserves are formed, the fossil record is laid down, sediment layers are built, and significant geological change occurs. At Genesis 1:3, the transition to 24-hour days occurs.

Between Genesis 1:3–31, God describes what He created previous to Genesis 1:3. The sequence in which God describes features of his finished creation does not reflect the sequence of events during creation. Nothing is created during the six-day

Genesis chronicle. The seven verses of Genesis 1:3, 6, 9, 11, 14, 20, and 24 are not creative commands, but declarative statements.

As mentioned, the six-day chronicle in Genesis 1:3–31 emphasizes five major themes: (1) God describes a mature Earth that has existed for some time. (2) God describes a world full of light and life in contrast to a lifeless, dark, water covered world portrayed in Genesis 1:2. (3) God identifies by name five features of His creative work. (4) God approves His creation as "good" and "very good." (5) God is proclaimed as sole creator in contrast to the polytheistic beliefs of the Egyptians and subsequent cultures.

The above five themes could have been presented without being structured in a six-day work format followed by a seventh day of rest. So why six, numerically increasing, sequential days each bounded by evening and morning? Why a rigid seven-day format? The most logical reason is to support observance of the Sabbath. Keep in mind that Moses wrote both Genesis and Exodus, containing the creation story and the Ten Commandments.

Genesis 2:4–25 describes when God *did* things to the Earth and heavens. The first event was planting the garden (Gen. 2:8) and growing trees for the garden (Gen. 2:9). Logically, the garden would have been prepared before man was created. From that point onward, God formed man (Gen. 2:7), breathed life into man (Gen. 2:7), put man in the garden (Gen. 2:8), formed animals for the garden (Gen. 2:19), brought the animals to Adam for naming (Gen. 2:19), built Eve from Adam's rib (Gen. 2:22), and united Adam and Eve in marriage (Gen. 2:22–24). Genesis Chapter 2 flows in a simple narrative style that does not beak until Genesis 4:26.

Synthesis

Theologians and Hebrew scholars have debated for years about the differences between Genesis Chapter 1 (Gen. 1:1–2:3) and Chapter 2 (Gen. 2:5–25). Liberals and skeptics say the chapters represent two conflicting creation accounts written by different authors. Conservatives claim Chapter 1 as the real creation story, while Chapter 2 supplies additional detail, albeit with some thorny problems. *Answers to Tough Questions Skeptics Ask About the Christian Faith* by apologist Josh McDowell discusses these two viewpoints (the longest section in his book) in an attempt to reach a satisfactory answer.[22] Both liberals and conservatives agree the two chapters are radically different.

Genesis Chapter 1 is rigidly structured and highly stylized. In Genesis 1:3–31, all events occur in a six-day format. At the beginning of each day, God makes a descriptive statement about his creation. On the first three days, God calls out (identifies) the common name of the described feature. In five instances, God is proclaimed as maker or creator of the described feature (a parallelism). Each daily narrative is closed with a reference to evening and morning, with the day being enumerated. The six-day chronicle clearly establishes God as a powerful maker and creator.

In contrast, Genesis Chapter 2 flows in a casual narrative style where the order of events is sometimes ambiguous. No rigid time frame exists and no reference is made to specific days, months, or years. The term "create" is meticulously avoided when describing God's creative work. Yahweh is introduced as the name for God.

In Genesis 2:5–25, the narrative is simple and straightforward, something expected of a historical account of this antiquity. Adam describes the location of the Garden of Eden with respect to nearby rivers, but is unable to tell us the time frame, an understandable omission. Simple language is used throughout the narrative. For example, the word "create," which has developed into quite a theological term, is not used. Instead, the actions of Yahweh God are described using the verbs "form, breathe, plant, put, grow, bring, and build." History begins with the forming of Adam, the building of Eve, and the planting and growing of the garden in which they live. Adam's narrative narrowly focuses on mankind with total disregard to the bigger picture. He recounts history as he sees it, without addressing past events or related theological considerations.

Numerous individuals contributed to the writing of Genesis. *Exemplar* creation explains the creation narrative in Genesis 2:5–4:26 as originating with Adam. Multiple individuals are responsible for the material found in Chapters 5–11. The first eleven chapters of Genesis represent memorized history. Before the development of writing, designated historians carefully memorized history and accurately passed it on, a feat well within human capability. The explosion of detail, beginning with Genesis Chapter 12, represents the development of writing and the recording of events as they occurred. The Patriarchs, beginning with Abraham, had their history written down. Genesis 2:5–50:26 represent written history given to Moses. Under the direction of the Holy Spirit, Moses compiled and edited the written material he received to create the book of Genesis.

Imagine for a moment the Bible began at Genesis 2:5. Although accurate and true, the story begs several important questions? To begin with, there is no historical setting. Is the Earth relatively new, or has it been around for a while? Who created the heavens, Earth, Sun, and Moon? Where did the birds, land animals, and marine creatures come from? Who is Yahweh God and what are his attributes and accomplishments? In Genesis Chapter 1, Moses answers all these questions and more.

Moses wrote Genesis 1:1–2:3 as a sophisticated preamble to Adam's simple, historical narrative. Moses theologically introduces the creation of man with a preamble about a single, powerful, creator God in refutation of polytheistic belief. Moses wrote Chapter 1 to establish God as sole creator of the heavens and Earth and all therein. Major features in heaven and on Earth are described and attributed to God's creative power, rather than the pagan gods of the Egyptians, Sumerians, Babylonians, and Assyrians.

Moses received the basis for Genesis Chapter 1 while on Mount Sinai. During a period of six days, God described the heavens, Earth, and other pertinent features. In some instances, God called out (identified) specific features by name. On the seventh day, God did not speak. Moses took the actions of God during these seven days and developed a creation preamble centered around the Sabbath. God himself provided an example for mankind by working six days and then resting on the seventh. The preamble of Genesis Chapter 1 supports observing the Sabbath codified in Exodus 20:8–11, 31:12–17, and Deut. 5:12–15.

In Genesis 1:1–2:3, sixty percent of the words are from the writer, while only forty percent reflect the direct words of God. The first two verses (Gen. 1:1–2), are statements by Moses. Each day of the six-day chronicle begins with God uttering a descriptive statement. In five instances, Moses follows with a parallel statement proclaiming God as maker and creator of the feature described. God is the one who made the expanse (Gen. 1:7), made two great luminaries (Gen. 1:16), created great reptiles, marine creatures, and winged fliers (Gen. 1:21), made the land animals, (Gen. 1:25), and created man (Gen. 1:27). On the seventh day (Gen. 2:1–3), all of the narrative is supplied by Moses. God totally rests and does not speak.

Exemplar creation attributes Moses as the author of Genesis Chapter 1 and the editor of Genesis Chapter 2. The Bible clearly teaches that Moses wrote the Pentateuch (the five books of law). The Pentateuch itself identifies Moses as its writer: Exodus 17:14, 24:4, 34:27, Num. 33:1–2, and Deut. 31:9–11. Eight other books in the Old Testament name Moses as writer of the Pentateuch: Joshua 1:7, 8:31–32, 1 Kings 2:3, 2 Kings 14:6, 21:8, 1 Chron. 22:13, Ezra 6:18, Neh. 13:1, Dan. 9:11, and Malachi 4:4. Six books in the New Testament refer to Moses as writer of the law: Matt. 19:8, Mark 12:26, John 5:45–47, 7:19, Acts 3:22, Romans 10:5, and 1 Cor. 9:9. Some selected sample verses are:

(1) Exodus 17:14 Then the LORD said to Moses, "Write this as a memorial in a book and recite it in the ears of Joshua." (ESV)

(2) Joshua 1:7 Only be strong and very courageous, being careful to do according to all the law that Moses my servant commanded you. (ESV)

(3) 1 Kings 2:3 And keep the charge of the LORD your God, walking in his ways and keeping his statutes, his commandments, his rules, and his testimonies, as it is written in the Law of Moses. (ESV)

(4) 1 Chronicles 22:13 Then you will prosper if you are careful to observe the statutes and the rules that the Lord commanded Moses for Israel. (ESV)

(5) Nehemiah 13:1 On that day they read from the Book of Moses in the hearing of the people. (ESV)

(6) Malachi 4:4 Remember the law of my servant Moses, the statutes and rules that I commanded him at Horeb for all Israel. (ESV)

Exemplar creation attributes Genesis 2:4, a transitional verse, to Moses. He combined the words "create" and "Yahweh" in the same verse. In Gen. 1:1–2:3, Moses uses the word "create" and never uses the term "Yahweh." In Gen. 2:5–4:26, Adam never uses the word "create" and freely uses the term "Yahweh" for God's name. Moses left distinctive clues to separate material he authored from Adam's account.

Conclusion

When Genesis Chapters 1 and 2 are properly understood, they fully complement each other. They are not two conflicting creation stories. Rather, they form a logical, integrated, historically accurate, and theologically sound account about the origin of the universe, Earth, its biosphere, and mankind. In addition, no inherent conflict exists with scientific evidence in regard to time.

Genesis Chapter 3 continues Adam's historical narrative of events in the Garden of Eden. Through Satan's influence, Adam and Eve disobey God and eat of the tree of knowledge of good and evil. They are punished and cast out of the garden, never to return. Adam and Eve give birth to two sons, Cain and Abel, and the elder kills the younger in the first recorded murder in history. Adam and Eve conceive another son, Seth, in addition to many more sons and daughters (Gen. 5:4). Cain and Seth marry their immediate relatives (sisters) and begin having sons and daughters. From that point onward, mankind continues to multiply and fill the Earth.

The complete Genesis creation story has several levels of complexity capable of appealing to a wide reading audience, ranging from a small child to the scientist and theologian. On the surface, Genesis is a simple story of an omnipotent God and how He created the heavens, Earth, and all therein. On a deeper level, there are significant implications about the creation of man in the image of God, the building of Eve from Adam's rib, the establishment of marriage, the Garden of Eden as a protective enclosure, Adam's assigned job of cultivating the garden, the two special trees in the center of the garden, human free will, effects of the first sin, Satan's influence, and man's punishment for sinning. On a still deeper level are implications concerning the lifeless, dark, water covered Earth (Gen. 1:2), great reptiles (Gen. 1:21), the trinity (Gen. 1:26), the dominion mandate (Gen. 1:28), and the messianic prophecy for the coming of Christ (Gen. 3:15). On all three levels, the Genesis story is true.

Exemplar creation is based on a careful study of the Hebrew text of the Old Testament and presents the Genesis creation story as an abbreviated, non-technical, historical account of origins that is truthful and trustworthy. The creation story and scientific evidence do not conflict where they intersect. Special revelation and general revelation can be harmonized in regard to significant time. Genesis Chapters 1 and 2 can be accepted by intelligent, educated, biblically knowledgeable, scientifically literate Christians as a credible explanation of origins.

"The world wants to be deceived."
Martin Luther (1483—1546)

Chapter 3

Roots of Deception

Time: 600–300 BC
Place: Somewhere on the Arabian Peninsula

An imposing figure moved through the narrow streets. His gait was slow but not labored, more of a stroll than someone bent on a destination. He smiled broadly, greeting those he met. A man at peace with fellow men. Occasionally he stopped and exchanged pleasantries. Short conversations sprinkled with terms of admiration and praise. He was obviously well-liked and respected, if not fawned upon by his admirers.

The Sabbath had come to a close, night was fast approaching. Shadows grew and deepened in the shelter of the tightly packed houses, soon to be swallowed in darkness.

His pace quickened. The neighborhood through which our figure trod might be best described as typical middle-class for its time and period. The simply built, mud brown houses were small, cramped, and colorless. They provided basic shelter and a place to call home. Dogs, goats, and other family pets roamed the streets. The cries of hungry children echoed among the barren walls.

This soon gave way to structures whose inhabitants were obviously more prosperous. The white-washed houses gleamed in the fading light. The cobblestone streets were swept clean, lest their occupants soil the bottoms of their robes. A sense of dignity and affluence permeated the air. Although not yet dark, lamplight streamed from the windows, clearly an extravagance and a sign that servants were eager to please.

Finally, the lone figure stopped before a thick, oil polished, cedar door. Pausing briefly to admire its combination of strength and beauty, he entered. Two servants waited in the anteroom. Speaking sharply of a desire to begin the after-Sabbath meal, he strode purposefully to his bed chamber. Anticipating his arrival, three lamps had been lit. Better to waste oil than want light, or incur the master's wrath.

He quickly stripped off his ceremonial robe, made of the finest Egyptian linen. The garment had cost him a small fortune, but was well worth the expense. The en-

tire outfit consisted of a head scarf, sash, and robe, embellished with fringe, tassels, and pockets, in addition to ornate embroidering. None of the other teachers wore anything comparable. His followers admired him all the more, while jealousy infected the competition.

As he slipped into a freshly washed, plainly functional robe, his visage became more apparent in the lighted room. He was a tall man, with a robust physique. He had a well-proportioned face, accented with a strong chin, firm cheeks, and an aquiline nose, all covered with unblemished skin. An expanding waistline testified of good food and better wine. The eyes radiated alertness and intelligence. Combined with a powerful voice, quick mind, and dignified mannerisms, he was an impressive figure. A modest assessment, of which the owner was proud.

His mind wandered over the day's events. His reputation as a teacher of the Torah was growing along with a faithful following. Each Sabbath day his audience was larger and, more importantly, so were the offerings. The money bag he was obliged to carry home grew heavier each week. But then, expenses kept increasing. Adjusting one's lifestyle to meet the rising expectations of an influential position was a burden. And there was always the obligatory public offering for the poor (they seemed to always be in need). At least no one knew what coins he dropped in the box.

A recent speech given by an orator in the public square came to mind. The heathen claimed the Gentile gods were powerful. Each god was responsible for creating some plant, beast, or bird, in addition to the sky, sun, and moon. The pagan's tale had kept the audience in rapt attention. In spite of his mesmerizing story, Aaliyah wanted to stone him, but the civil authorities forbade such action.

The story of beginnings in the Torah recounted six days when Yahweh described, named, and blessed all that he had created—not impressive at all. All agreed the story was open to interpretation, and Aaliyah had been working on an improved version. With his new explanation, Yahweh commanded rather than described. God commanded and created for six days and then rested on the Sabbath. On the first day, He commanded light into existence. On the second day, He commanded and separated the water above from the water below. On the third day, He commanded and separated land from water. On the fourth day, Yahweh commanded the sun, moon, and stars into existence. Being all-powerful, God simply spoke to create the birds of the sky, the beasts of the field, and the fish of the sea. Finally on the Sabbath, Yahweh rested from his labors.

He absent-mindedly fingered the large gold ring adorning his left hand. However, reality returned with the aroma of cooked lamb and a growling stomach. A sumptuous if not lavish meal awaited his presence, followed by an evening of pleasure with his favorite concubine.

He would give his new interpretation additional thought. By slightly changing the pronunciation, he could attach a new meaning to the troublesome verbs he had identified. There would be no need to change the written text of Moses—anathema to *such an idea. And who was going to oppose him, the most respected teacher in the entire city? His changes were a masterpiece of subtlety and allowed for a revolutionary explanation. The ignorant would readily accept his teaching while the literate might take slightly more convincing. He could hear the coins tinkling in the box.*

Epilogue: Two Sabbaths later, Aaliyah presented his highly embellished interpretation. The response was more than gratifying; they loved it! Yahweh was all-powerful and stronger than any of the heathen gods. Now highly praised, word of his message quickly spread. In time, his distorted explanation would become the accepted belief of all Jews and set the Bible on a collision course with empirical science two thousand years in the future.

Biblical Authority as the Basis for Christian Belief

To say we have been deceived about Genesis, implies knowledge of a correct account. To identify deception, legitimacy must be established as a benchmark. To state that Christians have been misled about the creation story, requires recognition of a truthful account.

The Bible is God's message to humanity, containing both historical and doctrinal information. Traditional Christian belief (taught in the Bible) is that God inspired selected men to write the Old and New Testament. The original manuscripts have been copied and passed down through the centuries to establish the basis for the Bible we have today. During thousands of years, God's providence has protected the Bible against corrupting influences and concerted attempts to destroy it.

The Bible is the final authority for Christian belief, worship, and practice. Church traditions, ecclesiastical authorities, elected or appointed spiritual leaders, church councils, human creeds, religious declarations, philosophies, extra-biblical writings, personal revelations, and self-proclaimed prophets do not replace biblical authority. While elements of our religious heritage may be enlightening, they must be subservient to scripture. From inception, the Bible has remained steadfast throughout cultural, moral, religious, philosophical, political, scientific, and technological change. Centuries of history have established God's word as the only steadfast guide for the church and its theology. The Bible was written to be relevant throughout mankind's past, present, and future.

The Bible stands above all other secular and religious books in the world for its authorship, content, claims, and antiquity. *Evidence That Demands a Verdict* by Josh McDowell is a timeless commentary about the Bible. He discusses its authors, their professions, and the times in which they wrote. McDowell details the manuscripts on which the Bible is based and convincingly points out that more ancient copies of the New Testament exist today than any other document of antiquity. By careful comparison, scholars have been able to verify the faithful reproduction of essentially all the original New Testament writings. Copies of manuscripts in the Hebrew language of the Old Testament and Greek of the New Testament serve as the basis for today's English translation of the Bible.

The Bible is the only true and dependable source for the Christian church's theology and belief. As Dr. Harold Lindsell points out in *The Battle for the Bible*, establishing the Bible as the ultimate authority for religious information is of paramount importance for the person who believes in God. Church teaching should support the Bible rather than destroy its credibility.

The Genesis creation story has a huge impact on our acceptance of the Bible as true. As John MacArthur says, "If the biblical creation account is in any degree unreliable, the rest of Scripture stands on a shaky foundation."[1] If the Genesis creation story is rejected, can we believe other supernatural acts of God in the Bible? If we disallow the miracles of Jesus Christ, can we logically accept Him as the son of God with power to forgive sins? If we accept Darwinian evolution and see ourselves as evolved primates, are right and wrong, sin and punishment, or heaven and hell relevant issues? To a large extent, our belief in the Bible stands or falls on our view of God as an omnipotent creator who made the heavens, Earth, and all therein. When God is firmly established as our creator, other teachings of the Bible (especially the miracles) become credible and readily acceptable.

Although the Bible is the basis for Christian belief, we are given a stern warning about false beliefs taught by deceitful teachers based on their incorrect interpretation of scripture. In 2 Timothy 2:15, the apostle Paul says, "Study to shew thyself approved unto God, a workman that needeth not to be ashamed, rightly dividing the word of truth." As Bible believers, we are challenged to carefully study the word of God to determine its true teachings.

Biblical Inerrancy as the Basis for Christian Belief

The Bible testifies to its own authority and truthfulness, as revealed by a study of pertinent verses. As stated in 2 Timothy 3:16, "All scripture is given by inspiration of God, and is profitable for doctrine, for reproof, for correction, for instruction in righteousness." Additional verses in Titus 1:2 and Hebrews 6:18 point out that God cannot lie. It logically follows that when God inspired men to write the Bible, what He directed them to say was true and without error.

In 1988, the International Council on Biblical Inerrancy sponsored a meeting in Chicago to discuss biblical inerrancy. The Chicago Statement on Biblical Inerrancy resulted and was signed by around 300 evangelical biblical scholars. Included in this statement are Articles of Affirmation and Denial comprised of nineteen proclamations regarding the authority, inspiration, and inerrancy of the Bible. Article X states: "Inspiration, strictly speaking, applies only to the autographic text of Scripture, which in the providence of God can be ascertained from available manuscripts with great accuracy. We further affirm that copies and translations of Scripture are the Word of God to the extent that they faithfully represent the original."

When the nineteen articles are carefully analyzed, inspiration and inerrancy are limited to the original autographs of the inspired writers. The original writings no longer exist. Since biblical inerrancy is based on the original manuscripts, the Article X statement cannot be disproved.

The original inspired writings of the Old Testament have been carefully copied and passed down through history. Based on a thorough analysis, surviving copies show a high degree of agreement. However, a minuscule number of scribal errors are found in the Hebrew text. For example, in 2 Chronicles 22:2 the KJV says that Ahaziah, king of Judah (not to be confused with Ahaziah the king of Israel), was 42 years old when he began to reign, based on the Hebrew text. In contrast, 2 Kings 8:26 gives an age of 22 years when Ahaziah began to reign.

A small number of intentional scribal changes have been found. For example, the age when Saul began reigning and his age at death are missing from the Old Testament. This information appears to have been intentionally deleted from the original Hebrew text in 1 Samuel 13:1, deduced by comparing the verse format with 2 Samuel 2:10 and 5:4 (the format is identical except for the deleted ages). Critics typically identify these as major errors in the Bible.

Bible scholars have used a combination of Septuagint manuscripts, Syriac translations, and New Testament references in an attempt to correct scribal errors and deletions. Regardless, microscopic changes of this nature do not necessarily correlate to an error in the original manuscript.

Today, *perceived errors* in understanding the Bible are the main challenge to biblical inerrancy—with the creation account being foremost. We are faced with the issue of whether our understanding agrees with the real message of the text. When viewing a particular passage, does our perception agree with reality—the original written word based on normal rules of speech, grammar, context, and syntax?

In regard to the Old Testament, today's Hebrew Bible is the basis for modern English translations. The *Biblia Hebraica* (Hebrew Bible) is based on original manuscripts, some from the dawn of writing, that have been copied and passed down through the centuries. Minor errors have occurred through repetitive copying and, in some instances, intentional change. Textual criticism and painstaking comparison among ancient manuscripts have been used to correct discernible errors and reconstruct the text of the original writers as closely as possible.[2]

In some cases, our knowledge of the Old Testament writers' message is less than clear. Our understanding of the Bible has been affected by a general loss of information throughout time. Some Hebrew words and their meaning in reference to animals, plants, minerals, objects, geographical features, cities, and personal names have been lost in history. The precise meaning of some ancient Hebrew verbs, nouns, and other words are not understood with certainty. Some colloquial Hebrew expressions, poetical statements, and metaphorical sayings are ambiguous. Because of these effects, certain words, terms, and verses are translated from Hebrew into English on a best effort basis. The mature believer can easily accept minor textual uncertainties and interpretative problems without having a disparaging view of the Old Testament.

In addition, we can acknowledge variations in writing style and a lack of standardized grammar, without accusing scripture of being in error. We can accept a non-chronological style of writing about historical events, without saying the author is wrong. We can recognize the use of informal quotes from other passages of scripture, without saying the writer made a mistake. We can understand that two accounts of the same event may differ in detail, without necessarily being in conflict. We can acknowledge that the translation of some words and names from one language to another (e.g., Hebrew to Greek) was not standardized and varied among writers.

Added to the above, are issues influenced by tradition and theology. This is especially true of the Genesis creation account. Theologians have traditionally had a specific way of explaining certain key words in the creation story, although their explanation is not supported by the rest of the Old Testament. This has led to the perception that Genesis Chapters 1 and 2 conflict with scientific evidence, and the creation story is false.

When examined objectively, the Hebrew Bible is a phenomenal book. For example, the writers of the Old Testament span roughly one thousand years (Moses to Nehemiah) and represent thirty-two or more authors. The message recorded in the 39 books they wrote is amazingly coherent. By far, the Old Testament is the oldest book in the world. In considering the antiquity of the creation account, when properly understood, it is sophisticated by today's standards and significantly different from pagan stories and mythological ramblings. We can accept that God inspired the writing of the Hebrew Bible in its original form. Beginning at inception, its copying, understanding, and translation have deteriorated to a minuscule extent because of the influence of fallible men, their errant ideas, and the passing of time. Man has definitely been a corrupting influence. Today, through careful study we can be confident of the message God intended us to have—especially the Genesis account.

Alternates to the Bible as the Basis for Religious Belief

Accepting the Bible as the inerrant, inspired word of God and the authority for Christian belief is an important issue. New Testament Christians during the first century after the time of Christ accepted scripture as their only authority. The writings of the God-inspired apostles and prophets were the basis for their belief. However, both then and now, some have strayed from this practice.

First among religious groups that challenge the Bible as the sole authority for Christian belief is the Roman Catholic Church and, with more than one billion members, is a force to be reckoned with. The Catholic Church accepts the Bible and eleven apocryphal books as one authority, but also church tradition and the ruling pope.

So the Bible, church tradition and around 266 popes (decreeing with papal infallibility) form the basis of Catholic belief. The church claims a succession of popes back to the apostle Peter,[3] although this claim is not supported by the Bible or secular history.[4] The Catholic Church alleges to be the one, holy, apostolic, universal church founded by Jesus Christ.

Popes have had a major influence in developing Roman Catholic Church theology. The pope claims to speak in behalf of Jesus Christ and is considered infallible when speaking *ex cathedra* (a belief imposed by Vatican I in 1870). The pope has primacy in the church and is often referred to as the Vicar of Christ. However, history reveals that popes are quite human. As pointed out in *Vicars of Christ: The Dark Side of the Papacy*, a number of popes between 500 and 1600 AD are best described as corrupt. They sold church positions for profit, were materialistic, politically ruthless, abused their power, neglected their spiritual duties, pursued sensual pleasures, and enjoyed numerous concubines, prostitutes and, in some cases, homosexual partners. Laying aside their moral failings, "Many popes have made astonishing [doctrinal] errors. They have repeatedly contradicted one another and the Gospel. Far from championing the dignity of man, they have times without number withheld from Catholics and non-Catholics the most elementary rights."[5]

Teachings and practices of the Catholic Church often conflict with the Bible. For example, Catholics pray to Mary and worship her as the "Mother of God." There is no mention or command in the New Testament to worship or pray to Mary. In contrast, Jesus is the only mediator between man and God (1 Timothy 2:5) and we are to pray in his name (John 14:13–14). Other beliefs and practices essentially unique to Catholics are penitence (in contrast to repentance), indulgences for the dead (burning candles and offering mass), praying to Catholic saints, priestly confession, the priestly absolution of sins, a requirement of celibacy for priests (not to be equated with chastity), belief in purgatory, rote prayers, and the belief Mary remained a virgin her entire life. Catholics believe in transubstantiation, a doctrine that the bread and wine literally turn into the blood and body of Christ during the Holy Eucharist (communion). In 401 AD, St. Augustine published his treatise, *On the Good of Marriage*, and argued that sexual relations in marriage between husband and wife were sinful, except for begetting children, a view still dominant within church leadership. Catholic doctrine forbids the use of modern contraceptives for birth control. Using St. Augustine's reasoning, allowing a married couple to use a contraceptive would condone sinful sex.

The Mormon Church is a highly visible American religion, claiming a membership of more than thirteen million. This group was started by Joseph Smith, Jr. (1805–1844), best described as a charismatic, opportunistic, deceitful, sexually promiscuous, ego maniac who created a religious following. He practiced polygamy and had around thirty-four wives, eleven of whom were married to other men.[6] As a teenager, Joseph Smith was allegedly directed by the angel Moroni to find a set of buried golden plates near his farm home. He eventually retrieved the plates, written in "reformed

Egyptian," and translated them into the *Book of Mormon*, first published in 1830. More of the teachings of Joseph Smith were printed in *Doctrine and Covenants*, first published in 1835. In 1851, Franklin D. Richards published a number of additional writings by Joseph Smith and others in *The Pearl of Great Price*. Mormons consider these three books equal or superior to the Bible.

Mormons differ from orthodox Christian doctrine on many issues. They believe that salvation can only be obtained by accepting Joseph Smith, and the Church of Jesus Christ of Latter-day Saints as the only true church.[7] The most outlandish belief is that God was once a man with a physical body. Faithful Mormon men can likewise become gods through their obedience to Mormon requirements and good deeds. Other beliefs unique to the Mormon Church are baptism for the dead, celestial marriage, and belief in three heavens. Baptism for the dead is a major practice and allows a Mormon in good standing to be baptized for a dead loved one or other unrelated persons (thus their intense interest in genealogy) in a temple ceremony to obtain a greater degree of glory in heaven.

Jehovah's Witnesses, another American religion, claim a worldwide membership of more than seven million adherents. This group had its beginning as Zion's Watch Tower Tract Society started by Charles Taze Russell (1852–1916). Russell was a charismatic figure and a prolific writer who viewed himself as "God's mouthpiece." He taught that Christ would return in 1874 and 1878 (two failed prophecies). He was serious about pyramidology and believed the Great Pyramid of Giza was built by the Hebrews and contained biblical-related information. After Russell's death, his followers fragmented into a number of groups, with Jehovah's Witnesses eventually becoming the most successful.[8]

Foremost among Jehovah's Witnesses doctrinal teachings are denial of both the trinity and the deity of Jesus Christ. God the Father created Jesus. Only their religion represents true Christianity. They do not believe in hell as a place of punishment; instead, unbelievers die and cease to exist. According to their teaching, only 144,000 will go to heaven and all other faithful Jehovah's Witnesses will live forever in an earthly paradise. Organization leadership predicted Armageddon and the establishment of Christ's kingdom on Earth in 1914, 1925, and 1975 (all failed prophecies). Jehovah's Witnesses believe Christ died on a single upright pole rather than a cross. Faithful members do not celebrate birthdays, Christmas, Easter, Independence Day, Thanksgiving, and other holidays. They reject military service and refuse to salute the American flag, recite the Pledge of Allegiance, or sing the National Anthem. They decline use of the word "church" and meet in "Kingdom Halls." They forbid members to have blood transfusions and at one time forbade them to have vaccinations and organ transplants. Official doctrinal position is disseminated through two magazines, *Awake* and *The Watchtower*, from their headquarters in Brooklyn, New York. They have translated their own Bible, called the "New World Translation of the Holy Scriptures," that emphasizes use of the name "Jehovah" for God, in addition to other unique doctrinal teachings.[9]

The Church of Christ, Scientist (or Christian Science), a fading religion, was founded by Mary Baker Eddy in 1866. She wrote *Science and Health with Key to the Scriptures*, published in 1875, to explain her beliefs and give insight to the Bible. Her book is the primary source of doctrine for her followers, first organized as a church in 1879. Christian Scientists see spiritual reality as the only reality, and material reality is an illusion. Physical healing through the right spiritual and mental attitude is stressed. Sickness is the result of fear, ignorance, or sin. Neither hell as a place of eternal punishment nor heaven as a place of eternal reward are taught. A person who dies, simply adjusts to another level of consciousness. The Christian Science religion does not have trained pastors but instead relies on "Readers," lay members voted into office by the local congregation to teach for a period of time.

The Seventh-day Adventist Church, with a current membership of around fourteen million, was formally organized in 1863. At that time, its most prominent members were Ellen G. White, James White, and Joseph Bates. Ellen White rose to prominence in the church after convincing fellow Adventists about her gift of prophecy. She claimed to have received a number of visions from God. She was a charismatic speaker in addition to a prolific writer and published more than 40 books and 5,000 periodical articles (the most prolific non-fiction female writer of all time). According to Adventist doctrine, keeping the Sabbath holy as taught in the Old Testament is binding on all Christians today. For this reason, Adventists meet on the seventh day of the week. Followers of Ellen White believe the wicked will be destroyed in the lake of fire described in Revelation, rather than suffer eternally in hell (there is no eternal punishment). Death results in an unconscious state. Until they are resurrected, both the righteous and unrighteous are unconscious (soul sleep).

In addition to the above five religions, a host of other Bible-related religions have developed in America during the last two centuries and include the Unitarian Church, Worldwide Church of God by Herbert W. Armstrong, Church of God International by Garner Ted Armstrong, Philadelphia Church of God by Gerald Flurry, Community of Christ (RLDS), the Unification Church of Sun Myung Moon, and Aryan Nations Church by Dr. Wesley Swift. Portions of their doctrines depart significantly from orthodox Christian belief. Several non-biblical-based religions have sprung up, one of the most visible being The Church of Scientology, based on the teachings of science fiction writer L. Ron Hubbard.

One common theme among all the above churches is that they were established by strong, if not charismatic leaders, often claiming visions, revelations, and divine authority. Most leaders were prolific writers and established their unique beliefs through books they wrote, apart from the Bible. They saw themselves as chosen of God. Most claimed the Bible as their authority and taught some biblical doctrine; however, they all developed extra-biblical or counter-biblical theology not found in scripture.

As illustrated by this brief discussion, when we fail to use the Bible as our sole religious authority, we are cast adrift in a world of charlatans, deceivers, egotists, and power mongers. About any belief or practice imaginable can become legitimatized. A number of the above religions claim to be the "true church" whose leaders say they are spokesman for God. History is replete with charismatic leaders who claim to be God's prophet of the day, ready to dispense their truth to the world.

For Christians, accepting the Bible as the foundation for our religious belief is the most important doctrine we can hold. The Old Testament tells us about Yahweh, details the creation story, and gives a history of the Hebrew people. The New Testament records the life and ministry of Jesus Christ, provides a history of the early church, and defines Christianity. The Bible is the only dependable source of information concerning religious belief and practice. If the Bible did not exist, there would be no Jews, Catholics, or Protestants. We would be atheists, animists, ancestor worshipers, idolaters, or pagans. Our religions would be characterized by Buddhism, Hinduism, Sikhism, Shintoism, Jainism, and Scientology.

When Christians use the Bible as their sole authority for belief and practice, they can easily reject spurious religious teachings. This does not necessarily mean Christians will agree on every subject (there are legitimate biblical interpretative issues), but common ground can be established on the clear teaching of scripture. Without the Bible as our sole religious authority, doctrine is bounded only by the limits of human imagination. The ignorant and trusting are easily drawn to esoteric, mystical, unusual, radical, sensational, and bizarre beliefs, especially when taught by a charismatic leader with an air of sophistication. In contrast, educated Christians with an intellectual mindset can be led astray by popular social agendas, appealing philosophies, doctrinal rationalization, and self-serving causes.

In closing this section, I want to emphasize that I have no axe to grind about the specific religions mentioned above. I have no interest in becoming embroiled in their theological beliefs and use them only to clearly illustrate what happens when we go beyond the Bible in teaching and practice. This applies to whether we add, delete, misinterpret, or embellish the biblical text. This is a major issue for Christians who believe traditional young-Earth creation theology represents a correct translation and explanation of the Genesis creation story.

Historical Hebrew Beliefs

We tend to think that believers around the time of the birth of Jesus Christ were highly uniform in their doctrine. After all, they accepted the written word of the prophets, strongly believed in God, and were 2,000 years closer to when the Old Testament was given. In truth, people before, during, and after Christ's ministry held a variety of beliefs and were often divided. Some different views within the church today reflect beliefs held during the New Testament period.

The Sadducees represented the wealthy upper class of Jewish society during the time of Christ. Sadducees derived their name from Zadok, the high priest of the first temple built during the time of Solomon.[10] Descendants of Zadok served as high priest until Solomon's temple was destroyed. The Sadducees strictly observed the written law. They rejected the immortality of the soul (the soul ceased to exist at death). Likewise, bodily resurrection was denied, along with any punishment for evil after death. They believed in human free will.[11]

The Pharisees represented the middle and lower classes of Jewish society during Christ's earthly ministry. Most were officials, bureaucrats, judges, and educators. They derived their name from the Hebrew term *perushim* which means "separate."[12] They were scrupulous in their observance of the written law (Pentateuch) and oral law. The oral law was an interpretation of written law, developed by successive generations of teachers. Pharisees believed in the providence of God and His interference in human affairs. They believed in a bodily resurrection. Men would be rewarded or punished after death based on their deeds. Adherents tithed and followed purification rituals.[13] They believed the Messiah would set up His kingdom on Earth and bring world peace.

Although not mentioned in the Bible, the Essenes are another important Jewish religious group during the New Testament period. What we know about their beliefs and practices comes from extra-biblical sources such as Josephus and the Dead Sea Scrolls. Essenes believed in communal living, and when a new member joined, he gave his land and money to the community. They practiced celibacy, and the Qumran community that copied and hid the Dead Sea Scrolls was composed of all male celibates. Doctrinal beliefs included immortality of the soul, a resurrection, and final judgment. Physical purity through bathing was emphasized. The use of oil as an ointment was rejected because it defiled the body.[14]

By the time of Christ, there were a number of contradictory Jewish beliefs, some of which are not taught in the Old Testament. Based on a combination of written and oral law, opposing beliefs among Jewish sects included such topics as the state of the dead, resurrection from the dead, hell as a place of punishment, forgiveness, divorce, rules for observing the Sabbath, personal cleansing, male celibacy, the existence of angels, personal free will, predestination, and God's involvement in the affairs of men. Also predominant during this time was young-Earth creation theology, the belief that God spoke the heavens and Earth into existence in six literal days.

Fundamental Principles of Biblical Creation

Because of controversy about the creation story, any search for truth must have a solid foundation. As illustrated by the above, several errant teachings have been around since before the time of Christ. Some are deeply entrenched within current religious belief. The Genesis creation story ranks among the most troublesome issues. A combination of special revelation (the Bible) and general revelation (evidence about the physical world) establish the basis for resolving this problem.

My search for a credible translation and explanation of Genesis is based on four fundamental principles: (1) God created the heavens and Earth. (2) God inspired a written account of what He created. (3) His inspired written account will not conflict with His physical creation. (4) Any perceived disagreement between the two is mankind's responsibility.

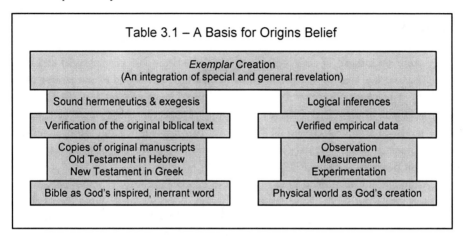

Truth cannot conflict with truth. Special revelation and general revelation should not clash. In reality, orthodox English translations of the Bible strongly conflict with general revelation in regard to time.

God is neither dishonest nor incompetent. Apparent conflict between the Genesis creation story and general revelation cannot be blamed on God. He did not give us false information in the Bible, nor falsify physical evidence to mislead us. He is not a deceiver. The blame for any error lies solely on mankind, rather than God.

Table 3.1 illustrates the basis on which Bible students and Christians can form their beliefs about origins. The foundation consists of the Bible as God's word and the physical universe as His creation. Parallel lines of information and reasoning build upwards and merge at the top as an integrated explanation of origins based on special and general revelation.

Traditional Young-Earth Creation Theology

Conservative Hebrew scholars consider Moses as the author of the first five books of the Old Testament, often called the Pentateuch (or *Torah* by the Jews). Numerous passages in Exodus, Numbers, and Deuteronomy point to Moses as the author. Additional references in Joshua, 1 Kings, 2 Kings, Ezra, Nehemiah, Daniel, and Malachi refer to Moses as the author. In John 7:19, Jesus refers to Moses as writer of the Pentateuch. In regard to Genesis, Moses compiled and edited written history passed down from Adam, Noah, Abraham, Isaac, Jacob, and their descendants.

(Some young-Earth creationists believe that writing is nearly as old as the human race and that Genesis 1:1 to 5:1 was written during Adam's lifetime.[15]) When Moses wrote Genesis, what he penned in Hebrew on the original manuscripts was inspired of God and without error.

Young-Earth creationists claim their theology has been the accepted belief throughout history, and work from the *past to the present* to prove their point. God spoke the heavens, Earth, and all therein into existence during six 24-hour days around 4004 BC according to Ussher.[16] Moses recorded this event in the book of Genesis. The Hebrews were God's chosen people who preserved and copied the Pentateuch and other books of the Old Testament. Around 275 BC, the Septuagint translation was begun when Jewish scribes translated the first five books of the Old Testament (the Pentateuch) from Hebrew into Greek. This major work strongly supports traditional young-Earth creation theology. Further along in history, the writings of Philo (20 BC–50 AD) and Josephus (37–100 AD) reveal that young-Earth creation theology was an accepted belief at that time. Moving on to 500 AD, the Masoretic scribes began adding vowel points and accent marks to the Hebrew text. These vocalization marks support young-Earth creation theology. Jerome's translation of the Bible into Latin supports this theology, followed centuries later by German, French, and English versions.

Proponents view the above historical continuum as overwhelming confirmation of the truth of their position. From their perspective, traditional young-Earth theology is supported by more than twenty-two hundred years of translation, commentary, and belief.

Roots of Deception

A second line of reasoning, counter to the above, works from the *present backward to the past*. This position is skeptical of traditional young-Earth theology and focuses on pointing out (1) how this theology conflicts with scientific evidence in regard to time, (2) how this errant belief was added to the Bible, and (3) how we can appeal to the Hebrew text for our understanding of Genesis.

Starting around 1700, scientists began to question a young age for the Earth. Up until that time, traditional young-Earth creation theology had been the reigning biblical paradigm, and had never been seriously challenged. As scientific knowledge grew, so did physical evidence in support of an old age for the Earth. Newly discovered evidence conflicted with young-Earth creation theology. During the last 300 years, empirical evidence in support of an old age for the universe, Earth, and its biosphere has accumulated to the point it will never be overturned. Orthodox translations of the Bible and young-Earth creation theology are in irreconcilable conflict with scientific evidence in regard to time.

As we go back in time, the Masoretic Text appears as a key piece of evidence.

The Old Testament we have today is translated from the Masoretic Text, produced by the Masoretes (a group of Hebrew scribes) who faithfully copied and preserved the Hebrew Bible after the time of Christ. To understand what they did wrong, we must first understand the language of Genesis.

The Old Testament was written primarily in Hebrew, with a small amount in Aramaic, using twenty-two alphabetic characters. There are no vowels in biblical Hebrew, and all letters are consonants. During the time of Christ, when Hebrew was read aloud, the speaker put vowels into the words. To standardize the pronunciation of words, Masoretic scribes added vowel points and accent marks (small dots, dashes, and other symbols above, below, and within the Hebrew letters) to the text.

Several sources help identify when vocalization marks were added. According to *The Anchor Bible Dictionary*, between 500 and 700 AD, Hebrew scribes developed vowel points and accent marks to aid in the reading of Hebrew text.[17] Another source, *The New Encyclopedia Britannica,* states that the Masoretic text was meticulously assembled and codified and supplied with diacritical marks to ensure correct pronunciation. This work began around the 6th century and was completed in the 10th century, by scholars at Talmudic academies in Babylonia and Palestine.[18] A third source, *The Text of the Old Testament* by Ernst Würthwein, says vowel points and accent marks originated between 650 and 750 AD.[19]

The work of the Masoretes raises several important issues. First, vocalization marks were added 500 years or more after Christ's ministry, proven by the Dead Sea Scrolls and other archaeological discoveries. *Vocal marks were not in the original text and are uninspired additions to the Bible.* Secondly, traditional young-Earth creation theology was the dominant origins belief of the day, and the Masoretes fully accepted it. Vocal marks they added support their theology. Thirdly, vowel points and accent marks control the interpretation of some key verbs in the Genesis creation account. By the seemingly innocuous addition of vocal marks, Masoretic scribes helped embed young-Earth creation theology into the biblical text.

As we go back in time, the writings of Flavius Josephus (37–100 AD), a Jewish historian, attest to the dominance of young-Earth creation theology immediately following Christ's ministry. Josephus wrote extensively about Jewish beliefs and history, and commented on the Old Testament. In regard to the Genesis creation story, Josephus explained that creation occurred in six days. Heaven and earth were created on the first day. Earth was in a thick darkness and a wind moved across the surface. God created light and separated it from darkness. He named night and day. On the second day, God placed the heaven over the whole world and determined that heaven should stand by itself. He placed a firmament around the earth and made it agreeable as a source of moisture, rain, and dew. On the third day, God appointed dry land to appear with the sea round about it. He made the plants and seeds spring up. On the fourth day, He "adorned" the heaven with the Sun, Moon, and the other stars, and appointed their motions and courses. On the fifth day, God "produced" the living creatures that swim in the sea and fly in the air. On the sixth day, God made the four-footed beasts, both male and female. He also formed man. In six days, God made the world and all therein. The seventh day was a time of rest called the Sabbath.[20] Josephus' account of creation essentially agrees with traditional young-Earth theology as taught today.

Philo of Alexandria (20 BC–50 AD) was also a Jewish historian. He lived in Alexandria, Egypt, which had a large Jewish population at the time. Philo gave a detailed commentary on the Genesis creation story, generally supportive of traditional young-Earth creation theology. According to Philo, during the first three days God separated light from darkness. The whole body of water in existence was spread out over all the earth and penetrated its parts like a sponge soaked with moisture. Earth was swampy land and deep mud. The elements of earth and water were mixed up and combined together in one confused mass of an "undistinguishable and shapeless nature." God caused the salt water to be gathered together.[21] God began to "adorn" the land and bade it bring forth grass, corn, herbs, fodder for cattle, and food for man. He commanded every kind of tree to spring up, both wild and cultivated. The earth produced full grown trees with fruit. On the fourth day, He "adorned" the heavens. The earth brought forth all kinds of plants and fruits before the Sun and Moon existed.[22] God created stars perceptible by the external senses.[23] On the fifth day, God proceeded to create the "races of mortal creatures." He created the aquatic animals, including the "races of fish and sea monsters," followed by the "races of birds." On the sixth day, God had the earth bring forth cattle and beasts and creeping things of each kind. Man was created on the sixth day, the last of God's created creatures.[24] Philo's rambling commentary of the creation account appears to be a mixture of scripture, bad theology, and an active imagination.

As we retreat backward in time, the Septuagint (a Greek translation of the Old Testament) becomes the next significant document. As mentioned, the first five books of the Old Testament (the Pentateuch) were translated from Hebrew into Greek by Jewish scribes in Alexandria, Egypt, around 275 BC.[25] *The Anchor Bible Dictionary* gives the third century BC as a general date for translation of the *Torah* into Greek.[26] The remaining books of the Old Testament were translated at various times during the next 100–300 years. Translation of the Old Testament from Hebrew into Greek was a response to the spread of the Greek language due to the conquests of Alexander the Great. The Septuagint allowed Jews and proselytes who did not speak Hebrew to study the Old Testament in their native Greek tongue.

The Septuagint raises several significant issues. First, the Septuagint is not a dependable translation, as pointed out in the introductory remarks to *A New English Translation of the Septuagint*.[27] Some words are not translated, poorly translated, mistranslated, or added to the Hebrew text. Secondly, the Septuagint is not inspired. There is no inspired translation of the Old Testament into any language—Greek, Syrian, Latin, German, English, or otherwise. Thirdly, the Hebrew scribes who translated the Septuagint believed in traditional young-Earth creation theology and used their work to embed their beliefs into the Bible. For example, in Genesis 1:9 an entire extra sentence is inserted to reinforce the belief that God spoke and separated the water from dry land on the third day.[28] The scribes who translated the Septuagint were familiar with the native Hebrew and Greek languages of the day and were conceptually capable of making a good translation; however, their poor scholarship and theological beliefs produced a less than accurate work.

Today, except Bible students, few people have heard of the Septuagint; however, this has not always been the case. At one time, the Septuagint was accepted as the authoritative account of the Old Testament. Jerome (347–420 AD) translated the Old Testament from Hebrew into Latin. Jerome realized that the Hebrew text should be the basis for any translation. At the time, many believed the Septuagint was inspired of God and criticized Jerome for not using it as the basis for his translation. The Septuagint was accepted above the Hebrew text. Although the Septuagint has faded from the public eye, its influence is still quite prevalent, especially in regard to the creation account.

As we go further backwards in history, we can theorize that sometime between 600–300 BC traditional young-Earth creation theology developed among the Hebrews. During this time, a charismatic leader emerged and began teaching a new, exciting interpretation of the creation story (as illustrated by the fictitious account of Aaliyah at the beginning of this chapter). God created the heavens and Earth and all therein during six days. In this new theology, God simply spoke and brought things into existence. This new explanation was viable in light of the miracles of the Old Testament when God killed the Egyptian first born, parted the Red Sea, supplied manna from heaven for 40 years, and gave the Israelites victory over their enemies. Unfortunately, this embellished creation account set the Bible on a collision course with empirical science two thousand years in the future.

A brief look at Hebrew history provides a framework for speculating when young-Earth creation theology developed. The original creation story remained intact during the life of Moses, Joshua, the time of the judges, and the first three kings of Israel (Saul, David and Solomon). Based on the revealing poetical account given in Psalms 104:5–9, David correctly understood the creation story. Following the reign of Solomon, the kingdom was divided into Judah and Israel. The resulting two kingdoms repeatedly strayed away from God into idolatry and sinful practices. Eventually Israel was carried away into captivity in 721 BC, and Judah followed in 587 BC.[29] In 536 BC, the Jews returned to Israel, and in 516 BC the second temple was dedicated. Nehemiah returned to Jerusalem in 445 BC and began to repair the city wall.[30] By 275 BC, around when the first five books of the Septuagint were translated, young-Earth creation theology was an established belief. We can speculate that during this time of turmoil new creation theology emerged.

As we continue back in time, we finally come to the Pentateuch written by Moses. Genesis Chapters 1 and 2 are essentially identical in all reliable Hebrew manuscripts. With certainty, we have the words penned by Moses thirty-five hundred years ago. When the Septuagint translation and Masoretic vocalization marks are laid aside as a controlling influence, the original Genesis creation story is allowed to surface. When the language of the creation story is connected with the rest of the Old Testament, mistranslated words and phrases soon come to light. When scientific evidence is used to help build an explanatory framework in regard to the timing of past events, a Genesis creation story emerges that is fully truthful and trustworthy.

Deception Becomes Paradigm

Regardless of when or why young-Earth creation theology developed, once established it became the theological paradigm of biblical origins. The Hebrews passed the story down from generation to generation. Jews who converted to Christianity passed their creation beliefs to the early New Testament Christian church.

Although the early Christian church (33–100 AD) no doubt believed in young-Earth creation theology, the Holy Spirit kept any specific endorsement of this belief out of the apostles' writings. In the New Testament, God is identified as creator of the heavens and Earth. The creation of Adam and Eve, Adam's sin, Abel's sacrifice, the slaying of Abel by Cain, and Seth as the son of Adam are clearly taught in the New Testament as historical. However, no New Testament scripture specifically states that God *created* the heavens and Earth *in six days*, instantly spoke them into existence, or created them from nothing.

Moving beyond the New Testament period, the young-Earth interpretation of Genesis became a part of Roman Catholic Church theology, Muslim writings and belief, and Protestant doctrine. Today, all three religious groups have adherents of this theology to one extent or another, and struggle with reconciling scripture and scientific evidence in regard to significant time.

Young-Earth creation theology has had a significant influence on all translations of the Old Testament. Starting with the Greek Septuagint, its effect is also seen in early translations of the Latin Vulgate, the Syriac Peshitta, and a number of targums. This theology is found in English translations, starting with the hand-copied Wycliffe Bible of 1384. Young-Earth creation theology influenced William Tyndale's translation of the Pentateuch into English, first published in 1530. The effect of young-Earth theology can be found in the Myles Coverdale Bible of 1535, the Matthew's Bible of 1537, the Great Bible of 1539, the Geneva Bible of 1560, the Bishop's Bible of 1568, and the King James Version of 1611.[31] All subsequent English translations of the Bible have been affected by this theology.

Present-day scholars and theologians rely heavily on the Septuagint translation and to a lesser extent the Masoretic vocalization marks for their understanding of the Genesis creation story. Hebrew scholars use these two works (and traditional theology) as the basis for their translation and explanation of the Hebrew text. Although the

Septuagint and Masoretic works are not inspired, they are accepted as authoritative in regard to the creation account. Traditional logic is that the Hebrews were God's chosen people, they spoke the native languages, and were the copiers and keepers of the Old Testament; therefore, what they believed must be correct.

Conclusion

God does not want Christians to be deceived about spiritual matters. The apostle Paul warned believers, "Let no one deceive you" (2 Thessalonians 2:3). In Acts 20:29–30, Paul warned the elders at Ephesus that deceivers within the church would attempt to gain a following by teaching false doctrine. Not only does the Bible warn about deception, but gives an example of how to counter it. The Bereans were noble people who received Paul's teaching with an open mind; however, they searched the scripture each time they were taught to verify his message (Acts 17:11). Christians have the tools to avoid religious deception, but careful study of the Bible is required.

Deceivers fool others by passing off fake and false material as the real thing. They try to imitate the genuine article as closely as possible. For example, if counterfeiters want to pass off fake one hundred dollar bills, they do not print Donald Duck's picture on purple paper. Instead they attempt to duplicate a true bill.[32] In a similar manner, charlatans and hucksters deceive people by appearing truthful, genuine, and sincere. Part of what they say may be true; however, the real focus of their message is false.

As anyone, Christians can be deceived. Anyone who accepts or trusts others can be misled. We have neither the time nor energy to verify everything we hear, read, or see to determine if it is true. We all tend to trust teachers, authority figures, professionals, and people who appear knowledgeable about a subject.

However, Christians have additional issues to deal with. The foundation of the Christian life is faith-based belief. We are to have faith in God, and the Bible as the word of God. Unfortunately, Christians sometimes place their faith in false teachers who claim to be purveyors of biblical truth. The Bible makes it abundantly clear that we should believe the right things. As one commentator has said, "We cannot just believe anything. Our objects of faith must be God and His Word, not mere men or wild claims."[33]

Christians are commanded to love one another. On the down side, love tends to be accepting and is willing to overlook.[34] Love can be blind to obvious defects and inconsistencies. Deceitful teachers can use Christian love to manipulate and lead others astray. However, true love will not tolerate lies, deception, and false teaching that in the end will hurt and destroy others.

Christians tend to believe their spiritual leaders.[35] Church members want to respect their leaders as biblically educated, righteous, and trustworthy. However, followers have an obligation to ensure that trust placed in a spiritual leader is be backed up by their moral conduct (they should walk the talk). Their teaching should agree with what is taught in the Bible. Leadership must be accountable.

When betrayed in a relationship, restoration is not easy. Putting trust in someone and then having that trust betrayed is painful. When the deception becomes known, the immediate reaction is hurt followed by anger. As emotions subside, intense distrust becomes the predominant reaction. Restoring the relationship may take years of hard work. Trust is rebuilt slowly in small steps over time, and the wound may never completely heal.

In my personal Christian walk, I feel betrayed and hurt. I have been misled by conservative Christians who claim to accept the Bible as the inspired, inerrant word of God, yet hold to a creation account that contradicts God's word and His work. I have been hurt by liberals who claim to be people of faith, yet attack the Genesis creation story as myth and deny God as our creator. This experience has made me skeptical of all theology related to origins not clearly taught in the Bible. It has made me skeptical of all scientific theory related to origins driven by philosophical naturalism. Similar to the Bereans, I find myself immersed in study both inside and outside scripture to verify my beliefs.

Bible believers have been deceived about the Genesis creation story. To many, this deception is very painful and quite personal. Regardless, because of the importance of the creation issue, we must stay the course. Rebelling against God, denying the truth of the Bible, and walking away from our Christian faith is not the answer. The correct course lies in remaining faithful to God and seeking to understand what the Bible truly teaches about origins. Firm scientific evidence regarding time and past events can be used as an aid.

The original perpetrators of the Genesis deception are long dead, in fact more than twenty-two hundred years have passed since their demise. We do not know who the architects of this embellished account were. They could have been ethnic Hebrews or Jewish proselytes from Egypt, Palestine, or Syria. Regardless of whom they were, our only recourse is forgiveness.

We cannot go backwards and undo the past, but only forward. Progress begins by accepting the fact that our understanding of Genesis Chapters 1 and 2 has been wrong for more than twenty-two hundred years. The Septuagint translation of the Genesis account is seriously in error, heavily influenced by the incorrect theology of the day. The Septuagint has been the primary influence in steering origins theology in the wrong direction, resulting in the current incorrect English translation of Genesis. We must lay aside our parochial attitudes, private ambitions, and personal pride. Our goal is the pursuit of truth based on special and general revelation. We have been wrong, we acknowledge our error, we accept the truth, and we will change. The future of Christianity will be heavily influenced by how well churches, seminaries, colleges, and schools accept and propagate the truth of Genesis.

The story about Aaliyah at the beginning of this chapter is fictitious; however, it helps illustrate how the false interpretation of Genesis Chapter 1 may have originated and, in general, how false religious beliefs begin. Typically, extra-biblical and counter-biblical teaching begins with a single individual. In most instances, the individual is respected and recognized as a spiritual leader by his followers. Motivations can include fame, fortune, power, and the desire to develop something new, exciting, or different. They want to distinguish themselves as an exceptional religious leader. In my opinion, most false teachers are obsessed with their self-importance and have little real respect for biblical authority. Doctrinal error they develop is not the result of an honest mistake.

Have I therefore become your enemy because
I tell you the truth? (Galatians 4:16) NKJV

Chapter 4

Evidence of Age

Any biblical view of origins, with aspirations of being credible, must consider the impact of science on present-day thinking. Scientific evidence is observable, repeatable, factual, and the basis of our modern technology. Applied science has significantly reduced the effects of pestilence, disease, famine, and natural catastrophe. Applied science has made possible for mankind to have the highest standards of transportation, communication, housing, clothing, food, medical care, entertainment, and comfort the world has ever known. As Phillip Johnson has rightly observed, science is the only universally valid form of knowledge within our culture. For these reasons, a serious attempt must be made to reconcile scientific evidence in regard to time and the Genesis creation account.

The orthodox belief of the church throughout past centuries has been traditional young-Earth creation theology. According to this theology, the heavens and Earth are relatively young. Using the genealogies given in the Old Testament, Anglican Archbishop James Ussher (1581–1656) calculated a widely accepted creation date of 4004 BC. During six days, God created the heavens, Earth, and all therein.

When calculating the Earth's age, Ussher treated the genealogies of Genesis Chapters 5 and 11 as complete, without gaps. Based on a correct understanding of scripture and scientific evidence, this was a mistake. A study of the genealogies in the Bible reveals they were often abbreviated to aid in memorization. Disreputable people were often intentionally omitted. In addition, when used within the context of a Hebrew genealogy, "beget" does not necessarily mean a direct father-to-son relationship, but can indicate a father-to-descendant relationship. Gaps can be allowed in the Genesis genealogies, and the creation of Adam and Eve (the first humans) can be easily extended backwards to 15,000–30,000 BC.

In addition, Ussher made several other mistakes. He viewed Genesis 1:3, 6, 9, 11, 14, 20, and 24 as commands, rather than declarative statements, being misled by the "jussive/command" verb. He failed to realize that in Genesis 1:3–31 God was describing a mature creation that had existed for some time. He also failed to realize that the seven-day account given in Genesis 1:3 to 2:3 was structured to support six days of work followed by a day of rest, codified in the Ten Commandments for observing the Sabbath.

In the eighteenth century, scientists began to seriously dispute Ussher's creation date as they discovered evidence to the contrary. Geologists came to realize that multilayered rock formations, fossilized remains, uplifted mountains, and severe erosion required significant time to occur by natural means. As science continued to mature, more objective data became available. Scientists discovered evidence in starlight, Antarctic ice layers, lake sediments, radiometric isotope decay, tree-ring chronologies, and carbon-14 decay that strongly support significant age and conflict with young-Earth creation theology.

Because of the perceived conflict between the Genesis creation account and scientific evidence in regard to time, many people have come to doubt the Bible's credibility. Disagreement has affected not only their belief in the creation story, but the remainder of scripture. A credible solution to the time conflict is sorely needed to reverse this trend.

According to *Exemplar* creation, Genesis Chapters 1 and 2 present an abbreviated, non-technical, historical account of what God did, but little about the actual process. The exact time and method God used to create the heavens and Earth are not revealed in scripture, and man is left to his own resources to fill in the details. If God chose to form the heavens in a series of creative events throughout billions of years, that is within His purview. If God opted to make plants and animals during multiple creative events separated by millions of years, that is His prerogative. If Yahweh decided to develop a mature Earth during significant time, before creating Adam and Eve, that is fully within His right. Theologians have no grounds to demand that God act in a specific manner in the absence of explicit biblical teaching. This is doubly true, when there is compelling evidence to the contrary. God is capable of rapid, individual creative events (e.g., the forming of Adam and Eve), yet the sum total of all His creative events extend throughout billions of years. With Him, time has little significance.

Exemplar creation proposes that a combination of special and general revelation best explain origins. The Bible clearly teaches that God created the heavens and Earth. Solid scientific evidence clarifies the time involved in this process. When combined together, scripture identifies God as the creative agent and scientific evidence clarifies the time.

Apparent Age

Apparent age is the realization that when God instantaneously creates something, the object created can, but not necessarily, represent a developmental process requiring significant time. For example, God created Eve as an adult, yet a baby takes years to grow into an adult. Jesus turned water into wine at the wedding feast in

Cana of Galilee, yet grapes require time to grow and grape juice requires time to ferment, age, and turn into fine wine (John 2:1–11). God caused Aaron's staff to bud, blossom, and produce almonds in a single night, a feat that normally takes years (Num. 17:8). These miracles illustrate that God has the ability to quickly create items that would otherwise require significant time through normal growth processes.

Young-Earth creationists often use the above examples to reject evidence of age. God simply made the Earth and universe look old, although they are not. While this argument sounds plausible, closer examination reveals some serious flaws. For example, when God created Eve, she appeared to be a young adult with a normal growth history. In reality, she may have been only a few hours old. The creation of Eve as an adult is accepted; however, in examining her closely, she does not exhibit the normal wear and tear of an adult her age. The bottoms of her feet have no thick calluses from walking barefooted. She has no cracked or broken toenails. There are no scratches, cuts, or scars on her arms and legs. Her hands are not callused from working nor are any fingernails chipped. Sunlight has not aged her skin. She has no facial wrinkles and her teeth are perfect without cavities, decay, stains, chips, or wear. A more in-depth examination shows that her heart, lungs, kidneys, thyroid, and liver appear to be in perfect condition.

In examining the concept of apparent age, we should distinguish between *essential* and *nonessential functions*. When God created Eve as the first woman, all essential functions were present. Eve had a brain, arms, legs, heart, circulatory system, and other body parts to function as an adult. However, it is inconceivable that God would have artificially aged Eve's body by producing nonessential scars, sun damaged skin, tooth decay, and high blood pressure to give the appearance of physical deterioration over time. Apparently Eve was created full grown; however, it is unthinkable God would have implanted false memories of childhood and adolescence.

The Earth serves as another example of essential and nonessential function. We can accept God as having the power to rapidly create our planet, with the essentials for life, consisting of upraised continents, mountains, deserts, soil for growing plants, ocean basins, abundant water, and an oxygen-nitrogen atmosphere. However, we cannot believe God would create nonessential layers of sediments containing fossils and minerals that would normally take millions of years to accumulate. We cannot believe He would create nonessential tree-ring chronologies, radiometric decay samples, and meteor impact craters to falsify evidence of significant age.

A number of time indicators are discussed in this chapter and include distant stars, information within starlight, Moon impact craters, the absence of Earth impact craters, Antarctica and Greenland ice layers, Antarctica coal and fossils, the radiometric dating of igneous rocks, the carbon-14 dating of organic material, tree-ring growth, and lake sediment layers. Some people attempt to explain away all these age indicators by saying God made the heavens and Earth to appear old. He made them with a false appearance of age. While God no doubt has the ability to falsify evidence of this nature, a brief analysis proves He would not.

Assume for a moment Genesis truly teaches a recent Earth as proposed by traditional young-Earth creation theology. The Earth and all therein were created within six days around 4004 BC. God then *intentionally falsified physical evidence* to make our planet appear old. Contradictory actions of this nature do not make sense. Why would God want His written word to disagree with physical evidence? Why would God want to create conflict between special revelation and general revelation? There is no rational answer for such action.

If the Earth was recently created as proposed by traditional young-Earth creation theology and God intentionally falsified evidence to indicate the appearance of great age, *then He is a deceiver.* Rather than being someone who cannot lie, God takes on the attributes of Satan and becomes a liar (John 8:44). Such actions are completely contradictory to His nature.

The most cogent answer for most evidence supporting an old universe is that the evidence is true. We can agree that some data in regard to time is imprecise and some inferences lead to questionable conclusions. However, other data is accurate and the inferences based thereon are entirely logical. The following highly reliable evidence points to an old heavens, Earth, and biosphere, and easily reconciles with the *exemplar* translation and explanation.

Measuring Distance to Stars and Galaxies

Stars have always intrigued mankind. How did they originate? How do they work? How far away are they? Present-day astronomy can now answer some of these questions. For example, astronomers have developed techniques and technology that allow accurate distance measurements to some stars and galaxies. This capability has been developed through intensive effort involving thousands of scientists and technicians during the last one hundred years.

Trigonometric methods can be used to measure the distance to stars within roughly 300 light years of Earth. Using trigonometry, if the length of one leg and the acute angle opposite that leg are known, the size of the resultant triangle can be determined. For measuring the distance to a star, the Earth's average orbital diameter about the Sun of 298 million kilometers (186 million miles) is used as one leg of the triangle.

Measuring the acute angle to a star (target star) from Earth is slightly more involved. The angle to a target star is measured in relation to a distant reference star that is so far away it appears to be stationary when viewed from Earth. At a specified point in the Earth's orbit, the angle between the target star and reference star is measured. Six months later, when the Earth is on the opposite side of its orbit, the angle between the target star and reference star is measured again. The smaller of the two angles is subtracted from the larger to obtain the acute angle (parallax angle) to the target star. The distance to the target star can be calculated by dividing Earth's orbital diameter of 298 million km by the sine of the parallax angle. This is called the *trigonometric parallax* method.[1]

A precisely measured parallax angle (acute angle) is key to accurately calculating the distance to a star. Technology has been developed to permit the measurement of parallax angles in milliarc seconds. One thousand milliarc seconds equal one arc second. In turn, 60 arc seconds equal one arc minute, 60 arc minutes equal one arc degree, and 360 arc degrees equals a full circle.

In 1989, the Hipparcos Mission satellite was launched by the European Space Agency and remained active until communication was terminated in 1993. From space, Hipparcos measured 118,218 stars for their parallax angles.[2] (This data is available to the public in the Hipparcos Data Catalog on its website.) The angles measured are very small, with the smallest listed at around 10 milliarc seconds. For example, star number 1340 has a parallax angle of 10 milliarc seconds (mas), which calculates to a distance of 326 light years.

Another technique used for measuring the distance to stars millions of light years from Earth is based on absolute brightness and the inverse square law. This method uses the three characteristics of (1) apparent brightness, (2) absolute brightness, and (3) color index. The first characteristic, *apparent brightness*, is the brightness of a star as viewed from Earth. The farther away a star is, the less its apparent brightness. The second characteristic, *absolute brightness*, is a measure of the total light produced by a star, similar to a 100 watt light bulb. Regardless of how near or far away the light bulb, it always gives off the same amount of light. The third characteristic is the *color index* of a star. Stars range in color from blue, to blue-white, white, yellow-white, orange, and red. Blue stars are the hottest in temperature and red stars are the coolest. Star color can be precisely measured and assigned a color index.

Astronomers have discovered that the color index of a star is approximately proportional to its absolute brightness. This relationship applies to stars identified as *main sequence stars*. The correlation of color index to absolute brightness was discovered independently by astronomers Ejnar Hertzsprung and Henry Norris Russell around 1912.[3]

The principle behind measuring the distance to a main sequence star is based on the inverse square law. As a main sequence star gets farther from Earth, its apparent brightness decreases as the square of the distance. For example, suppose a star one light year from Earth has an apparent brightness of one. The same star two light years from Earth will have one-fourth the brightness. The same star three light years from Earth will have one-ninth the brightness. This relationship continues until the star can no longer be seen. The inverse square relationship of apparent brightness to distance is used to determine how far away a star is from Earth.

For main sequence stars, the color index is approximately proportional to its absolute brightness. Regardless of the distance from Earth, if a star is visible, its color index can conceptually be measured and thus its absolute brightness determined. By comparing the absolute brightness of a main sequence star (determined by its color index) against its apparent brightness (determined by direct measurement), the distance to a star can be calculated. This technique can be used to measure individual stars out to one million light years or more from Earth. No extrapolation of data is required, and the physics behind this procedure have been verified on Earth.

Stars in the Andromeda Galaxy (M31), approximately 2.5 million light years away, have been measured using the inverse square technique. In 2005, astronomer Ignasi Ribas of the Catalonia Institute for Space Studies in Bellaterra, Spain and his colleagues announced they had used this technique to precisely determine the distance to two binary stars in the Andromeda Galaxy. The stars were calculated to be 2.52 million light years away from Earth (meaning their light took 2.52 million years to reach Earth) within an accuracy of six percent.[4] Precisely determining the color index and apparent brightness of the stars proved to be the greatest difficulty.

Measuring the distance to stars by the inverse square law is not related to popular cosmological theories. Measurements based on this technique are unrelated to ideas about the ultimate size of the universe, the age of the universe, or Big Bang theory. This type of measurement is independent of spectral redshift explanations. Astronomers who are both Bible believers and non-believers accept the inverse square method and acknowledge that stars exist more than one million light years from Earth.

Starlight and Time

Old starlight from distant stars challenges the credibility of traditional young-Earth creation theology in regard to time. Light from distant stars is just now reaching Earth. For example, light from a star two million light years away must travel two million years to reach our planet. On reaching Earth, events recorded in the starlight two million years ago can be observed. The distance starlight travels and the information contained therein, conflict with the belief that all stars were created in 4004 BC.

What do young-Earth creationists say about this evidence? At first, they questioned the techniques used to measure the distance to stars, such as the trigonometric parallax and inverse square method. Their objections fell by the wayside as astronomers who believed in traditional young-Earth creation theology came forward and supported these measurement methods.

The argument then developed that God instantly created starlight between the Earth and distant stars. The problem with this idea is that starlight contains unique information about specific events such as novae, luminosity variations, and regular cyclic fluctuations. For example, in 1987, a supernova was discovered in the Tarantula Nebula, an estimated 170,000 light years away—meaning the actual event occurred 170,000 years ago. Many supernovae occur every year, and in 2006 alone 551 were identified.[5] All of them represent stored information within starlight from past events just now reaching Earth.

If God created starlight and falsified the information contained therein, then He is a great deceiver. Ken Ham, a leading young-Earth creationist, has rejected the idea that God instantly created starlight between the Earth and distant stars.[6]

Time dilatation is another argument developed by those who believe God created the stars 6,000 years ago. *Starlight and Time* by D. Russell Humphreys, PhD, hypothesizes that massive time dilatation occurred because of a white hole.[7] While the first four creation days ticked away on Earth, billions of years passed out in the universe among the stars.

Humphreys' hypothesis is based on the observation that a clock within a high gravity field will run slower than one subject to lower gravity. For example, a clock on the surface of the Earth will run more than 38 milliseconds per day slower than one in a geosynchronous orbiting satellite, where gravity is weaker. This difference is very small, but nevertheless real. The time dilation hypothesis proposes that our planet was subject to an immense gravity field, causing time to pass slowly, while time among the stars occurred at a normal rate. The universe aged billions of years, while only a few days passed on Earth. Time dilation of this magnitude is completely speculative.

Dr. Humphreys uses the time dilation hypothesis in an attempt to harmonize starlight, time, and a 6,000 year old universe.[8] His interpretation of Genesis 1:1–19 ranks among the most bizarre yet conceived. Humphreys' idea is repeatedly trotted out as the answer to the starlight problem[9] in a desperate effort to salvage traditional young-Earth creation theology. His explanation violates the assertion that young-Earth theology is based on a straight forward, literal reading of the biblical text.

Another idea proposed to solve the starlight problem requires a change in the speed of light, hypothesized to have decreased over time. The speed of light was allegedly faster in the past.[10,11] A faster speed of light permitted starlight from distant stars to arrive at Earth in significantly less time. There is nothing to support this belief other than inaccurate measurements made by previous investigators. Precise experiments prove that the speed of light in a vacuum is constant. In addition, for light to reach Earth from distant stars within the first four days of creation, the speed of light would have been millions of times more than it is today—not just a few percent. According to Answers in Genesis, a ministry supportive of young-Earth theology, arguments relying on a change in the speed of light should not be used.

In the final analysis, traditional young-Earth creation theology is in direct conflict with starlight and an old age for the stars. This theology has a significant problem with time. Significant time is needed for starlight to reach Earth from stars created in the remote regions of space. A 6,000 year old universe does not allow adequate time. In contrast, *exemplar* creation allows time in the indefinite past prior to Genesis 1:3 for starlight to reach Earth. *Exemplar* creation easily harmonizes with this firm scientific evidence.

Moon Impact Craters

Impact craters present a serious challenge to the credibility of traditional young-Earth creation theology in regard to time. Since the Moon and Earth are linked together, their history in some respects is similar. Impact craters on the Moon are a reflection of impact events on Earth. Six thousand years is not adequate time for impact craters to occur on Earth and then be removed by weathering.

Close examination of the Moon reveals its surface is pockmarked with craters as a result of meteor impacts throughout time. Craters range from less than a foot in size to the Ptolemaeus impact basin, 164 km (102 miles) in diameter. In many areas there are craters within craters. Owing to the absence of an atmosphere on the Moon, craters formed in the distant past are still present today. There is no wind or water to erode them away or fill them in with sediment, and they provide a clear record of past impact events. The *Encyclopedia of Earth Sciences* hypothesizes that most craters were formed early in the Moon's history more than 3 billion years ago.[12] The *Age of the Earth* hypothesizes that the majority of Moon craters were formed between 3.5 and 4.6 billion years ago.[13]

Extensive observations have been made of Moon craters. A merge of the NASA-RP-1097 and USGS crater data lists 8,596 lunar craters more than 1 km (0.62 miles) in diameter, by latitude, longitude, name, size, and identification number. This includes 1,088 lunar craters more than 50 km (31 miles) in diameter.[14] Table 4.1 gives the distribution by size of Moon craters from 1 km (0.62 mile) to 600 km (373 miles) in diameter.

When compared with the Moon, the Earth has few impact craters. The Earth Impact Database lists a total of 174 confirmed meteorite craters in the world.[15] Of that number, 155 are above one kilometer in diameter. A well-recognized crater in America is the Barringer Meteor Crater, located twenty miles west of Winslow, Arizona. This crater has a classic shape and is approximately 1.25 km (4,100 ft) in diameter and 174 meters (571 ft) deep. The edge of the crater rises approximately 46 meters (150 ft) above the surrounding terrain.

Based on their relationship, the Earth and Moon have been subjected to the same meteor activity in the past. Earth was hit by proportionally more meteors because of its larger size. The Moon has 8,596 meteorite craters, more than one kilometer in diameter, that correspond to approximately 115,500 meteor impacts on Earth, based on the ratio of their surface areas. The 1,088 meteorite craters on the Moon, more than 50 km in diameter, equate to approximately 14,620 meteor impacts on Earth. Early in its history, our planet's surface was completely molten and meteor impacts left no permanent mark. As the crust solidified, impacts left massive craters, but weathering and other natural processes have erased any remains except for 174 known craters.

Traditional young-Earth creation theology has no time to fit this number of meteor impacts into 6,000 years of Earth's history. For example, for 115,500 impacts to occur before Noah's flood (between 4004 and 2349 BC according to Ussher[16]) would have required 70 meteor impacts per year more than one kilometer in diameter and 8.8 impacts per year more than 50 km in diameter. It is doubtful civilization could have survived this level of meteor impacts. To have the impact rate then drop dramatically after Noah's flood to 0.040 per year (represents 174 impacts during 4,350 years) is without a plausible explanation.

Table 4.1 – Moon Impact Crater Size Distribution
(Arranged in decreasing order by diameter size)

Diameter Size Range (kilometers)	Quantity	Diameter Size Range (kilometers)	Quantity	Diameter Size Range (kilometers)	Quantity
501-600	2	151-160	10	71-80	134
401-500	1	141-150	13	61-70	234
301-400	6	131-140	22	51-60	287
201-300	19	121-130	31	41-50	468
191-200	5	111-120	31	31-40	711
181-190	8	101-110	52	21-30	1211
171-180	8	91-100	84	11-20	2027
161-170	10	81-90	93	1-10	3129

Reference: McDowell, Jonathan (2007). A merge of NASA-RP-1097 (Anderson and Whitaker 1982) and USGS lunar crater data.

The time Noah was in the ark represents a second possible period for meteor impacts. Any hypothesis that 115,500 meteor impacts occurred during Noah's flood presents several problems. This number of meteor strikes in 375 days (the time Noah was in the ark) would have been devastating and represents 308 meteor strikes per day, including 39 strikes more than 50 km in diameter. It is doubtful Noah's ark could have survived the devastation caused by this level of meteor activity.

In addition to the above problems are the meteors themselves. For all meteors to strike Earth during the time Noah was in the ark, requires a continuous swarm of meteors for at least 28 days. This is the time necessary for one complete revolution of the Moon as it orbits the Earth (to expose its entire circumference). A minimum of one orbit is required to achieve a distribution of meteor impacts over the Moon's surface. A swarm of meteors extending the diameter of the Moon's orbital plane, 812,000 km (504,577 miles), would have been needed for a minimum of 28 days. In addition, two other swarms would have been required. Craters on the Moon are the result of meteors from at least three different directions: the equatorial plane, the north pole, and the south poles. From what scientists know about our solar system, it is highly implausible three meteor swarms would occur and converge on the Earth from three different directions within a 375 day period.

A third possible period for meteor impacts is after Noah's flood. If this happened, most impact sites would be visible today, since not enough time has elapsed for erosion and weathering to remove them. There would be thousands of impact sites, rather than the 174 meteorite craters currently identified.

To explain Moon craters, some proponents of traditional young-Earth creation theology use the argument of apparent age. We can readily accept God as having the ability to rapidly create the Moon with its current mass, size, shape, and orbit—all essential functions. However, covering the lunar surface with a multitude of different size meteor impact basins would be nonessential. Adding nonessential features to cause the Moon to appear old makes God a great deceiver. If the Moon were truly 6,000 years old, it should have essentially no meteor impact craters. The idea of apparent age should not be used to solve problems traditional young-Earth creation theology has with lunar impact craters.

In summary, evidence of 8,596 Moon impact craters is compelling proof that a proportional number of impacts also occurred on Earth. Within the past, approximately 115,500 meteors with the capability of forming a one kilometer diameter crater or larger have struck Earth. Six thousand years does not allow enough time for this number of meteor impacts to occur and then be removed by natural processes. In contrast, *exemplar* creation allows time in the indefinite past prior to Genesis 1:3 for these impact events. *Exemplar* creation easily harmonizes with this scientific evidence and its logical inferences.

Antarctica and Greenland Ice Cores

Ice core data present a serious challenge to the credibility of traditional young-Earth creation theology in regard to time. In certain parts of the world, snow piles up on a continual basis. Summers are cold enough to keep winter snowfall from melting, which has resulted in snow accumulation to enormous depths. Two of the most notable areas on Earth where this has occurred are Greenland and Antarctica. Snow has collected in some areas on these two continents to more than 3,000 meters (9,843 ft) thick. As snow has accumulated, pressure has turned it into ice. A count of annual layers within this ice gives a physical record going back more than 100,000 years.

Annual layers are formed by snow that falls throughout the year in Antarctica and Greenland. Most snow accumulates during winter, with less during summer. Dust builds up on the snow during summer and provides a dirty film so that annual layers can be visually distinguished. Non-visual effects also occur, based on the temperature difference between winter and summer snow. Non-visual effects that are a permanent part of the ice record include the amount of deuterium (heavy hydrogen), oxygen-18 isotopes, CH_4, and carbon dioxide contained in the snow. Non-visual effects can be measured to confirm visual effects when counting ice layers.

Annual ice layers represent physical evidence of past climatic change. Scientists study the ice record to understand past planetary heating and cooling fluctuations. Other motivations include an attempt to accurately date past volcanic eruptions, such as the Minoan eruption of Thera (an island in the eastern Mediterranean Sea) that occurred roughly around 1600 BC.

Drilling an ice core is a huge project, normally accomplished under challenging conditions. Ice cores are typically drilled at locations where the average temperature ranges between –25° and –65° F. A combination of temperature, wind, and isolation make for difficult living conditions. All crew members, food, living quarters, support supplies, and drilling equipment must be transported either by air or overland to the core site. Drilling can take several years to complete and may be limited to the summer seasons. A core drilling project is an expensive, large undertaking and normally requires government funding. Logistics support is typically supplied by the United States Air Force. Scientific personnel for the project usually come from a number of universities and scientific organizations.

Ice cores are drilled, handled, stored, and analyzed with specialized equipment. Drilling is done with a hollow core drill, in some instances thermally heated. Ice core sections range from 3 to 6 meters (9.8 to 19.7 ft) in length and have a typical diameter of 10 cm (4 in). Each section is carefully stored in a custom made container and identified. Containers are kept refrigerated at a point well below freezing during ground and air transport for thousands of miles. At the research center (such as The National Ice Core Laboratory in Lakewood, Colorado) they are stored in freezers prior to examination.

The examination process for ice cores is extensive. Cores are sliced lengthwise using a paper thin saw blade into different sections, similar to cutting a log into boards. One thin, lengthwise piece is used to visually count annual layers in the core. Pieces are mounted on a special viewing table, with controlled backlighting, to aid in counting the dust bands. Other complete lengthwise pieces are analyzed for electrical conductivity. Lengthwise pieces may be further cut into small crosswise pieces for isotope, gas, ion, and dust analysis. Most work is accomplished in a clean room atmosphere, under conditions approximating the inside of a deep freeze.

As depth increases in an ice pack, annual layers become thinner. Pressure causes ice to flow horizontally to the sides of the glacier, resulting in thinning of the lower layers. Increasing depth is accompanied by progressively thinner layers that are more difficult to count.

Table 4.2 lists the major ice cores drilled in the world. The year completed, ice depth, and core depth are a matter of public record. The two far right columns list the number of counted or estimated annual ice layers at a specific depth in the ice core.

The first major ice core drilled, and the first to reach bedrock in Antarctica, was completed on January 29, 1968, at Byrd Station. The core was drilled with a cable-suspended electromechanical hollow rotary drill. Byrd station is located at 80° 01′ S, 119° 31′ W near the southwest corner of Antarctica at an altitude of 1,530 meters (5,020 ft) above sea level. Vertical thickness of the ice at this location is 2,164 meters (7,100 ft). Although no specific annual layers were counted for the Byrd core, the project obtained important data about the ice—it was indeed thick.

Dome C (old) ice core was drilled during 1977–1978 using a thermally heated core drill.[17] The full core depth was 906 meters (2,973 ft). Dome C is located at 74°

39′ S, 124° 10′ E at an elevation of 3,240 meters (10,630 ft). Average air temperature at this site is –64.3° F and is among the coldest drilling sites in Antarctica. The core was analyzed for deuterium, oxygen-18 isotopes, CO_2, and CH_4. Non-visual indicators were used to count 39,515 annual layers at a depth of 903.4 meters (2,964 ft). Based on present moisture measured in one year of snow fall at this site, with no thinning of annual ice layers, it would take approximately 113,000 years to accumulate an ice thickness of 3,400 meters.

The Vostok ice core drilling project was completed in January of 1998 in Antarctica, and was a joint effort between Russia, France, and the United States.[18] The Vostok core is the deepest ice core ever recovered, with a length of 3,623 meters (11,887 ft). Drilling stopped 120 yards short of a subterranean lake the size of Lake Ontario, as scientists did not want to contaminate the water with drilling fluids. No visual layer counting was performed on the Vostok ice core. Non-visual isotope measurements, glacial modeling, and other methods were used to estimate 422,766 annual layers at a depth of 3,310 meters (10,860 ft). Based on present moisture measured in one year of snow fall at this site, with no thinning of annual ice layers, it would take roughly 123,000 years to accumulate an ice thickness of 3,700 meters.

Drilling at Dome C (EDC3) was started in 1999 and completed in 2003.[19,20] Dome C is located at 75° 06′ S, 123° 21′ E in Antarctica at an altitude of 3,233 meters (10,607 ft). The ice core was 3,260 meters (10,696 ft) long and represents an estimated 800,000 annual layers. No visual layer counting was performed on the Dome C core. Isotope measurements, modeling, and other methods were used to estimate the number of annual layers. Based on present moisture measured in one year of snow fall at this site, with no thinning of annual ice layers, it would take about 108,000 years to accumulate an ice thickness of 3,260 meters.

The Greenland Ice Core Project (GRIP) completed its drilling phase in 1992.[21] The drill site is located at 72° 35′ N, 37° 38′ W, at an altitude of 3,230 meters (10,598 ft). The core hole was 3,029 meters (9,938 ft) deep and ended at bedrock. This was the first major core to be extensively analyzed for annual layers. Manual counting identified 60,000 annual layers in the first 2,495 meters (8,186 ft) of the core. The manual counting of visual layers was cross checked against annual isotope cycles and other methods. The average layer thickness at 2,495 meters was 0.684 cm (0.269 in). At depths below 2,495 meters, the ice layers became progressively thinner and manual counting became difficult. The GRIP ice core is 2,983.2 meters (9,788 ft) long and contains an estimated 248,763 annual layers.

The Greenland Ice Sheet Project Two (GISP2) completed its drilling phase on July 1, 1993, by drilling 3,053 meters (10,017 ft) through the Greenland Ice Sheet into bedrock.[22] GISP2 is located at 72° 36′ N, 38° 30′ W in central Greenland at an altitude of 3,208 meters (10,525 ft), approximately 30 km (18.6 miles) from the GRIP site. Using annual dust layers, the GISP2 core was manually counted for the first 37,900 layers. The GISP2 ice core is 2,792 meters (9,161 ft) long and contains approximately 108,857 annual layers, when counted using annual isotope cycles.

The first 100,000 annual layers of electrical conductivity and oxygen isotope data for the Greenland GISP2 and GRIP cores have been compared, and their curves match very closely. For the same depth in meters, the GRIP core has more than twice as many layers as the GRISP2 core because of ice thinning.

Table 4.2 – Major Greenland and Antarctica Ice Cores						
Continent	Ice Core Location	Date Completed (year)	Total Ice Thickness (meters)	Annual Moisture (cm/yr)	Annual Ice Layers	At Core Depth (meters)
Antarctica	Byrd Station	1968	2,164	15.0	---	---
Antarctica	Dome C (old)	1978	3,400	3.0	39,515	903.4
Greenland	GRIP	1992	3,029	25.0	248,763	2,983.2
Greenland	GISP2	1993	3,053	25.0	108,857	2,792.0
Antarctica	Taylor Dome	1994	1,811	2.5	214,760	554.0
Antarctica	Vostok	1998	3,700	3.0	422,766	3,310.0
Antarctica	Dome C	2003	3,300	3.0	800,000	3,260.0
Greenland	NorthGRIP	2003	3,085	19.0	123,000	3,080.0

Notes:
(1) The annual moisture accumulation is in centimeters of water per year.
(2) Dome C completed in 2003 is also known as EDC3.
(3) The annual ice layers listed occur up to the core depth in meters listed. Beyond that point layers become uncertain. For example, GRIP had 248,763 layers at a core depth of 2,983.2 meters.

The North Greenland Ice Core Project (NorthGRIP) completed its drilling phase in July 2003, after six years.[23] The core was drilled at 75.1° N, 42.3° W (north of the GRIP and GISP2 sites) to a depth of 3,085 meters (10,122 ft) where the drill hit bedrock. The core drill itself was 11 meters (36 ft) long and hung from a cable during drilling. Each ice core section was 3.5 meters (11.5 ft) long and 9.8 cm (3.86 in) in diameter. The clear, regular, annual layers in the core were visible down to 2,600 meters (8,531 ft), representing approximately 80,000 annual layers.[24] The NorthGRIP core has been cross-dated to the GRIP core back to 105,000 years before present using isotope data.

Scientists have analyzed the NorthGRIP core using several isotope and ion measurements to precisely count the number of annual layers. As mentioned, the concentration of several isotopes and ions in snow fluctuate on an annual basis because of the temperature difference between winter and summer. In the NorthGRIP core, oxygen isotopes, deuterium, calcium ions, and sodium ions were cross checked against visually counted annual layers. This core provides a record of annual layers back to more than 100,000 years before present.

At 3,085 meters (10,122 ft), the NorthGRIP drill bottomed out on bedrock. When the drill was retracted, some organic material was found stuck to the drill tip. According to James White, professor of Geological Sciences at the University of

Colorado at Boulder, the pieces looked like blades of grass or pine needles.[25] This organic material is evidence that plants existed on the Earth more than 100,000 years ago.

Ice core data confirm that Antarctica and Greenland have been covered with ice for more than 100,000 years. GRIP, GISP2, Taylor Dome, Vostok, Dome C, and NorthGRIP are solid evidence that the Earth is substantially older than 6,000 years. The cross correlation of data among different cores adds weight to the validity of this conclusion.

What do supporters of traditional young-Earth creation theology say about this evidence? Critics of ice core data say annual layers are actually sub-annual layers.[26] Critics hypothesize that multiple snow falls during the winter season show up as sub-annual layers, indistinguishable from annual layers. The fallacy of this argument is that oxygen isotopes, deuterium, calcium ions, and sodium ions in snow vary according to temperature. Winter snow has a different concentration of molecules than summer snow because of temperature effects. Annual snowfall accumulation based on non-visual measurements can be matched with the visual counting of ice layers. For example, the number of manually counted layers compared against the number of oxygen-18 isotope annual temperature cycles easily agree within five percent. This is conclusive evidence these layers represent more than 100,000 years of Earth history.

Michael Oard, a young-Earth creationist, hypothesizes that the huge accumulations of ice in Greenland and Antarctica are because of heavy snows that started immediately after the flood of Noah, approximately 4,350 years ago.[27] He says present accumulations are the result of 500 years of heavy snows and cold temperatures because of post flood effects, and represent the start of the ice age.[28] There is no evidence in the ice core record to support his belief.

In summary, more than 100,000 annual layers observed in ice cores are physical evidence of an old Earth. Multiple drilling sites and different personnel on two different continents, at different times, confirm the validity of this evidence. *Exemplar* creation allows time in the indefinite past prior to Genesis 1:3 for the accumulation of significant ice in Antarctica and Greenland. *Exemplar* creation easily harmonizes with this firm scientific evidence.

Antarctica Coal and Fossils

Ernest Shackleton was the first to discover coal in Antarctica. During the 1907–1909 expedition, Shackleton took his ship, *Nimrod,* into the Antarctic where he set up base camp at Cape Royds on Ross Island, located in McMurdo Sound. In an attempt to reach the South Pole, his group traveled south across the Ross Ice Sheet and through the Transantarctic Mountains on the Beardmore Glacier. They were within 97 nautical miles (180 km) of being the first to reach the South Pole, when they stopped and began retreating.[29]

On the return trip from their historic attempt, Shackleton and his group made an interesting discovery 350 miles from the South Pole. As they left the Polar Plateau and were crossing the Beardmore Glacier, they discovered coal at an altitude of 3,100 meters (10,200 ft). Shackleton's party brought back samples and mapped the vein, located near Mount Buckley.

The Transantarctic Mountains in western Antarctica, immediately east of the Ross Ice Sheet, form one of the world's great mountain chains, extending for more than 2,200 km (1,370 miles) in length. Many mountain peaks exceed 4,000 meters (13,000 ft) in height[30] and contain numerous exposed coal seams.[31]

Coal has also been found in the Prince Charles Mountains located in eastern Antarctica at approximately 70° S, 70° E. Within these mountains, the Amery Oasis (near the junction of the Lambert Glacier and the Amery Ice Shelf) lies at an altitude ranging from 400 to 1,300 meters (1,300 to 4,300 ft) above sea level. The Bainme-dart Coal Measures at the Amery Oasis contain significant deposits of coal, with some seams more than 3 meters (10 ft) thick.[32]

Coal in Antarctica is physical evidence of past abundant plant life, before the climate turned deadly cold. Coal may be formed in swamps where vegetation accumulates over time and becomes compacted. Coal can also be formed when vegetation is stripped from the land, collected at settling points, covered with sediment, and then compacted. Regardless of the formation process, coal is compelling evidence of climatic conditions favorable to plant growth.

Several notable animal fossils have been found in Antarctica. During a 1990–1991 expedition, William R. Hammer, a paleontologist at Augustana College discovered a new dinosaur. The dinosaur skeleton was found at an altitude of 3,800 meters (12,450 ft) on Mount Kirkpatrick located in the Transantarctic Mountains near the Beardmore Glacier. Professor Hammer's dinosaur, named Cryolophosaurus, meaning "frozen crested reptile," is a large crested meat-eating theropod with two large hind legs for walking and two small fore limbs for grasping prey. Cryolophosaurus is the first carnivorous dinosaur found in Antarctica.[33] Remains of three other dinosaurs were also found, consisting of a very large prosauropod (a long-necked, small-headed, semi-bipedal, herbivorous dinosaur), a small pterosaur (a flying reptile), and another unknown theropod (a bipedal dinosaur with a three toed foot and considered carnivorous).

On December 7, 2003, while on another fossil hunting expedition in Antarctica, Professor Hammer found a sauropod pelvis at an altitude of 3,900 meters (12,800 ft) on Mount Kirkpatrick.[34] The pelvis measured about a meter across and belonged to a sauropod estimated to be between 1.8 and 2.1 meters (5.9 to 6.9 ft) tall and up to 9 meters (29.5 ft) long. Sauropods were quadruped, herbivorous dinosaurs with a long neck and tail, and a small head. They are the largest dinosaurs to have roamed the Earth.

A variety of plant remains have been found in the Ohio Range of the

Transantarctic Mountains, including fossilized tree trunks and ferns. The Ohio Range is known for its highly picturesque, thick layers of massively eroded sedimentary rock.

Animal and plant fossils are firm evidence that at one time abundant life existed in Antarctica. Today, except for marine life, essentially nothing lives there owing to the extreme cold. In the past, Antarctica's climate was substantially different and was warm enough to allow dinosaurs, trees, ferns, and other vegetation to grow. Temperatures somehow dropped from an estimated average of +60° F in the past to an average of –50° F today. When this happened, animal and plant life disappeared and ice began to accumulate.

How did the Antarctic climate change from warm to bitter cold? This is an intriguing question. The leading theory proposes that at one time Antarctica was closer to the equator where it received more sunlight. Because of continental drift, Antarctica moved to its present location throughout vast time.

What do proponents of traditional young-Earth creation theology say about this information? Some hypothesize that originally the Earth had a different atmosphere, resulting in a mild climate over the entire Earth. Proponents say that after Noah's flood, approximately 4,350 years ago, the global climate changed to its present state. This hypothesis conflicts with the ice cores of Greenland and Antarctica, that prove conclusively these two continents have been very cold for more than 100,000 years.

Apparent age should not be used to explain Antarctic coal and fossils. We can readily accept God as having the ability to rapidly create the Earth with its current mass, size, shape, atmosphere, and orbit about the Sun—essentials for a life supporting planet. However, creating coal, dinosaur remains, and plant fossils in Antarctica would not have been necessary. Adding nonessential features to create the appearance of age makes God a great deceiver.

In summary, significant time is necessary to allow the warm climate animals of Antarctica to grow, mature, die, and become fossilized. Significant time is needed for warm climate plants to grow, accumulate, and form thick coal beds. Significant time is needed for the continent of Antarctica to drift to its present location and become drastically colder. Significant time is required for ice to accumulate to great thickness in Greenland and Antarctica. *Exemplar* creation allows time in the indefinite past prior to Genesis 1:3 for these events to occur. *Exemplar* creation easily harmonizes with scientific evidence and its logical inferences.

The Green River Formation

The Green River Formation represents the accumulation of millions of years of sediment. Formations of this nature are a serious challenge to traditional young-Earth creation theology in regard to time. A thick sedimentary deposit extending over a large area, formed within a common time frame, and related to a common cause may be called a *formation*. A formation may be composed of several different types of layered sedimentary rock.

Sedimentary rock, as opposed to igneous or metamorphic rock, is the most common rock on the Earth's surface. Common sedimentary rocks include shale, sandstone, carbonates, evaporites, and coal. Shale is a sedimentary rock composed of clay-like, fine-grained mineral particles. Sandstone is sedimentary rock composed mainly of sand-sized minerals or rock grains. Carbonate sedimentary rocks, which include limestone, dolomite, calcite, and chalk, are formed from accumulated organic material supplied by marine life. Evaporites (mineral deposits formed by the evaporation of water) include gypsum, rock salt, borax, and epsomite. Coal forms from accumulated organic material supplied typically by land plants and animals.

Table 4.3 – Estimated Rate of Accumulation of the Varved Rocks of the Green River Formation			
	Thickness of Varves (millimeters)		Time necessary to accumulate 1 foot (years)
	Range	Average	
Sandstone, fine-grained	0.6 – 9.8	1.16	250
Marlstone and related rocks	0.014 – 0.370	0.167	2,000
Oil shale, moderately good	0.03 – 0.114	0.065	4,700
Oil shale, rich	0.014 – 0.153	0.037	8,200
Weighted average		0.018	2,200
Reference: Bradley, Wilmot H. (1929). The Varves and Climate of the Green River Epoch, *U.S. Geological Survey Professional Paper 158-E*, Page 99.			

The Green River Formation is found in the basins of three separate ancient lakes located in southwestern Wyoming, northwestern Colorado, and northeastern Utah. The first is Lake Gosiute, which includes the Green River Basin, Washakie Basin, Great Divide Basin, and Sand Wash Basin. The second is Fossil Lake, containing Fossil Basin, which lies to the west of Lake Gosiute. The third is Lake Uinta, containing the Uinta Basin and Piceance Basin, which lie south of Lake Gosiute.

The Green River Formation has been extensively studied by geologists because of its deep sedimentary deposits. Henry W. Roehler, a geologist for the U.S. Geological Survey, has written several professional papers about the area described as Lake Gosiute. At one location in Lake Gosiute, about 30 miles west of the southern part of the Rock Springs Uplift, he found sedimentary rock about 1,800 feet deep attributed solely to the Green River Formation (consisting of the Luman Tongue, Scheggs Bed of Tipton Shale, Rife Bed of Tipton Shale, Wilkins Peak Member and Laney Member).[35] Deposits at this location consist of fresh water oil shale, salt water oil shale, numerous mineral evaporites, and other sediments.

Millions of varves (very thin sediment layers), formed at the bottom of the three identified ancient lakes, represent one of the unique features of the Green River Formation. "The usual type of varve consists of a pair of laminae [couplet], one of which is distinctly richer in organic matter than the other."[36] The contact surface between the two parts of a varve and adjacent varves are generally sharp and regular.

Wilmot H. Bradley, another U.S. Geological Survey geologist, used the varved deposits of the Green River Formation to estimate its age. Bradley theorized that varves formed on the lake bottom from particles that slowly settled out of the lake water. Bradley measured the thickness of varves in four basic types of rock at several different locations. From this, he determined the average varve thickness and estimated the number of years to accumulate one foot of rock as shown in Table 4.3. Bradley discovered that the Green River Formation along Parachute Creek in Garfield County, Colorado (located in the Piceance Basin of Lake Uinta) is about 2,600 feet thick.[37] He determined that the varved sediments at Parachute Creek are composed of 7 percent fine-grained sandstone, 76 percent marlstone, 13 percent moderate oil shale, and 4 percent rich oil shale. Based on the estimated time to accumulate one foot of rock given in Table 4.3, Bradley calculated that the Green River epoch lasted about 6,500,000 years.[38] Based on Bradley's data, the number of varves in 2,600 feet of sedimentary rock at Parachute Creek is estimated at 6,096,013 as shown in table 4.4.

Table 4.4 – Estimated Number of Varves of the Green River Formation in 2,600 feet of Varved Rocks at Parachute Creek, Colorado (Piceance Basin of Lake Uinta)			
	Average Varve Thickness (millimeters)	Type of Rock (percent of total thickness)	Number of varves in each type of rock
Sandstone, fine-grained	1.16	7%	47,822
Marlstone and related rocks	0.167	76%	3,606,496
Oil shale, moderately good	0.065	13%	1,584,960
Oil shale, rich	0.037	4%	856,735
			Total 6,096,013
Reference: Bradley, Wilmot H. (1929). The Varves and Climate of the Green River Epoch, U.S. Geological Survey Professional Paper 158-E, Page 99, 107			

Oil shale varves are theorized to have formed by the accumulation of organic material and fine-grained mineral particles that settled to the bottom of the lake. Bradley believes the organic material was supplied by minute planktonic organisms with an average size of 50 microns and an average specific gravity of 1.05.[39] In contrast, the fine-grained mineral particles are as small as 5 microns in diameter and most have a specific gravity of 2.0 or greater. Based on Stokes' Law, the more dense fine-grained minerals tend to settle out first to form the bottom of a varve, while the less dense organic material settles out last to form the top. As mentioned, a varve consists of a pair of dark and light laminae and by definition represents one year of time; however, there may be circumstances where a couplet may form in less time.

One of the issues regarding the Green River Formation, is whether fine shale laminae couplets are formed annually or sub-annually. In other words, does a varve represent one year of time similar to a tree-growth ring? In 1988, geologists Paul Buchheim and Robert Biaggi published the results of their study of two volcanic ash (tuff) layers in Fossil Lake. The two tuffs were caused by two separate volcanic eruptions, whose ashes subsequently blew onto the lake and settled to the bottom. Each tuff is about two to three centimeters thick and separated by a group of oil shale varves. Buchheim and Biaggi measured 1,089 varves in the center of Fossil Basin and 1,566 varves around the basin margins, located between the two tuffs.[40] Varves around the basin margins tended to be thicker. They theorized that seasonal factors were the primary cause of varves at the lake center, whereas a combination of inflow events related to local storms and seasonal factors caused varve deposition near the margins.[41] Based on this data and their logic, around thirty-five percent of the varves (laminae couplets) around the edges of Fossil Basin were due to storm water inflow and represent sub-annual layers.

What do proponents of traditional young-Earth theology say about this information? They believe that most sedimentary deposits were formed by an Earth covering Noah's flood, although a few deposits may have been formed by post-flood events.[42] In attacking the data from the Green River Formation, they say that a varve does not necessarily represent one year. While this statement is true in some instances, the 2,600 feet of sedimentary rock containing approximately 6,000,000 varves (laminae couplets) at Parachute Creek in Lake Uinta easily represent more than three million years of accumulation.

Young-Earth creationists say that fossils found in the Green River Formation represent rapid burial by Noah's flood. Typically, unless dead plants and animals are rapidly buried, they decay or are eaten by scavengers. However, fossils can be formed by slow burial if conditions are right. Cold temperatures, thermal stratification, oxygen-deficient water, or hydrogen sulfide on the bottom of a lake can provide proper conditions for the preservation of organic material until it becomes covered by slowly accumulating sediment.

The most condemning evidence against Noah's flood as an explanation for the Green River Formation is the depth of the sediments. Noah was in the ark for a total of 375 days, so all sediments had to be formed within that time or less. The 2,600 feet of sediment in Lake Uinta would have required the formation of 6.93 feet of sediment per day—an impossible occurrence for oil shale.

Alternating layers of different sedimentary rock, formed by different mechanisms, defy a simple Noah's flood explanation. One section of the Wilkins Peak Member of the Green River Formation reaches a maximum thickness of about 1,300 feet.[43] At one location, the Wilkins Peak Member contains 77 beds of oil shale stacked one on top of the other, separated by sedimentary rock, which in some instances are evaporite beds (sediments formed by the evaporation of water).[44] At Blacks Fork Corehole No. 1, the total thickness of all 77 oil shale beds is 262 feet. Each bed ranges in thickness from less than 1 foot to more than 16 feet.[45] Keep in mind that each bed contains thousands of varves. At another location, the Wilkins

Peak Member contains around 40 beds of trona and halite (two mineral evaporites) stacked one on top of the other, separated by sedimentary rock, which in some instances are oil shale beds. The trona beds range in thickness from less than 1 foot to about 35 feet, while the halite beds range in thickness from less than 1 foot to about 20 feet.[46] Alternating layers of mineral evaporites (trona, halite and salt) and oil shale cannot be formed by a single catastrophic flood (i.e., Noah's flood). Mineral evaporites are formed by the slow evaporation of mineral laden water. A 35 foot thick layer of trona requires significant time. On the other hand, oil shale is formed by the slow accumulation of small organisms and fine-grained mineral particles as they settle out of water. A 16 foot thick accumulation of oil shale represents thousands of years. The formation of mineral evaporites and oil shale require significant time and represent radically different depositional environments.

Another feature of the Green River Formation that defies a Noah's flood explanation, is the presence of distinct layers of volcanic tuff (volcanic ash) separated by oil shale varves. For example, in Fossil Lake oil shale varves occur above, between, and below one tuff pair. In a turbulent Earth covering flood lasting forty days, followed by an eleven month period of calm water, sediment layers of this type would never develop.

In summary, the 2,600 feet of sedimentary rock in the Green River Formation at Parachute Creek in the Piceance Basin of Lake Uinta contain an estimated 6,000,000 oil shale varves—compelling evidence of extensive time significantly beyond three million years. Young-Earth creationists have no plausible explanation for this evidence within the time frame of Noah's flood and a 6,000 year old Earth. On the other hand, *exemplar* creation allows time in the indefinite past prior to Genesis 1:3 for large sedimentary deposits such as the Green River Formation to develop. *Exemplar* creation easily harmonizes with this scientific evidence.

Radiometric Dating Igneous Rocks

A precise method of determining the Earth's age has been a pursuit of scientists for many years. Radiometric dating is the result of that quest and indicates the Earth is billions of years old. This dating technique presents a serious challenge to the credibility of traditional young-Earth creation theology in regard to time.

Before radiometric dating was developed, several methods were used to estimate the Earth's age. Processes extrapolated to determine age include planetary cooling, sedimentation, salt and mineral accumulation in the oceans, helium diffusion, and the decay of Earth's magnetic field. Extrapolations of these phenomena begin with certain assumptions, potential causes for error, and known inconsistencies. Dates range from a few thousand to millions of years.[47]

To better understand extrapolation, the accumulation of salt in the Dead Sea serves as a good example. Scientists can calculate the amount of water and salt currently in the Dead Sea. In addition, they can measure the amount of water received annually from the Jordon River and the amount of salt in each cubic foot of incoming water. From this information, the total amount of salt added to the Dead Sea in one year can be calculated. Using this information, scientists can compute the sea's saltiness 1,000 years in the past or future.

The problem with using extrapolation to determine the past or future saltiness of the Dead Sea is that conditions may change. The climate may change and subsequently affect the amount of rain and salt flowing into the Jordan River. The type of vegetation and amount of cleared land may vary throughout time and influence water runoff. The quantity of water removed from the Jordan River for irrigation may be altered. The inflow of salt from subterranean springs that flow directly into the Dead Sea may fluctuate. In the long term, many variables can affect the amount of water and salt flowing into the Dead Sea to make this an unreliable extrapolation over thousands of years.

On the other hand, radiometric dating, based on the extrapolation of isotope decay, has proven to be reliable. An atomic isotope is one form of an element. For a specific element, all isotopes have the same number of protons and electrons, but a different number of neutrons. An unstable isotope may decay into another isotope of the same element or a completely different element. Isotope decay is the most consistent type of natural change known and is unaffected by non-nuclear processes acting near the surface of the Earth such as heat, cold, pressure, magnetism, centrifugal force, shock, and chemicals.

Isotope decay rates have been carefully measured and are stated in half-life, which is the length of time required for one-half of the isotope atoms within a sample to decay into another form. By precisely measuring the isotopes and decay products in an igneous rock, its age since solidification can be determined. In essence, when an igneous rock solidifies, it becomes a ticking clock that can be read at some future date.

Radiometric dating applies to the dating of igneous rocks (rocks that were once completely molten). Magma from within the Earth and volcanoes are the most common source. In contrast, sedimentary rocks have never been molten and cannot be dated; however, individual igneous rocks or grains of rock contained within sediments can be dated. Radiometric dating cannot be used to directly date plant and animal fossils, but a lava flow on top of a fossil, or beneath it, can be dated to give an upper or lower age limit.

Five of the better known radiometric techniques for dating igneous rocks are rubidium-strontium, samarium-neodymium, potassium-argon, argon-argon, and uranium-lead. The rubidium-strontium, uranium-lead, and samarium-neodymium techniques are preferred because no knowledge of the original rock content is needed. (For a short discussion of these dating techniques, an Internet article by Dr. Roger C. Wiens is recommended.[48]

One of the most significant books written about our planet's age is *Age of the Earth* by G. Brent Dalrymple, PhD, research geologist at the U.S. Geological Survey and retired professor from Oregon State University. In his book, Dr. Dalrymple discusses radiometric dating and presents an extensive compilation of information from different sources. Table 4.5 gives a summary of the oldest igneous rocks provided in his book.

		No. of		
Book Table	Description	Sample Dates	Dating Details	Age Range (billions of yrs)
4.1	West Greenland	476	43 avg. ages	2.52 to 3.81
4.1	Labrador	131	12 avg. ages	2.52 to 3.76
4.2	Superior Province, North America	130	15 avg. ages	2.32 to 3.68
4.4	Pilbara Block, Western Australia.	175	19 avg. ages	2.61 to 3.57
4.6	Barberton Mountain Land, S. Africa	247	33 avg. ages	2.73 to 3.56
5.5	Lunar Mare basalt rocks	62	Dated 14 rocks	3.09 to 3.95
5.6	Oldest lunar rocks	30	Dated 13 rocks	3.90 to 4.51
6.3	Old meteors	67	Dated 42 rocks	4.29 to 4.60

Table 4.5 – Radiometric Ages of Early Rocks
(A compilation of radiometric dates from *The Age of the Earth*)

Reference: Dalrymple, G. Brent (1991). *The Age of the Earth.*

Dalrymple gives a total of 1,159 sample dates from five major locations on Earth with an age spread of 2.32 to 3.81 billion years. Since publication of his book, rocks dated up to 4 billion years old have been found in Greenland, the Canadian Shield near Lake Superior in Canada, Transvaal Province of South Africa, and Western Australia.[49]

Age of the Earth also lists information collected from dating Moon rocks and meteorites. Dalrymple gives a number of dates from lava flows (basalt rocks) on the Moon between 3.09 to 3.95 billion years old.[50] Some of the oldest Moon rocks date from 3.90 to 4.51 billion years old.[51] He gives 67 dates from 42 different meteorites between 4.29 and 4.60 billion years old.[52]

Dalrymple discusses lead isotopes and their use in dating the Earth. Based on the Holmes-Houtermans model, lead isotope decay gives a calculated Earth age of 4.54 billion years.[53] He says that naturally occurring long-lived radioactive isotopes lead to the incontrovertible conclusion that the solid bodies of the Solar System formed 4.54 billion years ago.[54] Based on this and direct radiometric measurements, an age of 4.6 billion years is often quoted for the Earth.

Prevalent theory proposes that meteors and the Earth were formed at the same time. Molten material within the meteors cooled first, because of their smaller size, and started the clock ticking. Earth, starting as a molten ball, took roughly 700 million years to cool enough to retain the first rocks. The earliest rocks found on our planet's surface are approximately 3.8 to 4.0 billion (3,800,000,000–4,000,000,000) years old. Rocks older than this are theorized to have been recycled by subduction, when they slid back into the molten mantle and remelted.

The controversy concerning radiometric dating has been fueled to an extent by occasional inconsistent measurements, often used by critics to attack its credibility. Inaccurate results have occurred because of the initial immaturity of the process stemming from poor laboratory techniques, lack of process knowledge, improper sample preparation, and poor sample selection. As the technology for radiometric measurement has matured, it has become more reliable.

Accepting radiometric dating as a credible process does not mean it is infallible. Several factors can affect the accuracy of dates obtained from igneous rocks. Exacting laboratory procedures are a basic requirement. Igneous rocks to be dated must be carefully selected, and rocks not fully melted or contaminated by their surroundings can give incorrect dates. Reheated igneous rocks may give inaccurate results since the clock is incompletely reset. Both the original formation date of the rock and the reheating event date may be wrong.

In summary, radiometric dating is not based on visual evidence equivalent to starlight, Moon craters, or ice cores. Radiometric dating is the measurement of isotope decay, undetectable by the human senses, extrapolated backward in time. However, based on precise measurements using sensitive instrumentation and a consistent decay process, extrapolation is highly credible. Igneous rocks that have been fully melted, uncontaminated while melted, solidified, and not reheated are excellent candidates for dating. Trustworthy average dates can be obtained as evidenced by the analysis of multiple samples taken from a specific rock outcrop using different dating techniques and different laboratories. Radiometric dating is compelling evidence that the Earth is billions of years old. *Exemplar* creation allows time in the indefinite past prior to Genesis 1:3 for significant radioisotope decay to occur. *Exemplar* creation easily harmonizes with this scientific evidence.

Carbon-14 Dating Organic Material

Radiocarbon dating presents a serious challenge to the credibility of traditional young-Earth creation theology in regard to time. Carbon-14 dating is a method of determining the age of once living plants and animals (organic materials). This technique cannot date rocks. Completely fossilized plant or animal remains are not good candidates for dating. Evidence from research about radiocarbon dating indicates life has existed on Earth back to 30,000 years and beyond.

The radiocarbon dating of organic materials is based on decay of the carbon-14 isotope extrapolated backward in time (similar to the radiometric dating of igneous rocks). Accuracy depends on the consistency of all variables affecting the process.

The carbon family has three naturally occurring isotopes: carbon-12, carbon-13, and carbon-14. Carbon-12 comprises 98.892% of the total carbon in the atmosphere, while carbon-13 accounts for 1.108% of the total.[55] Carbon-14 comprises about 0.00000000010% of the carbon in the atmosphere.[56] Carbon-12 and carbon-13 are stable and used as a reference, while carbon-14 is unstable and is the basis for radiocarbon dating.

The origin and decay of carbon-14 begins when nitrogen-14 atoms in the upper atmosphere are struck by cosmic rays. When a nitrogen atom has one proton removed and one neutron added, one carbon-14 atom is formed. Starting with a given amount of carbon-14 in a sample, approximately 5,730 years are required for one-half of the starting amount to decay and turn into another form (this determines its half-life).[57]

Once carbon-14 is formed, it combines with oxygen in the atmosphere to make carbon dioxide, which descends to the Earth's surface and is picked up by plants. During photosynthesis, the carbon atom is separated from the two oxygen atoms. Carbon becomes a permanent part of the plant's structure, while oxygen is released back into the atmosphere. When animals eat plants, the carbon contained therein becomes a part of their bodies, residing in their bones, teeth, horns, claws, and other tissues.

When a plant or animal dies, intake of all carbon ceases and their remains become a ticking clock as carbon-14 slowly decays. Conceptually, by measuring the ratio of carbon-12 or carbon-13 to the remaining carbon-14, the time since death can be determined.

Three major techniques have been developed for carbon-14 dating: the gas counting method, the liquid scintillation method, and the accelerator mass spectrometry method. The newest method, accelerator mass spectrometry (AMS), has an advantage over the others because small samples from one gram to a few milligrams can be analyzed. The AMS method is able to count all carbon-14 atoms in a specimen at one time, rather than counting their decay rate (in small samples, the number of individual carbon-14 atoms that decay in an hour may only be a few).

The basics of radiocarbon dating are easy to understand; however, taking a concept and turning it into a reliable dating method is more difficult. Many factors in radiocarbon dating can significantly affect its accuracy. The precision of radiocarbon dating becomes increasingly uncertain above 10,000 years because of the rapidly decreasing percentage of carbon-14 in a sample. As shown in Table 4.6, after five half-lives, or 28,650 years, only 3.12% of the original carbon-14 remains. The basic physics limit the process. In addition, several other known variables can affect the precision of radiocarbon dating.

(1) Atmospheric carbon – The first major variable in radiocarbon dating is the amount of carbon-14 in the Earth's atmosphere. Since carbon-14 in the air is the source of carbon for plants and animals, if the amount in the atmosphere varies over time, then the amount retained by a living organism will also vary. Scientists believe that any change in Earth's magnetic field affects carbon-14 production by offering more or less protection from cosmic rays. Changes in the Sun can also vary the intensity of cosmic radiation bombarding Earth and influence carbon-14 production. Regardless of the cause, scientists know that the percentage of carbon-14 in the Earth's

atmosphere has changed throughout time. The amount has been higher in the past, which causes radiocarbon dated objects to appear younger than they really are.

Tree-ring dating (dendrochronology) has been used for many years to correlate radiocarbon dates. Scientists have counted tree rings and measured their radiocarbon ages to develop correlation curves. Using this technique, Dr. C. W. Ferguson at the University of Arizona, Tucson built a tree-ring chronology from bristlecone pine trees in the White Mountains of California going back almost 8,000 years.[58]

Table 4.6 – Carbon-14 Half-Life and its Decay in a Sample over Time
(Based on a half-life of 5,730 years)

Number of C-14 Half-Lives	Percent of Original Carbon-14	Percent of Original Carbon-13	Percent of Original Carbon-12	Number of Years Before Present
0	100.000%	100%	100%	0
1	50.000%	100%	100%	5,730
2	25.000%	100%	100%	11,460
3	12.500%	100%	100%	17,190
4	6.250%	100%	100%	22,920
5	3.120%	100%	100%	28,650
6	1.563%	100%	100%	34,380
7	0.781%	100%	100%	40,110
8	0.391%	100%	100%	45,840
9	0.195%	100%	100%	51,570
10	0.098%	100%	100%	57,300

Scientists have built standardized calibration curves that permit correcting radiocarbon dates affected by carbon-14 variation in the atmosphere. In 1998, the IntCal98 radiocarbon calibration curve was released, based on a partial tree-ring serie.. An updated version, IntCal04 was released in 2004, based on a complete tree-ring chronology of German pine, German oak, Irish oak, and Pacific Northwest Douglas fir going back 12,410 calendar years before present (BP).[59] Beyond this, corals were used to extend the curve back to 26,000 calendar years BP. The complete IntCal04 calibration curve permits the correction of carbon-14 dates to a maximum of 26,000 years. Based on this calibration curve, 22,000 radiocarbon years are equivalent to 26,000 calendar years.[60]

A radiocarbon correlation curve back to 50,000 years was built by Dr. Richard Fairbanks at Columbia University and his associates based on coral. Corals were obtained from Barbados in the western tropical Atlantic, the Kiritimati Atoll in the central equatorial Pacific, and the uplifted reefs of Araki Island in the western Pacific. This correlation curve is based on ^{230}Th $/^{234}U/^{238}U$ radiometric measurements of coral compared against carbon-14 measurements. The first 12,410 years of the IntCal04 radiocarbon tree-ring dendrochronology curve and the coral curve are essentially identical.[61] From 12,410 to 26,000 calendar years BP, the majority of the IntCal04 curve is based on coral analysis from this study.

An additional correlation curve was developed by measuring the age of organic material in alternating layers of sediment in Lake Suigetsu, Japan. Small white blooms grow on the lake each year. At the end of their annual life cycle, the blooms settle to the bottom and form a white layer. During the remainder of the year, black sediment collects on the lake bottom. Alternating layers of black sediments and white blooms permit a visual count of annual layers. Scientists counted 29,100 alternating layers and built a radiocarbon correlation curve from 8,830 to 37,930 calendar years before present.[62] For the period of time they overlap, the Lake Suigetsu correlation curve and the IntCal04 calibration curve are essentially identical.

(2) Fractionation – A second important variable in radiocarbon dating is fractionation.[63] Earth's atmosphere contains a given ratio of carbon-12, carbon-13, and carbon-14. Fractionation occurs when living things retain carbon in a ratio different from the atmosphere. This happens because plants discriminate against slight chemical and physical differences among the three different isotope forms.

The amount that plants discriminate against carbon-13 has been measured. Plants classified as C4 plants such as maize, sorghum, amaranth, millet, buffalo grass, pigweed, and sugar cane use the Hatch-Slack cycle during photosynthesis and retain an average of 13% less carbon-13 than found in the atmosphere. Plants classified as C3 plants such as rice, wheat, oats, soybeans, and potatoes use the Calvin-Benson cycle during photosynthesis and retain an average of 26% less carbon-13 than found in the atmosphere.[64] Humans and animals that feed on these plants end up with a fractionation effect in their bones, teeth, fingernails, horns, claws, and other tissues.

A third group of plants that show strong fractionation (normally not used for food), include warm evergreens, cool deciduous, hardwood, and conifer trees. These trees retain approximately 27% less carbon-13 than found in the atmosphere.[65] Fractionation effects are retained in charcoal when wood is burned (carbonized) in short term experiments.[66]

The physical properties of carbon-14 cause it to have different fractionation values than carbon-13. The fractionation effect of carbon-14 in a sample is considered to be twice that of carbon-13.[67,68] Fractionation makes things look older than they really are, and when dates are corrected in radiocarbon dating they are always younger (more recent). Fractionation effects can cause significant dating error.

(3) Matter transfer – A third variable in radiocarbon dating is the transfer of material in or out of a sample. In radiometric dating, when an igneous rock cools it becomes a sealed unit. Unless the rock is heated to its melting point or near its melting point, none of the radioactive isotopes can leave the rock. This ensures an accurate clock. This is not the case with organic material. Foreign matter can infiltrate organic material such as wood or bone to the extent they becomes completely fossilized. When wood and bone are buried in soil and begin to decay, atoms and molecules transfer in and out of their structures. Carbon, calcium, proteins, and amino

acids are removed from bone as it slowly decays. Organic materials stored in dry, protected surroundings have potential for giving the best radiocarbon dates.

(4) Laboratory procedures – A fourth variable in radiocarbon dating is the facility performing the analysis. Readings among laboratories may vary depending on the accurate calibration of equipment. The handling of samples during cleaning, preparation, and analysis will vary among laboratories. Samples must typically be cleaned to remove contamination in the form of carbonates, fluvic acids, soil humics, and other soluble organic matter absorbed from their surroundings.[69] All effects combined cause variation in the measured age, when multiple laboratories date the same object.

Knowledgeable individuals whose business is radiocarbon dating are aware of all four of the variables mentioned. Some of these variables can be accounted for, controlled, and monitored—while others cannot. This dating method is similar to any other emerging technology, becoming more dependable as it matures.

What do proponents of traditional young-Earth theology say about carbon-14 dating? Young-Earth creationists, Ken Ham and Don Batten, discuss radiocarbon dating in *The Revised & Expanded Answers Book* and *The New Answers Book*.[70,71] Except for a couple of simple straw man concerns, there is little criticism. Apparent age is not used as an argument to attack radiocarbon dating results.

The radiocarbon dating of archaeological artifacts is often used to support the Bible. For example, the first Dead Sea Scrolls were discovered in Cave No. 1 during the final months of 1946. One of the artifacts found was the Great Isaiah Scroll. The scroll is written in 54 columns, contains all 66 books of Isaiah, and is complete except for some damage around the edges. Isaiah is probably the most significant prophetical book in the Old Testament about the coming of Jesus Christ, His life, and death. Material from the scroll was AMS radiocarbon dated by two prestigious laboratories in Zurich, Switzerland and Tucson, Arizona. At a two sigma level, the Zurich date was 230–48 BC and Tucson reported 230–53 BC.[72] The correlation was almost perfect. An average date of 140 BC is often quoted for the scroll.

Radiocarbon dating has been used to discredit spurious religious claims. For example, the Shroud of Turin is claimed to be the burial cloth of Christ and considered a sacred relic by some. The cloth bears blood stains of a man who appears to have been whipped. Samples of the shroud were sent to AMS laboratories in Zurich, Switzerland and Tucson, Arizona and Oxford, England for carbon-14 dating. Three other datable artifacts with a known archaeological date were sent along as control samples. Radiocarbon dating gave a ninety-five percent confidence level of 1260–1390 AD for the shroud.[73] The Shroud of Turin is not the burial cloth of Christ, yet this spurious relic continues to be promoted as a biblical artifact.

In summary, radiocarbon dating supports the existence of life on Earth substantially before 4004 BC in contradiction to traditional young-Earth creation theology. The carbon-14 decay process has been directly checked against tree-ring chronologies and annual lake sediment accumulations. The resultant calibration and correlation curves are strong evidence of life on Earth up to 30,000 years and beyond. *Exemplar* creation easily harmonizes with the scientific evidence of carbon-14 dating (within inherent limitations of the technique).

Radioactive Halos

Dr. Robert V. Gentry, a nuclear physicist and young-Earth creationist, wrote *Creation's Tiny Mystery,* where he claims that polonium-218 radiohalos in Precambrian granites prove the fiat creation of planet Earth within three minutes in the recent past. Gentry's work is often cited by supporters of traditional young-Earth creation theology to support their belief in a young Earth.[74]

Gentry's theory is based on a combination of known evidence about radioactive isotope decay and unknown phenomena. Theoretically, radiohalos are formed by alpha particles released during the decay of radioactive isotopes concentrated at a point source in granite. The alpha particles of a specific energy level radiate out from the point source and leave a characteristic concentric ring. The distance an alpha particle travels is proportional to its energy level, which in turn is a function of the specific decaying isotope. The cross section of a halo looks similar to a series of concentric rings. Typical three ring halos are quite small with a diameter of around 0.068 mm (0.0027 inch) and must be viewed under a microscope.

Table 4.7 – U-238 Alpha Particle Decay Series			
Element	Isotope	Age in Half-Life	Energy in MeV
Uranium	U-238	4,470,000,000 yrs.	4.196
Uranium	U-234	245,400 yrs.	4.856
Thorium	Th-230	75,400 yrs.	4.771
Radium	Ra-226	1,599 yrs.	4.870
Radon	Rn-222	3.82 days	5.590
Polonium	Po-218	3.04 min.	6.114
Polonium	Po-214	163 microseconds	7.833
Polonium	Po-210	138.4 days	5.409
Lead	Pb-206	Stable	0
Reference: Lide, David R., ed. (2008). *CRC Handbook of Chemistry & Physics*, 88th ed. pp11-182 to 11-195.			

The decay of uranium-238 and its resultant products are well understood. When uranium decays, it emits alpha and beta particles as it changes from one isotope to another. Since radiohalos are theorized to be caused *only by alpha particles*, isotopes that release beta particles are typically omitted from the decay series. As shown in Table 4.7, the eight-step alpha particle decay series progresses from uranium U-238 to lead Pb-206, a stable element.

Theoretically, a radiohalo formed by the U-238 through Pb-206 decay series has eight concentric rings surrounding the isotope point source as shown in Figure 4.8.

Normally only five rings are actually distinguishable under an optical microscope. Typically the U-234, Th-230, and Ra-226 rings are so close together they cannot be identified separately since their alpha particle energy decay levels are similar. Additionally, the Rn-222 and Po-210 rings appear as a single ring.

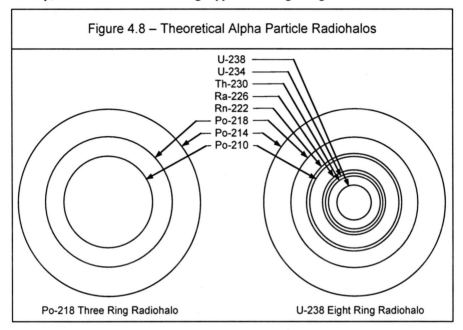

Figure 4.8 – Theoretical Alpha Particle Radiohalos

U-238
U-234
Th-230
Ra-226
Rn-222
Po-218
Po-214
Po-210

Po-218 Three Ring Radiohalo   U-238 Eight Ring Radiohalo

Theoretically, a radiohalo formed by the Po-218 through Pb-206 decay series should have three rings, consisting of Po-218, Po-214, and Po-210, surrounding the isotope point source as shown in Figure 4.8. The final decay product, Pb-206, is stable and does not emit any alpha particles.

According to Gentry, radiohalos found in granite that exhibit three rings were formed from Po-218. Gentry believes polonium-218 came into existence when God created the Earth in the recent past. Consequently, Po-218 had no precursor isotopes and was not part of a normal U-238 decay series. Since polonium-218 has a half-life of 3.04 minutes, he hypothesizes that Earth's primordial granites formed and solidified in less than three minutes.

Although Gentry's conclusions have gained acceptance among proponents of traditional young-Earth creation theology, his idea is rejected by essential all other scientists knowledgeable of the subject. Gentry's conclusions are criticized for a number of reasons.

(1) Precambrian granite and newer granite – According to Gentry's hypothesis, only "primordial granites" contain radiohalos, and they should be absent in newer granites. Gentry says that Precambrian granites are primordial rocks (or Genesis rocks), which are the foundation rocks of the continents. Gentry found halos in a

number of granite samples sent to him from different parts of the world; however, he did not distinguish the local or regional geological setting of his samples.[75] Not all granites found on Earth are of the same age. For example, the Columbia River Plateau contains newly formed granites less than 17 million years old compared to 3.8 billion year old granites found in Greenland based on radiometric dating. At a minimum, no granites that lie above sedimentary or fossil bearing rocks should contain halos. Gentry has failed to prove that halos only occur in "primordial basement granites" and that none appear in newer granites.

(2) Unusual halos – Dwarf and giant halos have been found in minerals, and their size cannot be reconciled with any known alpha decay energies. The formation of these halos defies a simple alpha particle decay explanation. Other halos have ghost rings that do not correspond to any known alpha decay energy. The current state of knowledge about radioactive elements does not suggest a plausible explanation.[76]

(3) Assumed alpha particle effects – Gentry assumes that granite halos are all due to the effect of alpha particles during isotope decay. Beta particles are not considered to have an effect. However, beta particles cannot totally be ruled out. Experiments have revealed that high energy beta particles can break molecular bonds. A combination of alpha and beta decay particles may be hypothesized as the cause of the observed mineral discoloration halos.[77]

(4) Three and five ring halos – Both three and five ring halos have been observed. Three ring halos are believed to represent the Po-218 through Pb-206 decay series, with their corresponding short half-lives. On the other hand, five ring halos (theoretically eight rings) are believed to represent the U-238 through Pb-206 decay series.[78,79] The half-life for the decay of U-238 is 4.47 billion years. Five ring halos indicate a long age of millions of years and conflict with Gentry's interpretation of three ring halos.

(5) Radon gas – Gentry believes three ring halos are the result of isotope decay in the Po-218 through Pb-206 series. Rn-222, also known as radon gas, decays into Po-218. Radon gas is often found in granite and can permeate through rock. A hypothesis counter to Gentry's is that radon gas could migrate through rock and collect at a specific point, whereupon it would decay into Po-218 and form a three ring halo. This hypothesis has not been demonstrated experimentally.

(6) A one-time effect – According to Gentry, three ring halos are a short term, one-time effect that occurred within 3.04 minutes. The halos developed when God created the primordial basement rocks, an act that will never be repeated. On the other hand, most legitimate age measurement processes are connected to a continuous,

verified annual effect measured over time. For example, the radiometric dating of rocks is based on known isotope decay on a *yearly* basis extrapolated backward in time. Dendrochronology is based on known *yearly* tree-ring growth throughout hundreds of years. The age of starlight is based on the speed of light and the distance it can travel within a *year*. Ice cores are based on the *yearly* accumulation of snow throughout time. All these yearly effects are observed today, and are the basis of the credible dating techniques discussed.

In summary, dwarf halos, giant halos, three ring halos, and five ring halos have all been observed. Isotope decay and associated alpha particles are hypothesized to be the cause of some halos; however, they cannot plausibly explain all halos. The full range of halo phenomena is not well understood and is on the edge of scientific knowledge. Gentry's interpretation of halos as proof that Earth's Precambrian granites were all created in less than three minutes in the recent past is pure speculation. In addition, for young-Earth creation theology to be true, all of the evidence presented elsewhere in this chapter in support of significant time must be overturned.

Conclusion

In regard to time, the real issue is not the *absolute* age of the universe, our solar system, or life on Earth. The real issue is compelling scientific evidence that traditional young-Earth creation theology is terribly wrong in regard to time. The heavens, Earth, and its biosphere are much older than 4004 BC.

A number of physical indicators prove the Earth and universe are older than the date calculated by Archbishop James Ussher. The measured distance to stars and the speed of light prove the heavens are millions of years old. Impact craters illustrate the implausibility of a 6,000 year old Earth and Moon. Ice cores from Greenland and Antarctica confirm the Earth is more than 100,000 years old. Coal, in addition to animal and plant fossils, in Antarctica prove it had a warm climate before the temperature plunged and ice began accumulating more than 100,000 years ago. The Green River Formation easily represents more than three million years of oil shale laminae accumulation. The oldest igneous rocks on Earth have been radiometric dated around 3.9 billion years old. Tree-ring chronologies calibrated against carbon-14 decay go back 12,410 calendar years. The scientific evidence in support of significant time is overwhelming and will never be overturned.

Keep in mind that significant time in a building process is not equivalent to naturalistic evolution. For example, the Great Pyramid of Khufu in Giza, Egypt was built during a twenty year period, and an estimated 2.3 million blocks of cut stone were used in its construction.[80] No one denies the Great Pyramid is due to intelligent cause rather than natural cause. However, suppose the pyramid builders were immortal and laid one block every 100 years to take a total of 230 million years for its construction. In considering this amount of time, could we rightfully say the Great Pyramid had evolved? Of course not! Regardless of the time taken to build the Great Pyramid, it is undeniably a product of intelligent cause. Given billions of years, natural cause cannot build the Great Pyramid. Natural mechanisms alone are incapable of cutting 2.3 million stone blocks to the required shape, transporting them to the job site, and then assembling them in a pyramid structure.

Promoters of traditional young-Earth creation theology, in addition to naturalistic evolutionists, have repeatedly equated billions of years with evolution. For this reason, an old age for the universe is very disturbing to many Christians. Although unsettling, we should reject the notion that if the Earth is billions of years old then evolution must be true. We must realize that more than enormous time is needed. Evolutionary formation of the first stars from hot hydrogen and helium gases by self-gravity, the solar nebular hypothesis, chemical evolution, and biological evolution lack a plausible natural constructive mechanism, and can be rejected.

Empirical science based on observation, measurement, and experimentation has determined that natural cause is severely limited as a constructive mechanism. Random, naturally directed, purposeless, mechanistic change is incapable of creating design information, complex functional systems, mathematically improbable structures, and fine-tuned arrangements—even given billions of years. Time is not a magic wand capable of curing the severe limitations of natural cause.

On the other hand, God as an eternal, omnipotent creator could easily have built galaxies, stars, our solar system, Earth, and its biosphere when given millions of years of time. God could have widely spaced many creative events throughout time. Although discrete creative events no doubt occurred quite rapidly (e.g., species created in the Cambrian explosion), they may have been separated from other creative events by significant time.

Exemplar creation offers a solution to the time problem that respects the integrity of the Bible and easily harmonizes with scientific evidence. Where the Genesis creation story and scientific evidence intersect, they can be harmonized in regard to time. *Exemplar* creation permits the occurrence of events requiring significant time in the indefinite past prior to Genesis 1:3.

Hope for the Bible believing community lies not in attempting to overturn the massive amount of evidence accumulated by scientists in support of an old universe. The road to success does not require Christians to challenge science in a head-to-head confrontation over time—a fight they will continue to lose. Instead, victory rests in a proper translation and explanation of the creation story. When key words and phrases in Genesis are proper translated, *exemplar* creation emerges as a biblically sound explanation.

*These were more noble than those in Thessalonica, in that they
received the word with all readiness of mind, and searched the scriptures daily, whether those things were so. (Acts 17:11) KJV*

Chapter 5

Key Words in Genesis

The Old Testament was written in Hebrew, and biblical Hebrew (compared to Modern Hebrew) is often quite limited in its choice of nouns, pronouns, adjectives, verbs, and adverbs. The common language of Moses' day, reflected in the Bible, is inadequate to describe complex actions, physical phenomena, and scientific concepts. *Strong's Exhaustive Concordance of the Bible* lists 8,674 Hebrew words in its Hebrew and Chaldee Dictionary that represent most of the words in the Old Testament. On the other hand, *Merriam-Webster's Collegiate Dictionary* contains roughly 200,000 English words. With such a disparity, properly translating the Old Testament can be problematic. A single word in Hebrew may be capable of being translated into two, three, or more English words having a specific meaning. For example, in the King James Version, the Hebrew word *erets* is translated in descending frequency as "land, earth, country, and ground," all of which have a fairly precise connotation in English. How *erets* is translated can influence our understanding of a verse. In the story of Noah's flood, does *erets* refer to land or the entire Earth as a planet? The translation of *erets* dramatically affects our view of this event.

When the context of a sentence forces a Hebrew word to be translated a specific way, proper selection from multiple choices is not difficult. Problems arise when the context is neutral, and the entire meaning of a sentence hinges on a single word—a major issue in translating some key words in the Genesis creation account. If a word can be legitimately translated two or three different ways, then selection becomes a judgment call when the context is neutral.

Both English and Hebrew have homographs; words spelled the same, but with a different meaning. For example, the statement, "The leader of the *band* wore a wedding *band* on his finger." A musical band and a wedding band are totally different, yet have the same spelling.

Both English and Hebrew can also have heteronyms: words spelled the same, but with a different meaning *and pronunciation* (heteronyms are a subcategory of homographs). For example, "The lead pack mule was carrying the miner's lead ore." In English, context determines how these two words are pronounced. In biblical Hebrew, vocal marks added by the Masoretes often determine the pronunciation and meaning of a word. This is a critical issue for some words in Genesis.

The Hebrew Bible (*Biblia Hebraica*) presented in *The Lexham Hebrew-English Interlinear Bible* by Logos Research Systems of Bellingham, Washington is the basis for the *exemplar* translation of Genesis Chapters 1 and 2. The Lexham Bible was translated by the University of Stellenbosch in South Africa and uses *The Biblia Hebraica Stuttgartensia* (the Masoretic text) as its basis. Each Hebrew word is retained in its verse structure, with the corresponding English translation below. The Hebrew text is presented in a right to left format (opposite the English style), identical to that found in the *Biblia Hebraica*.

One of the main advantages of the Lexham Bible (first released in 2004) is its electronic format designed for the personal computer. Hebrew-English interlinear Bibles have been around for a long time; however, their print is often small and they lack search capability. In contrast, the Lexham Bible gives a clear presentation of the Hebrew text and allows for rapid searches using Boolean operators on Hebrew words and roots of interest. This permits the serious Bible student to quickly, accurately, and comprehensively study translation issues. The Bible student is able to examine all occurrences of a specific Hebrew word in a matter of minutes, a task that would normally take weeks or months.

In conjunction with the Lexham Bible, a *Strong's Exhaustive Concordance of the Bible* (primarily an electronic version) was used for word studies. Strong's concordance contains every English word in the King James Version of the Bible and assigns a numerical identifier that corresponds to the Hebrew or Greek on which the English is based. Strong's numbers provide a common method of identifying specific words in the Hebrew text without resorting to the Hebrew alphabet and are used throughout Chapters 5 and 6. The eliyah.com Internet version was used for most word studies. This electronic version allows the serious student to quickly find all occurrences of an English word in the Bible (and its Hebrew equivalent), a task that would normally take hours or days.

Several Hebrew words in Chapters 5 and 6 and Appendix B are represented using phonetic spelling. For example, phonetic spelling of the Hebrew word (ברא), meaning "create," is *bârâ*. The phonetic spellings given in *Strong's Exhaustive Concordance of the Bible* are generally used, since it is the most well-known biblical Hebrew reference book. The English phonetic spelling and pronunciation of a Hebrew word will often vary among authorities.

Some key words in Genesis deserve an in-depth study and their proper understanding is essential for a correct translation of the Hebrew text. Keep in mind that words used to describe the Genesis account have no special meaning applicable only to the creation story. They were words commonly used in the Hebrew language of the day and occur throughout the Old Testament.

The basis of study for the following key words in Genesis is *not to explore every possible meaning*, but to ensure that specific words used in the *exemplar* translation are legitimate and well-supported elsewhere in the Old Testament. With this approach, Hebrew words and their frequency of translation into English are often analyzed. For example, Hebrew words based on the root *bânâh* occur 376 times in the Old Testament and are translated 366 times as "build" in the KJV. Therefore, the translation of *bânâh* as "made" in Genesis 2:22 is replaced with "built" in the *exemplar* translation. Although the average person may not appreciate the small difference between *made* and *built*, such subtleties are the basis for current errant translations of the Genesis account and its conflict with scientific evidence in regard to time.

Bârâ – Create

The Hebrew word *bârâ* (Strong's 01254) occurs seven times in the first two chapters of Genesis and is consistently translated "create." The Brown-Driver-Briggs Hebrew Lexicon gives the English word "create" as an acceptable translation of the verb *bârâ*,[1] underlined and accompanied by its Strong's number in superscript in the *exemplar* translation below:

• Genesis 1:1 In the beginning, God created[01254] the heavens and the Earth.

• Genesis 1:21 And God *is the one who* created[01254] the great reptiles.

• Genesis 1:27 And God *is the one who* created[01254] man in His image, in God's image created[01254] him, male and female *God* created[01254] them.

• Genesis 2:3 All work that He created[01254] to do.

• Genesis 2:4 These accounts *that follow are about* the heavens and the Earth at their creation[01254].

The root word *bârâ* (Strong's 01254) occurs 54 times in the Old Testament and is translated "created" 33 times, "create" 8 times, and "creator" 3 times, in addition to other miscellaneous words in the KJV.[2] In the Pentateuch, *bârâ* is specifically reserved for actions performed by God and is translated "create" in the KJV except in two instances (Exodus 34:10 and Num. 16:30). *Bârâ* can be legitimately translated create in the Genesis story.

Âsâh – Do, Did and Doing

The Hebrew word *âsâh* (Strong's 06213) occurs twelve times in the first two chapters of Genesis and can be translated a number of ways. The Brown-Driver-Briggs Hebrew Lexicon gives the English words "do" and "make" as primary translations of the verb *âsâh*.[3] An understanding of *âsâh* is essential for its proper translation in the Genesis creation story.

The word *âsâh* (Strong's 06213) occurs approximately 2,633 times in the Old

Testament and is translated "do, did, done, or doing" 1,333 times, "make or made" 653 times, "wrought" 52 times, "deal" 52 times, "commit" 49 times, "offer" 49 times, "execute" 48 times, "keep" 48 times, "shew" 43 times, "prepare" 37 times, "work" 29 times, "do so" 21 times, "perform" 18 times, "get" 14 times, "dress" 13 times, "maker" 13 times, and "maintain" 7 times, in addition to other miscellaneous words in the KJV.[4]

In view of the many different translations of *âsâh,* what does it really mean? The basic meaning of *âsâh* is equivalent to the English word "do," a general word that specifies the performance or execution of an action.

In the English language, the words "do, did, done, or doing" can refer to a multitude of actions. For example, we might say, "Jane is doing her hair." In this sentence *doing* is a general word that indicates some type of action is being performed. Jane's actions can include washing, rinsing, dyeing, drying, curling, combing, brushing, teasing, or straightening her hair. We could say, "Karen is doing the dishes." In this case, Karen's actions can include picking up, scraping, rinsing, washing, drying, or putting dishes away. We could say, "John is doing drugs," which might refer to sniffing, inhaling, smoking, swallowing, or injecting drugs. The word "do" and its tenses in the English language can refer to an unlimited number of activities permissible within the context of a statement.

The general meaning of *âsâh* results in it being translated a number of different ways in the Old Testament, based on verse context and the translator's judgment. The problem occurs when the context of a verse is neutral and does not suggest a specific meaning. The translation of *âsâh* within a neutral context causes a small amount of confusion in understanding the Genesis creation story.

The Hebrew words *bârâ* and *âsâh* have different meanings. *Bârâ* means "create" and in the Pentateuch is normally reserved to describe a creative act of God. *Âsâh* is a general word to denote some kind of action, which can include the action of creating. *Âsâh* is never translated "create" in the KJV, but nevertheless can refer to a creative act of God as in Genesis 1:31.

Âsâh is often translated "made." *Âsâh* is used to describe the building of the tabernacle in Exodus 36:11–37, when the workman *made* loops, curtains, coverings, boards, bars, veils, and pillars for the tabernacle. *Âsâh* is used to describe things God *made* in the Genesis creation story.

The word *âsâh* occurs twelve times in Genesis Chapters 1 and 2, underlined and accompanied by its Strong's number in superscript in the *exemplar* translation below:

- Genesis 1:7 And God *is the one who* made[06213] the expanse.
- Genesis 1:11 And the fruit tree making[06213] fruit.
- Genesis 1:12 And the trees making[06213] fruit.
- Genesis 1:16 And God *is the one who* made[06213] two great luminaries.
- Genesis 1:25 And God *is the one who* made[06213] the animals of the Earth.

• Genesis 1:26 And God said, Man, made[06213] in our image.
• Genesis 1:31 And God saw all that *He had* done[06213] and behold *it was* very good.
• Genesis 2:2 And on the seventh day God finished His work that *He had* done[06213] and rested on the seventh day from all His work that *He had* done[06213].
• Genesis 2:3 All His work that He *had* created *and* done[06213].
• Genesis 2:4 In the days Yahweh God did[06213] *the* Earth and heavens.
• Genesis 2:18 For him I *shall* make[06213] as his counterpart a helper.

The above verses represent a range of acceptable English translations for *âsâh*. Each word translation is based on the context of the verse and the explanatory framework of the chapter. In cases where there is legitimate doubt as to word selection, *âsâh* is translated "did" or "done" such as in Genesis 2:2–4. Translating *âsâh* in this manner permits application to a wide range of possible actions.

In addition to the above, two other important verses contain *âsâh* in regard to the Genesis creation account.

• Exodus 20:11 For in six days the LORD made[06213] heaven and earth, the sea, and all that in them is, and rested the seventh day: wherefore the LORD blessed the sabbath day, and hallowed it. (KJV)

• Exodus 31:17 It is a sign between me and the children of Israel for ever: for in six days the LORD made[06213] heaven and earth, and on the seventh day he rested, and was refreshed. (KJV)

The above verses are used by proponents of traditional young-Earth creation theology to support belief that the heavens and Earth were created in six 24-hour days. Actually these verses are stating that God *did* (rather than made or created) the heavens, earth, sea, and all therein in six days. The context of these two verses is a discussion of work and the Sabbath—not a discussion of how the universe was created. Primary focus is on the Ten Commandments.

In the above two verses, the writer of Exodus discusses working six days and resting on the Sabbath. Work God did includes describing, identifying, distinguishing, approving, and blessing. The best translation for *âsâh* to describe the many things God accomplished in Genesis Chapter 1 is the general word "did." Keep in mind that in the KJV, *âsâh* is predominately translated "do, did, done, or doing" in the Old Testament.

In Exodus 20:10–11 quoted below, man is commanded to work six days and rest on the Sabbath, similar to when God worked and *did things* for six days and rested on the seventh. When describing the six-day Genesis chronicle, *âsâh* is used to explain a broad range of activities that God *did*, equated with work. Also notice the expression "For in six days" in the KJV is changed to "For six days" in the *exemplar* translation of Exodus 20:11. The word "in" is clearly absent from the Hebrew text.

• Exodus 20:10 But the seventh day is the sabbath of the LORD thy God: in it thou shalt not do any work[04399], thou, nor thy son, nor thy daughter, thy manservant, nor thy maidservant, nor thy cattle, nor thy stranger that is within thy gates. (KJV)

• Exodus 20:11 For six days Yahweh did[06213] the sky[08064] and land[0776] the sea[03220] and all that is in them, and rested on the seventh day: wherefore Yahweh blessed the Sabbath day, and hallowed it. (ET)

In Exodus 31:15–17, the Hebrews were again commanded to keep the Sabbath, and the six-day Genesis chronicle is repeated as an example of resting from labor. *Âsâh*, translated *did* (rather than made), is used to explain a broad range of activities equated with work. The expression "for in six days" in the KJV is changed to "for six days" in the *exemplar* translation of Exodus 31:17. The word "in" is clearly not a part of the Hebrew text.

• Exodus 31:15–16 Six days may work[04399] be done; but in the seventh is the sabbath of rest, holy to the LORD: whosoever doeth any work[04399] in the sabbath day, he shall surely be put to death. Wherefore the children of Israel shall keep the sabbath, to observe the sabbath throughout their generations, for a perpetual covenant. (KJV)

• Exodus 31:17 It is a sign between me and the children of Israel forever; for six days Yahweh did[06213] the heavens[08064] and Earth[0776], and on the seventh day He rested, and was refreshed. (ET)

Tôhûw and Bôhûw – Vacant and Empty

The two Hebrew words *tôhûw* (Strong's 08414) and *bôhûw* (Strong's 0922), found in Genesis 1:2, occur only one time in the first two chapters of Genesis. These words are best translated "vacant" and "empty" to describe the complete absence of life on early Earth. Compare the KJV against the *exemplar* translation below.

• Genesis 1:2 And the earth was without form[08414] and void[0922] and darkness was upon the face of the deep. And the Spirit of God moved upon the face of the waters. (KJV)

• Genesis 1:2 And the Earth was vacant[08414] and empty[0922] *of life*. And darkness *was* over the surface of the deep *waters*. And the Spirit of God hovered over the surface of the waters. (ET)

Of these two words, *bôhûw* is the least controversial. The Wilhelm Gesenius Lexicon gives "emptiness" and "voidness" as the only two translations of the noun *bôhûw*.[5] The Brown-Driver-Briggs Hebrew Lexicon gives "emptiness" as the only translation of the noun *bôhûw*.[6] The word *bôhûw* (Strong's 0922) occurs 3 times in the Old Testament in Genesis 1:2, Isaiah 34:11, and Jeremiah 4:23, and is translated "void" 2 times and "emptiness" 1 time in the KJV.[7] In Genesis 1:2, *bôhûw* is translated "empty" or "void" by essentially all English translations of the Bible.

Tôhûw is the more problematic of the two words. Most of the difficulty in understanding this word is due to the influence of theology. Theological persuasion has resulted in the incorrect translation of *tôhûw* as "without form" in Genesis 1:2 and Jeremiah 4:23 in all orthodox translations of the Bible. The Brown-Driver-Briggs Hebrew Lexicon gives the English word "emptiness" as an acceptable translation of the noun *tôhûw*.[8] Based on its usage in the Old Testament, the basic meaning of *tôhûw* is "empty" or "vacant."

The KJV and other orthodox Bible versions translate *tôhûw* in an inconsistent manner. *Tôhûw* (Strong's 08414) occurs twenty times in nineteen verses in the Old Testament.[9] When referring to a place that is physically empty, *tôhûw* is often translated "wilderness, waste, empty place, barren, nothing, desert place, desolate, or uninhabited." When *tôhûw* refers to moral or intellectual emptiness, it is often translated "vain, vanity, void, nothing, or useless."

Various Bible versions are quoted below to illustrate how *tôhûw* has been properly translated in some instances. Outside Genesis Chapters 1 and 2, *tôhûw* occurs nineteen times in eighteen verses. Notice how *tôhûw* is rendered based on its basic meaning of *empty* or *vacant*. The expression "without form" will not fit into the majority of these verses.

(1) Deuteronomy 32:10 He found them in a desert land, in an <u>empty</u>[08414], howling wasteland. He surrounded them and watched over them; he guarded them as he would guard his own eyes. (NLT)

(2) 1 Samuel 12:21 And do not turn aside after <u>empty</u>[08414] things that cannot profit or deliver, for they are <u>empty</u>[08414]. (ESV)

(3) Job 6:18 Turn aside do the paths of their way, They ascend into <u>emptiness</u>[08414], and are lost. (Young's Literal Translation, 1898[10])

(4) Job 12:24 Turning aside the heart of the heads of the people of the land, And he causeth them to wander in <u>vacancy</u>[08414]—no way! (Young's Literal Translation)

(5) Job 26:7 He stretcheth out the north over the <u>empty</u>[08414] *place*, and hangeth the earth upon nothing. (KJV)

(6) Psalm 107:40 He is pouring contempt upon nobles, And causeth them to wander in <u>vacancy</u>[08414]—no way. (Young's Literal Translation) [The second half of this verse is identical to the second half of Job 12:24.]

(7) Isaiah 24:10 The ruined city lies <u>desolate</u>[08414]; the entrance to every house is barred. (NIV) [This is a perfect description of a defenseless town affected by

war. Prior to the battle, the people lock their houses and flee the oncoming conflict. After the battle, the ruined city is empty of inhabitants.]

(8) Isaiah 29:21 Who make a man an offender by a word, And lay a snare for him who reproves in the gate, And turn aside the just by empty[08414] *words.* (NKJV)

(9) Isaiah 34:11 But pelican and hedgehog will possess it, And owl and raven will dwell in it; And He will stretch over it the line of desolation[08414] And the plumb line of emptiness. (NASB) [This describes Edom as a destroyed, deserted, and empty place. An object of God's judgment.]

(10) Isaiah 40:17 All the nations are as nothing before him, they are accounted by him as less than nothing and emptiness[08414]. (ESV)

(11) Isaiah 40:23 Who brings princes to nothing, and makes the rulers of the earth as emptiness[08414]. (ESV)

(12) Isaiah 41:29 Behold, all of them are false; Their works are worthless, Their molten images are wind and emptiness[08414]. (NASB)

(13) Isaiah 44:9 Framers of a graven image are all of them emptiness[08414], And their desirable things do not profit, And their own witnesses they are, They see not, nor know, that they may be ashamed. (Young's Literal Translation, 1898)

(14) Isaiah 45:18 For thus says the Lord, who created the heavens (he is God!), who formed the earth and made it (he established it; he did not create it empty[08414], he formed it to be inhabited!): "I am the Lord, and there is no other." (ESV) [This verse points out that the Earth was made to be inhabited rather than remain empty.]

(15) Isaiah 45:19 I have not spoken in secret, in a dark place of the earth: I said not unto the seed of Jacob, Seek ye me in vain[08414]: I the LORD speak righteousness, I declare things that are right. (KJV)

(16) Isaiah 49:4 Then I said, I have laboured in vain[08414], I have spent my strength for nought, and in vain: *yet* surely my judgment *is* with the LORD, and my work with my God. (KJV)

(17) Isaiah 59:4 No one calls for justice, Nor does any plead for truth. They trust in empty[08414] words and speak lies; They conceive evil and bring forth iniquity. (NKJV)

(18) Jeremiah 4:23 *I* saw the land and *it* looked vacant[08414] and empty[0922] and to the heavens there was no light. (ET) [This is a prophecy from Jeremiah against the Hebrew people and Jerusalem because of their disobedience to God. A future time is described when the land would be empty owing to its people being carried off as prisoners of war. This verse has nothing to do with the creation or destruction of the Earth. All English Bibles mistranslate this verse due to the influence of traditional young-Earth creation theology, since the expression *tôhûw* and *bôhûw* is the same as found in Genesis 1:2.]

When the Genesis creation story is reconnected with the remainder of the Old Testament, the meaning of *tôhûw* can be readily determined. From the above verses, the basic meaning of *tôhûw* is "vacant or empty," and especially so when referring to a physical place. Isaiah 45:18 clearly points out that the Earth was made to be inhabited, rather than remain empty.

Use of the words *tôhûw* and *bôhûw* in Genesis 1:2 represent a style commonly found in the Old Testament. When Hebrew writers wanted to emphasize a point, they sometimes used two words with a similar meaning joined by a conjunction. Further emphasis was achieved through rhyming words, as demonstrated by *tôhûw* and *bôhûw*. This style is often used in the English language. For example, when packing for a trip we may "cram and jam" our clothes into a suitcase. A common expression found in Genesis 1:22 and elsewhere in the Old Testament is "be fruitful and multiply," based on the Hebrew *râbâh* (Strong's 06509) and *pârâh* (Strong's 07235). In 2 Chronicles 1:10, the expression "wisdom and knowledge" is based on the Hebrew *chokmâh* (Strong's 02451) and *maddâe* (Strong's 04093). In 1 Chronicles 16:27, the translation "glory and honor" is based on *hôwd* (Strong's 01935) and *hâdâr* (Strong's 01926). In Hebrew, the words in each of these expressions have a similar meaning and a poetic quality. When translated into English, a significant loss of impact occurs when the rhyming sound is destroyed.

In summary, *tôhûw* and *bôhûw* can be translated "vacant and empty" in the creation story with full biblical support. The illegitimate translation of *tôhûw* as "without form" in Genesis 1:2 and Jeremiah 4:23 besmirches the integrity of biblical scholarship and is due to errant theological influence. This illicit translation is found in essentially all English Bibles. The Hebrew words *tôhûw* and *bôhûw* correctly describe the complete absence of life on Earth sometime after its formation.

Tehôwm – Deep

The Hebrew word *tehôwm* (Strong's 08415) occurs one time in the first two chapters of Genesis and is translated "deep." There is no need to complicate translation of this word based on theology. "Deep" followed by the explanatory "waters" is proposed as the best translation of *tehôwm* in Genesis 1:2. Compare the KJV against the *exemplar* translation below.

• Genesis 1:2 And the earth was without form and void, and darkness was upon the face of the deep[08415]. And the Spirit of God moved upon the face of the waters. (KJV)

• Genesis 1:2 And the Earth was vacant and empty *of life*. And darkness was over the surface of the deep[08415] *waters*. And the spirit of God hovered over the surface of the waters. (ET)

Brown-Driver-Briggs Hebrew Lexicon gives the noun *tehôwm* as meaning "deep of subterranean waters," "deep overwhelming sea," "abyss of sea," "deep of primeval ocean", and "deep depth of river."[11] The word *tehôwm* (Strong's 08415) occurs 36 times in the Old Testament and is translated "deep" 20 times, "depth" 15 times, and "deep places" 1 time in the KJV.[12]

Several pertinent verses in the Bible contain *tehôwm,* where it is used in reference to deep water. English words translated from *tehôwm* are underlined and identified by their Strong's number in superscript in various translations below:

- Deuteronomy 8:7 For Jehovah thy God bringeth thee into a good land, a land of water-brooks, of springs, and of deep[08415] waters, that gush forth in the valleys and hills. (Darby, 1890[13])

- Job 38:30 The waters are hid as with a stone, and the face of the deep[08415] is frozen. (KJV) [The face of the deep can be frozen, which implies the deep is water.]

- Psalm 106:9 He rebuked the Red Sea, and it became dry, and he led them through the deep[08415] as through a desert. (ESV) [The bottom of the Red Sea is described as the deep.]

- Isaiah 51:10 Art thou not it which hath dried the sea, the waters of the great deep[08415]; that hath made the depths of the sea a way for the ransomed to pass over? (KJV) [Waters of the great deep were dried up by God so the Israelites could pass through the Red Sea.]

- Isaiah 63:13 That led them through the deep[08415], as an horse in the wilderness, that they should not stumble? (KJV) [This verse describes Moses when he divided the waters of the Red Sea and led the nation of Israel through the deep.]

- Ezekiel 26:19 For thus saith the Lord God; When I shall make thee a desolate city, like the cities that are not inhabited; when I shall bring up the deep[08415] upon thee and great waters shall cover thee. (KJV) [God is threatening to cover the city with deep water.]

- Jonah 2:5 The waters surrounded me, even to my soul; The deep[08415] closed around me; Weeds were wrapped around my head. (NKJV)

Use of *tehôwm* in the above verses refers to (1) a place where water came from, (2) the Red Sea, and (3) waters that covered Jonah. When the Genesis creation story is reconnected to the remainder of the Old Testament, the meaning of *tehôwm* becomes apparent.

By translating *tehôwm* as "deep" in Genesis 1:2, followed by the explanatory word "waters," clarity is added. Translating *tehôwm* only as "deep" leaves the reader wondering what is meant. Is Moses referring to the depths of a formless, dark, watery void? Is he describing a black, chaotic, fluidic mass? Such translations give expositors reason to wax eloquent to the total confusion of all who listen.

In ancient times, man did not have the same concept of the oceans that we have today. Humans were not capable of diving to the bottom of the deep seas or oceans to explore them. Deep waters were an unknown quantity, and a mystery described simply as the "deep." This is contrasted by shallow streams, rivers, and ponds that could be investigated and held no mystery.

Many mythological and pagan religious beliefs about the deep have been found in ancient Babylonian and Ugaritic writings.[14] Although the word "deep" occurs in the Genesis creation story, it is not used in reference to these beliefs. Pagan mythology was kept out of the Bible and is not the basis for the creation account. A correct understanding of the word "deep" in Genesis 1:2 is based on its usage elsewhere in the Old Testament.

Shâmayim – Heaven and Sky

The Hebrew word *shâmayim* is translated either "heaven" or "air" by the KJV in the first two chapters of Genesis. In comparison, the New International Version translates *shâmayim* as "sky" six times in Genesis Chapters 1 and 2.

The word *shâmayim* (Strong's 08064) occurs 420 times in the Old Testament and is translated "heaven" or "heavens" 398 times, "air" 21 times, and "astrologers" 1 time in the KJV.[15] The King James Version never translates *shâmayim* as sky. The English Standard Version translates *shâmayim* as sky two times, while the New International Version has the same rendering approximately forty-five times.[16]

As used in the Old Testament, "heaven" has three meanings. Heaven can mean the sky where birds fly, from which rain falls, and where clouds exist. Secondly, heaven can mean the cosmic heavens where the Sun, Moon, planets, and stars are seen. Thirdly, heaven is God's abode.

The following two verses refer to heaven as a place where the birds fly and from which the rain falls.

• Jeremiah 15:3 And I will appoint over them four kinds, saith the Lord: the sword to slay, and the dogs to tear, and the fowls of the heaven[08064], and the beasts of the earth, to devour and destroy. (KJV)

• Deuteronomy 11:11 But the land, whither ye go to possess it, is a land of hills and valleys, and drinketh water of the rain of heaven[08064]. (KJV)

The following two verses refer to heaven as a place where the Sun, Moon, and stars exist, visible from the surface of the Earth.

• Genesis 22:17 That in blessing I will bless thee, and in multiplying I will multiply thy seed as the stars of the heaven[08064], and as the sand which is upon the sea shore; and thy seed shall possess the gate of his enemies. (KJV)

• Deuteronomy 4:19 And lest thou lift up thine eyes unto heaven[08064], and when thou seest the sun, and the moon, and the stars, even all the host of heaven[08064], shouldest be driven to worship them. (KJV)

The following two verses refer to heaven as the abode of God. Heaven is a place above the Earth where God has His throne and looks down on man.

• Psalm 11:4 The Lord is in his holy temple, the Lord's throne is in heaven[08064] his eyes behold, his eyelids try, the children of men. (KJV)

• Psalm 53:2 God looked down from heaven[08064] upon the children of men, to see if there were any that did understand, that did seek God. (KJV)

The context of a verse determines whether *shâmayim* should be translated "heaven" or "sky." If the context does not imply a specific meaning, then translation becomes a judgment call.

When ancient man looked up at the sky, he saw a continuum from the surface of the Earth to distant galaxies—identical to what we see today. However, because he was ignorant of barometric pressure, knowledge of our atmosphere, the arrangement of our solar system, the stars, the Milky Way, and other galaxies, his understanding was radically different from ours. Twenty-first century scientific knowledge can be used to more precisely translate *shâmayim* as either sky or heaven.

Erets — Land and Earth

The Hebrew noun *erets* is translated primarily as "land" or "earth" in the King James Version. *Erets* (Strong's 0776) occurs 2,504 times in the Old Testament and is translated "land" 1,543 times, "earth" 712 times, "country" 140 times, "ground" 98 times, and "world" 4 times, in addition to other miscellaneous words in the KJV.[17]

Based on early man's knowledge of the Earth, *erets* should normally be translated "land." Translation of *erets* as "Earth" should rarely be done and only when referring to the entire planet from our current perspective. Ancient man (prior to 1000 BC) did not understand the concept of Earth as a planet. Adam did not know the Earth was one of eight planets in our solar system. Noah did not know the Earth was a giant sphere orbiting the Sun, in turn orbited by the Moon. Abraham did not know the Earth was a huge ball 7,900 miles in diameter, with 70 percent of its surface area covered by water. Jacob did not know the Earth had seven continents surrounded by four oceans. Moses did not know the Earth was a huge rotating globe, with an equator and a spin axis passing through the north and south poles.

To ancient man, *erets* was the land on which he lived and traveled. *Erets* consisted of the forests, fields, deserts, and mountains that man had knowledge of and where he had journeyed. *Erets* was where the plants grew and a place where the animals roamed. The birds of the sky flew over the *erets*. When man climbed to the top of the highest mountain, *erets* was all that he could see. *Erets* confined the waters of the deep and continued beyond the horizon where man had never ventured.

The following are a few of the many verses in the Bible that illustrate how ancient man's concept of *erets* was equivalent to our modern concept of land.

- Genesis 11:28 And Haran died before his father Terah in the land[0776] of his nativity, in Ur of the Chaldees. (KJV)

- Genesis 12:1 Now the LORD had said unto Abram, Get thee out of thy country[0776], and from thy kindred, and from thy father's house, unto a land[0776] that I will shew thee (KJV) [*Erets* is translated both "country" and "land" in this verse. Abram was moving from one land to another land.]

- Genesis 12:10 And there was a famine in the land[0776] and Abram went down into Egypt to sojourn there; for the famine was grievous in the land[0776]. (KJV) [There was a famine in the land of Canaan, not the whole Earth.]

- Genesis 13:12 Abram dwelled in the land[0776] of Canaan, and Lot dwelled in the cities of the plain, and pitched his tent toward Sodom. (KJV) [*Erets* obviously means land rather than Earth.]

- Exodus 10:5 And they shall cover the face of the earth[0776], that one cannot be able to see the earth[0776]. (KJV) [This verse is talking about locusts covering the land during the plagues in Egypt and is obviously not referring to the entire Earth.]

The Hebrew word *erets* should be translated "land" in the vast majority of occurrences in the Old Testament. When referring to land, ground, territory, terrain, or country, *erets* should not be translated "earth" or "Earth."

We can use twenty-first century knowledge to translate *erets* as either land or Earth, depending on context. *Erets* should only be translated "Earth" when referring to the entire planet. Some verses of the Bible definitely apply to all the land. For example, the rigid translation of *erets* as "land" in the first eleven chapters of Genesis seriously distorts the creation account.[18] God's actions cannot be constrained because of limited human understanding during Moses' day.

Qâvâh – Wait

The Hebrew word *qâvâh* (Strong's 06960) is of significant importance in properly understanding the six-day Genesis chronicle. The Brown-Driver-Briggs Hebrew Lexicon gives "wait" as the primary translation of the verb *qâvâh*.[19] The Wilhelm Gesenius Lexicon gives "to await" as an acceptable translation.[20]

In Genesis 1:9, *qâvâh* is translated "let be gathered together" in the KJV, but should be translated "wait." This word has been mistranslated for more than twenty-two hundred years due to the influence of traditional young-Earth creation theology. Compare the KJV against the *exemplar* translation.

• Genesis 1:9 And God said, <u>Let</u> the waters under the heaven <u>be gathered to-gether</u>[06960] unto one place, and let the dry land appear: and it was so. (KJV)

• Genesis 1:9 And God said, "The waters under the sky <u>wait</u>[06960] in one place, and the dry ground *is* seen." And *it* was so. (ET)

Table 5.1 – Occurrences of the Hebrew Verb Qâvâh in the Old Testament
Strong's 06960, based on the root (קוה)

Strong's No. with Suffix	Complete Hebrew Term	Basic Hebrew Word	KJV Translation	Verse Location
06960A	יקוו	קוו	let be gathered together	Genesis 1:9
06960A	יקוו	קוו	wait	Isaiah 51:5, 60:9
06960A	קוו	קוו	wait	Psalm 56:6, 119:95
06960A	לקוו	קוו	wait	Lamentations 3:25
06960A	ונקוו	קוו	shall be gathered	Jeremiah 3:17
06960A	קוו	קוו	waited	Job 6:19
06960B		קוה	wait, look, patiently, tarrieth	Job 7:2, 17:13; Psalm 27:14, 37:34, 40:1, 52:9, 69:20; Prov. 20:22; Isaiah 59:9, 59:11, 64:3; Jer. 8:15, 14:19, 14:22; Hosea 12:6; Micah 5:7
06960C		קוי	wait, look	Gen. 49:18; Job 30:26; Psalm 25:3, 25:5, 25:21, 37:9, 39:7, 40:1, 69:6, 130:5; Isaiah 5:4, 8:17, 25:9, 26:8, 33:2, 40:31, 49:23; Jer. 13:16; Lam. 2:16
06960D		קו	look, wait	Job 3:9; Ps. 130:5; Isaiah 5:2, 5:7

References:
(1) Eliyah.com (2006). Online Strong's Concordance.
(2) van der Merwe, Christo, ed. (2004) *The Lexham Hebrew-English Interlinear Bible.*

Jeremiah 3:17 is the second occurrence in the Bible where *qâvâh* is mistranslated "shall be gathered," rather than correctly translated "wait." This verse is one of many that teach waiting on Yahweh, and its mistranslation is without excuse. Compare the KJV against the *exemplar* translation below.

• Jeremiah 3:17 At that time they shall call Jerusalem the throne of the LORD; and all the nations <u>shall be gathered</u>[06960] unto it, to the name of the LORD, to Jerusalem: neither shall they walk any more after the imagination of their evil heart. (KJV)

• Jeremiah 3:17 At that time they shall call Jerusalem the throne of Yahweh. And all nations will <u>wait</u>[06960] to name Yahweh in Jerusalem and go no longer after the stubbornness of their evil heart. (ET)

Forty-nine words, identified by Strong's number 06960, are listed in Table 5.1. *Qâvâh* is translated "wait or waited" 31 times, "look, looked, or looketh" 14 times, "gathered" 2 times, "patiently" 1 time, and "tarrieth" 1 time in the KJV.[21] *Qâvâh* is consistently translated "wait, look, patiently, and tarrieth" in 47 out of 49 occurrences, or 96% of the time in the KJV. In two verses, Genesis 1:9 and Jeremiah 3:17, *qâvâh* is translated "let be gathered together" and "shall be gathered" respectively. The translation in both of these verses is illegitimate as the following illustrates.

In the Old Testament, several Hebrew words are translated "gather." The five most common words translated "gather," arranged in descending order are:

• *Âcaph* (Strong's 0622) – This Hebrew word occurs 200 times and is translated "gather" 86 times, "together" 51 times, and "assemble" 15 times, in addition to other miscellaneous words in the KJV.[22]

• *Qâbats* (Strong's 06908) – This Hebrew word occurs 127 times and is translated "gather" 70 times, "gather together" 42 times, "assemble" 6 times, and "gather up" 3 times, in addition to other miscellaneous words in the KJV.[23]

• *Lâqat* (Strong's 03950) – This Hebrew word occurs 37 times and is translated "gather" 23 times, "glean" 12 times, and "gather up" 2 times in the KJV.[24]

• *Kânac* (Strong's 03664) – This Hebrew word occurs 11 times and is translated "gather" 5 times, "gather together" 4 times, "heap" 1 time, and "wrap" 1 time in the KJV.[25]

• *Qâshash* (Strong's 07197) – This Hebrew word occurs 8 times and is translated "gather" 6 times and "gather together" 2 times in the KJV.[26]

Several scriptures in the Old Testament clearly describe a gathering of people in Israel and Jerusalem. The following are a collection of prophetic verses that describe a gathering. Notice these verses do not use *qâvâh*. The Hebrew words *âcaph* (Strong's 0622) and *qâbats* (Strong's 06908) are used exclusively.

• Isaiah 43:9 All the nations gather together[06908] and the peoples assemble[0622]. Who among them can declare this, and show us the former things? Let them bring their witnesses to prove them right, and let them hear and say, It is true. (ESV)

• Ezekiel 11:17 Therefore say, Thus saith the Lord GOD; I will even gather[06908] you from the people, and assemble[0622] you out of the countries where ye have been scattered, and I will give you the land of Israel. (KJV)

• Ezekiel 20:34 And I will bring you out from the people, and will gather[06908] you out of the countries wherein ye are scattered, with a mighty hand, and with a stretched out arm, and with fury poured out. (KJV)

• Ezekiel 20:41 I will accept you with your sweet savour, when I bring you out from the people, and gather[06908] you out of the countries wherein ye have been scattered; and I will be sanctified in you before the heathen. (KJV)

• Ezekiel 22:19 Therefore thus saith the Lord GOD; Because ye are all become dross, behold, therefore I will gather[06908] you into the midst of Jerusalem. (KJV)

• Ezekiel 36:24 For I will take you from among the heathen, and gather⁰⁶⁹⁰⁸ you out of all countries, and will bring you into your own land. (KJV)

• Micah 4:11 Now also many nations are gathered⁰⁶²² against thee, that say, Let her be defiled, and let our eye look upon Zion. (KJV)

• Micah 2:12 I will surely⁰⁶²² gather⁰⁶²² all of you, O Jacob; I will surely bring together the remnant of Israel. I will bring them together like sheep in a pen, like a flock in its pasture; the place will throng with people. (NIV) [The Hebrew text repeats the word "gather" for emphasis and actually says, "I will gather gather all of you."]

• Zechariah 12:3 On that day I will make Jerusalem a heavy stone for all the peoples. All who lift it will surely hurt themselves. And all the nations of the earth will gather⁰⁶²² against it. (ESV)

• Zechariah 14:2 For I will gather⁰⁶²² all nations against Jerusalem to battle; and the city shall be taken, and the houses rifled, and the women ravished; and half of the city shall go forth into captivity, and the residue of the people shall not be cut off from the city. (KJV)

• Zechariah 14:14 And Judah also shall fight at Jerusalem; and the wealth of all the heathen round about shall be gathered together⁰⁶²², gold, and silver, and apparel, in great abundance. (KJV)

Just as the idea of a *gathering* is taught in the Old Testament, the idea of *waiting* is also taught. Seventeen scriptures strongly promote the idea of waiting on Yahweh (commonly translated LORD). The following, including Jeremiah 3:17, are a sample of verses that teach this concept. The Hebrew word *qâvâh* (Strong's 06960) is used exclusively to indicate waiting.

• Psalm 25:5 Lead me in thy truth, and teach me: for thou art the God of my salvation; on thee do I wait⁰⁶⁹⁶⁰ all the day. (KJV)

• Psalm 27:14 Wait⁰⁶⁹⁶⁰ on the LORD, be of good courage, and he shall strengthen thine heart, wait⁰⁶⁹⁶⁰ I say, on the LORD. (KJV)

• Psalm 52:9 I will praise thee for ever, because thou hast done it: and I will wait⁰⁶⁹⁶⁰ on thy name; for it is good before thy saints. (KJV)

• Psalm 69:6 Let not them that wait⁰⁶⁹⁶⁰ on thee, O Lord GOD of hosts, be ashamed for my sake; let not those that seek thee be confounded for my sake, O God of Israel. (KJV)

• Proverbs 20:22 Say not thou, I will recompense evil; but wait⁰⁶⁹⁶⁰ on the LORD, and he shall save thee. (KJV)

• Isaiah 8:17 And I will wait⁰⁶⁹⁶⁰ upon the LORD, that hideth his face from the house of Jacob, and I will look for him. (KJV)

• Isaiah 25:9 And it shall be said in that day, Lo, this is our God; we have waited[06960] for him, and he will save us: this is the LORD; we have waited[06960] for him, we will be glad and rejoice in his salvation. (KJV)

• Isaiah 33:2 O LORD, be gracious unto us; we have waited[06960] for thee: be thou their arm every morning, our salvation also in the time of trouble. (KJV)

• Isaiah 40:31 But they that wait[06960] upon the LORD shall renew their strength; they shall mount up with wings as eagles; they shall run, and not be weary; and they shall walk, and not faint. (KJV)

• Jeremiah 3:17 At that time they shall call Jerusalem the throne of Yahweh. And all nations will wait[06960] to name Yahweh in Jerusalem and go no longer after the stubbornness of their evil heart. (ET) [All English Bibles incorrectly translate "wait" as "gather" in this verse.]

• Lamentations 3:25 The LORD is good unto them that wait[06960] for him, to the soul that seeketh him. (KJV)

• Hosea 12:6 Therefore turn thou to thy God: keep mercy and judgment and wait[06960] on thy God continually. (KJV)

Some Hebrew verbs clearly describe inactive behavior, while others describe physical action. *Qâvâh* is translated "wait, look, patient, and tarry" in the KJV and denotes inactive behavior. In contrast, Hebrew verbs such as *âcaph* and *qâbats*, translated "gather" in the KJV, denote physical action to collect things and describe gathering food (Gen. 41:48), gathering fruit (Exodus 23:10), gathering quails (Num. 11:32), gathering ashes (Num. 19:9), gathering corn (Deut. 11:14), gathering the spoil of battle (Deut. 13:16), and gathering grain (Ruth 2:7).

An examination of the Hebrew text gives additional proof for translating *qâvâh* in Genesis 1:9 as "wait." Forty-nine occurrences in 45 verses identified by Strong's number 06960 are translated from the Hebrew root (קוה). Word variations and their spelling based on this root are identified in Table 5.1.

Eight verses, including Genesis 1:9 and Jeremiah 3:17, contain identical spelling for *qâvâh* and are identified as Strong's 06960A in Table 5.1. Six of these eight verses translate *qâvâh* as "wait." These six verses give compelling support for translating Genesis 1:9 and Jeremiah 3:17 as "wait" rather than "gather."

• Job 6:19 The troops of Tema looked, the companies of Sheba waited[06960A] for them. (KJV)

• Isaiah 51:5 My righteousness is near; my salvation is gone forth, and mine arms shall judge the people; the isles shall wait[06960A] upon me, and on mine arm shall they trust. (KJV)

• Isaiah 60:9 Surely the isles shall wait[06960A] for me, and the ships of Tarshish first, to bring thy sons from far, their silver and their gold with them, unto the name of the LORD thy God, and to the Holy One of Israel, because he hath glorified thee. (KJV) [The isles are an inanimate object and can only wait.]

• Psalm 56:6 They gather themselves together, they hide themselves, they mark my steps, when they wait[06960A] for my soul. (KJV)

• Psalm 119:95 The wicked have waited[06960A] for me to destroy me: but I will consider thy testimonies. (KJV)

• Lamentations 3:25 The LORD is good unto them that wait[06960A] for him, to the soul that seeketh him. (KJV)

In respect to the selected eight verses, the influence of the Septuagint can be clearly seen. In Isaiah 51:5, Isaiah 60:9, Psalm 56:6, Psalm 119:95, and Lamentations 3:25, *qâvâh* is translated in the Septuagint[27] as "wait" (identical to the KJV). In Genesis 1:9 and Jeremiah 3:17, the Septuagint translates *qâvâh* as "gathered" (identical to the KJV). In Job 6:19, *qâvâh* is not translated by the Septuagint (it was left out), while translated "wait" in the KJV.

In summary, several verses in the Old Testament teach both gathering and waiting. In reference to a gathering in Israel, Jerusalem, or elsewhere, all verses use the Hebrew words *âcaph* (Strong's 0622) or *qâbats* (Strong's 06908). Many verses in the Old Testament teach the idea of waiting on Yahweh and use the Hebrew word *qâvâh* (Strong's 06960). *Qâvâh* should be translated "wait" in Jeremiah 3:17.

The incorrect translation of *qâvâh* represents the pervasive influence of traditional young-Earth creation theology. The mistranslation of "gather" in Genesis 1:9 and Jeremiah 3:17 in the Septuagint are fabrications without biblical support. This illegitimate translation is reflected in all English Bibles. Regardless of the good intentions of those involved, this rendering is a stain on the integrity of biblical scholarship.

The correct translation of *qâvâh* as "wait" in Genesis 1:9 is overwhelmingly supported by its usage elsewhere in scripture. When the Genesis creation story is reconnected to the remainder of the Old Testament, the true meaning of *qâvâh* becomes apparent. On the third day, God observed the waters under the sky waiting in one place. He was describing a passive scene. There was no "gathering together" of the waters on that day.

Miqveh — Collection

The best translation for the Hebrew *miqveh* (Strong's 04723) in Genesis 1:10 is "collection." Unfortunately, *miqveh* is translated "gathering together" in the KJV to support the belief that God gathered the waters together on the third day. Compare the KJV against four other translations where *miqveh* is underlined and correctly translated "collection:"

• Genesis 1:10 And God called the dry land Earth; and the gathering together[04723] of the waters called he Seas: and God saw that it was good. (KJV)

• Genesis 1:10 And God calleth to the dry land "Earth," and to the collection[04723] of the waters He hath called "Seas;" and God seeth that it is good. (Young's Literal Translation, 1898)

• Genesis 1:10 And God called the dry land Earth, and the collection[04723] of waters he called Seas: and God saw that it was good. (Webster's Translation, 1833[28])

• Genesis 1:10 And the Lord called the dry land Earth, and the place of the collection[04723] of waters He called Sea. And the Lord saw that it was good. (Targum of Onkelos, English translation by J. W. Etheridge, 1862)

• Genesis 1:10 And God called the dry ground "land" and called the collection[04723] of waters "seas." And God saw that *it was* good. (ET)

Table 5.2 – Occurrences of the Hebrew Verb Miqveh in the Old Testament (Strong's 04723 and 04724)					
Strong's Number	Complete Hebrew Term	Basic Translation	Basic Hebrew Word	No.	Verse Location
04723	וּלְמִקְוֵה	and to collection	מִקְוֵה	1	Genesis 1:10
04723	מִקְוֵה	collection	מִקְוֵה	1	Exodus 7:19
04723	מִקְוֵה	collection	מִקְוֵה	1	Leviticus 11:36
04723	וּמִקְוֵה	and collection	מִקְוֵה	2	1 Kings 10:28
04723	מִקְוֵה:	collection	מִקְוֵה	1	1 Chronicles 29:15
04723	וּמִקְוֵא	and collection	מִקְוֵא	2	2 Chronicles 1:16
04723	מִקְוֵה	collection	מִקְוֵה	1	Ezra 10:2
04724	מִקְוֵה	collection	מִקְוֵה	1	Isaiah 22:11
04723	מִקְוֵה	collection	מִקְוֵה	3	Jeremiah 14:8, 17:13, 50:7

References:
(1) Eliyah.com (2006). Online Strong's Concordance.
(2) van der Merwe, Christo, ed. (2004) *The Lexham Hebrew-English Interlinear Bible*.

The Brown-Driver-Briggs Hebrew Lexicon gives "collection" as the only translation of the noun *miqveh*.[29] The word *miqveh* (Strong's 04723 and 04724) occurs 13 times in the Old Testament and is translated "linen yarn" 4 times, "hope" 4 times, "gathering together" 1 time, "pool" 1 time, "ditch" 1 time, "plenty" 1 time, and "abiding" 1 time in the KJV.[30] The inconsistent translation of *miqveh* in the KJV totally obscures its meaning.

In most verses where *miqveh* occurs, it can be translated "collection" for improved clarity and consistency. Keep in mind that *miqveh* can refer to a collection of water (cistern, spring, pool, or reservoir), a collection of people (the nation Israel), a collection of belief (consensus of opinion), a collection of goods (herd of horses), and a collection of money (an offering).

Table 5.2 and the following ten verses illustrate how *miqveh* can be translated "collection" in the Old Testament. *Miqveh* is identified by the underlined words and their accompanying Strong's number in superscript.

• Exodus 7:19 Yahweh said to Moses, "Say to Aaron, Take your staff and stretch out your hand over the waters of Egypt, over their streams, over their rivers, over their ponds and over all collections[04723] of their water. And be blood and be blood in all the land and in all the wood *vessels* and all the stone *vessels*." (ET) [The expression "and be blood" is repeated for emphasis in the Hebrew text. All collections of water in Egypt would turn to blood.]

• Leviticus 11:36 Only a fountain or pit, a collection[04723] of water, is clean, but that which is coming against their carcass is unclean. (Young's Literal Translation, 1898) [A fountain (spring) and pit (cistern) represent a collection of water.]

• 1 Kings 10:28 And Solomon brought out horses from Egypt. And from a collection[04723] *of horses,* the king's traders took from the collection[04723] at a price. (ET) [As described in this verse, a collection of horses were brought out of Egypt and Solomon's traders took horses from that collection for the king's use. His traders probably received first pick from any herd of horses imported into Israel. Solomon paid for the horses that he took at an agreed upon price. In businesses where the quality of a product naturally varies, such as gemstones, vegetable produce, livestock, or lumber, preferred customers are often given first pick of new merchandise.]

• 1 Chronicles 29:15, 16 For we are strangers before thee, and sojourners, as were all our fathers: our days on the land are as a shadow and without a collection[04723] *for you.* Yahweh our God, as for all this abundance that we have provided for building you a temple for your Holy Name, it comes from your hand, and all of it belongs to you. (ET) [Verses 29:7–10 discuss the collection of money and materials given by David and the people of Israel for the building of the temple by Solomon, while 29:11–19 is a prayer about this offering.]

• 2 Chronicles 1:16 And Solomon brought out horses from Egypt. And from a collection[04723] *of horses,* the king's traders took from the collection[04723] at a price. (ET) [This verse is essentially the same as 1 Kings 10:28.]

• Ezra 10:2 And Shechaniah the son of Jehiel, one of the sons of Elam, answered and said unto Ezra, We have trespassed against our God, and dwell with strange wives of the people of the land. And now there is a collection[04723] *of belief* in Israel concerning this thing. (ET) [Collection is used in the sense of a *consensus of belief* about the strange wives they had married and the course of action to take. The strange wives were subsequently put away.]

• Isaiah 22:11 You made a collection[04724] between the two walls for the water of the old pool. But you did not look to him who did it, or see him who planned it long ago. (ET) [Collection is translated "ditch" in the KJV and "reservoir" in the NKJV, NIV, ESV, RSV, ASV, and NASB in this verse.]

• Jeremiah 14:8 O collection[04723] of Israel, He saves in time of trouble. Why be as a stranger in the land and like a wanderer spread out to spend the night? (ET) [The expression "congregation of Israel" or "congregation of the children of Israel" appears more than 39 times in the Old Testament. In this instance, Jeremiah uses the expression "collection of Israel."]

• Jeremiah 17:13 O collection[04723] of Israel, all who forsake Yahweh are ashamed, disloyal and departed. May it be written in the land, they have forsaken Yahweh the fountain of living water. (ET)

• Jeremiah 50:7 All *who* found them devoured them. And their enemies said, "We are not guilty *for destroying them*, for they have sinned against Yahweh. Righteous habitation and collector[04723] is their father Yahweh." (ET) [This is a poetical verse. God is the collector of the Hebrew people, providing a righteous abode for them. They would otherwise be as scattered sheep.]

In summary, all uses of the word *miqveh* relating to water refer to a "collection of water" rather than a "gathering together of water." Reconnecting the Genesis creation story to the rest of the Old Testament helps clarify this word. On the third day, God called the collection of waters "seas."

Hâyâh — Be

Hebrew verbs based on the root *hâyâh* (היה) occur several times in Genesis Chapters 1 and 2. The Wilhelm Gesenius Lexicon gives "to be" and "to exist" as the first meanings of the root *hâyâh*.[31] The Brown-Driver-Briggs Hebrew Lexicon gives "be" and "exist" as two acceptable translations of *hâyâh*.[32]

Verbs in the English language can be categorized as either dynamic or stative. *The Oxford Dictionary of English Grammar* points out that dynamic verbs imply action or change.[33] Stative verbs express a state or condition.[34] According to the *American Heritage College Dictionary,* stative English verbs include the words "be, is, was, were, been, am, and being."[35] In addition, "are" is a tense of "be."[36] The word "exist" is a stative verb and defined in current dictionaries as: "To have actual being, be real."[37]

Stative verbs can be further classified as state-of-being verbs, and include "are, is, am, were, was, be, being, and been." The root *hâyâh* (היה) and its derivatives are often translated into English as stative verbs that indicate state-of-being.

Hâyâh (Strong's 01961) and its many derivatives occur approximately 3,482 times the Old Testament.[38] Table B.1 in Appendix B lists forty-six derivative verbs based on the Hebrew root (היה) and the number of times each occurs in the Bible. *Strong's Exhaustive Concordance* gives the English translation of some occurrences. For example, *hâyâh* is translated "been" 75 times in the KJV."[39]

The derivatives (יְהִי), (וַיְהִי), (וְהָיוּ), (וְהָיָה), (יְהִיֶה), (הֱיוֹת), and (הָיְתָה) from the Hebrew root *hâyâh* (הָיָה) occur in several verses in the first two chapters of Genesis. (To simplify discussion of these derivatives, they will be referred to as *hâyâh* followed by their Hebrew spelling.)

A word search using a Strong's online concordance shows that *hâyâh* (Strong's 01961) occurs only four times in the first two chapters of Genesis. In contrast, a search of the Hebrew text reveals that *hâyâh* occurs 33 times in 23 separate verses.[40] Some of the more significant verses in the first two chapters of Genesis containing *hâyâh* are given below. Words in the *exemplar* translation have been replaced with "be" to illustrate the nature of this stative Hebrew verb.

- Genesis 1:2 And the Earth be[01961] vacant and empty of life.
- Genesis 1:3 And God said, "be[01961] light and light be[01961]."
- Genesis 1:5 And evening be[01961] and morning be[01961]—day one.
- Genesis 1:6 And God said, "Be[01961] an expanse in the middle of the water, and it be[01961] to separate between water *above* from water *below*."
- Genesis 1:8 And evening be[01961] and morning be[01961]—second day.
- Genesis 1:14 And God said, "Be[01961] luminaries in the expanse of the heavens to distinguish between the day and between the night, and *they* be[01961] for a sign for appointed times and for days and years."
- Genesis 1:15 And luminaries be[01961] in the expanse. And *it* be[01961] so.
- Genesis 1:29 For you, *they* be[01961] for food.
- Genesis 1:31 And evening be[01961] and morning be[01961]—the sixth day.
- Genesis 2:5 And every bush of the field be[01961] not yet on the land.
- Genesis 2:7 And the man be[01961] as a living creature.
- Genesis 2:18 God said, "*It is* not good *for* the man to be[01961] alone."
- Genesis 2:24 And they *shall* be[01961] as one flesh.
- Genesis 2:25 And the two be[01961] naked, the man and his wife.

What is the most important single word in the Genesis creation story? Some people will identify the words "create, make, or beginning" as the most important. Others mention "day" or perhaps "evening and morning." In truth, the Hebrew verb *hâyâh* is probably the most significant word in the creation account and is one of the keys to properly understanding this story. To grasp the importance of *hâyâh*, we need to know some of its history and usage.

Gap theology proposes that between Genesis 1:1 and 1:2 there was an enormous period of time. Significant time is allowed for geological change and the fossil record to occur. As mentioned in Scofield's notes on Genesis, at the end of this time the face of the Earth underwent a cataclysmic change as the result of divine judgment.[41] God destroyed the Earth's surface and then began reforming it, starting with Genesis 1:3. Gap theology came into prominence in the early 1800s; promoted by Thomas Chalmers in an attempt to harmonize the Bible and a long age for the Earth.[42]

To make scripture support gap theology, a different rendering for Genesis 1:2 was proposed. The new translation said, "But the earth *had become* a ruin and a desolation,"[43] in contrast to the KJV which says, "And the earth *was* without form and void." A stative verb, indicating state-of-being, was replaced by verb that appears to indicate action.

Table 5.3 – Verbs Based on the Hebrew Root Hâyâh in the Creation Story (Strong's 01961)			
Scripture	Complete Hebrew Term	Basic Translation	Exemplar Translation (context of verb use)
Genesis 1:2	הָיְתָה	be	Was vacant and empty
Genesis 1:3	יְהִי	be	There is light
Genesis 1:3	וַיְהִי־אוֹר	and be light	And light exists
Genesis 1:5	וַיְהִי־עֶרֶב	and be evening	And there was evening
Genesis 1:5	וַיְהִי־בֹקֶר	and be morning	And there was morning
Genesis 1:6	יְהִי	be	There is an expanse in the middle
Genesis 1:6	וִיהִי	and be	And it exists to separate between
Genesis 1:7	וַיְהִי־כֵן	and be so	And it was so
Genesis 1:14	יְהִי	be	There are luminaries
Genesis 1:14	וְהָיוּ	and be	And *they* are a sign for appointed
Genesis 1:15	וְהָיוּ	and be	And luminaries exist
Genesis 2:7	וַיְהִי	and be	And the man existed as a living
Genesis 2:24	וְהָיוּ	and be	And they shall be as one flesh
Reference: van der Merwe, Christo, ed. (2004) *The Lexham Hebrew-English Interlinear Bible.*			

Arthur C. Custance wrote *Without Form and Void* in support of gap theology and the new translation required. His entire book focuses on promoting the translation of *hâyâh* (הָיְתָה) in Genesis 1:2 as "had become" rather than "was." In his translation, Custance replaces a stative verb with one that appears to indicate action. The acceptance of gap theology is based on a desperate attempt to harmonize scripture with science, rather than sound biblical hermeneutics and exegesis. Most people knowledgeable of both Hebrew and science reject this translation.

Hâyâh (הָיְתָה), translated "was" in Genesis 1:2, is listed in Table 5.3. This specific Hebrew word occurs 116 times in the Old Testament, and its occurrences are listed in Table B.2 of Appendix B. *Hâyâh* (הָיְתָה) is translated in the KJV using the stative verbs "was, had, is, been, be, and are" in 90 out of 116 times. *Hâyâh* (הָיְתָה) is translated "became" in only four instances.

Derivatives of *hâyâh* occur in key places in Genesis 1:3, 6, and 14 as shown in Table 5.3. The KJV and other versions translate these verses in a misleading manner to indicate action is occurring, when it is not (similar to what gap theology proposes for Genesis 1:2). These three verses are traditionally explained as commands—God speaks and things are instantly created from nothing. The word "let" is added to indicate a command in the expression, "Let there be."

Hâyâh, identified as (יהי) and (ויהי) and (והיו), occur in seven key places in Genesis 1:3, 6, 14, and 15 as follows:

- Genesis 1:3 And God said, <u>Let there be</u> light <u>and there was</u> light. (KJV)

- Genesis 1:6 And God said, <u>Let there be</u> a firmament in the midst of the waters <u>and let</u> it divide the waters from the waters. (KJV)

- Genesis 1:14–15 And God said, <u>Let there be</u> lights in the firmament of the heaven to divide the day from the night; <u>and let them be</u> for signs, and for seasons, and for days, and years. <u>And let them be</u> for lights in the firmament of the heaven to give light upon the earth. (KJV)

Compare the KJV above with the *exemplar* translation below where the derivatives of *hâyâh* are properly translated as non-command, stative verbs. Notice these are declarative statements and no action is indicated.

- Genesis 1:3 And God said, "<u>There is</u> light, <u>and</u> light <u>exists</u>." (ET)

- Genesis 1:6 And God said, "<u>There is</u> an expanse in the middle of the water, <u>and</u> *it* <u>exists</u> to separate between water *above* from water *below*." (ET)

- Genesis 1:14–15 And God said, "<u>There are</u> luminaries in the expanse of the heavens to distinguish between the day and between the night, <u>and *they*</u> are for a sign for appointed times and for days and years. <u>And</u> luminaries <u>exist</u> in the expanse of the heavens to give light over the Earth." (ET)

Genesis 1:3 describes the existence of light and nothing more. Nothing is being created, made, or formed in this verse. Bible translators have incorrectly taken this simple declarative statement and turned it into a command. Orthodox translations treat the first *hâyâh* (יהי) as a command by adding the word "let." The second *hâyâh* (ויהי) is correctly treated as stative.

Genesis 1:6 describes the existence of an expanse (firmament). The first occurrence of *hâyâh* (יהי) is translated "let there be" in the KJV to indicate a command. Worse yet, the second occurrence of *hâyâh* (ויהי), translated "and let," implies an additional command. Orthodox translations incorrectly treat both occurrences as "jussive/command" verbs indicating action by adding the word "let."

Genesis 1:14–15 mentions the existence of two luminaries in the heavens. God describes the existence of the Sun and Moon—not their creation. The KJV translates *hâyâh* (יהי) as "let there be" and turns this verse into a command. The two occurrences of *hâyâh* (והיו) are translated "and let them be" and turn two declarative statements into commands.

Hâyâh (היה) in the above three verses occurs 50 times in the Old Testament and its occurrences are listed in Table B.3 of Appendix B. This specific verb is translated the stative "be" 18 times, in addition to "let be" 15 times, "let there be" 5 times, and "let" 2 times. All these occurrences can easily be translated as stative verbs that indicate state-of-being.

The English words "are, is, am, were, was, be, being, and been" are eight stative verbs that indicate state-of-being. They do not switch back and forth between stative and dynamic. If they are the only verbs in a sentence, the sentence will be stative. For example, in the English language it is difficult if not impossible to construct a sentence showing action which uses only the verb "be." *Hâyâh* in Genesis 1:3, 1:6, and 1:14 is a stative verb that indicates state-of-being.

In summary, *hâyâh* in Genesis 1:2 can be translated as the stative verb "was" to indicate state-of-being in rejection of gap theology. Likewise, in Genesis 1:3, 1:6, and 1:14 *hâyâh* can be translated as a stative verb in rejection of traditional young-Earth creation theology. Reconnecting the Genesis account with the rest of the Old Testament helps in understanding and properly translating this verb.

It is interesting to note that all Hebrew lexicons give "exist" as a legitimate translation of the verb *hâyâh*. However, in approximately 3,482 occurrences of the root *hâyâh* (היה) and its derivatives, they are not translated "exist" in a single instance in the King James Version and other popular English translations. The *exemplar* translation has several verses where *hâyâh* is appropriately translated "exist."

The Basics of Hebrew Verbs

Hebrew verbs comprise one of the more complicated verbal systems in existence. They consist of a root plus seven stems. Each *verb stem* is developed from the same root. The seven verb stems for Hebrew strong verbs are qal, niphal, piel, pual, hiphil, hophal, and hithpael.[44,45] The spelling for the qal stem is identical to the root, from which the other six stems are derived.[46]

In addition to the above, each verb has several *verb states* (sometimes called tenses), which include perfect, imperfect, imperative, infinitive, participle, and jussive.[47] Also included in verb states are the masculine, feminine, singular, plural, first person, second person, and third person. This permits building a verb table based on a matrix of verb stems and verb states. A single root can have more than 170 *verb forms* when all stems and states are considered.[48]

Most verb forms are constructed by adding a prefix or suffix to the root, though in some instances no change in spelling occurs. For example, standard tables for strong verbs show that some imperfect and jussive verbs have the same spelling.[49] For verbs forms that are spelled the same, determining a specific verb form is based on sentence context and can be a judgment call.

The astute Bible student will notice that verb forms with the same spelling in a verb table can have different vowel points and accent marks. For example, qal jussive, niphal jussive, and piel jussive strong verbs are spelled the same, but have different vowel points and accent marks[50] (small dots, dashes and other symbols added above, below or within the letters). The primary purpose of these marks is to guide the pronunciation of words when the Hebrew Bible is read aloud. As previously mentioned, vocalization marks were not a part of the original Hebrew text and were added by Masoretic scribes starting around 500 AD.

Hebrew verbs can be totally intimidating; however, help is available to aid to their study. The *Old Testament Parsing Guide* by Beall, Banks, and Smith lists every single verb in the Old Testament and is a good starting point in the study of verb stems, verb states, and verb forms. Several Hebrew grammar books provide additional help. Understanding verb forms is absolutely essential for a correct translation of the Genesis creation story.

Alleged Command Verbs in Genesis

Ten key verbs in Genesis 1:3, 6, 9, 11, 14, 20, and 24 control our understanding of the Genesis creation story. These verbs are traditionally classified as jussive (meaning they are command verbs) and transform the seven verses in which they occur into commands. Each verse begins with the expression, "And God said." God speaks and allegedly commands things into existence. These ten "jussive/command" verbs form the foundation for the incorrect translation of the six-day Genesis chronicle written by Moses.

As mentioned in Chapter 3, the Septuagint is the basis for traditional thinking about the Genesis creation account. The first five books of the Old Testament (the Pentateuch) were translated around 275 BC. Jewish scribes, familiar with the Hebrew and Greek languages of the day, were ideally suited for this task; however, their poor scholarship and theological beliefs resulted in a less than accurate translation. They used this opportunity to embed their theology into the Old Testament for all time by translating ten key verbs and seven verses as commands. These translators helped establish an interpretive paradigm that has continued for more than twenty-two hundred years. Today, the Septuagint is a key influence in the errant translation of the Genesis creation story.

The *exemplar* translation explains Genesis 1:3, 6, 9, 11, 14, 20, and 24 as seven declarative statements made by God. Appendix B discusses in detail the alleged ten "jussive/command" verbs found in these verses. Justification is given for treating them as perfect verbs (with no requirement for a command) based on their common usage throughout the Old Testament. Table 5.4 identifies these ten verbs and their correct translation. Below are eight reasons why these verses should be treated as statements and not commands.

(1) Not command verbs — Six of the ten verbs classified in Table 5.4 as "jussive" verbs are not used in commands in the vast majority of occurrences. Outside Genesis Chapter 1, more than 97% of the time these verbs are used in other than a command context in the Old Testament.

Table 5.4 – Ten Key Verbs in Seven Verses of Genesis Chapter One (Traditionally considered jussive/command verbs)					
Verse	Hebrew Term[1]	Verb Root[2]	KJV Translation	Traditional Assigned Verb Form[2]	*Exemplar Translation*
Gen. 1:3	יְהִי	הָיָה	let there be	Qal jussive	there is
Gen. 1:6	יְהִי	הָיָה	let there be	Qal jussive	there is
Gen. 1:6	וִיהִי	הָיָה	and let	Qal jussive	and exists
Gen. 1:9	יִקָּווּ	קָוָה	let be gathered together	Niphal jusm	wait
Gen. 1:9	וְתֵרָאֶה	רָאָה	and let appear	Niphal jusm	and is seen
Gen. 1:11	תַּדְשֵׁא	דָּשָׁא	let bring forth	Hiphil jussive	sprouting
Gen. 1:14	יְהִי	הָיָה	let there be	Qal jussive	there are
Gen. 1:20	יִשְׁרְצוּ	שָׁרַץ	let bring forth	Qal jusm	swarm
Gen. 1:20	יְעוֹפֵף	עוּף	that may fly	Polel jusm	flying
Gen. 1:24	תּוֹצֵא	יָצָא	let bring forth	Hiphil jussive	brings forth

Note: According to the *Old Testament Parsing Guide*, when the verb form is given as "jusm" rather than "jussive," the spelling of the word does not indicate jussive. The four verbs of Genesis 1:9 and 1:20 are not jussive based on spelling.
References:
(1) van der Merwe, Christo, ed. (2004). *The Lexham Hebrew-English Interlinear Bible.*
(2) Beall, Todd S. and William A. Banks, Colin Smith (2000). *Old Testament Parsing Guide: Revised and Updated Edition.*

(2) No jussive spelling — Based on spelling, four of the ten verbs listed in Table 5.4 are not jussive verbs. The four verbs in Genesis 1:9 and 1:20 are classified as "jusm" rather than "jussive" by the *Old Testament Parsing Guide*. Jusm is explained as: "jussive in meaning, but no unique form to indicate jussive."[51] In plain English, the spelling of these words (their unique form) does not show they are jussive, yet they have been assigned a jussive meaning.

(3) No command required — The seven key verses of Genesis 1:3, 6, 9, 11, 14, 20, and 24, that begin with the expression, "And God said," have no inherent requirement to be commands. Outside Genesis Chapter 1, the same expression where God is speaking occurs sixteen times.[52] A command is issued in eight verses in Genesis 6:13, 17:9, 17:15, 17:19, 21:12, 35:1, Exodus 3:14, and Numbers 22:12. A declarative statement is issued in the remaining eight verses of Genesis 9:8, 9:12, 9:17, 46:2, 1 Kings 3:5, 3:11, 2 Chronicles 1:11, and Jonah 4:9. These verses clearly show that a

command does not necessarily follow the expression, "And God said." It cannot be dogmatically required that Genesis 1:3, 6, 9, 11, 14, 20, and 24 be interpreted as commands.

(4) Use of stative verbs – In Genesis 1:3, 6, and 14, use of the stative verb *hâyâh* discredits the idea that God is creating anything. Stative verbs are used to describe the way things "are, is, am, were, was, be, being, or been" rather than to show action or change. *Hâyâh* in these three verses can mean "be or exist" and is primarily translated "be, is, was, or were" in the KJV of the Old Testament.

When God commands, the appropriate dynamic verbs are used rather than stative verbs. For example, dynamic verbs are used in eight verses outside Genesis Chapter 1 where the Hebrew expression, "And God said," is followed by a command. Dynamic verbs are used in commanding to "make thee an ark" (Gen. 6:13–14), "shall keep my covenant" (Gen. 17:9), "not call her name" (Gen. 17:15), "shall bear thee a son" (Gen. 17:19), "hearken to her voice" (Gen. 21:12), "arise and go" (Gen. 35:1), "thus shalt thou say" (Exodus 3:14), and "thou shalt not go and thou shalt not curse" (Num. 22:12).

(5) Missing dynamic verbs – In the seven key verses of Genesis 1:3, 6, 9, 11, 14, 20, and 24, God does not use the appropriate dynamic verbs to show that action is either expected or occurring. With the exception of Genesis 1:11, the Hebrew verbs translated "create, make, form, plant, grow, and build" are not used anywhere in these seven verses—important dynamic verbs are clearly missing.

When the seven alleged "command" verses are compared with true action verses in the creation account, the difference is striking. Notice the dynamic verbs used when God *created* the heavens and Earth (Gen. 1:1), when God *formed* man and *breathed* into his nostrils (Gen. 2:7), when God *planted* the garden (Gen. 2:8), when God *put* man in the garden (Gen. 2:8), when God *grew* trees for the garden (Gen. 2:9), when God *formed* the animals of the garden (Gen. 2:19), when God *brought* the animals to Adam for naming (Gen. 2:19), and when God *built* Eve from Adam's rib (Gen. 2:22). In these verses, the appropriate dynamic Hebrew verbs translated "create, form, breathe, plant, put, grow, bring, and build" are used to indicate past and present action. Also notice the expression, "And God said" is absent in all of these action verses.

(6) Comparison with known commands – The only two real commands in the first two chapters of Genesis are found in Genesis 1:28 and 2:16–17. These two commands use the dynamic verbs "be fruitful, multiply, replenish, subdue, have dominion, eat, and not eat" to express God's desires. None of these verbs are classified as jussive by the *Old Testament Parsing Guide*. Also notice the absence of "let" in English translations. The language of these two commands is significantly different from the alleged commands of Genesis 1:3, 6, 9, 11, 14, 20, and 24.

(7) Forced mistranslation – Treating Genesis 1:3, 6, 9, 11, 14, 20, and 24 as commands has forced the illegitimate or poor translation of several words in the creation story. For example, treating Genesis 1:9 as a command has forced Hebrew scholars to grossly mistranslate *qâvâh* as "let be gathered together" rather than "wait."

(8) Conflict with general revelation – Traditional theology considers Genesis 1:3, 6, 9, 11, 14, 20, and 24 as commands that resulted in creation of the heavens, Earth, and its biosphere during six days in 4004 BC. An incorrect explanation of the six-day Genesis chronicle causes special revelation to conflict with general revelation. The time frame forced on Genesis by traditional young-Earth creation theology irreconcilably clashes with firm scientific evidence.

Young-Earth creation theology and traditional thinking require that Genesis 1:3–31 be interpreted in a command context. By speaking, God created out of nothing (*creatio ex nihilo*). By commanding, God instantly brought the heavens, Earth, and all therein into existence during six 24-hour days. Outside Genesis Chapter 1, the following three verses are often quoted in support of this belief.

• Psalm 33:6 By the word of the LORD were the heavens made; and all the host of them by the breath of his mouth. (KJV)

• Psalm 148:5 Let them praise the name of the LORD: for he commanded, and they were created. (KJV)

• Hebrews 11:3 Through faith we understand that the worlds were framed by the word of God, so that things which are seen were not made of things which do appear. (KJV)

Psalm 33:6 and other poetical verses should not be used to explain God's method of creation. For example, pillars are described as supporting the Earth in 1 Samuel 2:8, Job 9:6, and Job 26:11. We know the Earth is not supported by pillars, and these verses are speaking metaphorically. In a general sense, Psalm 33:6 extols the majesty and power of God as maker of the heavens.

For those who believe Psalm 33:6 is a description of how God created the heavens and Earth, notice the term *made* (*âsâh*, Strong's 06213) is used rather than *create*. This verse can be legitimately translated, "By *His* word, Yahweh did[06213] the heavens." There is no mention of God doing the Earth (only the heavens). This verse says nothing about *creating* the heavens *in six days* or that God created the heavens *out of nothing*.

Psalm 148:5 says that Yahweh commanded and they were created. From the previous four verses of Psalms 148:1–4, we can assume "they" refers not only to the angels who praise the name of the LORD but also to the heavens containing the Sun, Moon, and stars. Notice there is no mention of God creating the Earth (only the term heavens is used). Likewise, this verse says nothing about creating the heavens *in six days* or that God created the heavens *out of nothing*.

Hebrews 11:3 says that the worlds were framed by the word of God. This is substantially different from saying God spoke and commanded the Earth to be created *instantly out of nothing*. Keep in mind the Greek word translated "worlds" is not equivalent to "Earth." According to this verse, "things seen" were made of things invisible (things that do not appear). Paul's statement can be explained in reference to atoms or sub-atomic particles such as protons, neutrons, and electrons. God made the worlds (i.e., universe) out of basic matter that cannot be seen.

The ancient Greek philosopher Democritus (460–370 BC) proposed that everything is made of atoms. The English word "atom" comes from the Greek *atomos*, meaning "uncuttable," and defined as the smallest indivisible elemental particle of matter. The Greek philosophers believed that all visible objects were made of invisible atoms. The Apostle Paul was no doubt aware of Greek thought and may have alluded to this explanation when writing Hebrews. God created the invisible, from which the visible is made.

If we objectively look at the above three verses and others in the Bible, they do not support the interpretation of Genesis 1:3, 6, 9, 11, 14, 20, and 24 in a command context. No scripture in the Bible specifically mentions that God *created* the heavens and Earth *in six days*. No scripture states that God *instantly created* the heavens and Earth. No scripture states that God created the heavens and Earth *from nothing*. We can reject the traditional "jussive/command" interpretation that has been forced onto Genesis 1:3–31.

Conclusion

The eighteen key words (6 nouns and 12 verbs) discussed in this chapter and their use in the *exemplar* translation is well-supported. Reconnecting these words with the rest of the Bible significantly aids in their proper understanding. In the *exemplar* translation, there are no metaphorical interpretations or special definitions that apply only to the creation account. There are no illegitimate or forced translations unsupported by the remainder of the Old Testament.

The most significant issue in regard to a correct translation of the creation story is the treatment of Genesis 1:3, 6, 9, 11, 14, 20, and 24 as declarative statements rather than commands. These seven verses and the ten alleged "jussive/command" verbs found therein form the backbone of current incorrect explanations. At best, treating these declarative statements as commands was a bad judgment call. More realistically, scripture was deliberately embellished and countless generations have been misled.

Key words in the Genesis account control its meaning. After God created the Earth, it was vacant and empty of life rather than "without form." The deep is a clear reference to the depths of the seas and oceans. On day one, God did not create light, but described its presence through use of the stative Hebrew verb *hâyâh*. On the second day, God did not create an expanse, but described its existence by using the stative verb *hâyâh*. On the third day, the waters calmly waited in one place, and there was no "gathering together." On the fourth day, God did not create the Sun and Moon, but described their existence through use of the stative *hâyâh*. .

Although not necessarily an exciting topic, a proper understanding of key Hebrew words is essential for a good translation of the Genesis creation story. The mistranslation of critical words and expressions has caused the current problem that has existed for more than twenty-two hundred years. When the above identified words are placed in their scriptural context, their significance becomes apparent. (As key words are reintroduced in Chapter 6, readers should reference the material herein.)

At this point, Hebrew scholars and serious Bible students should read Appendix B for additional discussion of the ten key verbs identified above. Because of the specialized academic nature of this material, it has been separated from the main text. Appendix B discusses in detail the ten "jussive/command" verbs listed in Table 5.4, that control translation of the six-day Genesis chronicle.

Lead me in your truth and teach me, for you are the God of my salvation; for you I wait all the day long. (Psalm 25:5) ESV

Chapter 6

Translating Genesis

The first two chapters of Genesis are a fascinating study, as attested by innumerable books and commentaries. As pointed out in Chapter 1, the Genesis creation story is a source of controversy, not only in the religious world, but also the secular. Theologians, philosophers, and scientists alike seek the story's meaning, yet a proper understanding has heretofore been elusive. Any explanation acceptable to Bible believers must treat the Old Testament as truthful, trustworthy, and inspired of God. On the other hand, Bible believing scientists expect special revelation and general revelation to harmonize in regard to time. *Exemplar* creation satisfies these fundamental requirements.

The development of the *exemplar* translation is explained in this chapter. *The Biblia Hebraica Stuttgartensia* (Masoretic text of the Hebrew Bible) presented in *The Lexham Hebrew-English Interlinear Bible* is the starting point. The Lexham translation is checked for accuracy on a word-for-word basis against the Hebrew text; however, any word translated from Hebrew into English must be supported elsewhere in the Old Testament. In a few instances, words are changed when the Lexham translation is not correct or an alternate rendering is justified. The King James Version (KJV) of the Bible is used as the standard reference for word translation. In some instances, the English Standard Version (ESV), New King James Version (NKJV), New American Standard Bible (NASB), New International Version (NIV), and other versions are referenced.

A small minority of people may object to using *The Biblia Hebraica Stuttgartensia* as the basis for my translation. *The Biblia Hebraica Stuttgartensia* is based on the Leningrad Codex, which is the Ben Asher Masoretic Text, and the basis for modern English translations. In contrast, when the KJV was translated in 1611, the Ben Chayyim Masoretic Text was used as the basis. Regardless, with respect to Genesis Chapters 1 and 2, I am not aware of any alphabet character differences between the Ben Asher Masoretic Text and the Ben Chayyim Masoretic Text. We have a reliable copy of the Hebrew text that Moses wrote.

The following format is used to show development from the Hebrew text to the *exemplar* translation. The A-form of the verse is directly copied from *The Lexham*

Hebrew-English Interlinear Bible, except presented in a left-to-right format rather than the reverse. The word-for-word order of the Hebrew text is retained, and slash marks separate each Hebrew word or term. The B-form of the verse reflects word changes from the Lexham version and all substitutions are underlined. Some simple verses may not have a B-form. The C-form of the verse rearranges the text into the English style and adds words enclosed in brackets to smooth out language flow. The D-form shows the completed version of the verse; brackets are dropped, final minor changes are made, and italics are added.

Progression from the A-form to the D-form allows the Bible student to follow verse development. Underlined words indicate changes from the previous verse form. A Strong's number is often attached in superscript to identify specific English words with their corresponding Hebrew word. In the final D-form, significant words not in the Hebrew text are identified by italics similar to the KJV.

The translation of some Hebrew words into English is a judgment call. A number of Hebrew words have legitimate multiple meanings (they are homographs) and selecting the corresponding English word is based on context. Some Hebrew words can have several legitimate shades of meaning, and choosing the appropriate one can be a judgment call. During translation, each Hebrew word must be narrowed to a corresponding English word. In the *exemplar* translation, word selection from available valid choices is controlled by (1) a strict appeal to the Hebrew text, (2) verse context, and (3) an explanatory framework guided by general revelation. As practiced in Chapter 5, Hebrew words and their frequency of translation into English are occasionally analyzed, with the KJV as a reference.

Hebrew verbs do not have a past, present, or future tense similar to verbs in the English language. Hebrew verbs can be divided into the *perfect* and *imperfect* state. The perfect expresses completed action or state-of-being, while the imperfect expresses incomplete action.[1] Neither the perfect nor imperfect have a tense (time of action) apart from context and issues of syntax.[2] When the context is unclear, determining past or present tense is a judgment call—a significant issue in translating Genesis Chapter 1. For example, in the *exemplar* translation of Genesis 1:7, 16, 21, 25, 26, and 27, "made" and "create" refer to actions that occurred in the past and are complete.

Keep in mind that Hebrew was written from right to left, opposite the English style. A sentence in Hebrew typically follows the order of verb-subject-object. In contrast, English sentence structure is typically subject-verb-object. When Hebrew is translated into English, the verb and subject order are normally reversed.

Hebrew lacks any punctuation to mark the end or beginning of a thought. There are no periods or question marks at the end of a sentence. In addition, no letters are capitalized at the beginning of a sentence. However, the Hebrew letter vav (ו), normally translated "and," often marks the beginning of a new thought. For this reason, many sentences and verses begin with "and" in the *exemplar* translation due to its highly literal nature. The Hebrew letter vav is also used as a conjunction when joining two nouns, verbs, or adjectives (e.g., be fruitful *and* multiply).

The Genesis creation story should not be interpreted in a historical and scientific vacuum. For example, it is impossible to know what a camel looks like from only reading scripture. Personal knowledge of the world helps flesh out this animal. In like manner, knowledge of general revelation is invaluable in helping us understand the creation account. I have no issue appealing to firm scientific evidence accumulated throughout the centuries. Romans 1:20 says, "For since the creation of the world God's invisible qualities—his eternal power and divine nature—have been clearly seen, being understood from what has been made, so that men are without excuse" (NIV). On the other hand, I do not appeal to undependable scientific theories driven by belief in philosophical naturalism.

The *exemplar* translation was developed with the goal of being a highly literal, yet understandable rendering of the Hebrew text. Although many Bible translations claim to be literal, those claims are debatable. For example, verses in the A-form copied from *The Lexham Hebrew-English Interlinear Bible* are literally translated, but normally quite difficult to read. Few languages translate into another in an easy flowing style. Words must be rearranged or added (often debatable) to improve readability and sentence structure. The remainder of this chapter presents the *exemplar* translation in detail; the most credible word-for-word translation of Genesis Chapters 1 and 2 yet developed in the English speaking world.

Genesis Chapter One

1:1A. In beginning/create/God/the heaven/and/the earth. (LHEIB[3])
1:1C. In [the] beginning[07225], God create[01254] the heaven[08064] and the Earth[0776].
1:1D. In the beginning, God created the heavens and the Earth.

This verse is traditionally translated:
• In the beginning God created the heaven and the earth. (KJV)
• In the beginning God made the heaven and the earth. (Septuagint[4])

As shown above, the Septuagint poorly translates this simple verse. In this verse and in Genesis 1:21, 27, and 2:4, the Hebrew word *bârâ* is mistranslated "made" rather than "create." In Genesis 2:3, the Septuagint does not translate *bârâ* at all, a clear illustration of its inaccuracy.

Dr. Bruce Waltke in *Genesis: A Commentary* says that some traditional theologians consider Genesis 1:1 as a summary of the entire six-day creation account that is to follow.[5] Placement of this verse at the beginning has no chronological significance. Genesis 1:1 and 1:2 are explained as non-chronological and must be shuffled around to achieve a logical flow of events.

Traditional young-Earth creation theology, proposed by Dr. Henry Morris, explains "heavens" in Genesis 1:1 as the equivalent of "space."[6] Initially space was empty and remained so until the fourth day. He says, "In like manner the term 'earth' refers to the component of matter in the universe. At the time of the initial creation, there were no other planets, stars, or other material bodies in the universe; nor did they come into being until the fourth day."[7] "So this verse [Genesis 1:1] must speak essentially of the creation of the basic elements of matter, which thereafter were to be organized into the structured earth and later into other material bodies."[8]

Exemplar creation does not require a metaphorical interpretation of heaven and Earth in Genesis 1:1. The heavens refer to everything ancient man could see when looking upward from the surface of the Earth. Today, the heavens are the galaxies, globular star clusters, nebulae, stars, solar systems, planets, and moons we can see with the naked eye, in addition to those observed by powerful telescopes. The Hebrew word *erets* (Strong's 0776), here translated Earth, refers to all the land ancient man walked on and knew about. From a twenty-first century knowledge perspective, "all of the land" is the planet Earth.

Dr. John Sailhamer points out that the word "beginning" in Genesis 1:1 is translated from the Hebrew *rê'shîyth,* and refers not to an instant in time but to an undefined period of time when God created.[9] *Rê'shîyth* can refer to a beginning period of time without specified limits. For example, in Genesis 10:10, the beginning of Nimrod's kingdom was Babel, Erech, Accad, and Calneh. These cities were built or acquired over a period of time. In Job 8:7, the beginning period of Job's life is mentioned as being small, but the latter end was to be greater.

Based on scientific evidence, the Earth, stars, and galaxies are of different ages and did not originate at the same moment in time. Evidence supports the explanation of *rê'shîyth* in Genesis 1:1 as referring to a period of time.

Genesis 1:1 attributes God as creator of the heavens and Earth, without defining the time of their creation. Undefined time could be one day or billions of years. The exact time, sequence, and method God used to create the heavens and Earth are not revealed in scripture, and man is left to his own resources to fill in the missing information.

• This is the first occurrence in the Bible of the Hebrew word *shâmayim* (Strong's 08064), here translated "heavens." *Shâmayim* occurs 420 times in the Old Testament and is translated "heaven" 398 times, "air" 21 times, and "astrologers" 1 time in the KJV.[10] See Chapter 5 for additional discussion of this word.

• This is the first occurrence of *bârâ* (Strong's 01254), here translated "create." In Genesis, *bârâ* occurs eleven times in Genesis 1:1, 1:21, 1:27, 2:3, 2:4, 5:1, 5:2, and 6:7 and is always translated create. See Chapter 5 for additional discussion of this word.

• This is the first occurrence of *rê'shîyth* (Strong's 07225), here translated "beginning." *Rê'shîyth* occurs 51 times in the Old Testament and is translated "beginning" 18 times, "firstfruits" 11 times, "first" 9 times, and "chief" 8 times, in addition to other miscellaneous words in the KJV.[11] The Brown-Diver-Briggs Hebrew lexicon gives "beginning" as an acceptable translations of the noun *rê'shîyth.*[12]

• This is the first occurrence of *erets* (Strong's 0776), here translated "Earth," which occurs 2,504 times in the Old Testament.[13] See Chapter 5 for additional discussion of *erets* and Earth.

1:2A. And the earth/be/formless/and empty/and darkness/over surface/the deep/and spirit/God/hover/over surface/the waters. (LHEIB)

1:2B. And the earth/be/<u>vacant</u>/and empty/and darkness/over surface/the deep/and spirit/God/hover/over surface/the waters.

1:2C. And the Earth^{0776} be^{01961} vacant^{08414} and empty^{0922} [of life]. And darkness^{02822} [was] over^{05921} [the] surface^{06440} [of] the deep^{08415} [waters]. And [the] spirit [of] God hover^{07363} over^{05921} [the] surface^{06440} [of] the waters.

1:2D. And the Earth <u>was</u> vacant and empty *of life*. And darkness *was* over the surface of the deep *waters*. And the Spirit of God hovered over the surface of the waters.

This verse has been translated:

• And the earth was without form and void; and darkness was upon the face of the deep. And the Spirit of God moved upon the face of the waters. (KJV)

• Yet the earth was invisible and unformed and darkness was over the abyss, and a divine wind was being carried along over the water. (Septuagint[14])

• Earth was a soup of nothingness, a bottomless emptiness, an inky blackness. God's Spirit brooded like a bird above the watery abyss. (*The Message*) [This version grossly mistranslates the Hebrew text]

• The erth was voyde and emptie ad darcknesse was vpon the depe and the spirite of god moved vpon the water. (William Tyndale, 1530[15])

• And ye earth was voyde and emptie, and darcknes was vpon the depe, & ye sprete of God moued vpo the water. (Myles Coverdale, 1535[16])

• And the earth was void and empty, and darkness was upon the face of the deep; and the spirit of God moved over the waters. (Douay-Rheims, 1899)

According to Bruce Waltke, some traditional theologians explain Genesis 1:1 as a summary of the entire six-day creation account that is to follow. Genesis 1:2 is a description of the chaotic state of the Earth immediately after its creation. Earth is described as an unproductive and uninhabited place.[17] The problem with this explanation is that Genesis 1:1 contains the only mention of God creating the Earth. If Genesis 1:1 is considered a summary of the entire creation account, then theologians admit that, "There is no word of God creating the planet earth or darkness or the watery chaos" as described in Genesis 1:2.[18]

In a similar vein, Sailhamer discusses Genesis 1:1 as a title for the creation account. If Genesis 1:1 is a summary of the first chapter, then the actual creation process starts with Genesis 1:2.[19] The story begins with an Earth that is without form and void. He says, "We are left with the uncomfortable discovery that the passage does not tell us when, or who, created the earth."[20] "Since the creation story starts with an unformed Earth, the traditional concept of "creation out of nothing" is not invalidated but is not taught in Genesis [Chapter] 1."[21]

Traditional young-Earth creation theology proposed by Henry Morris explains the "heavens and earth" in Genesis 1:1 as equivalent to "space and raw matter." In regard to Genesis 1:2, Morris says, "The matter so created was at first unformed and uninhabited."[22] His explanation of heaven and earth in Genesis 1:1–2 is metaphorical and not a literal, straightforward reading of the text as claimed.

The above explanations illustrate the confusion regarding the interpretation of these two verses. The KJV, Septuagint, and *The Message* represent traditional translations, all of which are incorrect. Theological influence has obfuscated the understanding of Genesis 1:1–2.

Exemplar creation explains Genesis 1:1 and 1:2 as occurring in chronological order. Genesis 1:1 describes the initial creation of the heavens and Earth in the past, without defining the time frame. Genesis 1:2 is a description of the Earth sometime after its creation, without defining the elapsed time. Time between the two verses could be one day or billions of years. At this point, the Earth is: (1) vacant and empty of life, (2) has deep water covered by darkness, and (3) the Spirit of God is hovering over the waters. No special or metaphorical meanings need be applied to any of the words.

What is meant by the statement, "And the Earth was vacant and empty?" The logical answer is that the Earth was empty *of life*, since living things are a primary topic of the six-day Genesis chronicle. In addition, Isaiah 45:18 specifically states that God did not create the Earth to be empty, but rather to be inhabited. The two rhyming Hebrew words, *tôhûw* (Strong's 08414) and *bôhûw* (Strong's 0922), strongly emphasize emptiness. See Chapter 5 for additional discussion of *tôhûw* and *bôhûw*.

In addition to the biblical text, scientific evidence indicates the Earth was once a molten ball of material, with an estimated surface temperature of 600° C. At that temperature, the Earth was completely sterile.

The translation of *tôhûw* as "without form" in the KJV is illegitimate, and a result of theological influence. A careful study of all verses in the Bible containing *tôhûw* shows it cannot be correctly translated in this manner. As quoted above, William Tyndale's Pentateuch of 1530, the Myles Coverdale Bible of 1535, and the Douay-Rheims version correctly translate *tôhûw* and *bôhûw* as "void and empty." Theological influence changed the translation to "without form and void" in the Geneva Bible of 1560, and most subsequent English Bibles adopted the same language.

• This is the first occurrence of the Hebrew verb *hâyâh* (Strong's 01961), here translated "was." When used as a stand-alone word or part of a Hebrew compound word, derivatives of the root *hâyâh* occur 33 times in 23 separate verses in Genesis 1:2, 3, 5, 6, 7, 8, 9, 11,13,14, 15, 19, 23, 24, 29, 30, 31, 2:5, 2:7, 2:10, 2:18, 2:24, and 2:25.

1:3A. And say/God/be/light/and be light. (LHEIB)
1:3C. And God say, "Be^{01961} light^{0216} and light^{0216} be^{01961}."
1:3D. And God said, "<u>There is</u> light, and light <u>exists</u>."

This verse is traditionally translated:
• And God said, Let there be light: and there was light. (KJV)
• And God said, Let there be light, and there was light. (Septuagint[23])
• God spoke: "Light!" And light appeared. (*The Message*)

Genesis 1:3 begins the first day narrative, traditionally explained as when God created light. In this verse, the Hebrew verb *hâyâh* (Strong's 01961) occurs two times. The first occurrence of *hâyâh* (יְהִי) is translated "let there be" in the KJV and traditionally assigned a jussive verb state.[24] When treated as jussive, the word "let" becomes a part of the translation. Jussive verbs are traditionally considered "command verbs" and turn this simple declarative statement into a command. The second occurrence of *hâyâh* (וַיְהִי) is translated "and there was" in the KJV and assigned an imperfect state (not a command). *The Message* represents conventional errant thinking about this text.

Traditional explanations of Genesis 1:3 have God creating some type of intermediate light on the first day, before the Sun is created on the fourth day; however, the details are rather vague. Was this light coming from the presence of God? Was this light from a distant point source similar to the Sun? Some have proposed that events on the first day are out of sequence and should be placed within the fourth day, when God created the Sun and Moon. As Waltke says, "Certain 'difficulties' in the order of the days seem clearly to represent a dischronologization."[25] An incorrect translation of Genesis 1:3, accompanied by a faulty explanatory framework, leads one down a path that only gets worse with subsequent verses.

Exemplar creation explains Genesis 1:3 as a statement by God about one of the most important phenomena in our solar system—abundant light. That light is coming from the Sun, which has been shining for many years. Nothing is created in this verse. The complete absence of dynamic Hebrew verbs in Genesis 1:3–5 shows God is not creating, making, forming, planting, growing, or building anything.

Exemplar creation views Genesis 1:3 as a declarative statement, rather than a command. Nothing is being created. This is the first of seven verses in Genesis 1:3, 6, 9, 11, 14, 20, and 24 that start with the expression, "And God said." This verse does not contain any dynamic verbs and does not follow the pattern of verses in Genesis when God is physically doing something such as when God *created* the heavens and Earth (Gen. 1:1), *formed* man of dust from the ground (Gen. 2:7), *breathed* life into man (Gen. 2:7), *planted* the Garden of Eden (Gen. 2:8), *put* man in the garden (Gen. 2:8), *grew* trees for the garden (Gen. 2:9), *formed* animals for the garden (Gen. 2:19), *brought* the animals to Adam for naming (Gen. 2:19) and *built* Eve from Adam's rib (Gen. 2:22). All these verses use dynamic Hebrew verbs to describe physical action. In Genesis 1:3, no action verbs are used and God is not commanding anything to happen.

The identical Hebrew expression translated, "And God said" is not restricted to the seven verses found in the six-day chronicle and is used elsewhere in the Old Testament. Outside Genesis Chapter 1, when God is speaking, this expression occurs sixteen times.[26] A command is issued in eight verses in Genesis 6:13, 17:9, 17:15, 17:19, 21:12, 35:1; Exodus 3:14, and Numbers 22:12. A statement is issued, with no action implied, in the remaining eight verses of Genesis 9:8, 9:12, 9:17, 46:2; 1 Kings 3:5, 3:11; 2 Chronicles 1:11, and Jonah 4:9.

In addition, the English expression, "The LORD said" occurs 219 times in the KJV of the Old Testament.[27] In the vast majority of occurrences, God is making a statement rather than issuing a command. When God speaks, a command does not necessarily follow.

We can reject dogmatic claims that Genesis 1:3 is a command based on (1) an analysis of verses containing the Hebrew expression, "And God said," (2) verses containing the English phrase, "The LORD said," (3) knowledge that *hâyâh* in Genesis 1:3 is a stative verb, and (4) information given in Chapter 5 and Appendix B.

Exemplar creation explains Genesis 1:1, 1:2, and 1:3 as occurring in chronological sequence, with the time between being undefined. In Genesis 1:1, God created the heavens and Earth. In Genesis 1:2, the Earth is described as a dark, empty of life and covered by deep water sometime after its formation. Between Genesis 1:2 and 1:3, God raised the continents and created plants, marine life, land animals, and flying creatures (not necessarily in that order). The transition from undefined time to literal days occurs at Genesis 1:3 as shown in Table 2.1. Genesis 1:3 is the first of six, chronological, 24-hour days during which God describes, identifies, distinguishes, approves, and blesses His work.

The time required for all of the events that occurred prior to Genesis 1:3 is undefined in scripture, and one day or billions of years may have transpired. General revelation reveals that significant time passed prior to Genesis 1:3. During this time God created the stars, galaxies, our solar system, and Earth. As discussed in Chapter 4, careful examination of these objects indicates significant time occurred.

Starting with Genesis 1:3, God describes the Earth and heavens during a six-day period. The sequence God used to *create things* prior to Genesis 1:3 is not necessarily the sequence used to *describe them* in Genesis 1:3–31. The exact time, sequence, and methods God used when creating are not revealed in scripture, and man is left to his own resources to fill in the missing information.

In the *exemplar* translation of Genesis 1:3, the first occurrence of *hâyâh* is translated "there is" and the second is translated "and exists." Both are stative, state-of-being verbs that denote the existence of light and nothing more. See Chapter 5 for additional discussion of the Hebrew verb *hâyâh*.

- This is the first occurrence of the noun *ôwr* (Strong's 0216), translated "light." In the first two chapters, *ôwr* occurs six times in Genesis in 1:3, 4, 5, and 18.
- *Ôwr* should not be confused with *mâ'ôwr* (Strong's 03974), translated in Genesis 1:14, 15, and 16 as "luminaries" or light giving bodies.
- In the Hebrew text, the pattern of Genesis 1:3 is reflected in Genesis 1:6. Notice the similar underlined structure, "<u>And God said, There is</u> an expanse. . . <u>and</u> <u>it exists</u> to separate between water *above* from water *below*."
- In the Hebrew text, the pattern of Genesis 1:3 is also reflected in Genesis 1:14–15. Notice the underlined structure, "<u>And God said, There are</u> luminaries. . . <u>And luminaries exist</u> in the expanse of the heavens. . ."

1:4A. And see/God/the light/that good/and cause to separate/God/between/the light/ and between/the darkness. (LHEIB)

1:4B. And <u>saw</u>/God/the light/that good/<u>and distinguish</u>/God/between/the light/and between/the darkness.

1:4C. And God saw that the light[0216] [was] good. And God distinguish[0914] between[0996] the light[0216] and between[0996] the darkness[02822].

1:4D. And God saw that the light *was* good. And God distinguished between the light and between the darkness.

This verse has been translated:
- And God saw the light, that it was good: and God divided the light from the darkness. (KJV)
- And God saw that the light was good. And God separated the light from the darkness. (ESV)
- And the Lord saw the light that it was good. And the Lord distinguished between the light and between the darkness. (Targum of Onkelos, English translation by J. W. Etheridge, 1862)

Traditional theology explains this verse as when God physically divided/separated light from darkness, rather than when God distinguished light from darkness.

In English, "separating" and "distinguishing" are two closely related words with a slight difference. Contrasting physical objects can be readily separated from each other. Goats can be separated from sheep. Wheat can be separated from chaff. Men can be separated from women. However, non-physical phenomena are normally distinguished. We distinguish between darkness and light, cold and heat, silence and sound. Darkness, cold, and silence are not substances. Darkness is the absence of light, cold is the absence of heat, and silence is the absence of sound.

Newer translations of the Bible such as the ESV, NKJV, and NIV recognize the subtle difference between separating and distinguishing. In Leviticus 10:10 and Ezekiel 22:26, the holy is *distinguished* from the common. In Leviticus 11:47 and 20:25, the clean is *distinguished* from the unclean.

The Hebrew word *bâdal* (Strong's 0914) has several different shades of meaning, and in Genesis 1:4 is best translated distinguish rather than divide or separate. *Bâdal* can mean to physically separate as in Numbers 16:21 when God told Moses and Aaron to *separate* from the people so He could destroy them. In Exodus 26:33, the veil of the tabernacle *divided* between the holy and the most holy. However, *bâdal* can be legitimately translated "distinguish" in the sense of distinguishing between holy and common, clean and unclean, or light and darkness.

In Genesis 1:4, God is doing nothing more than distinguishing light from darkness in preparation for calling (identifying) them as day and night. In the *exemplar* translation, *bâdal* is translated "distinguish" in Genesis 1:4, 14, and 18, while translated "separate" in 1:6 and 7.

- The word *bâdal* (Strong's 0914) occurs 42 times in the Old Testament and is translated "separate" 25 times, "divide" 8 times, "difference" 4 times, "sever" 3 times, and "asunder" 2 times, in addition to other miscellaneous words in the KJV.[28] In the first two chapters of Genesis, *bâdal* occurs in Genesis 1:4, 1:6, 1:7, 1:14, and 1:18.
- Gesenius' Hebrew Lexicon defines *bâdal* as primarily "to separate" or "to distinguish,"[29] Strong's Concordance defines *bâdal* as "to divide" and can mean literally or figuratively to separate or distinguish.[30]
- The English Standard Version (ESV) translates *bâdal* as "distinguish" in Leviticus 10:10, 11:47, and Ezekiel 22:26.
- The New King James Version (NKJV) translates *bâdal* as "distinguish" in Leviticus 10:10, 11:47, 20:25, and Ezekiel 22:26
- The New International Version (NIV) translates *bâdal* as "distinguish" in Leviticus 10:10, 11:47, 20:25, and Ezekiel 22:26.
- This is first occurrence of the Hebrew word *bêyn* (Strong's 0996), here translated "between." In the first two chapters, *bêyn* occurs nine times in Genesis 1:4, 1:6, 1:7, 1:14, and 1:18.

1:5A. And call/God/to the light/day/and to the darkness/call/night/and be evening/ and be morning/day/one. (LHEIB)

1:5C. And God call^{07121} to the light^{0216} day^{03117} and call^{07121} to the darkness^{02822} night. And evening be^{01961} and morning be^{01961}, day^{03117} one^{0259}.

1:5D. And God called the light "day" and called the darkness "night." And evening <u>was</u>, and morning <u>was</u>—day one.

This verse has been translated:
• And God called the light Day, and the darkness he called Night. And the evening and the morning were the first day. (KJV)
• And he called the light Day, and the darkness Night; and there was evening and morning one day. (Douay-Rheims, 1899)

In Genesis 1:5, God calls out (identifies) the light as "day" and the darkness as "night." One cycle of evening and morning defines one complete day. One cycle marks 24 hours of time, signifies one revolution of the Earth, and corresponds to three hundred sixty degrees of planetary rotation.

Traditional young-Earth creation theology, as explained by Henry Morris, has a major problem at this point. The first day is now complete. The Earth has been created and is rotating on its axis. The planet is being illuminated by some kind of temporary light source corresponding to the Sun. Light and darkness are occurring to produce day and night.[31] Everything appears logical except there is no mention of God creating the Earth. As explained by Morris, the word "earth" in Genesis 1:1–2 is the basic matter from which the planet Earth and universe are constructed.[32] According to his interpretative framework, Genesis *does not record creation of the Earth as a planet.*

The Hebrew expression translated into English in verse 1:5C above as, "And evening be and morning be, day one," is identical in the Hebrew text for all six days except for the numbers and "the" added in Genesis 1:31.

In Genesis 1:5, the Hebrew word *echâd* (Strong's 0259), meaning "one," is used to number the day. *Echâd* is a cardinal number employed for counting (one, two, three, etc.) in the Hebrew language.[33] On the remaining six days, ordinal numbers are used (second, third, fourth, etc.), indicating position in Hebrew.[34] This is *day one* of the six-day Genesis chronicle, rather than the *first day* of the universe. The Douay-Rheims Bible correctly translates this cardinal number as "one."

• This is the first occurrence of the Hebrew word *qârâ* (Strong's 07121), here translated "call." *Qârâ* occurs 735 times in the Old Testament and is translated "called" 528 times, "cried" 98 times, "read" 38 times, and "proclaim" 36 times, in addition to other miscellaneous words in the KJV.[35]
• In the first two chapters, "call" occurs eight times in Genesis 1:5, 1:8, 1:10, 2:19, 2:20, and 2:23. Typically, a name is called out.
• This is the first occurrence of *echâd* (Strong's 0259), here translated "one." *Echâd* occurs 952 times in the Old Testament and is translated "one" 687 times, "first" 36 times, "another" 35 times, "other" 30 times, and "any" 18 times, in addition to other miscellaneous words in the KJV.[36]

1:6A. And say/God/be/expanse/in middle/the water/and be/cause to separate/between/water/to water. (LHEIB)

1:6B. And say/God/be/expanse/in middle/the water/and be/<u>to separate</u>/between/ water/to water.

1:6C. And God said, "Be[01961] [an] expanse[07549] in [the] middle[08432] [of] the water, and [it] be[01961] to separate[0914] between[0996] water [above from] to water [below]."

1:6D. And God said, "<u>There is</u> an expanse in the middle of the water, and it <u>exists</u> to separate between water *above* from water *below*."

> This verse is traditionally translated:
> • And God said, Let there be a firmament in the midst of the waters, and let it divide the waters from the waters. (KJV)
> • And God said, Let there be a firmament in the midst of the water, and let it be a division between water and water, and it was so. (Septuagint[37])

Genesis 1:6 begins the second day narrative, traditionally explained as when God created an expanse and separated the waters. This interpretation is driven by more than twenty-two hundred years of errant young-Earth creation theology embedded within the Septuagint. In this verse, the Hebrew verb *hâyâh* (Strong's 01961) occurs twice. The first *hâyâh* (יהי) is translated "let there be" and the second (ויהי) is translated "and let" in the KJV. Both occurrences are traditionally assigned a jussive verb state.[38] When *hâyâh* is treated as a "jussive/command" verb, the word "let" becomes a part of the translation. The treatment of *hâyâh* as a command verb is misleading and turns a simple declarative statement of God into a command.

Exemplar creation explains Genesis 1:6 as a statement by God about Earth's atmosphere. The sky is a clear expanse that has existed for many years. Nothing is being moved around, separated, or reorganized. The complete absence of dynamic Hebrew verbs in Genesis 1:6 shows God is not creating, making, forming, planting, growing, or building anything.

Exemplar creation views Genesis 1:6 as a declarative statement, rather than a command. This is the second of seven verses in Genesis 1:3, 6, 9, 11, 14, 20, and 24 that start with the expression, "And God said." As pointed out in the discussion of Genesis 1:3, when God speaks, a command does not necessarily follow. Based on analysis given in Chapter 5 and Appendix B, we can reject claims that Genesis 1:6 must be a command.

In the *exemplar* translation, the first *hâyâh* (יהי) is translated "there is" and the second *hâyâh* (ויהי) is translated "and exists." The structure of this verse and the occurrence of *hâyâh* in two places are similar to Genesis 1:3. See Chapter 5 for additional discussion of the verb *hâyâh*.

> • The word *râqîya* (Strong's 07549) occurs 17 times in the Old Testament and is consistently translated "firmament" in the KJV.[39] The word "expanse" in the ESV, NASB, and NIV is more descriptive and used in the *exemplar* translation.

1:7A. And make/God/the expanse/and separate/between/the waters/which/from under/to the expanse/and between/the waters/which/from over/to the expanse/and be so. (LHEIB)

1:7C. And God [is the one who] make^{06213} the expanse^{07549} and separate^{0914} between^{0996} the waters which from under to the expanse^{07549} and between^{0996} the waters which from over^{05921} to the expanse^{07549}. And [it] be^{01961} so^{03651}.

1:7D. And God *is the one who* made the expanse and separated between the waters under the expanse and between the waters over the expanse. And *it* <u>was</u> so.

This verse is traditionally translated: "And God made the firmament, and divided the waters which were under the firmament from the waters which were above the firmament: and it was so." (KJV)

In orthodox translations, God repeats himself in four separate instances in Genesis 1:6–7, 1:14–16, 1:20–21, and 1:24–25. These purported repetitive creative events show the fallacy of traditional interpretations. In Genesis 1:6, God allegedly speaks the expanse into existence and then needlessly repeats the act in Genesis 1:7.

To believe Earth's atmosphere was created on the second day strongly conflicts with general revelation in regard to time. There is overwhelming evidence that our atmosphere has existed for more than 100,000 years. An incorrect explanation of the time issue makes the Genesis creation story equivalent to pagan mythology. Scientific evidence discussed in Chapter 4 supports an old age for the Earth and its atmosphere significantly beyond 4004 BC.

Exemplar creation explains Genesis 1:7 as occurring in a chronological sequence of events. God made the expanse prior to Genesis 1:3. On the second day in Genesis 1:6, God describes the expanse as separating water from water. In Genesis 1:7, God is identified as the one who made the expanse. Since the expanse is described as existing in Genesis 1:6, there is no need for God to make the expanse in Genesis 1:7.

This is the first occurrence of the Hebrew word *âsâh* (Strong's 06213), here translated "made." *Âsâh* can indicate many different types of action. The basic meaning if *âsâh* is "do;" however, "made" is a legitimate translation in this verse. See Chapter 5 for additional discussion of this word.

- In the first two chapters, the Hebrew word *âsâh* (Strong's 06213) occurs twelve times in Genesis 1:7, 1:11, 1:12, 1:16, 1:25, 1:26, 1:31, 2:2, 2:3, 2:4, and 2:18, and translated "made, make, making, and did" in the *exemplar* translation.
- This is the first occurrence of the term "and *it* was so" which occurs in Genesis 1:7, 1:9, 1:11, 1:15, 1:24, 1:30; Judges 6:38; 2 Kings 15:2, and Amos 5:14.[40]

1:8A. And call/God/to the expanse/heaven/and be evening/and be morning/day/ second. (LHEIB)

1:8C. And God call^{07121} to the expanse^{07549} heaven^{08064}. And evening be^{01961} and morning be^{01961} second day^{03117}.

1:8D. And God called the expanse "<u>sky</u>." And evening <u>was</u>, and morning <u>was</u>—second day.

This verse is traditionally translated: "And God called the firmament Heaven. And the evening and the morning were the second day." (KJV)

In the *exemplar* translation, the Hebrew word *shâmayim* (Strong's 08064) is translated "sky." This verse is obviously referring to the Earth's atmosphere. The expanse has water above and water below as described in Genesis 1:7. The word *shâmayim,* as used by the Hebrews in the Old Testament, could refer to: (1) The sky where birds flew and from which rain fell. (2) The cosmic heavens where the Sun, Moon, and stars were. (3) Heaven as the abode of God. See Chapter 5 for additional discussion of this word.

1:9A. And say/God/be gathered/the waters/from under/the heaven/to place/one/and be seen/the dry ground/and be so. (LHEIB)
1:9B. And say/God/<u>wait</u>/the waters/from under/the <u>sky</u>/to place/one/<u>and is seen</u>/the dry ground/and be so.
1:9C. And God said, "The waters from under the sky^{08064} wait^{06960} [in] to one place^{04725} and the dry ground^{03004} is seen^{07200}. And [it] be^{01961} so^{03651}.
1:9D. And God said, "The waters under the sky wait in one place and the dry ground is seen." And *it* <u>was</u> so.

This verse has been translated:
• And God said, "Let the waters under the heaven be gathered together unto one place, and let the dry land appear: and it was so." (KJV)
• And God said, "Let the water that is under the sky be gathered into one gathering, and let the dry land appear." And it became so. And the water that was under the sky was gathered into their gatherings, and the dry land appeared. (Septuagint[41])

Genesis 1:9 begins the third day narrative, traditionally explained as when God commanded the waters to separate from dry land to form the oceans and seas. The Hebrew word *qâvâh* (Strong's 06960) is translated "let be gathered together" and *râ'âh* (Strong's 07200) is translated "let appear" in the KJV. Both are traditionally considered "command" verbs and assigned a jussive verb state.[42] When *qâvâh* and *râ'âh* are treated as "jussive/command" verbs, the word "let" becomes a part of the translation. This interpretation is misleading and turns a simple declarative statement of God into a command.

In Genesis 1:9, the traditional translation of *qâvâh* (Strong's 06960) as "let be gathered together" is illegitimate. The Hebrew text of the Old Testament strongly supports the correct translation of *qâvâh* as "wait." See Chapter 5 for a discussion of this word.

As shown above, the Septuagint poorly translates the Hebrew into Greek, and we can see the language has clearly been expanded. An entirely new last sentence has been added to this verse, with an emphasis on the "gathering" of the waters. The Septuagint illustrates the influence of errant theology on Bible translation.

The Hebrew word *râ'âh* (Strong's 07200) can be legitimately translated several different ways, but in Genesis 1:9 is best translated "seen" rather than "appear." *Râ'âh* is translated "see, saw, seen, seest, and seeing" 67% of the time in the KJV and as "appear" only 5% of the time. Use of the word "appear" in this verse is misleading, since it implies ground is being thrust upward out of the water. The word "seen" more accurately describes this passive scene.

Exemplar creation explains Genesis 1:9 as a statement by God about the Earth's water and land. The waters are tranquilly waiting in one place and dry ground is visible. Earth's land masses and oceans have been in their respective positions for many years. Land is not being uplifted, nor are the waters being gathered together on the third day. The absence of required Hebrew verbs in Genesis 1:9–13 shows God is not creating, making, forming, planting, growing, or building anything.

Exemplar creation views Genesis 1:9 as a declarative statement rather than a command. This is the third of seven verses in Genesis 1:3, 6, 9, 11, 14, 20, and 24 that start with the expression, "And God said." As pointed out in the discussion of Genesis 1:3, when God speaks a command does not necessarily follow. Based on analysis given in Chapter 5 and Appendix B, we can reject claims that Genesis 1:9 must be a command.

- The word *râ'âh* (Strong's 07200), here translated "see," is found nine times in the first two chapters of Genesis in 1:4, 1:9, 1:10, 1:12, 1:18, 1:21, 1:25, 1:31, and 2:19. Hebrew words of various spelling, based on the root (ראה), occur approximately 1,313 times in the Old Testament and are translated "see, saw, seen, seest, seeing" 879 times, "look" 104 times, "behold" 83 times, "shew" 68 times, and "appear" 66 times, in addition to other miscellaneous words in the KJV.[43]
- The word *yabbâshâh* (Strong's 03004), here translated "dry ground," is found in Genesis in 1:9 and 1:10 of the creation account. *Yabbâshâh* occurs 14 times in the Old Testament[44] and can readily be translated dry ground in every single occurrence.

1:10A. And call/God/to the dry ground/land/and to collection/the waters/call/seas/ and see/God/that good. (LHEIB)
1:10C. And God call[07121] to the dry ground[03004] land[0776] and call[07121] to the collection[04723] [of] waters seas. And God see that [it was] good.
1:10D. And God called the dry ground "land" and called the collection of waters "seas." And God saw that *it was* good.

This verse has been translated:
• And God called the dry land Earth; and the gathering together of the waters called he seas: and God saw that it was good. (KJV)
• God called the dry ground "land," and the gathered waters he called "seas." And God saw that it was good. (NIV)

Traditional young-Earth creation theology uses this verse to support the belief that God "gathered the waters" in Genesis 1:9. However, the Hebrew word *miqveh* (Strong's 04723) is best translated "collection," rather than "gathering together." Chapter 5 discusses the translation of this word in detail. The Hebrew text of the Bible and general revelation support "collection" as a superior word choice. Based on scientific evidence, the continents and oceans have been in their current positions for millions of years.

In Genesis 1:10, God continues to call out names. The Hebrew word *erets* (Strong's 0776) is translated "land" in the *exemplar* translation rather than "Earth" in the KJV. God specifically calls (identifies) dry ground not covered by water as "land" and the collected waters as "seas." Most orthodox translations do not properly distinguish between "dry ground" (Strong's 03004) and "land" (Strong's 0776) in this verse. As quoted above, the phrase "God called the dry ground 'land'" is accurately rendered in the New International Version.

1:11A. And say/God/produce/the earth/green/plant/give seed/seed/tree/fruit/make/ fruit/according to kind/which/seed in/on the earth/and be so. (LHEIB)
1:11B. And say/God/sprouting/the land/sprouts/plant/seeding/seed/tree/fruit/make/ fruit/to kind/which/seed in/over the land/and be so.
1:11C. And God say, "The land^{0776} [is] sprouting^{01876} sprouts^{01877}: plants^{06212} seeding^{02232} seed^{02233} [and the] fruit^{06529} tree make^{06213} fruit^{06529} to which kind [is] in [the] seed^{02233} over^{05921} the land^{0776}." And [it] be^{01961} so^{03651}.
1:11D. And God said, "The land is sprouting sprouts: plants seeding seeds and the fruit trees making fruit—to which kind is in the seed—over the land." And *it* <u>was</u> so.

This verse is traditionally translated:
• And God said, Let the earth bring forth grass, the herb yielding seed, and the fruit tree yielding fruit after his kind, whose seed is in itself, upon the earth: and it was so. (KJV)
• And God said, "Let the earth sprout vegetation, plants yielding seed, and fruit trees bearing fruit in which is their seed, each according to its kind, on the earth." And it was so. (ESV)

Genesis 1:11 is traditionally explained as when God created all plants on the third day by speaking them into existence. The Hebrew word *dâshâ* (Strong's 01876) is traditionally assigned a jussive verb state[45] and translated "let bring forth" in the KJV. When *dâshâ* is treated as a "jussive/command" verb, the word "let" becomes a part of the translation. This interpretation is misleading and turns a simple declarative statement of God into a command.

Exemplar creation explains Genesis 1:11 as a statement by God about Earth's vegetation. Plants and trees cover the land, and their seeds have been sprouting for many years. Nothing is being created on the third day. The absence of required Hebrew verbs in Genesis 1:9–13 shows God is not creating, making, forming, planting, growing, or building anything.

Exemplar creation views Genesis 1:11 as a declarative statement rather than a command. This is the fourth of seven verses in Genesis 1:3, 6, 9, 11, 14, 20, and 24 that start with the expression, "And God said." As pointed out in the discussion of Genesis 1:3, when God speaks a command does not necessarily follow. Based on analysis given in Chapter 5 and Appendix B, we can reject claims that Genesis 1:11 must be a command.

Genesis 1:11 and 1:12 appear to be almost identical verses, with the only significant difference being the word *dâshâ* (Strong's 01876) in Genesis 1:11 and *yâtsâ* (Strong's 03318) in Genesis 1:12. In the *exemplar* translation, *dâshâ* and *yâtsâ* are respectively translated "sprouting" and "growing." In these two verses, God is describing the sprouting of sprouts and the growing of sprouts—two completely different mechanisms of plant development.

This is the first occurrence of *cognate accusatives* in Genesis. In English, some basic words can be modified and used as either a noun or verb. For example, "run" can refer to running (a verb) or a runner (a noun). We could say, "The running runner is moving very fast." Cognate accusatives in the Hebrew text often appear as verb and noun combinations of the same basic word. In Genesis 1:11 the land is "sprouting sprouts" and the plants are "seeding seeds." Other cognate accusatives when literally translated are "swarming swarmers" in Genesis 1:20, "flying fliers" in Genesis 1:20, and "moving movers" in Genesis 1:26.

• The words *dâshâ* and *deshe* (sprouting sprouts) are used together in Genesis 1:11 as cognate accusatives.
• The Hebrew word *dâshâ,* here translated "sprouting" and identified as Strong's 01876, is based on the Hebrew root (דשא). *Dâshâ* is used as a verb 2 times in Genesis 1:11 and Joel 2:22 in the Old Testament.[46]
• The word *deshe,* here translated "sprouts" and identified as Strong's 01877, is also based on the Hebrew root (דשא). *Deshe* is used as a noun 14 times and is translated "grass" 7 times, "herb" 6 times, and "green" 1 time in the KJV. *Deshe* occurs in Gen. 1:11, 1:12; Deut. 32:2; 2 Sam. 23:4; 2 Kings 19:26; Job 6:5, 38:27; Psalm 23:2, 37:2; Prov. 27:25; Isaiah 15:6, 37:27, 66:14, and Jer. 14:5 in the Old Testament.[47] *Deshe* refers to tender vegetation, green growth, or sprouts that have just emerged from the ground.

• The words *zâra* and *zera* (seeding seeds) are used together in Genesis 1:11, 12, and 29 as cognate accusatives.

• The word *zâra,* here translated "seeding" and identified as Strong's 02232, is based on the Hebrew root (זרע). *Zâra* is used as a verb 56 times in the Old Testament and is translated "sow" 47 times and "yielding" 3 times, in addition to other miscellaneous words in the KJV.[48]

• The word *zera,* here translated "seed" and identified as Strong's 02233, is also based on the root (זרע). *Zera* is used as a noun 229 times in the Old Testament and is translated "seed" 221 times in addition to other miscellaneous words in the KJV.[49]

• This is the first occurrence of the word *eseb* (Strong's 06212), here translated "plant." *Eseb* occurs 33 times in the Old Testament and is translated "herb" 17 times and "grass" 16 times in the KJV.[50] *Eseb* is found in Genesis 1:11, 1:12, 1:29, 1:30, and 2:5 and is translated "plant" in the first two chapters of Genesis in the *exemplar* translation. The word "plant" is more inclusive of Earth's growing things and superior to "grass" or "herb." Elsewhere, the term "plant of the field" is used to indicate plants used for food. In other instances, the terms "plants of the mountains" and "plants of the earth" refer to wild plants.

1:12A. And cause to go forth/the earth/green/plant/give seed/seed/according to kind/ and tree/make fruit/which/seed in/according to kind/and saw/God/that good. (LHEIB)

1:12B. And is growing/the land/sprouts/plant/seeding/seed/to kind/and tree/make fruit/which/seed in/to kind/and saw/God/that good.

1:12C. "And the land^{0776} is growing^{03318} sprouts^{01877}: plant^{06212} seeding^{02232} seed^{02233} [according] to [their] kind, and [the] tree make^{06213} fruit^{06529} in which seed^{02233} [is] to kind." And God saw that [it was] good.

1:12D. "And the land is growing sprouts: plants seeding seeds *according* to *their* kind, and the trees making fruit—in which seed is to kind." And God saw that *it was* good.

This verse is traditionally translated: "And the earth brought forth grass, and herb yielding seed after his kind, and the tree yielding fruit, whose seed was in itself, after his kind: and God saw that it was good." (KJV)

Traditionally, Genesis 1:11–12 are explained as two repetitious verses, albeit with some slight variation. In Genesis 1:11, God commands the earth to bring forth grass, herbs, and fruit trees. In Genesis 1:12, God describes the result of his previous command. The writer of Genesis tends to repeat himself.

Exemplar creation explains Genesis 1:11–12 as two different aspects of plant maturation that involve seed sprouting and sprout growth. Both processes are made possible by the information and complex structure within seeds.

To believe all plants were created on the third day strongly conflicts with general revelation in regard to time. Ice core data indicate plant life has existed on Earth for more than 100,000 years. An incorrect explanation of the time issue tends to make the Genesis creation story appear as myth to the scientific community. Evidence discussed in Chapter 4 supports an old age for the Earth and its plant life.

- The word *yâtsâ* (Strong's 03318), here translated "growing" (bring forth) occurs 1,069 times in the Old Testament and is translated ". . . out" in the sense of going out 518 times, ". . . forth" in the sense of going forth 411 times, "bring" 24 times, "come" 24 times and other miscellaneous words in the KJV.[51]

1:13A. And be evening/and be morning/day/third. (LHEIB)
1:13C. And evening be^{01961} and morning be^{01961} third day^{03117}.
1:13D. And evening <u>was</u>, and morning <u>was</u>—third day.

1:14A. And say/God/be/light source/in dome/the heaven/cause to separate/between/ the day/and between/the night/and be/as sign/and as appointed time/and as day/and year. (LHEIB)
1:14B. And say/God/be/<u>luminaries</u>/in <u>expanse</u>/the heaven/<u>to distinguish</u>/between/the day/and between/the night/and be/as sign/and as appointed time/and as day/and year.
1:14C. And God say, "Be^{01961} luminaries^{03974} in [the] expanse^{07549} [of] the heaven^{08064} to distinguish^{0914} between^{0996} the day^{03117} and between^{0996} the night, and [they] be^{01961} <u>for</u> [a] sign^{0226} and <u>for</u> appointed times^{04150} and <u>for</u> days^{03117} and years^{08141}."
1:14D. And God said, "<u>There are</u> luminaries in the expanse of the heavens to distinguish between the day and between the night, and *they* <u>are</u> for a sign for appointed times and for days and years."

1:15A. And be/as light source/in dome/the heaven/give light/on the earth/and be so. (LHEIB)
1:15B. And be/as <u>luminaries</u>/in <u>expanse</u>/the heaven/<u>to give light</u>/<u>over the earth</u>/and be so.
1:15C. "And as luminaries^{03974} be^{01961} in [the] expanse^{07549} [of] the heaven^{08064} to give light^{0215} over^{05921} the earth^{0776}." And [it] be^{01961} so^{03651}.
1:15D. "And luminaries <u>exist</u> in the expanse of the heavens to give light over the Earth." And *it* <u>was</u> so.

Genesis 1:14–15 are traditionally translated:
- 1:14 And God said, Let there be lights in the firmament of the heaven to divide the day from the night; and let them be for signs, and for seasons, and for days, and years: (KJV)
- 1:15 And let them be for lights in the firmament of the heaven to give light upon the earth: and it was so. (KJV)
- God spoke: "Lights! Come out! Shine in Heaven's sky! Separate Day from

Night. Mark seasons and days and years, Lights in Heaven's sky to give light to Earth." And there it was. (*The Message*) [This version grossly mistranslates the Hebrew text]

Genesis 1:14 begins the fourth day narrative, traditionally explained as when God created the Sun, Moon, and stars by speaking them into existence. Why create a "special light source" on the first day and then replace it with the Sun on the fourth day? Creating the Sun on the first day is more logical, shows superior planning, and better use of available resources. There is no mention in scripture of the alleged "special light source" being removed by God or replaced by the Sun.

In Genesis 1:14, the Hebrew verb *hâyâh* (Strong's 01961) occurs two times. In the KJV, the first occurrence of *hâyâh* (יהי) is translated "Let there be" and the second (והיו) is translated "and let them be." The Septuagint, KJV, and most other orthodox translations treat both occurrences as "jussive/command" verbs. When *hâyâh* is treated as a "jussive/command" verb, the word "let" becomes a part of the translation. In contrast, the *Old Testament Parsing Guide* assigns a jussive verb state to the first occurrence, but not the second;[52] therefore, the second occurrence of *hâyâh* is not included in Table 5.4.

In Genesis 1:15, the Hebrew verb *hâyâh* (Strong's 01961) also occurs two times. In the KJV, the first occurrence of *hâyâh* (והיו) is translated "And let them be" and the second (ויהי) is translated "and it was." The Septuagint, KJV, and other orthodox translations treat the first occurrence as a "jussive/command" verb through use of the word "let." However, the *Old Testament Parsing Guide* does not assign a jussive verb state to any verbs in this verse,[53] and they are not included in Table 5.4.

Exemplar creation explains Genesis 1:14–15 as a statement by God about the Sun, Moon, and stars. They have existed for many years and nothing is being created. The complete absence of dynamic Hebrew verbs in Genesis 1:14–15 shows God is not creating, making, forming, planting, growing, or building anything.

Exemplar creation views Genesis 1:14 as a declarative statement, rather than a command. This is the fifth of seven verses in Genesis 1:3, 6, 9, 11, 14, 20, and 24 that start with the expression, "And God said." As pointed out in the discussion of Genesis 1:3, when God speaks a command does not necessarily follow. Based on analysis given in Chapter 5 and Appendix B, we can reject claims that Genesis 1:14–15 must be a command.

In the *exemplar* translation, the stative English words "are" and "exist" are translated from the Hebrew verb *hâyâh* (Strong's 01961), meaning primarily to "be" or "exist." In Genesis 1:14–15, this verb denotes the existence of luminaries and nothing more. No dynamic action is occurring. See Chapter 5 for additional discussion of the verb *hâyâh*.

1:16A. And make/God/two/the light source/the great/the light source/the great/as authority/the day/and the light source/the small/as authority/the night/and/the stars. (LHEIB)

1:16B. And do/God/two/the luminaries/the great/the luminary/the great/to rule/the day/and the luminary/the small/to rule/the night/and/the stars.

1:16C. And God [is the one who] do^{06213} the two great^{01419} luminaries^{03974}: the great^{01419} luminary^{03974} to rule^{04475} the day^{03117} and the small^{06996} luminary^{03974} to rule^{04475} the night and the stars.

1:16D. And God *is the one who* <u>made</u> two great luminaries: the greater luminary to rule the day and the smaller luminary to rule the night and the stars.

> This verse has been translated a number of ways:
> • God made two big lights, the larger to take charge of Day, The smaller to be in charge of Night; and he made the stars. (*The Message*) [This version grossly mistranslates the Hebrew text.]
> • And God made two great lights; the greater light to rule the day, and the lesser light to rule the night: *he made* the stars also. (KJV) [The translators put the words "he made" in italics to show they are added to the Hebrew text. The Hebrew letter vav (ו), normally translated "and," is translated "also" in this instance. The word order is reversed from "and the stars" to "the stars also," which makes an unusual translation.]
> • God made the two great lights, the greater light to govern the day, and the lesser light to govern the night; {He made} the stars also. (NASB) [The words "He made" are in brackets to clearly identify them as additions to the Hebrew text.]
> • And the Lord made the two great luminaries: the greater luminary to rule in the day; and the smaller luminary to rule in the night, and the stars. (English translation of the Targum of Onkelos by J. W. Etheridge, 1862)
> • And God made two great lights: a greater light to rule the day; and a lesser light to rule the night: and the stars. (Douay-Rheims, 1899)
> • And God made the two great luminaries, the great luminary for rulership of the day and the lesser luminary for rulership of the night, and the stars. (Septuagint[54])
> • God made the two great lights: the greater light to govern the day, the smaller light to govern the night, and the stars. (New Jerusalem Bible, 1985)

Genesis 1:16 is traditionally explained as when God made the Sun, Moon, and stars on the fourth day. A careful reading of this verse reveals that only two lights are mentioned as being made on the fourth day—the greater light and the lesser light. All translations of this verse specifically state, "And God made two great lights." Stars are mentioned as existing on the fourth day, but not created.

This verse illustrates the error of treating Genesis 1:14 and 1:16 as creative acts. God allegedly commands the luminaries into existence in Genesis 1:14 and then needlessly repeats the act in Genesis 1:16. In orthodox translations, God repeats himself in four separate instances in Genesis 1:6–7, 1:14–16, 1:20–21, and 1:24–25.

Essentially all orthodox translations of the Bible struggle with Genesis 1:16 because of their faulty explanatory framework. Every translation scheme possible, short of deliberately falsifying the text, is used to support the belief that God created the stars on the fourth day. Of the above seven translations, the first three incorrectly attempt to show how God created the stars on the fourth day, while the last four properly translate the Hebrew text. As shown above, the Etheridge English version of the Targum of Onkelos (a Hebrew to Aramaic translation probably before 200 AD), the Douay-Rheims Bible (based on Jerome's translation from Hebrew to Latin in 405 AD), the Pietersma English translation of the Septuagint, and the New Jerusalem Bible are the most accurate.

Genesis 1:16 clearly states the function of the two identified luminaries—to rule. The larger luminary rules the day and the smaller luminary rules over the night and the stars. The Sun totally dominates the day with its brightness. The Moon, as the brightest object at night, dominates the dark night and the faint stars.

Exemplar creation explains Genesis 1:16 as occurring in a chronological sequence of events. God made the Sun, Moon, and stars prior to Genesis 1:3. On the fourth day in Genesis 1:14–15, God describes the Sun and Moon as existing to give light on the Earth. In Genesis 1:16, God is firmly identified as maker of the Sun and Moon. Since the Sun and Moon are described as existing in Genesis 1:14–15, there is no need for God to make them in Genesis 1:16.

To believe the Sun, Moon, and stars were created on the fourth day strongly conflicts with general revelation in regard to time. Starlight from distant stars and galaxies is millions of years old. An incorrect explanation of time tends to make the Genesis creation story appear mythological to most scientists. Overwhelming scientific evidence, discussed in Chapter 4, supports an old age for the universe, and indicates the Sun, Moon, and stars are significantly older than the 4004 BC creation date proposed by Archbishop James Ussher.

1:17A. And place/they/God/in dome/the heaven/give light/upon the earth. (LHEIB)
1:17B. And gave/they/God/in expanse/the heaven/to give light/over the earth.
1:17C. And God gave[05414] they in [the] expanse[07549] [of] the heaven[08064] to give light[0215] over[05921] the Earth[0776].
1:17D. And God gave them in the expanse of the heavens to give light over the Earth.

This verse is traditionally translated: "And God set them in the firmament of the heaven to give light upon the earth." (KJV)

Exemplar creation explains this verse as a companion to the previous verse. In Genesis 1:16 and 1:17, God is identified respectively as the *maker* and *giver* of these luminaries.

The KJV translation of this verse shows the influence of traditional young-Earth creation theology. The reader is led to believe God "set" or "placed" the Sun and Moon in the heavens on the fourth day. While "set" is a legitimate translation of *nâthan*, "gave" is a superior word choice in this instance.

The Hebrew word *nâthan* (Strong's 05414) has several legitimate shades of meaning. *Nâthan* is translated "gave" in the KJV 54% of the time and "set" only 5% of the time. *Nâthan* also occurs in Genesis 1:29, when God *gave* plants to man for food and in Genesis 3:6, when Eve *gave* the fruit from the tree of knowledge of good and evil to Adam. In Genesis 12:7, God *gave* the land of Canaan to Abraham. In the *exemplar* translation, the more common "gave" rather than "set" in used.

- This is the first occurrence of the Hebrew word *nâthan* (Strong's 05414), here translated "gave." *Nâthan* occurs 2,008 times in the Old Testament and is translated "give" 1078 times, "put" 191, "deliver" 174 times, "made" 107 times, "set" 99 times, and "up" 26 times, in addition to other miscellaneous words in the KJV.[55] In the first two chapters, *nâthan* occurs in Genesis 1:17 and 1:29.
- The Hebrew verb *ôwr* (Strong's 0215), here translated "give light," occurs in Genesis 1:15 and 17. *Ôwr* occurs as a noun (Strong's 0216) in Genesis 1:3, 4, 5, and 18, where it is translated "light."[56]

1:18A. And to rule/over the day/and over the night/and cause to separate/between/the light/and between/the darkness/and see/God/that good. (LHEIB)

1:18B. And to rule/in the day/and in the night/and to distinguish/between/the light/ and between/the darkness/and see/God/that good.

1:18C. And to rule[04910] in the day[03117] and in the night and to distinguish[0914] between[0996] the light[0216] and between[0996] the darkness[02822]. And God saw that [it was] good.

1:18D. And to rule in the day and in the night and to distinguish between the light and between the darkness. And God saw that *it was* good.

This verse has been translated:
- And to rule over the day and over the night, and to divide the light from the darkness: and God saw that it was good. (KJV)
- And to rule in the day and in the night, and to distinguish between light and darkness. And the Lord saw that it was good. (Targum of Onkelos, English translation by J. W. Etheridge, 1862)

The Hebrew word *bâdal* (Strong's 0914) can be legitimately translated several different ways, but in Genesis 1:18 it is best translated "distinguish" rather than "divide." The Sun and Moon do not divide light and darkness—they are incapable of dividing anything. The Sun distinguishes the day (light) and the Moon distinguishes the night (dark). In the *exemplar* translation, *bâdal* is translated "distinguish" in Genesis 1:4, 14, and 18 and "separate" in Genesis 1:6 and 7. As shown above, the English translation of the Targum of Onkelos by J. W. Etheridge correctly translates *bâdal* in Genesis 1:18 as "distinguish."

1:19A. And be evening/and be morning/day/fourth. (LHEIB)
1:19C. And evening be[01961] and morning be[01961] fourth day[03117].
1:19D. And evening <u>was</u>, and morning <u>was</u>—fourth day.

1:20A. And say/God/swarm/the waters/swarm/creature/living/and bird/fly/above the earth/across surface/dome/the sky. (LHEIB)
1:20B. And say/God/swarm/the waters/swarm/creature/living/and <u>flier</u>/fly/<u>over the land</u>/over surface/<u>expanse</u>/the sky.
1:20C. And God said, "The waters swarm[08317] [with] swarm[08318] [of] living[02416] creature[05315] and flier[05775] fly[05774] over[05921] the land[0776] [and] over[05921] [the] surface[06440] [of the] expanse[07549] [of] the sky[08064]."
1:20D. And God said, "The waters swarm *with* swarms of living creatures, and fliers flying over the land and over the surface of the expanse of the sky."

> This verse has been translated:
> • And God said, Let the waters bring forth abundantly the moving creature that hath life, and fowl that may fly above the earth in the open firmament of heaven. (KJV)
> • And God said, "Let the waters bring forth creeping things among living creatures and birds flying on the earth against the firmament of the sky." (Septuagint[57])
> • And God said, "Let the waters swarm with swarms of living creatures, and let birds fly above the earth across the expanse of the heavens." (ESV)
> • And God said, Let the waters swarm with swarms of living creatures, and let birds fly above the earth in the open firmament of heaven. (ASV)
> • God said, "Let the waters swarm with swarms of living creatures, and let birds fly above the earth in the open expanse of sky." (World English Bible)

Genesis 1:20 begins the fifth day narrative, traditionally explained as when God created marine life and flying creatures by speaking them into existence. In all orthodox translations, the Hebrew word *shârats* (Strong's 08317) and *ûwph* (Strong's 05774) are assigned a jussive verb state.[58] When *shârats* and *ûwph* are treated as "jussive/command" verbs, the word "let" becomes a part of the translation. This interpretation is misleading and turns a simple declarative statement of God into a command.

The expression "let the waters bring forth" in the Septuagint and KJV is a gross mistranslation and makes God's method of creation appear to be an evolutionary process. In fact, some theistic evolutionists interpret this verse to say God used evolution throughout millions of years as His method of creating marine life. From their viewpoint, the waters (primordial soup) brought forth (evolved) living creatures. As shown above, the English Standard Version, American Standard Version, and World English Bible more accurately translate this expression as "the waters swarm with swarms of living creatures."

Exemplar creation explains Genesis 1:20 as a statement by God about Earth's abundant marine life and flying creatures. The pure water and air support a multitude of biological species. However, nothing is being created. The complete absence of the necessary dynamic Hebrew verbs in Genesis 1:20 shows God is not creating, making, forming, planting, growing, or building anything.

Exemplar creation views Genesis 1:20 as a declarative statement rather than a command. This is the sixth of seven verses in Genesis 1:3, 6, 9, 11, 14, 20, and 24 that start with the expression, "And God said." As pointed out in the discussion of Genesis 1:3, when God speaks a command does not necessarily follow. Based on analysis given in Chapter 5 and Appendix B, we can reject claims that Genesis 1:20 must be a command.

This is the first occurrence of the Hebrew word *ôwph* (Strong's 05775), here translated "fliers." This same word also occurs in Genesis 1:21, 22, 26, 28, 30, 2:19, and 2:20, where it is translated fliers in all instances in the *exemplar* translation. The word *ôwph* properly applies to all flying or winged creatures, including bats, birds, and insects. Leviticus 11:20, 21, and 23 mention an *ôwph* with four legs. Other Hebrew words used to identify flying creatures are *tsippôwr* (Strong's 06833) translated "bird," *nesher* (Strong's 05404) translated "eagle", and *ôrêb* (Strong's 06158) translated "raven."

• The words *shârats* and *sherets* (swarming swarmers) are used together in Genesis 1:20, 7:21; Leviticus 21:29, 11:41, 11:42, and 11:43 as cognate accusatives. (See Genesis 1:11 in this chapter for a discussion of cognate accusatives.)
• The word *shârats,* here translated "swarm" and identified as Strong's 08317, is based on the Hebrew root (שׁרץ). *Shârats* is used as a verb 14 times in the Old Testament and is translated "creep" 6 times, "bring forth abundantly" 5 times, "move" 1 time, "breed abundantly" 1 time, and "increase abundantly" 1 time in the KJV.[59]
• The word *sherets,* here translated "swarms" and identified as Strong's 08318, is also based on the Hebrew root (שׁרץ). *Sherets* is used as a noun 15 times in the Old Testament and is translated "creeping thing" 11 times, "creep" 2 times, "creature" 1 time, and "move" 1 time in the KJV.[60] Swarming things can be found on land, in the air, or in water. In Leviticus 11:29, swarming things that live on *land* are mentioned. In Leviticus 11:20–21, swarming things can fly in the *air*. In Leviticus 11:10, swarming things inhabit the *waters*.
• The words *ûwph* and *ôwph* (flying fliers) are used together in Genesis 1:20 and Hosea 9:11 as cognate acusatives.[61]

• The word *ûwph,* here translated "flying" and identified as Strong's 05774, is based on the Hebrew root (עוּף). *Ûwph* is used as a verb approximately 30 times in the Old Testament and is translated as some form of "fly" 24 times in addition to other miscellaneous translations in the KJV.[62]

• The word *ôwph,* here translated "fliers" and identified as Strong's 05775, is also based on the root (עוּף). *Ôwph* is used as a noun approximately 71 times in the Old Testament and is translated "fowl" 59 times and "bird" 9 times, in addition to other miscellaneous translations in the KJV.[63]

1:21A. And create/God/the sea monsters/the great/and/every kind of creature/the living/the move/which/swarm/the waters/according to kind/and/every kind of bird/wing/according to kind/and see/God/that good. (LHEIB)

1:21B. And create/God/the <u>reptiles</u>/the great/and/<u>every creature</u>/the living/the move/which/swarm/the waters/<u>to kind</u>/and/<u>every flier</u>/wing/<u>to kind</u>/and see/God/that good.

1:21C. And God [is the one who] create[01254] the great[01419] reptiles[08577] and every[03605] move[07430] living[02416] creature[05315], [with] which the waters swarm[08317], [according] to [their] kind, and every[03605] wing[03671] flier[05775] [according] to [its] kind. And God saw that [it was] good.

1:21D. And God *is the one who* created the great reptiles and every moving living creature with which the waters swarm, *according* to *their* kinds, and every winged flier *according* to *its* kind. And God saw that *it was* good.

This verse has been translated:

• And God created great whales, and every living creature that moveth, which the waters brought forth abundantly, after their kind, and every winged fowl after his kind: and God saw that it was good. (KJV)

• So God created the great sea creatures and every living creature that moves, with which the waters swarm, according to their kinds, and every winged bird according to its kind. And God saw that it was good. (ESV)

Traditional explanations have Genesis 1:21 as a virtual repeat of Genesis 1:20. God creates all marine creatures and fliers in Genesis 1:20 by instantly speaking them into existence and then needlessly creates them again for good measure in Genesis 1:21. In both instances, God creates all animals *ex nihilo* (out of nothing). In orthodox translations, God repeats His creative acts in four separate instances in Genesis 1:6–7, 1:14–16, 1:20–21, and 1:24–25.

To believe the great reptiles, marine creatures, and winged fliers were created on the fifth day strongly conflicts with general revelation in regard to time. Evidence supports the existence of marine life on Earth for more than 100,000 years. An incorrect explanation of time makes the Genesis creation story an embarrassment to scientifically minded Bible believers. Evidence discussed in Chapter 4 supports an old age for the Earth and indicates animal life has existed on Earth much longer than 6,000 years.

Exemplar creation explains Genesis 1:21 as occurring in a chronological sequence of events. God created the great reptiles, marine creatures, and winged fliers during an indefinite period of time between Genesis 1:2 and 1:3. On the fifth day in Genesis 1:20, God describes swarming swarms of marine creatures and flying fliers (but no great reptiles). In Genesis 1:21, God is identified as creator of the great reptiles, swarms of marine creatures, and winged fliers. Since marine life and flying creatures are described as existing in Genesis 1:20, there is no need for God to create them in Genesis 1:21.

The Hebrew word *bârâ* (Strong's 01254), here translated "created," occurs first in Genesis 1:1 and not again until Genesis 1:21. "Create" is not used in any verse between Genesis 1:1 and 1:21. If God created things on the first, second, third, and fourth days, then why is the verb "create" not used in describing events on those days? Its absence strongly discredits the traditional interpretation of these verses.

In Genesis 1:20, God describes the existence of marine life and flying creatures on Earth, but not great reptiles. Yet God clearly created great reptiles (in the distant past) as proclaimed in Genesis 1:21. Based on scientific evidence, no great reptiles are mentioned in Genesis 1:20 because they were extinct by time of Moses. When Genesis 1:20 and 1:21 are carefully examined in the proper explanatory framework, they fully harmonize with firm scientific evidence.

The *exemplar* translation renders the Hebrew word *tannîyn* (Strong's 08577) as "reptiles" rather than "whales" found in the KJV. The key to understanding these two words is the description given to Moses' rod when he threw it down. Sometimes his rod was called a *tannîyn,* as described in Exodus 7:9, 10, and 12, while at other times it was called a *nâchâsh,* as in Exodus 4:3 and 7:15. Both words refer to the same animal. When Moses' rod miraculously changed, it was called both a *tannîyn* (reptile as a general term) and a *nâchâsh* (snake as a specific reptile).

The existence of great reptiles mentioned in Genesis 1:21 was unknown to scientists until relatively recently, and their discovery is confirmation of scripture. The great *tannîyn* mentioned in Genesis probably includes both dinosaurs and reptiles. Under the current taxonomic system, dinosaurs are classified separate from reptiles. Through Isaiah 27:1, the *tannîyn* can be connected to the leviathan described by God in Job 41:4.

• This is the first occurrence of the word *tannîyn* (Strong's 08577), here translated "reptiles." *Tannîyn* occurs 28 times in the Old Testament and is translated "dragon" 21 times, "serpent" 3 times, "whale" 3 times, and "sea monster" 1 time in the KJV.[64]

• In Exodus 7:9, 10, and 12 when Moses cast his rod down before Pharaoh it was called a *tannîyn.* Isaiah 27:1 says the *tannîyn* living in the sea will be slain. Psalm 91:13 predicts how a *tannîyn* will be trampled under the feet. Deuteronomy 32:33 references a *tannîyn* with poison. Often *tannîyn* are mentioned in describing a desolate place such as in Job 30:29, Isaiah 34:13, Isaiah 43:20, and Jeremiah 10:22. In general, reptiles such as lizards and snakes live in desolate places rather than towns and villages. *Tanniyn* is the general term given to reptiles.

• The word *nâchâsh* (Strong's 05175) occurs 31 times in the Old Testament and is translated "serpent" in every occurrence in the KJV.[65] *Nâchâsh* is a snake, a specific type of reptile.

• A *nâchâsh* (snake) tempted Eve to sin and was cursed by God to crawl on its belly in Genesis 3:1–14. In Exodus 4:3 and 7:15, Moses' rod turned into a *nâchâsh*. In Numbers 21:6–7, God sent *nâchâsh* among the people to bite them. In Numbers 21:9, Moses made a *nâchâsh* of brass and put the figure on a pole for the people to look at and be saved. In 2 Kings 18:4, Hezekiah destroyed the brass *nâchâsh* the people had been worshiping.

1:22A. And bless/they/God/say/be fruitful/and multiply/and fill/the waters/in the sea/ and the bird/multiply/on the earth. (LHEIB)
1:22C. And God bless they say, "Be fruitful[06509] and multiply[07235] and fill[04390] the waters in the sea and multiply[07235] the flier[05775] on the land[0776]."
1:22D. And God blessed them saying, "Be fruitful and multiply and fill the waters in the seas and multiply the fliers on the land."

God blesses the marine animals and flying creatures that fill the land. He commands them to be fruitful and increase from their present state. This concludes the activities of day five.

• The Hebrew words *râbâh* (Strong's 07235) and *pârâh* (Strong's 06509) are translated "be fruitful and multiply." These two words rhyme in Hebrew, have a very similar meaning and are used to emphasize the idea of reproducing. A similar phrase occurs in Genesis 1:22, 1:28, 8:17, 9:1, 9:7, 47:27; Jeremiah 23:3, and Ezekiel 36:11.[66]

• This is the first occurrence of the word *pârâh* (Strong's 06509), here translated "be fruitful." *Pârâh* occurs 29 times in the Old Testament and is translated "fruitful" 20 times and "increased" 3 times, in addition to other miscellaneous words in the KJV.[67]

• This is the first occurrence of the word *râbâh* (Strong's 07235), here translated "multiply." *Râbâh* occurs 226 times in the Old Testament and is translated "multiply" 74 times, "increase" 40 times, "much" 29 times, "many" 28 times, and "more" 12 times, in addition to other miscellaneous words in the KJV.[68]

1:23A. And be evening/and be morning/day/fifth. (LHEIB)
1:23C. And evening be[01961] and morning be[01961] fifth day[03117].
1:23D. And evening was, and morning was—fifth day.

1:24A. And say/God/bring forth/the earth/creature/living/according to kind/domestic animal/and creeping/and wild animal earth/according to kind/and be so. (LHEIB)

1:24B. And said/God/bring forth/the land/creature/living/to kind/beasts/and moving/ and animal land/to kind/and be so.

1:24C. And God said, "The land[0776] brings forth[03318] living[02416] creature[05315] [according] to [their] kind: beasts[0929] and moving[07431] [things] and animal [of the] land[0776] [according] to [their] kind." And [it] be[01961] so[03651].

1:24D. And God said, "The land brings forth living creatures *according* to *their* kind: beasts and moving *things* and animals of the land, *according* to *their* kind." And *it* <u>was</u> so.

This verse is traditionally translated:

• And God said, Let the earth bring forth the living creature after his kind, cattle, and creeping thing, and beast of the earth after his kind: and it was so. (KJV)

• And God said, "Let the earth bring forth the living creature according to kind: quadrupeds and creeping things and wild animals of the earth according to kind." And it became so. (Septuagint[69])

Genesis 1:24 begins the sixth day narrative, traditionally explained as when God created the land animals by speaking them into existence; an interpretation driven by more than twenty-two hundred years of errant young-Earth creation theology embedded within the Septuagint. The Hebrew word *yâtsâ* (Strong's 03318) is traditionally assigned a jussive verb state[70] and translated "let bring forth" in the KJV. When *yâtsâ* is treated as a "jussive/command" verb, the word "let" becomes a part of the translation. This interpretation is misleading and turns a simple declarative statement into a command.

Exemplar creation explains Genesis 1:24 as a statement by God about Earth's land creatures. The bounty of the land supports a multitude of beasts, moving things, and animals. Nothing is being created. The complete absence of required Hebrew verbs in Genesis 1:24 shows God is not creating, making, forming, planting, growing, or building anything.

Exemplar creation views Genesis 1:24 as a declarative statement rather than a command. This is the last of seven verses in Genesis 1:3, 6, 9, 11, 14, 20, and 24 that start with the expression, "And God said." As pointed out in the discussion of Genesis 1:3, when God speaks a command does not necessarily follow. Based on analysis given in Chapter 5 and Appendix B, we can reject claims that Genesis 1:24 must be a command.

• This is the first occurrence of the Hebrew word (חית) here translated "animal." This word occurs 55 times where it is translated "animal" by *The Lexham Hebrew-English Interlinear Bible.*[71] The KJV uses the term "beast" rather than animal.

1:25A. And make/God/wild animal/the earth/according to kind/and the domestic animal/according to kind/and/all creeping thing/the ground/according to kind/and see/God/that good. (LHEIB)

1:25B. And make/God/<u>animal</u>/the Earth/<u>to kind</u>/and the <u>beasts</u>/<u>to kind</u>/and/<u>every moving</u>/the ground/<u>to kind</u>/and see/God/that good.

1:25C. And God [is the one who] make^{06213} [the] animal [of] the Earth^{0776} [according] to [their] kind: and the beasts^{0929} [according] to [their] kind and every^{03605} moving^{07431} [thing upon] the ground^{0127} [according] to [its] kind. And God saw that [it was] good.

1:25D. And God *is the one who* made the animals of the Earth *according* to *their* kind: the beasts *according* to *their* kind and every moving *thing* upon the ground *according* to *its* kind. And God saw that *it was* good.

This verse is traditionally translated: "And God made the beast of the earth after his kind, and cattle after their kind, and every thing that creepeth upon the earth after his kind: and God saw that it was good." (KJV)

Traditionally, Genesis 1:24 and 1:25 are explained as two repetitious verses. God speaks and instantly creates all land animals *ex nihilo* in Genesis 1:24, and then proceeds to make them again in Genesis 1:25. In orthodox translations, God needlessly repeats himself in four separate instances in Genesis 1:6–7, 1:14–16, 1:20–21, and 1:24–25.

To believe all land animals were created on the sixth day, strongly conflicts with general revelation in regard to time. Fossil and ice core evidence indicate land animals have been on the Earth for more than 100,000 years. Orthodox translations make the Genesis creation story unbelievable to scientifically literate people. Scientific evidence discussed in Chapter 4 supports the appearance of land animals significantly before 4004 BC.

Exemplar creation explains Genesis 1:25 as occurring in a chronological sequence of events. God created all land animals between Genesis 1:2 and 1:3. On the fifth day in Genesis 1:24, He describes abundant animal life. In Genesis 1:25, God is firmly identified as their creator. Since the land animals are described as existing in Genesis 1:24, there is no need for God to create them in Genesis 1:25.

In the *exemplar* translation, words used to describe land animals in this verse are translated in the broadest terms possible since all land-dwelling creatures are being described. Terms such as domestic animals, cattle, livestock, or wild animals are too narrow and not used.

1:26A. And say/God/make/humankind/in image + we/according to likeness + us/and rule over/over fish/the sea/and over bird/the heaven/and over domestic animal/and over all the earth/and over all the creeping thing/the move/on the earth. (LHEIB)

1:26B. And <u>said</u>/God/<u>made</u>/<u>man</u>/in image + <u>our</u>/<u>after likeness + our</u>/and <u>has dominion</u>/<u>on</u> fish/the sea/and <u>on flier</u>/the <u>sky</u>/and <u>on beasts</u>/and <u>on</u> all the Earth/and <u>on</u> all the moving/the move/over the land.

1:26C. And God said, "Man, made[06213] in our image[06754] [and] after our likeness[01823], has dominion[07287] on fish [of] the sea and on fliers[05775] [in] the sky[08064], and on beasts[0929] and on all[03605] the Earth[0776] and on all[03605] the moving[07431] [things that] move[07430] over[05921] the land[0776]."

1:26D. And God said, "Man, made in our image *and* after our likeness, has dominion on fish of the sea and on fliers in the sky and on beasts and on all the Earth and on all the moving *things* that move over the land."

This verse is traditionally translated: "And God said, *Let us* make man in our image, after our likeness: and *let them* have dominion over the fish of the sea, and over the fowl of the air, and over the cattle, and over all the earth, and over every creeping thing that creepeth upon the earth." (KJV, italics added for emphasis)

In rendering this verse, the deletion of "let" is the most significant difference between the KJV and the *exemplar* translation. The expressions "let us" and "let them" are not in the Hebrew text. According to traditional interpretations of this verse, God is "proposing" to make man in His image and likeness. The Hebrew text does not support this translation or interpretation.

In this verse, the two occurrences of the word "let" are not based on alleged jussive/command verbs. No verbs are classified or claimed to be jussive.

• The most literal translation of the last section of Genesis 1:26 is, "And on all the Earth and on all the moving movers over the land."

• The words *râmas* and *remes* (moving movers) are used together in Gen. 1:26, 7:14, 8:17, 8:19, and Ezekiel 38:20 as cognate accusatives. (See Genesis 1:11 in this chapter for a discussion of cognate accusatives.)

• The Hebrew word *râmas,* here translated "move" and identified as Strong's 07430, is based on the Hebrew root (רמשׁ). *Râmas* is used as a verb 16 times in the Old Testament and translated "creep" 11 times and "move" 5 times in the KJV.[72,73]

• The word *remes,* here translated "moving things" and identified as Strong's 07431, is also based on the Hebrew root (רמשׁ). *Remes* is used as a noun 18 times in the Old Testament and translated primarily as "creeping thing" in the KJV.[74,75]

• The word *âsâh* (עשׂה) is often translated "make" and identified as Strong's 06213.[76] When the Hebrew letter nun (נ) is added as a prefix to the root (עשׂה), it becomes (נעשׂה), the verb found in this verse.

1:27A. And create/God/the humankind/in image + he/in image/God/create/he/male/ and female/create/they. (LHEIB)

1:27C. And God [is the one who] create[01254] the humankind in He image, in God image create[01254] he, male and female [God] create[01254] they.

1:27D. And God *is the one who* created <u>man</u> in His image, in God's image created him, male and female *God* created them.

This verse has been translated:
• So God created man in his own image, in the image of God created he him; male and female created he them. (KJV)
• And God made man, according to the image of God he made him, male and female he made them. (Septuagint[77])

As shown above, the Septuagint poorly translates this verse by rendering *bârâ* as "made" rather than "create" in three different places. Although there is a corresponding Greek word for "create," the text was not translated in this manner, clearly illustrating the inaccuracy of the Septuagint.

Genesis 1:27 attributes God as the creator of man. This verse is supported by Genesis 5:1–2 which says, "This is the book of the generations of Adam. When God *created* man, he made him in the likeness of God. Male and female he *created* them, and he blessed them and named them Man when they were *created*." (ESV, italics added for emphasis)

Chapter 1 contains five major parallelisms. Five direct quotations from God describe the expanse (sky), two great luminaries (Sun and Moon), marine creatures, fliers, land animals, and mankind. Each quotation is then followed by a statement from Moses proclaiming God as maker or creator. In contrast, orthodox translations treat the first four instances as repetitive creative actions. In the fifth instance, God allegedly proposes to make man and then proceeds to create him. The *exemplar* translation treats all five parallelisms the same as follows:

(1) God describes an expanse (Gen 1:6). God is identified as the one who made and separated the expanse (Gen. 1:7).

(2) God describes luminaries in the heavens (Gen. 1:14–15). God is identified as the one who made the two great luminaries (Gen 1:16) and gave them in the expanse to rule and distinguish (Gen. 1:17–18).

(3) God describes swarming water creatures and fliers (Gen. 1:20). God is identified as the one who created the great reptiles, swarming water creatures, and winged fliers (Gen 1:21).

(4) God describes land beasts and animals (Gen. 1:24). God is identified as the one who made the land animals, beasts, and moving things (Gen. 1:25).

(5) God describes man and his dominion over all living things (Gen. 1:26). God is identified as the one who created man in His image (Gen. 1:27).

1:28A. And bless/they/God/and say/to + they/God/be fruitful/and multiply/and fill/ the earth/and subdue/and rule/over fish/the sea/and over bird/the heaven/and over all animal/the move/on the earth. (LHEIB)

1:28B. And bless/they/God/and say/to + they/God/be fruitful/and multiply/and fill/ the earth/and subdue/and <u>have dominion/on</u> fish/the sea/and <u>on flier</u>/the <u>sky</u>/and <u>on</u> all <u>living</u>/the move/<u>over the land</u>.

1:28C. And God bless <u>them</u>, and God said to <u>them</u>, "Be fruitful[06509] and multiply[07235] and fill[04390] the Earth[0776] and subdue[03533] [it] and have dominion[07287] on fish [of] the sea and on flier[05775] [in] the sky[08064] and on all[03605] living[02416] [things that] the move[07430] over[05921] the land[0776]."

1:28D. And God blessed them, and God said to them, "Be fruitful and multiply and fill the Earth and subdue it and have dominion on fish of the sea and on fliers in the sky and on all living *things* that move over the land."

Genesis 1:28 is the first command given in the creation story (none of the previous verses are commands). The command language is quite clear both in Hebrew and English. This verse is significantly different from the declarative statements of Genesis 1:3, 6, 9, 11, 14, 20, and 24. The dynamic verbs "be fruitful, multiply, fill, subdue, and have dominion" indicate what God intends for man to do. Also notice the absence of "let" in English translations. The *Old Testament Parsing Guide* classifies the action verbs listed as qal imperative, and none are classified as jussive.

This verse is often considered a cultural mandate. God commands man to populate the Earth and, by implication, create civilization, governments, and social structures. Man is to dominate the land, sky, and marine animals, and by inference use them for food, clothing, and beasts of burden.

• The Hebrew word *chay* (Strong's 02416), here translated "living," occurs 501 times in the Old Testament and is translated "live" 197 times, "life" 144 times, "beast" 76 times, "alive" 31 times, and "creature" 15 times, in addition to other miscellaneous words in the KJV.[78]

1:29A. And say/God/look/give/to + you/every plant/give seed/seed/which/on surface/ all the earth/and every kind of the tree/which in/fruit tree/give seed/seed/for + you/ be/as food. (LHEIB)

1:29B. And say/God/<u>behold</u>/give/to + you/every plant/<u>seeding</u>/seed/which/<u>over sur-face</u>/all the <u>land</u>/<u>and every the tree</u>/which in/fruit tree/<u>seeding</u>/seed/for + you/be/<u>for</u> food.

1:29C. And God said, "Behold[02009], [I have] give[05414] to you every[03605] plant[06212] seeding[02232] seed[02233], which [is] over[05921] [the] surface[06440] [of] all[03605] the land[0776] and every[03605] tree in which tree fruit[06529] [is] seeding[02232] seed[02233]. For you, [they] be[01961] for food."

1:29D. And God said, "Behold, *I have* given to you every plant seeding seed which is over the surface of all the land, and every tree in which fruit is seeding seed. For you, *they* <u>are</u> for food."

1:30A. And to every kind of animal/the earth/and to every kind of bird/the heaven/ and to every kind of/moving/on the earth/which in/breath/life/every kind of green/ plant/as food/and be so. (LHEIB)

1:30B. And to every <u>animal</u>/the <u>land</u>/and to every <u>flier</u>/the <u>sky</u>/and to every/moving/ over the <u>land</u>/which in/<u>creature</u>/<u>living</u>/<u>every green</u>/plant/<u>for</u> food/and be so.

1:30C. "And to every^{03605} animal [of] the land^{0776} and to every^{03605} flier^{05775} [in] the sky^{08064} and to every^{03605} moving^{07430} [thing] over^{05921} the land^{0776} in which [is a] living^{02416} creature^{05315} [I have given] every^{03605} green^{03418} plant^{06212} for food." And [it] be^{01961} so^{03651}.

1:30D. "And to every animal of the land and to every flier in the sky and to every moving *thing* over the land, which is a living creature, *I have given* every green plant for food." And *it* <u>was</u> so.

Genesis 1:29–30 apply to the entire Earth. God gave seeds, fruit trees, and green plants to man and animals for food. Plants are the foundation of the food chain. We should not incorrectly infer these two verses apply strictly to the Garden of Eden. To say the human race was vegetarian until God specifically allowed the killing of animals after the flood in Genesis 9:3 is an unsupported assumption. Likewise, to require all animals on the entire Earth to be herbivorous before Adam sinned is unwarranted and speculative.

God created the garden to be a place of peace, safety, and security from the world outside. We can infer that no significant carnivorous or predatory animals existed within the garden. If there were predator-prey relationships, they existed on a small scale and were not a threat to man.

1:31A. And see/God/everything that/make/and look good/very/and be evening/and be morning/day/the sixth. (LHEIB)

1:31C. And God see <u>every</u>^{03605} that [He had] make^{06213} and <u>behold</u>^{02009} [it was] very good. And evening be^{01961} and morning be^{01961} the sixth day^{03117}.

1:31D. And God saw <u>all</u> that *He had* <u>done</u>, and behold *it was* very good. And evening <u>was</u>, and morning <u>was</u>—the sixth day.

In this verse, the Hebrew word *âsâh* (Strong's 06213) is translated "done" in reference to the many things God *did* that are described and attributed to the creative hand of God in Genesis Chapter 1.

Throughout Genesis Chapter 1, God follows a pattern of approving features of His creation as good. On day one, light is proclaimed as *good* (Gen. 1:4). On the third day, the waters and dry land are described as *good* (Gen. 1:10) and vegetation is called *good* (Gen. 1:12). On the fourth day, the Sun and Moon are recognized as *good* (Gen. 1:18). On the fifth day, marine life and flying creatures are labeled as *good* (Gen. 1:21). On the sixth day, land animals are identified as *good* (Gen. 1:25). Finally, God summarizes all His work as *very good* (Gen 1:31).

Genesis Chapter Two

2:1A. And be finished/the heaven/and the earth/and all array + they. (LHEIB)

2:1C. And the heaven[08064] and the Earth[0776] [were] <u>finished</u>[03615], and all[03605] <u>their ar-</u>ray[06635] [of miscellaneous things]

2:1D. And the heavens and Earth *were* finished, and all their <u>multitude</u> *of miscellaneous things*.

This verse is traditionally translated: "Thus the heavens and the earth were finished, and all the host of them." (KJV)

The expression "host of heaven" and "LORD of hosts" is used several places in the Old Testament. "Host" is also used in reference to armies or multitudes of fighting men. In this verse, *exemplar* creation views "host" as referring to a multitude of details not mentioned. Genesis Chapter 1 is an abbreviated, non-technical, historical account of God's activities and many minutiae are not discussed.

- This is the first occurrence of the Hebrew word *tsâbâ* (Strong's 06635), here translated "host." *Tsâbâ* occurs 485 times in the Old Testament and is translated "host" 393 times, "war" 41 times, and "army" 29 times, in addition to other miscellaneous words in the KJV.[79]

2:2A. And finish/God/on day/the seventh/work + he/that/do/and rest/on day/the seventh/from all work + he/that/do. (LHEIB)

2:2C. And on the seventh day God finish[03615] he work[04399] that [he had] do[06213], and rest[07673] on the seventh day[03117] from all[03605] he work[04399] that [he had] do[06213].

2:2D. And on the seventh day God finished His work that *He had* <u>done</u>, and rested on the seventh day from all His work that *He had* <u>done</u>.

Genesis 2:2 discusses the seventh day when God finished His work and rested. God's work consisted of things He *did*. The Hebrew word *âsâh* (Strong's 06213) is primarily translated "did" in the Old Testament and is translated "did" in this verse to indicate the broadest possible range of work. Work God *did* includes describing, identifying, distinguishing, approving, and blessing. The following is a list of the work God *did* during the six-day Genesis chronicle:

- Day one: God *describes* light and *approves* it as good. He *distinguishes* between light and darkness, and *identifies them as* "day" and "night."
- Second day: God observes and *describes* the expanse. He *identifies* the expanse as "sky."
- Third day: God *describes* the dry ground and the seas, and *approves* them as good. He *identifies* the dry ground as "land" and the collected waters as "seas." He observes and *describes* Earth's abundant vegetation and *approves* it as good.

• Fourth day: God observes the Sun and Moon and *describes* their function in regard to signs, seasons, days, and years and *approves* them as good.
• Fifth day: God observes and *describes* marine and bird life. He *approves* them as good and *blesses* them.
• Sixth day: God observes and *describes* the land animals. He *approves* them as good. He *blesses* man and *commands* him to be fruitful. God *approves* all that he has done as "very good."

2:3A. And bless/God/day/the seventh/and hallow/he/because/on + he/rest/from all work/that create/God/to do. (LHEIB)
2:3C. And God bless the seventh day^{03117} and hallow he, because on he [God] rest from all^{03605} work^{04399} that God [He] create^{01254} to do^{06213}.
2:3D. And God blessed the seventh day and <u>sanctified it</u>, because on it *God* rested from all work that He created to do.

2:4A. These/account/the heaven/and the earth/at create + they/on day/make/Yahweh/ God/earth/and heaven. (LHEIB)
2:4B. These/account/the heaven/and the earth/at create they/<u>in days</u>/<u>did</u>/Yahweh/ God/earth/and heaven.
2:4C. These account^{08435} [that follow are about] the heaven and the Earth^{0776} at they create^{01254} in [the] days^{03117} Yahweh God did^{06213} [the] Earth^{0776} and heaven^{08064}.
2:4D. These accounts *that follow are about* the heavens and the Earth at their creation—in the days Yahweh God did *the* Earth and heavens.

This verse has been translated:
• These are the generations of the heavens and of the earth when they were created, in the day that the LORD God made the earth and the heavens. (KJV)
• This is the account of the heavens and the earth when they were created. When the LORD God made the earth and the heavens. (NIV)
• This is the book of the origin of heaven and earth, when it originated, on the day that God made the heaven and the earth. (Septuagint[80])

The Hebrew word *tôwledâh* (Strong's 08435) is normally translated "generations" or "account." When *tôwledâh* is used, a genealogy often follows such as in Genesis 5:1, 10:1, 11:10, 11:27, 25:12, 25:19, 36:1, and 36:9. In some instances, a historical account is given such as the story of Noah in Genesis 6:9 and the story of Joseph in Genesis 37:2. In a similar manner, Genesis 2:5 begins a historical account that ends in Genesis 4:26. The details covered include the forming of man from the dust of the ground, the building of woman from man's rib, the temptation of man, Adam and Eve's sin, and their ejection from the Garden of Eden.

The NIV leaves out "day" in its translation of Genesis 2:4, yet (בימם) translated "in the days" plainly occurs in the text and is a combination of the noun day (יום)

and the letter (ב). The Hebrew term (ביום) occurs approximately 524 times as a standalone expression in *The Lexham Hebrew-English Interlinear Bible*.[81] In Genesis 2:4, the NIV deliberately deletes what the Bible clearly says. Supporters of traditional young-Earth creation theology embrace the NIV translation, because it supports their position by removing a problematic word.[82]

The term "days" used in Genesis 2:4 is a thorny problem for most explanations of Genesis Chapters 1 and 2. In the *exemplar* translation, "days" in this verse refers to a period of time and includes all events that occur between Genesis 2:5 through Genesis 4:26—a span of several years. The Hebrew word (יום) in this verse is often translated "days" depending on context (Genesis 14:1, 26:1; 26:15; 26:18; Judges 15:20; Ruth 1:1; I Sam. 17:12, I Chron. 5:10, etc.).

As shown above, the Septuagint translation of Genesis 2:4 is filled with inaccuracies. The word "account" is mistranslated "book of the origin." "Creation" is mistranslated "originated." The term "Yahweh God" is shortened to "God." The phrase "earth and heavens" is incorrectly reversed to "heaven and the earth."

The word order in the phrase "heavens and Earth" occurs 27 times in the KJV translation.[83] The reverse expression, "Earth and heavens" occurs only in Genesis 2:4 and in Psalm 148:13.[84] Normally, heavens are mentioned first because they are more significant. With an estimated 125 billion galaxies, and each galaxy containing an estimated 400 billion stars, the heavens are considerably greater than the Earth. Reversal of word order to "Earth and heavens" at the end of Genesis 2:4 indicates a reversal in significance and suggests God primarily "did things" to the Earth, and the heavens were of less importance.

- This is the first occurrence of the Hebrew word *tôwledâh* (Strong's 08435), here translated "account." *Tôwledâh* occurs 39 times in the Old Testament and is translated "generation" 38 times in the KJV.[85]
- *Tôwledâh* occurs 13 times in Genesis. In Genesis 2:4, the NIV, NASB, NLT, and NAS translate *tôwledâh* using the more descriptive term "account" rather than "generations."
- This is the first occurrence of the Hebrew word (יהוה), here translated "Yahweh" (Strong's 03068). C. John Collins says this special name is given to God, the covenant-making and covenant-keeping God who made promises to the patriarchs of Israel.[86]

2:5A. And all/plant/the field/not yet/be/in the earth/and all plants/the field/not yet/spring up/because/not/cause to fall rain/Yahweh/God/on the earth/and humankind/was not/cultivate/the ground. (LHEIB)

2:5B. And every/bush/the field/not yet/be/on the land/and every plant/the field/not yet/grow/because/not/cause rain/Yahweh/God/over the land/and man/was not/cultivate/the ground.

2:5C. And every[03605] bush[07880] [of] the field[07704] be[01961] not yet[02962] on the land[0776], and every[03605] plant[06212] [of] the field[07704] [did] not yet[02962] grow[06779], because Yahweh God [had] not cause rain[04305] over[05921] the land[0776] and [there] was not man [to] cultivate[05647] the ground[0127] [where the garden was to be].

2:5D. And every bush of the field <u>was</u> not yet on the land, and every plant of the field *did* not yet grow, because Yahweh God had not caused rain over the land and there was no man to cultivate the ground *where the garden was to be*.

This verse has been translated:
• And every plant of the field before it was in the earth, and every herb of the field before it grew: for the LORD God had not caused it to rain upon the earth, and there was not a man to till the ground. (KJV)
• When no bush of the field was yet in the land and no small plant of the field had yet sprung up—for the Lord God had not caused it to rain on the land, and there was no man to work the ground. (ESV)

According to traditional interpretations of this verse, the entire planet is barren of plants and bushes, no rain has fallen anywhere, and by implication the ground is so dry plants will not grow. Interpreting Genesis 2:5 in this manner, strongly conflicts with traditional explanations about the first three day of creation. For example, the Earth was allegedly a watery mass for the first two days. On the third day, the ground and water were separated and the Earth was covered with vegetation. Logically, there was enough residual moisture to keep bushes and plants alive on the fourth, fifth, and sixth days. There is no place in traditional explanations to fit an Earth with no plant life because of dry conditions.

Because God created a mist to water the dry ground in Genesis 2:6, some believe no rain fell on the entire planet until Noah built the ark. We can reject this assumption. An act of God would have been required to halt evaporation, condensation, and precipitation over the entire planet for this length of time. Scripture nowhere directly supports such a condition. Traditional explanations of this verse fall apart with a careful analysis.

C. John Collins says, the ESV translates the barren land in Genesis 2:5 without rain as applying to "some unnamed place where these conditions held."[87]

Exemplar creation explains this verse as applying to the land of the Garden of Eden, before God planted anything. There were no bushes or plants of the field on this piece of ground. The spot chosen for the garden was essentially without rain and probably a desert. We can hypothesize the location was in the Arabian desert on the Arabian Peninsula, which includes present-day Saudi Arabia, Oman, Yemen, Kuwait, and Qatar (all near the Cradle of Civilization). Since Adam and Eve initially wore no clothing, a location with a hot, dry climate would have been a logical choice. The statement, "there was no man to cultivate the ground" connects readily with Genesis 2:15, where Adam was to cultivate the garden.

• This is the first occurrence of the Hebrew word *tsâmach* (Strong's 06779), here translated "grow. *Tsâmach* occurs 33 times in the Old Testament and is translated "grow" 13 times, "spring forth" 6 times, "spring up" 4 times, "grow up" 2 times, "bring forth" 2 times, "bud" 2 times and "spring out" 2 times, in addition to other miscellaneous words in the KJV.[88] In the first two chapters of Genesis, *tsâmach* occurs in Genesis 2:5 and 2:9.

2:6A. And stream/rise/from the earth/and water/all surface the ground. (LHEIB)
2:6B. And mists/rise up/from the land/and water/all surface the ground.
2:6C. And mists^{0108} rose up^{05927} from^{04480} the land^{0776} and water all^{03605} [the] surface^{06440} [of] the ground^{0127} [where the garden was to be].
2:6D. And mists rose up from the land and watered all the surface of the ground *where the garden was to be*.

2:7A. And form/Yahweh/God/the man/dust/from the ground/and blow/in nostril/breath/life/and be/the man/as creature/living. (LHEIB)
2:7C. And Yahweh God form^{03335} the man [of] dust from^{04480} the ground^{0127} and blow in [his] nostril [the] breath [of] life^{02416}. And the man be^{01961} as [a] living^{02416} creature^{05315}.
2:7D. And Yahweh God formed the man *of* dust from the ground and <u>breathed</u> in his nostrils the breath *of* life. And the man <u>existed</u> as a living creature.

This verse is traditionally translated:
• And the LORD God formed man of the dust of the ground, and breathed into his nostrils the breath of life; and man became a living soul. (KJV)
• Then the LORD God formed the man of dust from the ground and breathed into his nostrils the breath of life, and the man became a living creature. (ESV)

The Hebrew verb *hâyâh* (Strong's 01961), here translated "existed," is a stative verb showing state-of-being. It is not a dynamic verb showing action. *Hâyâh* means primarily to "be" or "exist."

The words of Genesis 2:7 used to explain the origin of man are precise. Yahweh's actions in creating Adam are described using the two dynamic verbs "formed" and "breathed." The end result is depicted by the stative verb "exist." Prior to this event there was only dust, and now there is Adam the living creature.

Genesis 2:7 refutes Darwinian claims of human evolution. Animal hominids did not evolve during millions of years to *become* Adam the man. There is no hint that primates slowly changed through random mutation and natural selection to *become* Adam the human.

The word "formed" is often used in the Old Testament to describe a potter forming a clay pot with his hands. The elemental materials for Adam came from the dust of the ground, and God arranged them to make his body. The creation of the first human was an awesome display of intelligence and power. God is truly the potter and man is the clay.

In Genesis 2:7, "formed" is translated from the Hebrew *yâtsar,* and has no relation to the expression "without form" in Genesis 1:2 in the KJV. As discussed in Chapter 5, the translation of "without form" in Genesis 1:2 is illegitimate.

- This is the first occurrence of the Hebrew word *yâtsar* (Strong's 03335), here translated "formed." *Yâtsar* occurs 62 times and is translated "form" 26 times, "potter" 17 times, "fashion" 5 times, "maker" 4 times, "frame" 3 times, and "make" 3 times, in addition to other miscellaneous words in the KJV.[89]

2:8A. And plant/Yahweh/God/garden in Eden/in east/and put/there/the man/who/form. (LHEIB)

2:8C. And Yahweh God plant [a] garden from [the] east in Eden, and there [he] put the man who [he had] formed[03335].

2:8D. And Yahweh God planted a garden from the east in Eden, and there *He* put the man whom *He had* formed.

2:9A. And cause to grow/Yahweh/God/from the ground/every kind of tree/be pleasing/to sight/and good/for food/and tree/the life/in middle/the garden/and tree/the knowledge/good/and evil. (LHEIB)

2:9B. And grow/Yahweh/God/from the ground/every tree/desirable/to sight/and good/for food/and tree/the life/in middle/the garden/and tree/the knowledge/good/and evil.

2:9C. And Yahweh God grow[06779] from[04480] the ground[0127] every[03605] tree [that was] desirable[02530] to [the] sight[04758] and good for food; and the tree [of] life[02416] in [the] middle[08432] [of] the garden and the tree [of] knowledge [of] good and evil.

2:9D. And Yahweh God grew from the ground every tree *that was* desirable to the sight and good for food, and the tree of life in the middle of the garden and the tree of knowledge of good and evil.

This verse is traditionally translated: "And out of the ground made the LORD God to grow every tree that is pleasant to the sight, and good for food; the tree of life also in the midst of the garden, and the tree of knowledge of good and evil." (KJV)

Genesis 2:9 describes God growing trees from the ground in the Garden of Eden. In the KJV, the word "made" has been added, but is not in the Hebrew text. Growing trees was not a problem for God. He may have grown them rapidly similar to when He caused Aaron's staff to sprout, bud, blossom, and produce almonds in one night as described in Numbers 17:1–8. On the other hand, God may have grown them in a traditional manner over several years.

• This is the first occurrence of the word *châmad* (Strong's 02530), here translated "desirable." *Châmad* occurs 21 times in the Old Testament and is translated "desire" 11 times, "covet" 4 times, and "delight" 2 times, in addition to other miscellaneous words in the KJV.[90]

2:15A. And take/Yahweh/God/the man/he put/in garden Eden/to cultivate/and to keep + she. (LHEIB)
2:15C. And Yahweh God take the man [and] put he in [the] garden [of] Eden to cultivate[05647] and to keep[08104] it.
2:15D. And Yahweh God took the man and put him in the Garden of Eden to cultivate and to keep it.

This verse has been translated:
• And the LORD God took the man, and put him into the garden of Eden to dress it and to keep it. (KJV)
• And the Lord God took the man whom he had formed and put him in the orchard to till and keep it. (Septuagint[91])

As shown above, the Septuagint incorrectly adds, "whom he had formed," an expression not in the Hebrew text.

Adam was put in the Garden of Eden to cultivate the ground. Genesis 2:5 mentions that no man was available to *cultivate* the ground, followed by Genesis 2:15 which says man was put in the garden to *cultivate* it. The Hebrew word *abad* (Strong's 05647) occurs in Genesis 2:5, 2:15, 3:23, 4:2, and 4:12. In these verses, *abad* describes cultivating or tilling the ground.

2:16A. And command/Yahweh/God/to the man/say/from all/tree the garden/eat/you eat. (LHEIB)
2:16B. And command/Yahweh/God/<u>over</u> the man/say/from <u>every</u>/tree the garden/eat/you eat.
2:16C. And Yahweh God command[06680] over[05921] the man say, "From every[03605] tree [of] the garden, you [may] eat[0398]-eat[0398]."
2:16D. And Yahweh God commanded over the man saying, "From every tree of the garden, you *may* eat-eat."

2:17A. And from tree/the knowledge/good/and evil/not/eat/from + he/because/on day/eat + you/from + he/die/you die. (LHEIB)
2:17C. <u>But</u> from [the] tree [of] the knowledge [of] good and evil, [do] not eat from, because on [the] day[03117] you eat from <u>it</u> you [shall] die[01491] die[04191].
2:17D. "But from the tree of the knowledge of good and evil, *do* not eat from, because on the day you eat from it you *shall* die-die."

Genesis 2:16–17 constitute the second command given in the creation story (the first command is Genesis 1:28). The command language is clear and significantly different from the declarative statements of Genesis 1:3, 6, 9, 11, 14, 20, and 24. The dynamic verb "eat" occurs four times to indicate what God intends for man to do and not do. Also notice the absence of "let" in English translations. In Genesis 2:16–17, none of the verbs are classified as jussive by the *Old Testament Parsing Guide*.

Word repetition was commonly used by writers of the Old Testament to stress a point. A form of the expression "eat-eat," found in Genesis 2:16, occurs several times in the Old Testament. God wanted Adam to eat fully of the garden and repeated the word for emphasis.

The expression "die-die," found in Genesis 2:17, occurs more than twelve times in the Old Testament. Repetition of the word "die" was used to emphasize the certainty of Adam's death if he ate from the tree of the knowledge of good and evil. In the KJV, this Hebrew expression is typically translated "surely die." The following three examples contain the identical expression found in Genesis 2:17 and show how this expression was used by those in authority to emphasize the certainty of death as a punishment.

Abraham misled the king of Gerar by telling him that Sarah was his sister. As a result, Abimelech took Sarah to be his wife. God appeared to him in a dream and said to return her to Abraham. Genesis 20:7 says, "Now therefore restore the man his wife; for he is a prophet, and he shall pray for thee, and thou shalt live: and if thou restore her not, know thou that thou shalt <u>surely die</u>, thou, and all that are thine." (KJV)

When David was fleeing from King Saul, Ahimelech the priest gave David food and Goliath's sword. When Saul was told of this act of kindness, he was angry at Ahimelech. Saul's response is recorded in 1 Samuel 22:16 when he said, "Thou shalt <u>surely die</u>, Ahimelech, thou, and all thy father's house." (KJV)

King David's son, Absalom, and his followers attempted to take the throne by force. As David fled from Jerusalem during the initial conflict, he was cursed by Shimei, the son of Gera. David regained his throne and eventually his son Solomon became king. He confined Shimei to Jerusalem as punishment for his disrespect. In 1 Kings 2:37, King Solomon decreed, "For it shall be, on the day you go out and cross the Brook Kidron, know for certain you shall <u>surely die</u>; your blood shall be on your own head." (NKJV)

• This is the first occurrence of the Hebrew word *âkal* (Strong's 0398), here translated "eat." *Âkal* occurs 810 times in the Old Testament and is translated "eat" 604 times, "devour" 111 times, and "consume" 33 times, in addition to other miscellaneous words in the KJV.[92] The similar expression "eat-eat" found in Genesis 2:16 occurs in 1 Sam. 14:30, Ezek. 3:1, and Ezek. 16:13.

• This is the first occurrence of the word *mûwth* (Strong's 04191), here translated "die." *Mûwth* occurs 835 times in the Old Testament and is translated "die"

424 times, "dead" 130 times, "slay" 100 times, "death" 83 times, "surely" 50 times, and "kill" 31 times, in addition to other miscellaneous words in the KJV.[93]
• The identical expression in Genesis 2:17, containing the two Hebrew words "die" (מות) and "you die" (המות) occurs in 12 verses in Gen. 20:7; 1 Sam. 14:44, 22:16; 1 Kings 2:37, 2:42; 2 Kings 1:4, 1:6, 1:16; Jer. 26:8; Ezek. 3:18, 33:8, 33:14.[94] A similar expression occurs in Judges 13:22, 1 Sam. 14:39, 2 Kings 8:10, and 2 Sam. 12:14.

2:18A. And say/Yahweh/God/not good/be/the man/to alone/make for + he/helper/as counterpart + he. (LHEIB)
2:18C. And Yahweh God say, "[It is] not good [for] the man to be[01961] alone. For he [I shall] make[06213] as his counterpart[05048] [a] helper.
2:18D. And Yahweh God said, "*It is* not good *for* the man to be alone. For him *I shall* make as his counterpart a helper."

This verse has been translated:
• And the LORD God said, It is not good that the man should be alone; I will make him an help meet for him. (KJV)
• And Jehovah God saith, "Not good for the man to be alone, I do make to him an helper—as his counterpart." (Young's Literal Translation, 1898[95])

The Hebrew word *neged* (Strong's 05048), here translated "counterpart," occurs in Genesis 2:18 and 2:20 when referring to Adam's helper. The Hebrew text is essential to identify *neged* since it is not listed as occurring in this verse in most concordances. *Strong's Exhaustive Concordance* defines *neged* to mean a "counterpart" or "mate." Brown-Diver-Briggs Hebrew lexicon states that *neged* can mean "corresponding to" or "opposite to."[96] Dr. Allen P. Ross in *Creation and Blessing* points out that *neged* means "opposite, over against, or counterpart."[97]
Because of its descriptive nature, *The Lexham Hebrew-English Interlinear Bible* rendering of *neged* as "counterpart" is retained in the *exemplar* translation. In many respects, woman is sexually and emotionally the "opposite" or "other side" of man. Their strengths and weakness may be viewed as complementary in marriage.

• This is the first occurrence of the Hebrew word *neged* (נגד), here translated "counterpart." *Neged* occurs approximately 170 times in the Old Testament and is translated "before" 124 times, "opposite" 34 times, "front" 5 times, "nearby" 3 times, "counterpart" 2 times, and "side" 2 times in *The Lexham Hebrew-English Interlinear Bible*.
• *Neged* is often used in describing someone or something that is opposite. Joshua 5:13 says, "And it came to pass, when Joshua was by Jericho, that he lifted his eyes and looked, and behold, a Man stood opposite[05048] him with His sword

drawn in His hand. (NKJV)
• *Neged* is often used in describing someone or something that is on the other side. 2 Kings 3:22 says, "Then they rose up early in the morning, and the sun was shining on the water; and the Moabites saw the water on the <u>other side</u>[05048] as red as blood." (NKJV)

2:19A. And form/Yahweh/God/from the ground/all animal/the field/and/all bird/the heaven/and bring/to the man/see/what call to + he/and all/what/call to/the man/creature/living/that/name. (LHEIB)
2:19B. And form/Yahweh/God/from the ground/<u>every</u> animal/the field/and/<u>every</u> <u>flier/the sky</u>/and bring/to the man/<u>to see</u>/what call to + he/and <u>every</u>/what/call to/the man/creature/living/that/name.
2:19C. And Yahweh God form[03335] from the ground[0127] every[03605] animal [of] the field[07704] and every[03605] flier[05775] [of] the sky[08064] [that lived within the garden]. And [God] bring [them] to the man to see what he [would] call[07121] to [them] and what[0834] every[03605] the man call[07121] to the living[02416] creature[05315], that [was its] name[08034].
2:19D. And Yahweh God formed from the ground every animal of the field and every flier of the sky *that lived within the garden*. And *God* brought *them* to the man to see what he *would* call them and whatever the man called the living creature, that *was its* name.

The animals God formed in Genesis 2:19 were specifically for the Garden of Eden. Animals of the field and fliers of the sky are mentioned; however, no marine creatures are specified. If this verse was describing animals on the entire Earth, marine life would be included. Since the garden was located on arid land, the absence of marine animals in the garden is not unexpected and suggests there were no large bodies of water in the garden as a habitat.

2:20A. And call/the man/name/to all the domestic animal/and to bird/the heaven/and to all/animal/the field/and for Adam/not find/helper/as counterpart. (LHEIB)
2:20B. And call/the man/name/to all the <u>beasts/and to flier</u>/the sky/and to all/animal/the field/and for Adam/not find/helper/as counterpart + he.
2:20C. And the man call[07121] name[08034] to all[03605] the beasts[0929] and to [the] flier[05775] [of] the sky[08064] and to all[03605] animal [of] the field[07704] [that lived within the garden]. And for Adam [was] not find as he counterpart[05048] [a] helper[05828].
2:20D. And the man called names to all the beasts and to the fliers of the sky and to all animals of the field *that lived within the garden*. And for Adam *was* not found as his counterpart a helper.

2:21A. And cause to fall/Yahweh/God/deep sleep/upon the man/and sleep/and take/one/of rib + he/and close up/flesh/in place of. (LHEIB)

2:21B. And cause to fall/Yahweh/God/deep sleep/<u>over the man</u>/and sleep/and take/ one/<u>from rib</u> + he/and close up/flesh/<u>under</u>.

2:21C. And Yahweh God cause [a] deep sleep to fall over[05921] the man and [during] sleep and take from one [of] he rib and close up[05462] under[08478] [the] flesh.

2:21D. And Yahweh God caused a deep sleep to fall over the man and *during* sleep took from one of his ribs and closed up under the flesh.

Genesis 2:21 describes the creation of Eve. God did not need to take anything from Adam to create Eve. Yahweh could have created her out of dust from the ground, but apparently wanted to show a symbolic relationship.

Based on our knowledge of biotechnology, the biblical description of the making of Eve is entirely plausible. From our perspective, taking Adam's DNA and modifying it to make Eve would be easier than using elemental materials extracted from the ground. God could have used DNA from any cell in Adam's body, but chose a rib. Bones contain stem cells in their marrow that, from a human viewpoint, are easier to manipulate. God did not need an entire rib, but only material from a rib. A single stem cell would have been sufficient. The Hebrew text supports the explanation of taking material from one of Adam's ribs.

In reference to this verse, Matthew Henry said that the woman is "not made out of his [man's] head to rule over him, nor out of his feet to be trampled upon by him, but out of his side to be equal with him, under his arm to be protected, and near his heart to be beloved."[98]

Ideally, woman is a counterpart to man in the marriage relationship. Their roles are different, yet important. A man and woman bring different physical, mental, and emotional attributes to marriage, and these traits can complement each other to achieve success. Because of Eve's sin in eating of the tree of knowledge of good and evil, God changed woman's original role in marriage according to Genesis 3:16.

• The Hebrew word *tachath* (Strong's 08478), here translated "under," occurs 544 times in the Old Testament, although only a few occurrences are mentioned in most concordances.[99] *The Lexham Hebrew-English Interlinear Bible* translates *tachath* primarily as "under" and "in place of." In the first two chapters, *tachath* occurs in Genesis 1:7, 1:9, and 2:21.

2:22A. And build/Yahweh/God/the rib/which take/from the man/into woman/and bring + she/to the man. (LHEIB)

2:22C. And Yahweh God build[01129] which [he] take [of] the rib from the man into [a] woman, and bring she to the man.

2:22D. And Yahweh God built—which *He* took *of* the rib from the man—into a woman, and brought her to the man.

This verse is traditionally translated:
• And the rib, which the LORD God had taken from man, made he a woman, and brought her unto the man. (KJV)
• And the Lord God built the rib which he took from Adam into a woman: and brought her to Adam. (Douay-Rheims, 1899)

The KJV mistranslates the Hebrew word *bânâh* (Strong's 01129) in this verse. *Bânâh* means "build" rather than "made," and there is no need to hide its meaning because of theological influence. Noah *built* an altar in Genesis 8:20, Abraham *built* an altar in Genesis 22:9, Jacob *built* an altar in Genesis 35:7, the children of Israel *built* cities for Pharaoh in Exodus 1:11, and God as the Master Builder *built* Eve from Adam's rib in Genesis 2:22. As shown above, the Douay-Rheims Bible correctly translates *bânâh* as built.

• The Hebrew word *bânâh* (Strong's 01129), here translated "built," is used throughout the Old Testament to describe building altars, cities, and houses. *Bânâh* is also used in the sense of building children in Genesis 16:2 and Genesis 30:3. Words based on the root *bânâh* occur 376 times in the Old Testament and are translated "build" 340 times, "build up" 14 times, "builder" 10 times, and "built again" 2 times, in addition to other miscellaneous words in the KJV.[100]

2:23A. And say/the man/this/the time/bone/from bones + I/and flesh/from flesh + I/ for this/be called/woman/for/from man/be taken this. (LHEIB)
2:23B. And say/the man/this/<u>now</u>/bone/<u>from bones my</u>/and flesh/<u>from flesh my</u>/for this/<u>called</u>/woman/<u>because</u>/from man/<u>taken this</u>.
2:23C. And the man say, "This^{02063} [is] now^{06471} bone from my bones and flesh from my flesh; for this^{02063} [shall be] called^{07121} woman, because this^{02063} [was] taken from man."
2:23D. And the man said, "This is now bone from my bones and flesh from my flesh; for this *shall* be called woman, because this *was* taken from man."

2:24A. Therefore/leave man/father + he/and mother + he/and cling to/to wife + he/ and be/as flesh/one. (LHEIB)
2:24B. <u>Over so</u>/leave man/father + he/and mother + he/and <u>hold fast</u>/<u>on</u> wife + he/ and be/as flesh/one.
2:24C. So^{03651} over^{05921} [this reason a] man [will] leave he father and he mother and hold fast^{01692} on he wife. And [they shall] be^{01961} as one flesh.
2:24D. So over *this reason*, a man *will* leave his father and his mother and hold fast on his wife. And *they shall* be as one flesh.

God's original plan was for one man to be married to one woman for life, but man quickly violated this arrangement. Genesis 4:19 records Lamech as the first man to have more than one wife. The practice of having two or more wives at the same time, or having a succession of wives through marriage and divorce was not God's plan. This is emphasized by Jesus' teaching in Matthew 19:7–9, and by the requirements for elders (bishops) and deacons in 1 Timothy 3:1–13 and Titus 1:5–9. In the New Testament church, leaders were expected to live in accordance with God's original plan for marriage.

The Old Testament is filled with stories of jealousy and infighting because of the practice of polygamy. Wives fought for their husband's affection and a desire to be the favorite. Children fought for power, inheritance, and the right of succession. The problems Jacob and David had with their wives and children are a prime example of this conflict.

In addition to the above, sexual relations outside marriage violate God's plan and have led to a host of sexually transmitted diseases. Diseases transmitted only by sexual contact could be eliminated within one or two generations by strict adherence to a one-man, one-woman, permanent relationship.

2:25A. And be/two/naked/the man/and wife/and not/be ashamed. (LHEIB)

2:25C. And [the] two^{08147} be^{01961} naked^{06174}, the man and [his] wife, and not ashamed.

2:25D. And the two <u>were</u> naked, the man and *his* wife, and not ashamed.

Conclusion

In the biblical debate regarding origins, theology should be evaluated based on: (1) How well it accepts the Genesis story as a God-inspired account that is truthful and trustworthy. (2) How well the remainder of the Old Testament supports the translation of words in Genesis. (3) How well theology harmonizes special revelation with general revelation. God's word and His work should not conflict.

Exemplar creation is based on a credible translation and explanation of several key words in Genesis Chapters 1 and 2. In descending order of importance, nineteen significant differences distinguish the *exemplar* translation from the KJV as listed below. The treatment of Genesis 1:3, 6, 9, 11, 14, 20, 24 as declarative statements rather than commands, and rejection of the "jussive/command" verb, substantially exceeds all other items in significance.

(1) In Genesis 1:3, 6, 9, 11, 14, 20, and 24, seven alleged commands are replaced by declarative or descriptive statements.

(2) Orthodox translations treat Genesis 1:6–7, 14–16, 20–21, and 24–25 as repetitive creative actions. This interpretation is not supported by the Hebrew text of the Bible and rejected.

• In Genesis 1:6, God allegedly commands the expanse (sky) into existence and then in Genesis 1:7 makes it.

- In Genesis 1:14-15, God allegedly commands the luminaries into existence and then in Genesis 1:16 makes them.
- In Genesis 1:20, God allegedly commands the marine creatures and fliers into existence and then in Genesis 1:21 creates them.
- In Genesis 1:24, God allegedly commands the land creatures into existence and then in Genesis 1:25 makes them.

(3) In Genesis 1:26, the illegitimate terms "let us" and "let them" are not in the Hebrew text and are deleted. The alleged proposal to make man is replaced by a descriptive statement about the existence of man.

(4) Genesis 1:6–7, 14–16, 20–21, 24–25, and 26–27 represent five major parallelisms in Chapter 1. In each instance, a descriptive quote by God is followed by a statement from Moses proclaiming God as maker or creator.
- God describes an expanse (Gen 1:6). God is identified as the one who made and separated the expanse (Gen. 1:7).
- God describes luminaries in the heavens (Gen. 1:14–15). God is identified as the one who made the two great luminaries (Gen 1:16) and gave them in the expanse to rule and distinguish (Gen. 1:17–18).
- God describes swarming water creatures and fliers (Gen. 1:20). God is identified as the one who created the great reptiles, swarming water creatures, and winged fliers (Gen 1:21).
- God describes land beasts and animals (Gen. 1:24). God is identified as the one who made the land animals, beasts, and moving things (Gen. 1:25).
- God describes man and his dominion over all living things (Gen. 1:26). God is identified as the one who created man in His image (Gen. 1:27).

(5) In Genesis 1:7, 16, 21, 25, and 27 the verbs "make" and "create" refer to past events performed by God.

(6) In Genesis 1:2, the illegitimate term "without form" is replaced by "vacant."

(7) In Genesis 1:9, the illegitimate term "let be gathered together" is replaced by "wait."

(8) In Genesis 2:22, the illegitimate "made" is replaced by "built."

(9) In Genesis 1:20, the illegitimate phrase, "Let the waters bring forth abundantly the moving creature that hath life" is replaced by, "The waters swarm *with* swarms of living creatures."

(10) In Genesis 1:21, "great whales" are replaced by "great reptiles" as a more accurate translation.

(11) In Genesis 1:4, 14, and 18, "divide" is replaced by "distinguished" as a more accurate term.

(12) In Genesis 1:10, "gathering together" is replaced by "collection" as a more credible translation.

(13) In Genesis 1:17, "set" is replaced by "gave" as a more common translation.

(14) In Genesis 1:9, "appear" is replaced by "seen" as a more common translation.

(15) In Genesis 1:10, 11, 12, 20, 22, 24, 26, 28, 29, 30, 2:5, and 2:6, "earth" is replaced by "land" as a more specific term.

(16) In Genesis 1:1, 2, 15, 17, 25, 26, 28, 2:1, and 2:4, "earth" is replaced by "Earth" (to indicate the planet) as a more specific term.

(17) In Genesis 1:14, 15, and 16, "lights" are replaced by "luminaries."

(18) In Genesis 1:31, 2:2, 3, 4 "made" is replaced by the more general "did."

(19) In Genesis 1:5 "the first day" is replaced by "day one" to reflect a cardinal rather than an ordinal number.

All orthodox English translations of the Bible are seriously in error regarding the Genesis creation story. This error has been driven by traditional young-Earth creation theology for more than twenty-two hundred years. Starting in the 1700s, science began to challenge orthodox translations of the creation account. Physical evidence supported a growing belief that the Earth was significantly older than 6,000 years. This data has grown to the point where the traditional Genesis account is in irreconcilable conflict with scientific evidence in regard to time, in turn affecting the credibility of the entire Bible.

Sound hermeneutics and exegesis now challenge traditional translations of the Genesis creation story. At the heart of the problem is the Septuagint translation and to a lesser extent Masoretic vocal marks. Through their work, Hebrew scribes embedded traditional young-Earth creation theology into the Old Testament. They treated ten perfect verbs as "jussive/command" verbs and transformed seven declarative statements into commands. This in turn forced the illegitimate translation of several related words and phrases. These errors have resulted in a translation of Genesis that is indefensible based on the Hebrew text of the Bible and a study of general revelation.

Most Hebrew scholars and theologians are aware of some of the issues raised in this chapter. The majority view the Genesis creation account with absolute puzzlement over its conflict with science in regard to time, yet believe current translations are correct. A radical shift in mindset is needed. This begins by realizing the Septuagint translation is: (1) not inspired, (2) contains a number of errors, and (3) has distorted the creation story. The Septuagint has been the primary driver behind incorrect interpretations of the creation account and resulting English translations. This in turn has forced the layman to choose between rejecting overwhelming scientific evidence in regard to significant time or rejecting the integrity of scripture.

A concentrated study rather than casual reading is required to fully understand Chapters 2, 5, 6, and Appendix B of this book. A complete understanding of the information contained herein provides a firm basis for accepting *exemplar* creation as the original creation story that God inspired Moses to write. When properly translated and understood, the Genesis creation account is an abbreviated, non-technical, historical account that can be accepted as truthful and trustworthy without apology. Although of great antiquity, the creation story is logical, accurate, carefully structured, and sophisticated when judged by twenty-first century standards. The Genesis account of origins stands significantly above all other religious stories, philosophical ideas, cultural beliefs, and myths regardless of their age—including present-day evolutionary theories.

Although I have been critical of orthodox translations of the Genesis creation account, one should not infer from my comments that English translations of the Bible are filled with errors. Once past the Genesis creation story and Noah's flood, a significant amount of controversy over the Old Testament disappears. While there is room for improvement in current English Bibles (a more consistent translation of Hebrew words, the elimination of *ad hoc* word translations, and the identification of added English words), I am not aware of any significant beliefs that are misrepresented.

Additionally, I do not accuse present-day conservative Bible theologians and Hebrew scholars of intentionally embellishing, and thus misleading people in regard to the Genesis account. Their beliefs are the result of more than twenty-two hundred years of errant interpretation, translation, and teaching by respected Christian leaders. They have unknowingly inherited a false paradigm and mistakenly defend it as true.

Your faith should not stand in the wisdom of men,
but in the power of God. (1 Corinthians 2:5) KJV

Chapter 7

A New Paradigm of Biblical Origins

Prior to writing this book I was a young-Earth creationist. More than thirty-five years ago I developed an interest in the creation-evolution controversy soon after graduating from college. During that period I aligned myself with proponents of traditional young-Earth creation theology and provisionally accepted information found in their books, magazines, video tapes, and DVDs. I was aware of the conflict young-Earth theology had with scientific evidence regarding time, but held to my private beliefs. After all, my personal convictions were not open to public theological and scientific scrutiny. I did not need to defend them to anyone; however, I hoped that someday a brilliant theologian might develop a viable explanation for Genesis. One that respected the biblical text and was capable of withstanding scientific scrutiny.

A few years ago while reading the Genesis story to teenagers in Sunday school, a student said, "This doesn't make sense." Her comment was reinforced by a presentation to an adult class exploring contemporary religious issues. In addition, I had closely studied English translations of Genesis and was confused. In Genesis 1:3–5, there is no mention of God creating the Earth on the first day. In Genesis 1:3–20, the word "create" is not used during the first four days, although God is allegedly creating. Creation of the Sun on the fourth day is completely out of order—logically it would have been formed on the first day. The creation of plants and trees on the third day and the making of marine life on the fifth day are in reverse order (according to the geological record, marine life appeared first). In Genesis 2:5–6, I found it incomprehensible that the entire Earth was dry and barren of vegetation immediately after its creation. The naming of more than ten thousand animals (all diverse animal species) by Adam in one day seemed wrong. And of course, the conflict with science regarding time was a big issue. These experiences and others motivated me to seriously examine the Genesis creation story to determine if a viable solution was possible. As mentioned in Chapter 1, what I discovered during my attempt to verify English translations of the Hebrew text led to the writing of this book.

Present interpretations of Genesis cast doubt on the truthfulness and trustworthiness of scripture. If the Bible is true, why does Genesis conflict with firm scientific evidence in support of significant time? Certainly God knows Earth's history, so why the apparent conflict about the time and sequence of past events? Surely God could have inspired Moses to write a historical account capable of withstanding twenty-first century scientific inquiry.

I find it incomprehensible that God would not know the true account of how the heavens and Earth came about in regard to the time and sequence of past events. An eternal, omnipotent, creator God should be capable of inspiring Moses to write an accurate account of beginnings. The account might not necessarily be complete or provide enough detail to satisfy the curiosity of twenty-first century scientists, but what the particulars given should be true. The fundamentals should be correct. To believe Genesis 1 and 2 are wrong casts doubt on the very nature of God. If Genesis appears wrong, the error points to man and not God.

My views about biblical origins have changed significantly. I consider tradition-al young-Earth creation theology a bankrupt idea on two major accounts: (1) Young-Earth theology irrevocably conflicts with clear scientific evidence in regard to time. The heavens and Earth are much older than 6,000 years. (2) Young-Earth theology relies on an incorrect translation and explanation of Genesis, and represents an em-bellished distortion of the creation preamble written by Moses.

Since coming to understand the real Genesis creation story, my confidence in the integrity of scripture has increased significantly. The Bible has again proven itself to be true when compared against the real facts of science. I fully accept Genesis Chap-ters 1 and 2 as a credible account of origins.

Some view *exemplar* creation described herein as nothing more than a compro-mise position. Others view it as just another old-Earth idea. Still others view it as little more than a compilation of young-Earth creation theology, gap theology, day-age theology, and literary interpretations. As previously stated, the basis for the *ex-emplar* creation is a superior translation of the Hebrew text, rather than out-of-the-box thinking or an attempt to amalgamate existing beliefs. Faithfulness to the biblical text is paramount. Each significant word is supported by its usage elsewhere in the Old Testament (scripture is compared with scripture). Not a single word, phrase, or verse is treated as mythological, metaphorical, or untrue. Each verse in Genesis Chapter 1 occurs in chronological order. The text of the story is fully respected, and God is creator of the heavens and Earth. Natural cause (evolution) is not a powerful constructive mechanism, even given millions of years.

As one might expect, young-Earth creation, gap theology, day-age theology, and literary interpretations each contain a thread of truth. All four theologies recognize that in the beginning God created the heavens and Earth. The six 24-hour days stressed by young-Earth theology is true. Gap theology, day-age theology, and liter-ary interpretations recognize that Genesis 1:1 and 1:2 fall outside the rigid six-day time frame of the six-day Genesis chronicle. They recognize that Genesis 1:1, 1:2, and 1:3 occur in a chronological order and time is undefined between each verse. According to literary interpretations, the seven-day story describes the actions of a powerful creator God structured within six days of work and one day of rest to support the Sabbath. Proponents of all four theologies are able to view Genesis 2:5–25 as a detailed explanation of God's creative activities.

The legitimate textual and scientific objections to *exemplar* creation are insignificant; however, the emotional and political objections are monumental. Conservative Christians are quite comfortable with current orthodox translations of Genesis that support traditional young-Earth creation theology, and feel little compulsion to change. Liberals, who believe there are two contradictory creation accounts and reject Genesis as God inspired, also see no need to reverse their position.

The strengths and objections to *exemplar* creation, similar to the format given in Chapter 1, can be summarized as follows:

Strengths:

(1) Genesis 1:1 and 1:2 occur outside the rigid six-day time frame established in Genesis 1:3–31.

(2) Genesis 1:1, 1:2, and 1:3 occur in a chronological order.

(3) The six days described in Genesis 1:3–31 are six literal, consecutive, chronological, 24-hour days.

(4) The seven-day structure of Genesis 1:3–2:3 supports the Sabbath, codified in the Ten Commandments as six days of work and one day of rest.

(5) Genesis 2:4–25 can be readily viewed as a period of time during which God made the Garden of Eden, formed man, formed animals, and built woman.

(6) Genesis 2:5 applies to a land that was dry and barren where the garden was to be planted, rather than the entire Earth.

(7) The language of Genesis is fully respected. No words, phrases, or verses are treated as metaphorical, mythological, or untrue.

(8) *Exemplar* creation acknowledges the addition, mistranslation, and poor translation of key words in most English translations of Genesis Chapters 1 and 2. The "jussive/command" verb is a fabrication of biblical Hebrew grammar and rejected.

(9) The creation story records two commands in Genesis 1:28 and 2:16–17. The language of these commands is clear and significantly different from the alleged creation commands in Genesis 1:3, 6, 9, 11, 14, 20, and 24.

(10) Genesis 1:6–7, 14–16, 20–21, 24–25, and 26–27 represent five major parallelisms, rather than repetitive creation commands.

(11) God is creator of the heavens and Earth. Natural cause is not a significant constructive mechanism, even given millions of years.

(12) *Exemplar* creation allows for millions of years to occur prior to Genesis 1:3 and easily harmonizes with scientific evidence for significant time.

(13) An analysis of genealogies in the Old and New Testament shows that the lineages given in Genesis Chapters 5 and 11 do not require a direct father-to-son

relationship. Gaps between the listed descendants permit extending the appearance of anatomically modern man backward in time.

(14) God has full knowledge of our origins and inspired the writing of the Genesis account. The exact time and method God used to create the heavens, Earth, and all therein are not revealed in scripture, and man is left to his own resources to fill in the missing details.

(15) *Exemplar* creation supports Genesis Chapters 1 and 2 as being truthful and trustworthy.

(16) *Exemplar* creation provides a reliable framework around which to build new Bible-based theology and credible theory about origins in support of God as our creator.

Objections:

(1) Although orthodox translations of Genesis Chapters 1 and 2 are seriously in error, both conservatives and liberals are comfortable with their respective beliefs and have little motivation to change.

(2) The biblical community has accepted a misleading translation and explanation of Genesis for more than two thousand years, an embarrassing mistake.

Miscellaneous Questions

In a book of this nature, some topics mentioned in the normal flow of discussion deserve a more in-depth treatment. In addition, some questions tend to repeatedly surface during any serious dialogue. The following is a short discussion of some important questions related to *exemplar* creation and biblical origins.

(1) What is significant about the "beginning" in Genesis 1:1?

Genesis 1:1 begins with the simple statement that in the beginning God created the heavens and Earth. Both the heavens and Earth combined refer to the entire universe. As mentioned in Chapter 6, Dr. John Sailhamer points out that the term "beginning" as used in the Bible can indicate a span of time. Within that span of time, the universe had a definite starting point.

Scientists overwhelmingly accept the fact that the universe is expanding. Based on redshift, galaxies are moving apart and that movement can be logically extrapolated backward in time to when all matter in the universe was contained in a single, large, ultra dense, high temperature spherical mass. At that point, a simple extrapolation of movement breaks down and cannot account for how all the mass of the universe came into existence from absolutely nothing. An appeal must be made to other mechanisms.

How the original mass of the universe came into existence is a matter of debate.

Philosophical naturalists say that all matter popped into existence out of nothing within a three minute period during the Big Bang. All matter and energy evolved from nothing (*evolutio ex nihilo*). Theists can as readily say God created all original matter (*creatio ex nihilo*). One major point agreed on by both sides is that the universe had a *beginning*. The concept of a beginning taught in the creation account is supported by twenty-first century scientific theory. In the absence of compelling evidence to the contrary, we can accept Genesis 1:1 as an abbreviated, non-technical, historical account that is true.

(2) What is significant about the description of the Earth in Genesis 1:2?

The New Encyclopedia Britannica, supplemented by other sources, gives a good overview of factual information and current theory about the history of early Earth. Allegedly, our solar system formed according to the solar nebular hypothesis. The necessary materials came from a large interstellar cloud of gas, dust, and debris. During a period of roughly 100 million years, a protoplanetary disk formed by self-gravity with the Sun at its center. The planets then "accreted" out of materials in the rim. After enough solid material had collected by self-gravity to form Earth, the resultant mass was heated and melted by (1) the decay of short-lived radioactive isotopes, (2) gravitational energy released from sinking metals, and (3) the impact of small planets. Earth was a molten ball about 4.6 billion years ago with an estimated surface temperature of 600° C (the low end of the temperature range for melted magmas). Water, trapped in rock from which the Earth was formed, vaporized, and precipitated to the surface before the crust hardened. Other gases released into the atmosphere include carbon dioxide, carbon monoxide, and hydrogen sulfide. The Earth underwent extensive meteor bombardment during roughly the first 700 million years.[1] Due to its dense, high pressure, hot atmosphere, Earth's surface was much like that of present-day Venus.[2]

Unfortunately, *Britannica* is typical of scientific writing that mixes fact and conjecture, without making a serious effort to distinguish the difference. Because of this practice, scientific knowledge has been corrupted to an extent. When the two are indiscriminately mixed, separating them is important.

The solar nebular hypothesis is not supported by the basic laws of chemistry and physics, and represents a speculative idea based on a firm belief in natural cause. The nebular hypothesis cannot explain the collapse of hydrogen and helium gases by self-gravity to form the Sun (or any star). An interstellar cloud composed of only these gases will not collapse and agglomerate by self-gravity. Hydrogen and helium gas have a strong tendency to diffuse and disperse rather than coalesce. In addition, the solar nebular hypothesis cannot explain how the Sun ended up with 99.87% of the mass, yet less than 3% of the angular momentum. The mass/momentum problem alone totally discredits this hypothesis.

The three natural ideas proposed in *Britannica* about how Earth's initial raw materials were melted are primarily conjecture. (1) While short lived radioactive isotopes at one time existed, it is inconceivable they provided the necessary heat to melt the entire Earth. The two isotopes, iron-60 and aluminum-16, are sometimes mentioned as potential candidates. Solid evidence is lacking to show these two isotopes could have provided the necessary heat. In addition, if it took 100 million years for the gas, dust, and debris within an interstellar cloud to coalesce into a protoplanetary disk, all short-term isotopes would have essentially disappeared. (2) Gravitational energy is real, but converting all of it to heat energy is not plausible. For example, imagine an asteroid attracted to the Moon by gravity. Due to the absence of air, no heating occurs from atmospheric friction (the same conditions of early Earth). On impact, the asteroid fractures and displaces surface material to form a crater. In general, impacts of this type produce very little heat, and kinetic energy is dissipated through deformation, fracture, displacement, and vibration. Supporters of this idea have failed to explain the physics behind their belief. (3) The impact of small planets on early Earth is speculative and most likely would have been destructive rather than constructive. Such an event would have exploded the loosely joined materials similar to a fast moving golf ball hitting a packed sphere of wet sand.

Based on the laws of chemistry and physics, no plausible natural explanation has yet been developed for the Earth's initial formation and its subsequent heating to a molten condition. When carefully examined, all current ideas based strictly on natural cause have serious problems and are speculation.

In Genesis 1:1, God is identified as creator of the Earth, and we can readily accept this account. He gathered the required solid materials into a single mass and then melted them to form Earth as a molten ball. We do not know the details of this constructive process.

The radiometric analysis of igneous rocks indicates our solar system and Earth were formed about 4.6 billion years ago. This age is based on the radiometric dating of Earth rocks, Moon rocks (obtained from various Moon expeditions), and meteors that have impacted Earth. Meteorites are the oldest, followed by Moon rocks and then Earth magmas. According to theory, molten material within the meteors cooled first because of their smaller size and started the clock ticking. The Moon solidified next, followed by the Earth. The oldest rocks found on Earth are around 3.9 billion years old. Any surface rocks that formed during the first 700 million years recycled into the molten mantle until the planet cooled sufficiently.[3]

A molten condition is a basic requirement for the formation of a spherical planet or moon by self-gravity. For example, of the 162 confirmed moons in our solar system, 18 are spherical moons (Proteus is not counted as spherical) and the remaining 144 are irregular moons, considered captured asteroids. Whatever their origin, the irregular rocky moons have never been completely melted in their current state. The 8 planets (Pluto was demoted) and 18 spherical moons reflect a once totally melted condition. Enceladus, a moon of Saturn, is one of the smaller spherical moons with a radius of 250 km (155 miles).

A completely molten condition allowed self-gravity to form Earth into a sphere, essentially as round and smooth as a billiard ball. Due to its molten condition, there were no raised continents, deep valleys, or uplifted mountains.

A completely liquid state allowed Earth's metals and minerals to differentiate into three major zones, identified as the crust, mantle, and core, based on density effects. Our planet's density progressively increases from the crust to the core (the core is about four times as dense as the crust). For natural differentiation to have taken place, a fully melted condition, gravity, and significant time are required.

Earth's surface water supports our planet as being molten at some time in the past. Meteorite rocks contain a small amount of entrapped water. Our planet's original solid materials are believed to have likewise contained a small percentage of water (less than one percent). As these materials were compacted and melted, a combination of pressure, gravity, temperature, and density effects forced vaporized water to the surface. Since Earth's surface was quite hot, all water remained in vapor form, creating an atmosphere saturated with water.

In regard to water sources, icy comets and erupting volcanoes are often hypothesized as a source for Earth's surface water. They may have contributed a small amount, but cannot account for the large quantity of water found on our planet.

The atmosphere on early Earth was dramatically different from today's, as shown by a quick analysis of three important facts. First, if our planet's surface were perfectly smooth, present surface water would cover Earth to a depth of 2.72 kilometers (1.69 miles). Second, the surface temperature of early Earth is conservatively estimated at 600° C. Third, when heated above its critical temperature of 374° C (705° F), water will remain in vapor form and may be compressed to any density without liquefying.[4] The typical density of water vapor is 0.325 gm/cm^3 at its critical temperature and pressure[5] (almost one-third the density of liquid water). Based on this information, *all surface water was kept in vapor form* because of the hot planetary surface. The high temperatures and pressures resulted in a significantly deeper atmosphere (the atmosphere expanded outward). Conditions on Earth were no doubt more extreme than found on Venus today, where the surface temperature is around 450° C (842° F) and the pressure is 90 bars (1,305 psi).

In summary, the conditions on early Earth were dominated by high temperature and water. The Earth's surface temperature was 600° C or more. All water forced from the interior of the planet to the surface was held in the atmosphere as vapor. At that point, Earth was in the grip of a massive self-sustaining greenhouse effect. We can hypothesize that Divine action was required to halt this effect and begin cooling. As the planet slowly cooled, hot vapor condensed into water to form a single ocean that covered the entire planet. With no upraised continents or mountains, Earth was essentially as smooth and round as a billiard ball. At most, some upraised impact craters or volcanic cones may have existed. The ocean was hot enough to keep the atmosphere saturated with moisture (imagine an ocean temperature of 200° F). As a result, continuous clouds covered the entire planet and blocked out the sunlight.

At the time described in Genesis 1:2, Earth was vacant and empty of life, and darkness reigned over its deep surface water—a better description than given in the 15th edition of *The New Encyclopedia Britannica.* We can fully accept Genesis 1:2 as an accurate, abbreviated description of early Earth.

(3) What is significant about the great reptiles mentioned on the fifth day?

What we know about dinosaurs is found in the fossil record. They lived and died a long time ago, significantly before the appearance of man on Earth. Some were enormous creatures. Today scientists have divided these large prehistoric animals into dinosaurs and reptiles. Large marine reptiles include the mosasaurs, icthyosaurs, and plesiosaurs. Large amphibious reptiles include the kronosaurus, while flying reptiles are represented by the pterosaurs.

From a scientific viewpoint, the discovery and explanation of dinosaurs is relatively recent. The word dinosauria was coined by anatomist Sir Richard Owen in a report he published in 1842, from the Greek word *deinos* "terrible, powerful" combined with *sauros* "lizard."[6] Dinosaur and large reptile bones were essentially unknown to scientists until the early 1800s when they began to be noticed and then sought after. Prior to 1800, people occasionally found dinosaur fossils, but were unable to rationally explain their findings.

The *exemplar* translation of Genesis reveals some unique historical information about large reptiles. On the fifth day in Genesis 1:20, the Earth is described as supporting abundant aquatic life and flying creatures. No great reptiles are mentioned. In Genesis 1:21, God is credited with *creating* the great reptiles in addition to the aquatic life and flying creatures previously mentioned. These two verses are accurate statements about the absence of large reptiles on the Earth when God spoke these words (probably to Moses) and the existence of great reptiles in the past as a creation of God. These verses are unique and support the Genesis account as an abbreviated, non-technical, historical account that is true.

(4) What is significant about the timing of man's appearance in Genesis?

According to current scientific evidence, anatomically modern man appears to be the last significant species to appear on Earth. New species of animals have developed since the appearance of man due to separation, isolation, and random change; however, these species are quite similar to the original. For example, we can hypothesize that all dogs came from a single gray wolf species based on mitochondrial DNA, yet today they represent in excess of 175 domestic dog breeds.

According to the Genesis story, man was the last species created on Earth, except for a small number of animals and birds created for the Garden of Eden (Genesis 2:19). Animal species found in the fossil record clearly predate the appearance of anatomically modern man. Genesis gives an accurate statement about the appearance of man and woman in relation to animals. Their correct order of appearance supports Genesis as a true historical account.

Fossil and archaeological evidence support the recent appearance of anatomically modern man roughly 15,000–30,000 years ago. The establishment of permanent cities and villages, beginning with Abu Hureyra on the Euphrates River around 11,000 BC, mark the rise of civilization.

Strong scientific evidence supports the existence of hominids before the appearance of anatomically modern man. Although the precise time for the appearance of many hominids is questionable (due to the limitations of carbon-14 dating and the absence of other reliable direct dating methods), fossil remains firmly confirm their presence. Prior to anatomically modern man, Neanderthal, proto-Neanderthal, and other hominids walked the Earth. Because of their inability to survive, they became extinct. They were inferior to anatomically modern man when judged by their tools, weapons, shelter, art, and burial practices (or the lack thereof). We can conclude that Adam and Eve were the first anatomically modern humans and the first hominids on Earth created in the image of God. All hominids created prior to Adam were not in the image and likeness of God (Genesis 1:26). Regardless of their capabilities, they lacked the distinctive characteristics given to Adam.

(5) What is significant about Adam cultivating the ground of the garden?

The Garden of Eden had several purposes, other than only a place for Adam and Eve to enjoy. Foremost, the garden was a sinless environment where man communed directly with God. On a more practical level, the garden was a place of security and safety from the predatory animals that roamed outside its boundaries. The garden was also a training environment where Adam was taught to cultivate the ground (Genesis 2:15) and grow food to survive.

When seriously considered, the logic for the Garden of Eden is readily apparent. God created Adam, but he had no inherent skills or experience. Without protection the garden afforded, Adam would have easily succumbed to wild animals. Without training, he would have starved once cast out of the garden. So the garden provided a place for Adam to learn, adjust to his surroundings, and become prepared for the world outside. We can accept the Garden of Eden as a requirement for the survival of newly created man.

(6) How could God call His creation "very good" in Genesis 1:31 if there had been millions of years of death and disease?

Proponents of traditional young-Earth creation theology say that God could not have called His creation "very good" in Genesis 1:31 if there had been millions of years of disease, pain, suffering, death, and extinction.[7] From their viewpoint, the expression "very good" indicates no animal death occurred on Earth before the fall of Adam (his sin and punishment).[8] According to their belief, no animals died or killed each other for food.[9] Earth was perfect before the fall.[10] Supporters of this theology say that before the fall there were no thorns or thistles, no struggle for survival, no carnivorous animals, no predator-prey relationships, and no death on the entire planet.

The no-death-before-Adam's-sin theology has been refined over the years. According to this belief, the curse (due to Adam's sin) affected the physical elements, the animal kingdom, and mankind.[11] Vertebrate animals (including fish) did not die before the fall; however, invertebrates and insects were killed and eaten.[12] No vertebrates were diseased, died of natural causes, or were killed by predators before Adam sinned.[13] Plants died naturally and were eaten. This theology is founded primarily on Romans 5:12, 1 Corinthians 15:20–22, Rom. 8:19–23, and Genesis 1:31.

Romans 5:12 says, "Therefore, just as sin came into the world through one man, and death through sin, and so death spread to all men because all sinned" (ESV). This verse clearly teaches that sin entered the world by one man and death came to all men because of Adam's sin. Animals are not mentioned in this verse. There is no statement that Adam's sin caused animals to die. There is no implication that animals sin or die because they sin.

1 Corinthians 15:21–22 says, "For as by a man came death, by a man has come also the resurrection of the dead. For as in Adam all die, so also in Christ shall all be made alive" (ESV). This verse says that death came to all mankind through Adam. Animals are not a topic in this verse. There is no mention that Adam's sin caused animal death or that animals can be made alive through Jesus Christ.

Romans 8:18–23 says, "For I consider that the sufferings of this present time are not worth comparing with the glory that is to be revealed to us. For the creation waits with eager longing for the revealing of the sons of God. For the creation was subjected to futility, not willingly, but because of him who subjected it, in hope that the creation itself will be set free from its bondage to corruption and obtain the freedom of the glory of the children of God. For we know that the whole creation has been groaning together in the pains of childbirth until now. And not only the creation, but we ourselves, who have the firstfruits of the Spirit, groan inwardly as we wait eagerly for adoption as sons, the redemption of our bodies" (ESV).

The above scripture is similar to Psalms 102:25–26 which says, "Of old you laid the foundation of the earth, and the heavens are the work of your hands. They will perish, but you will remain; they will all wear out like a garment. You will change them like a robe, and they will pass away" (ESV).

Contrary to young-Earth belief, the language of Romans 8:18–23 does not connect well with the language of Genesis regarding the fall of man. There is no declaration that bondage to corruption started in the Garden of Eden. There is no reference to Adam's sin and punishment. There is no specific statement that Adam's sin caused the bondage to corruption the creation is experiencing. As Dr. C. John Collins points out, the terms of Genesis 3:16–19 are not used in these verses.[14]

A combination of scripture and general revelation give the best explanation of Romans 8:18–23 about the decay of God's creation. These verses say "creation was subjected to futility," creation is in the "bondage to corruption," and creation has been groaning in "pains of childbirth." We can explain these statements in reference to the initial creation of the heavens and Earth as described in Genesis 1:1. Since the very beginning, the universe has been deteriorating and running down. The Second Law of Thermodynamics has always applied. God subjected our universe to decay at its inception.

We can view Romans 8:18–23 as a comparison between creation (the universe) and our human bodies. God made them both. Just as creation is in bondage to corruption, so also are our bodies to sin. Someday in the future, creation will be set free from its bondage and in like manner our bodies will be redeemed.

Genesis 1:31 says, "And God saw all that *He had* done, and behold *it was* very good." God's pronouncement of very good on the sixth day was a summarizing statement about the beautiful, well-functioning, highly complex world He had created. Very good summarizes what was described on the preceding days.

- On day one, light is proclaimed as *good* (Gen. 1:4).

- On the third day, the waters and dry land are described as *good* (Gen. 1:10) and vegetation is called *good* (Gen. 1:12).

- On the fourth day, the Sun and Moon are recognized as *good* (Gen. 1:18).

- On the fifth day, marine life and flying creatures are labeled *good* (Gen. 1:21).

- On the sixth day, land animals are identified as *good* (Gen. 1:25).

Exemplar creation proposes that animals existed on Earth for an undefined period of time previous to the creation of Adam and Eve. Animals were created by God between Genesis 1:2 and 1:3. Animal struggle, disease, pain, suffering, death, and extinction occurred from inception.

If Earth had been a perfect place, the Garden of Eden would have been unnecessary. Obviously, there was death and danger in the world because God made a protected enclosure where man could develop. He created a place where food was plentiful, without thorns and thistles. Only animals harmless to man lived in the garden. There were no dangerous bears, lions, tigers, hyenas, wolves, poisonous spiders, and venomous snakes. We can infer from scripture that no significant predator-prey relationships existed in the garden.

In Genesis 2:16–17, Adam is commanded to not eat of the tree of knowledge of good and evil, and warned that if he eats of the tree he will die. There is no mention of animals being instructed to not eat of the tree of knowledge. In fact, animals are incapable of discerning good from evil.

In Genesis 3:14–19, Adam, Eve, and the serpent are the only ones mentioned as being punished after disobeying God's command. As part of Adam and Eve's punishment, they were cast out of the garden into a harsh world of sweat and toil. The prevalence of thorns and thistles describe the "cursed ground" they were to cultivate. The serpent was punished and condemned to crawl on its belly. Except for the serpent, there is no mention of other animals being cursed. Animals outside the garden were completely unaffected by Adam's fall. We should not mistakenly assume that all animals on the Earth were cursed along with the serpent.

God's relationship in the Bible is primarily with humans—not animals. Man communed with God in the garden, not animals. Man sinned against God, not animals. Man was cast out of the garden, not animals. Man was given the Ten Commandments, not animals. Man was commanded to offer sacrifices for sins in the Old Testament, not animals. Jesus Christ came to die for the sins of mankind, not animals. There is no hint in scripture that animals follow a moral code, sin when killing each other, or need redemption from sin.

Many animals are obviously predators, and if traditional young-Earth creationists are correct, substantial redesign would have been required after Adam's sin. Lions have powerful jaws, large fangs, sharp claws, and powerful leg muscles to make them good predators. Venomous snakes have sharp fangs, poison sacs, and deadly venom to kill prey. Spiders weave webs and paralyze prey with their poisonous bite. If these animals were not meant to be predators, why were they created this way? No-death-before-Adam's-sin theology cannot explain the physical features of these animals. This theology requires predatory animals to have acquired their features after Adam's fall.[15] The most plausible explanation is that God created these animals with all their predatory features at inception, long before Adam sinned.

Without predatory animals, Earth's biology would quickly become unbalanced. Rabbits, rats, mice, and other fast multiplying animals would quickly overrun the land. Ultimately, starvation would be the primary means for restricting population growth. Predator-prey relationships are the chief method of population control.

When God described the Earth in Genesis 1:31, it was "very good." The Earth and its fine-tuned biosphere were working as planned. Plants were sprouting and growing in abundance as designed. Marine life and birds moved about in swarming swarms. Animals filled the land and reproduced faithfully after their kind. A multitude of carefully balanced dependent, symbiotic, and synergistic relationships were working as conceived. Predator-prey relationships existed as part of a food chain ultimately based on plant life. Millions of complex plants and animals were growing and reproducing as intended. Although not perfect, God was pleased with what He saw and called it "very good."

In summary, no-death-before-Adam's-sin theology is a prime example of thinking gone awry. This theology is little more than religious philosophy and is not directly supported by either the Bible or general revelation. The absence of animal violence, disease, and death on the entire Earth before the fall negates the reason for building the Garden of Eden as a protective enclosure for Adam and Eve. This theology supposes that animal death and predator-prey relationships are evil and sinful, and misinterprets God's approval of "very good" on the Earth. (*Peril in Paradise* by Mark Whorton gives a more complete discussion of this issue.)

The view supported by both scripture and general revelation is that the universe has been deteriorating since the beginning. At inception God subjected His creation to physical decay. On Earth, God created animals that experienced disease, pain, suffering, death, and extinction. The Garden of Eden was a protected place from the violence, danger, thorns, thistles, and cursed ground outside. Mankind was given a means of escaping decay through access to the tree of life. If Adam and Eve had never sinned, from a distance they could have looked at the world outside and not been subject to its harmful effects. Having fallen, they were thrown out of the garden into a world of predatory animals and dangerous things.[16] The great evil was not the events taking place outside the garden, but Adam and Eve's personal sin which caused them to suffer the judgment of God in being cast out of paradise.

(7) Does Genesis shed any light on the problem of pain, suffering, and evil?

The existence of pain, suffering, and evil in the world is an important theological issue of our time. When American adults were polled by George Barna about what question they would ask God if they had the opportunity, the overwhelming choice was, "Why is there so much suffering in the world?"[17] We often hear people blame God for permitting war, the death of a loved one, or a tragic disaster.

Several theologians and writers have addressed the issue of suffering. C. S. Lewis wrote about the subject more than 70 years ago in *The Problem of Pain*. More recently this topic is addressed in *When Bad Things Happen to Good People* by Rabbi Harold S. Kushner, *When God Doesn't Make Sense* by Dr. James Dobson, and *Trusting God: Even When Life Hurts* by Jerry Bridges. Two additional books are *Why Do Bad Things Happen if God is Good?* by Dr. Ron Rhodes and *Is God to Blame* by Dr. Gregory A. Boyd.

Philosophers have also addressed the issue of pain, suffering, and evil. Biblical skeptics and atheists typically use disease, destruction, disaster, and death to attack the nature of God. Philosophers from David Hume[18] to Arthur Schopenhauer[19] have questioned how God could be wise, loving, benevolent, and all-powerful with so much misery in the world—a question often posed to first year philosophy students. If God is loving and kind, why is there so much pain and suffering? If God is the sovereign ruler of the universe, why do bad things happen? The atheist's answer is that God does not exist, while others say God does not care or is powerless to do anything.

As discussed in *When God Doesn't Make Sense* by Rabbi Harold S. Kushner, when we experience pain and suffering, God seems distant and impersonal. Kushner says it is hard to live with the idea that things happen for no reason, that God has lost touch with the world, and nobody is in the driver's seat.[20] Pointless suffering is hard to bear. According to Kushner, when bad things happen to good people this inevitably raises questions about the goodness, kindness, and existence of God. Random things happen and randomness is a key philosophical issue.[21] The laws of nature are necessary, but they do not make exceptions for good, useful, or nice people.[22] Humans are made in the image of God and have free choice. Their actions can be good or bad.[23] Kushner believes that miracles happen, but not as an answer to prayer or because of God.[24] This perspective leads one to believe we must suffer and persevere without much hope. For those who adopt Kushner's viewpoint, God is distant and impersonal.

A substantially different position is taken in *Trusting God: Even When Life Hurts* by author Jerry Bridges. He says God is sovereign and rules absolutely over His creation to control it.[25] Bridges believes that no one can act outside God's sovereign will or against it.[26] By extension, God controls everything that happens including rape, murder, robbery, accidents, war, natural disasters, and disease. According to Bridges' logic, although God loves us, He specifically causes all bad things that happen. Rather than recognizing this theological contradiction, Bridges views it as a mystery known only to God. Humans were created with free will. According to Bridges, God permits people to act contrary to *His revealed will* (the Bible), but not His *sovereign will* (God's detailed scripted plan for each human).[27] As before, rather than identifying this as a theological contradiction, Bridges sees it as a mystery known only to God. He says things do not just happen in the world—God controls all.[28] Bridges says that God never explains what He is doing to us or why.[29] God's ways are incomprehensible to man (Deut. 29:29, Isaiah 55:8).[30] Bridges' explanation of suffering appears to be from a strong Calvinistic perspective. God is sovereign and uses His power to control every aspect of our life. He causes all pain, suffering, and evil. For those who adopt this viewpoint, life is fatalistic since everything is foreordained, predestined, and scripted by God.

A third contrasting view of the sovereignty of God and human suffering is given in *Is God to Blame: Moving Beyond Pat Answers to the Problem of Evil* by Dr. Gregory A. Boyd. He rejects blueprint theology that claims God uses His power to control (micromanage) every individual and everything that happens in the world. Boyd says blueprint theology engenders bitterness towards God when bad things happen to us.[31] Jesus' actions on Earth indicate what God is like—loving, merciful, kind, and empathetic to human suffering.[32] God is sovereign.[33] God as creator established the laws of nature to create an orderly stable world.[34] Boyd says God gave irrevocable free will to humans, the Devil and angels[35] and God is at warfare with Satan and his followers. Free will can be used for good or evil. Boyd believes that God's actions are self-constrained by what He established at creation. The constraints of a stable world and irrevocable free will are strong enough to prevent God from always unilaterally intervening to prevent evil and suffering.[36] According to Boyd, God orchestrates events to happen. God's actions can be influenced by prayer and He can intercede for our benefit. Sometimes God intervenes and sometimes He does not—a mystery known only to Him. We know what God is like through Jesus Christ (John 10:30,

14:7). God through Jesus Christ has great compassion and love for people (Matthew 8:16, 12:22, 14:14, 15:30, 15:32, 19:2, 20:34; John 3:16, 15:9; Ephesians 2:4, 3:9, 5:2; Titus 3:4; 1 John 3:16, 4:8, 4:19). God fully understands the human condition through Jesus who experienced pain, suffering, and death.

With these three different viewpoints as a reference, can a rational explanation be given for pain, suffering, and evil in the world? Is there an answer that respects God as a loving, kind, powerful creator, yet allows for misfortune? Understanding Genesis Chapters 1–3 and its implications are essential to properly answer this important question. Twelve key reasons have been identified as follows:

(1) Impartial laws – God, as Creator and Designer of the universe, established the laws of chemistry and physics. The consistent operation of basic physical phenomena is a requirement to have order and stability. Systems established by God are overwhelmingly beneficial in making the Earth habitable for life. For example, the law of gravity is essential for the proper operation of our solar system, Earth, and its biosphere. If gravity did not exist, the planets could not orbit the Sun, the Moon could not orbit Earth, our atmosphere would quickly be lost to the vacuum of space, and everything on Earth would die. Unfortunately, gravity has its down side and people can be injured or killed by its effects. Laws are impersonal and affect everyone the same. As mentioned in Matthew 5:45, God causes the sun to shine on both the good and the evil, and He sends rain on the just and the unjust.

(2) Competing factors – When God created Earth's biosphere, competing factors were an integral part of its design. As every engineer knows, design of a complicated system normally involves a balance of competing factors. In human designs, weight, size, cost, function, durability, aesthetics, and technological improvement must be integrated together in the final product.

One of the competing factors among animals involves predator-prey relationships and death. Free reproduction and population growth in animals must be balanced by death caused by aging, disease, sickness, starvation, accidents, and predators. If predators did not exist, then an increase in death due to other causes would be required. God designed predators as the primary means of controlling animal population size.

Some sensitive individuals are bothered by predator-prey relationships and animal death. They are repulsed by killing behavior. In their self-righteousness, God is condemned as cruel for designing animals that kill. Regardless, the Bible does not teach that the killing of one animal by another is evil or sinful. God established predator-prey relationships as the primary means to prevent overcrowding and starvation among animals, while permitting free reproduction.

(3) Paradise lost – God originally created the Garden of Eden as a protective enclosure for Adam and Eve to live in. The garden was a controlled environment where food was abundant, the animals harmless, and the weather favorable. Adam sinned and as a result was cast out, never to return. Outside the garden, predatory animals, harmful plants, thorns, thistles, and weeds were the norm. Mankind strug-

gled to survive against disease, plague, pestilence, and famine. Man was pummeled by natural disasters in the form of tornadoes, hurricanes, earthquakes, volcanoes, tsunamis, and floods. Adam, endowed with free will and intelligence, was fully responsible for being cast out of the garden.

(4) Sin and death – Adam and Eve sinned by disobeying God and were condemned to die. Subsequently, the curse of death passed to all humanity. Death is a fact of life. Based on the Bible, we can firmly say that: (a) God told Adam and Eve they would die if they ate of the tree of knowledge of good and evil. (b) Eve and Adam subsequently ate of the forbidden tree. (c) Adam and Eve were cast out of the garden and banned from the tree of life. (d) Adam and Eve physically died. (e) All subsequent humans have been subject to physical death.

We are not guilty of Adam and Eve's sin, but we are subject to the consequences of their sin—physical death. We all understand the consequences of other people's irresponsible actions. For example, a driver who falls asleep can injure a law abiding pedestrian. A disease carrier can infect a host of healthy individuals. Unsanitary conditions in food processing can make thousands of trusting customers sick. Most people can accept the unfortunate *consequences* of other people's actions, but refuse to accept *responsibility* for those actions without personal involvement. Lest we judge Adam and Eve too harshly, we would undoubtedly make the same decision if placed in the same circumstances. Some key verses related to death are:

• Therefore, just as through one man sin entered the world, and death through sin, and thus death spread to all men, because all sinned. For until the law sin was in the world, but sin is not imputed when there is no law. Nevertheless death reigned from Adam to Moses, even over those who had not sinned according to the likeness of the transgression of Adam, who is a type of Him who was to come. (Romans 5:12–14, NKJV)

• For if by the one man's offense death reigned through the one, much more those who receive abundance of grace and of the gift of righteousness will reign in life through the One, Jesus Christ. (Romans 5:17, NKJV)

• For as in Adam all die, even so in Christ all shall be made alive. (1 Corinthians 15:22, NKJV)

• And as it is appointed for men to die once, but after this the judgment. (Hebrews 9:27, NKJV)

(5) Consequences of death – The dying process involves infection, disease, malignancy, mutation, weakness, pain, and suffering. These conditions are a result of the curse placed on Adam, and an inherent part of physical death. From a human perspective, we would like to live fourscore and ten years in perfect health and then die quietly in our sleep. Although possible, this rarely happens.

(6) Human free will – Genesis Chapters 1–3 clearly teach that God gave man free will to choose, which includes the ability to disobey. In the Garden of Eden, man

had only one prohibition—not to eat of the tree of knowledge of good and evil. God could have excluded Lucifer and the tree of knowledge of good and evil from the garden, but did not. He could have insulated man from evil and temptation, making it essentially impossible to disobey. God gave Adam both the ability and means to make choices.

God has extended free will to all mankind throughout history. People like freedom to choose and want the ability to accept or reject God. Individuals want to control their own destiny.

Unfortunately free will has a down side. With universal free will extended to all humanity, it can be used for unspeakable evil. As C. S. Lewis said, we have abused our free will. Man's inhumanity to man is legend throughout history as millions have died due to crime, war, and genocide. During the twentieth century alone, more than 90 million people were killed due to political purges, ideological purification, and racial cleansing—rather than war with another country.[37] Essentially all genocide occurred in Communist and totalitarian regimes, as opposed to democratic nations with a strong Christian influence. People killing their fellow countrymen made the last century one of the bloodiest in world history. Man is truly his own worst enemy and God cannot be blamed for the misery caused by the abuse of free will.

(7) Satan's influence – Evil is an important concept taught in Genesis and is represented by a literal Devil in rebellion against God. Although Satan is discussed elsewhere in the Bible, his major effect on humanity is recorded in Genesis. The Devil, in the form of a serpent (Genesis 3:1–7, 2 Corinthians 11:3, Revelation 20:2), influenced Eve to eat of the tree of the knowledge of good and evil. Through Adam and Eve's disobedience, their lives were radically changed for the worse.

The Devil's influence in the world continues to worsen the state of man. He promotes disobedience and rebellion against God. He promotes lying, theft, murder, self-harm, sexual violence, hatred, war, and genocide. Why are there mass murders? Why are there sexual predators? Why are there terrorists? In part, because man has free will and his actions are influenced by the ultimate purveyor of evil—the Devil.

Currently, God significantly restrains the Devil's actions. In the book of Job, God allowed the Devil to take away Job's property and children. The Devil was then allowed to afflict Job's body, but was forbidden to take his life. Although free to influence man's thinking, God restrains the Devil's physical actions against us.

(8) Sowing and reaping – We are subject to the law of cause and effect. "Be not deceived; God is not mocked: for whatsoever a man soweth, that shall he also reap." (Galatians 6:7)

As individuals we often bring bad things on ourselves by our own sinful or foolish actions. The sexually promiscuous person who contracts AIDS has only himself to blame. The person who takes an illegal drug that destroys his body must accept personal responsibility. The drunken driver who causes an automobile accident is guilty as charged. The man who ruins his liver through excessive drinking can only accuse himself.

(9) Random events – A certain amount of randomness happens in the world. Our driving route to work on a given day may determine whether we are involved in a collision. The restaurant selected for a meal may determine if we get food poisoning. Personal contact with others may determine if we get a cold. Carelessness while working may result in an accident. A certain amount of randomness occurs based on human behavior, time, and location. Hurricanes, tornadoes, blizzards, earthquakes, tsunamis, and other natural phenomena are significantly random.

(10) Chastisement – God has the ability to chasten those He loves when they sin. Hebrews 12:5–11 speaks about the chastening hand of God. We are chastened by God similar to a father correcting his son for disobedience. Chastening helps us become holy, righteous, and obedient people. As explained in Revelation 3:19, "As many as I love, I rebuke and chasten: be zealous therefore, and repent."

(11) God's providence – God desires specific events to occur and uses His power to accomplish His will. For example, God promised Abraham that he would have offspring and caused Sarah to become pregnant. God orchestrated events to bring Joseph into a position of authority in Egypt. God delivered the children of Israel from Egypt. God raised up various judges to free Israel from their oppressors. Throughout history God has protected the Bible from attempts to destroy it. God interferes in the affairs of men to accomplish His will.

(12) Righteous prayer – God is influenced by and hears the prayer of the righteous. "The effectual fervent prayer of a righteous man availeth much." (James 5:16) In the Old Testament, God answered Hannah's prayer for a son, Solomon's prayer for wisdom, Hezekiah's prayer for healing and Elijah's prayer to withhold rain. In the New Testament, God answered Zacharias' prayer that Elizabeth might conceive a son (Luke 1:13), the church's prayer for the release of the imprisoned Peter (Acts 12:5), a prayer of boldness for the believers (Acts 4:29–31), and Peter's prayer for Tabitha to be healed (Acts 9:40).

Christians have full authority to pray directly to God. "Seeing then that we have a great high priest, that is passed into the heavens, Jesus the Son of God, let us hold fast our profession. For we have not an high priest which cannot be touched with the feeling of our infirmities; but was in all points tempted like as we are, yet without sin. Let us therefore come boldly unto the throne of grace, that we may obtain mercy, and find grace to help in time of need." (Hebrews 4:14–16)

Through Jesus Christ, God understands the human condition and is sympathetic. Christians can pray about their concerns and troubles. "Do not be anxious about anything, but in everything, by prayer and petition, with thanksgiving, present your requests to God." (Philemon 4:6) God can intervene in the decisions of men and the impartial actions of nature to answer our prayers.

So why do bad things happen? The answer is significantly more complex than saying, "God is sovereign." The real issue is *how God uses His power and authority.*

Based on the above twelve reasons, we are often unable to specifically determine why some bad things happen. In other instances, the cause is crystal clear. Man's continued sinful rebellion against God's moral code results in a significant amount of pain, suffering, and evil in the world today. Man's selfish desires have caused untold misery. Short sightedness and poor judgment cause a substantial amount of grief for ourselves and others. The consequences of personal anger, hatred, revenge, and intense jealously are normally regrettable.

From the above, what general statements can be made about God? We can correctly say that God allows pain, suffering, and evil in the world. Nothing happens that He does not allow. Most likely, God does not specifically cause the trouble we experience. In all likelihood, bad things that happen are not a direct result of the chastening hand of God. Although God can use the evil actions and intentions of wicked men to accomplish His desires, we should not accuse God of evil. For example, because of their hatred and jealously, Joseph's brothers sold him into slavery. Because Potiphar's wife falsely accused Joseph of sexual assault, he was cast into prison. God used these events and, in combination with dreams He revealed to Joseph, brought him into a position of power in Egypt. We should not accuse God of directly causing Joseph's brothers or Potiphar's wife to sin.

God is sovereign and ultimately in control, but for the present allows events to occur that are contrary to His holy, loving, and compassionate nature. His actions are self-constrained because of previous decisions. The laws of chemistry and physics are impersonal, and we can be harmed by them. Currently, the Devil influences human thinking to promote rebellion and sin. At present, men are able to use their personal freedom for evil purposes. In this world, we are subject to death, random events, and the impartial forces of nature.

Life may be likened to being a participant in a long-term spiritual contest (similar to Job). The good news is that God has revealed himself to us as the creator and controller. Through the Bible, He has shown us how to handle difficulties and live with hope. God fully understands the struggles and temptations we face. He is sympathetic to our fate. He wants us to believe in Him. By accepting Jesus Christ, we can have forgiveness of personal sin, freedom from guilt, a moral compass, and real purpose in living. God hears the Christian's prayer and can intervene. God is fully knowledgeable of man's actions, thoughts, and intentions. Eventually, all men, good and evil, rich and poor, will stand before God and be judged for their deeds. Those who have accepted Jesus Christ as their creator, redeemer, savior, and lord will be rewarded. Those who have rejected God and lived lives of selfishness, rebellion, and sin will be cast into everlasting torment reserved for the Devil and his angels. At the judgment, the evil will be punished and the righteous rewarded as clearly taught in Matt. 11:22, 12:36, 13:40–43, 13:47–50, 25:41, 25:46, 2 Thess. 1:5–9, Rom. 2:1-9, 14:10–12, 2 Pet. 2: 4–10, Rev. 20:10, 20:12–15.

Although the subject of pain, suffering, and evil is complex, the Bible gives a reason why most bad things happen. Genesis should be a major part of any biblical explanation, and we should be skeptical of any theology that ignores this portion of scripture. Accepting Genesis Chapters 1–3 as truthful and trustworthy permits the development of credible theology to explain God's influence in the world.

(8) Why has Genesis been translated wrong for the past two hundred years?

During the last two hundred years, newly discovered scientific evidence supports the Earth as being more than 6,000 years old; however, this information has not resulted in a credible explanation of biblical origins. The reigning theological paradigm has not appreciably changed. What has happened in theology is best illustrated by what has occurred in science.

The chemical evolution of life is a scientific paradigm. Chemical evolution proposes that the first microscopic life in the universe developed from non-life due to natural cause alone. Known materials and mechanisms available for chemical evolution include basic elements, simple inorganic molecules, random molecular combinations, and mechanistic phenomena acting throughout significant time. The first life evolved on Earth or within the universe at large.

Charles Darwin published *On the Origin of Species by Means of Natural Selection* in 1859 and planted the seeds of an evolutionary paradigm for biology. He gave a completely naturalistic explanation for Earth's species. From that time forward, ideas based on natural cause gained influence, and intelligent cause lost ground. Darwin did not explain the origin of the first single-celled microscopic organism, but simply accepted it as a given. His ideas of species development became widely accepted in scientific circles, as did his assumption of chemical evolution.

Chemical evolution is not a plausible idea when analyzed in the light of twenty-first century scientific knowledge. Chemical evolution is driven by philosophical naturalism and is strictly a faith-based belief. Origin of life experiments, when properly understood, completely discredit chemical evolution. The idea that life originated from a primordial soup deep in Earth's past is fraught with insurmountable problems, including the lack of evidence for the alleged oceans of chemical broth.

Nevertheless, biology textbooks are typically supportive of chemical evolution. The Miller-Urey experiment is presented in a positive light, all the while ignoring a host of negative implications. Speculation about the origin of life is given free rein. Conjecture typical of the National Academy of Sciences is given: "For those who are studying the origin of life, the question is no longer whether life could have originated by chemical processes involving non-biological components. The question instead has become which of many pathways might have been followed to produce the first cells."[38] For scientists knowledgeable of origin of life experiments and the complexity of single-celled life, this statement is not remotely credible.

In general, educational institutions train and graduate students who reflect their beliefs and values. The apple normally doesn't fall far from the tree. Most science educators believe that real science demands natural explanations. Eager, impressionable young students readily accept this approach and the necessity of believing in chemical evolution. In college, students majoring in biology are surrounded by professors who accept evolution. In fact, their academic course of study may be in evolutionary biology. The truth of biological and chemical evolution is a dominant theme, with essentially no dissenting thought. Due to time constraints and a lack of skepticism, students accept what is taught. And so, it is no surprise that most biology majors have a strong faith-based belief in natural cause, which includes chemical evolution. This belief perpetuates itself as students become assistant professors, professors, and tenured faculty—in turn teaching other students.

When viewed skeptically, we can reject chemical evolution as a self-perpetuating error within science education. Unfortunately, religious education has a similar problem with its explanation of the Genesis creation account. At the heart of the issue is how to discourage false or heretical teaching, while at the same time allowing truth to emerge.

Why has Genesis been translated wrong for the past two centuries? We can understand how that prior to 1700, traditional young-Earth creation theology was the dominant belief. There was no good reason to doubt it. After 1700, when challenged by scientific evidence supporting an old heavens, Earth, and biosphere, new ideas were developed (gap theology, day-age theology and literary interpretations) to accommodate new information. Unfortunately, these new ideas were at the expense of scripture—if not its outright rejection. Theologians and Hebrew scholars have been unable to view the translation of Genesis with any significant difference. They have failed to get beyond the "jussive/command" verb and associated errant thinking that controls the translation of Genesis. Trusting laymen, pastors, teachers, religious leaders, and academics have simply accepted the established paradigm.

(9) If the universe is millions of years old, then isn't evolution true?

Evolution is derived from the Latin word *evolutio* meaning to "unroll." As time unrolls due to its one-way flow, change occurs. Both creationists and evolutionists agree that things have changed over time. The disagreement is whether change has been due to *natural cause* or *intelligent cause*. Naturalistic evolutionists believe that all change has been due to natural cause alone. In the evolutionist's mind, natural cause provides a logical all-encompassing explanation of origins—although with some significant problems yet to be resolved. They believe that random, naturally directed, purposeless, mechanistic change is a powerful constructive mechanism when given significant time.

As previously mentioned, proponents of naturalistic evolution often say, "Evolution is a fact." However, when we understand the three different types of natural cause, this statement loses essentially all its force. Natural cause may be easily divided into three categories.

(1) Destructive Mechanism – Natural cause as a destructive mechanism is fully capable of wearing away, deteriorating, and randomizing—a fact.

(2) Weak Constructive Mechanism – Natural cause as a weak constructive mechanism is capable of building simple structures represented by snowflakes, mineral crystals, concretions, freeze-thaw rock circles, sand dune formations, caves, dried mud crack patterns, eroded structures, sand particles, salt grains, rocks, and basic molecules—a fact.

(3) Powerful Constructive Mechanism – Natural cause as an alleged powerful constructive mechanism has not demonstrated the ability to create design information, complex functional systems, mathematically improbable structures, and fine-tuned arrangements that we observe in nature—also a fact.

We can readily accept natural cause as an explanation for rusting iron, crumbling rocks, decaying plants, water erosion, lightning strikes, earthquakes, fires, tsunamis, hurricanes, and floods. Mechanistic processes can rationally explain stellar aging, stellar novae, meteor impacts, and planetary cooling. Naturally directed change can logically explain genetic mutations, limited species divergence, new viral strains, and the emergence of new antibiotic resistant bacteria. Purposeless change can credibly explain continental drift, ocean floor spreading, mountain erosion, volcanic mountain building, river delta formation, and sedimentary strata.

Natural cause as an alleged powerful constructive mechanism requires significant time. Conceptually our solar system condensed out of an interstellar cloud during millions of years. Speculatively, millions of years passed before the first single-celled life evolved from non-living materials. Hypothetically, biological evolution took millions of years to create Earth's many species. Improvements due to evolution are assumed to occur in small, incremental steps throughout vast time.

Intelligent design and time have no firm relationship. Design can occur quickly or over great periods of time. For example, the great pyramids of Egypt, Taj Mahal of India, Great Wall of China, Alaska Pipeline, English Channel Tunnel, and Petronas Towers of Malaysia represent great human design achievements. The time taken to build these structures represents the resources, priorities, and self-imposed schedule of the builders. The complex nature of these structures, not the time, is what identifies them as products of design. Conceptually, whether these structures were built in a day or a million years is irrelevant. If built over a million years time span, they would still be a product of intelligent cause. Natural cause is totally incapable of building these structures, even given billions of years.

Design information, complex functional systems, mathematically improbable structures, and fine-tuned arrangements are quite evident in the world about us— occurring both in nature and as man-made objects. Evolution has not demonstrated the ability to create these phenomena. On the other hand, design engineers readily create products such as cell phones, plasma televisions, automobiles, and computers that exhibit these characteristics. Humans with their limited intelligence and power can easily create items completely beyond the ability of natural cause. Likewise, an omnipotent creator identified in the Bible as God could easily have built galaxies, stars, our solar system, Earth, and its biosphere when given millions of years. Although many objects attributed to God's creative hand are of different ages and widely spaced throughout time, most discrete creative events no doubt occurred quite rapidly (e.g., the creation of Eve).

Answers in Genesis and The Institute for Creation Research (two organizations that promote young-Earth creation theology) have done an excellent job of emphasizing the complexity of biological life. For example, the book *Made in His Image* by Dr. Randy J. Guliuzza, discusses the complexities of the human body. The DNA information, complex interrelationships, feedback mechanisms, precise control, and intricate detail found within human systems defy an evolutionary explanation. When combined with knowledge of Michael Behe's Principle of Irreducible Complexity, the average person can understand why these systems could not have evolved in a random, step-by-step process.

On the down side, promoters of traditional young-Earth creation theology have repeatedly equated billions of years with naturalistic evolution. For this reason, an old age for the heavens and Earth is very disturbing to many Christians. However, we must realize that more than enormous time is needed. Evolution must have a plausible constructive mechanism in addition to millions of years. Time alone is not a magic wand capable of curing the severe limitations of natural cause.

(10) What is the real Genesis creation story?

The real Genesis creation story begins in Genesis 2:5 with mankind. This simple story tells of God planting and growing trees for the Garden of Eden, forming man, placing man in the garden, forming animals for the garden, and building Eve from Adam's rib. Yahweh God is recognized as man's creator. Chapter 2 is a straightforward, unembellished, historical account as told by Adam. The language is simple, as expected from a story of such great antiquity.

Designated historians carefully memorized Adam's account and accurately passed it on. The long ages of those who lived between Adam and Abraham allowed the number of historians involved in this process to be kept at a minimum to reduce error. Eventually mankind developed writing, the account was written down, and passed on to Moses. Under the direction of the Holy Spirit, Moses edited Adam's account and included it in the book of Genesis.

Moses then wrote a sophisticated prelude to Adam's historical account, which we now call Genesis Chapter 1. This God-inspired story readily reflects Moses' education, training, and sharp intellect, and is a masterpiece of prose.

Most of Chapter 1 (Gen. 1:3–2:3) is set within a rigid seven-day format divided into six days of work and one day of rest to support the Sabbath. This pattern of work and rest was later codified in the Ten Commandments in Exodus 20:8–11, 31:12–17, and Deuteronomy 5:12–15. God set an example that man was required to follow.

Chapter 1 alternates between statements made by God and creative works attributed to him. God spoke to Moses while he was on Mount Sinai. During six 24-hour days God described the Earth and heavens, and Moses recorded those statements in Genesis 1:3, 6, 9, 11, 14–15, 20, 24, and 26. When Moses wrote Chapter 1, he identified God as maker of the expanse (Gen. 1:7), maker of the two great luminaries (Gen. 1:16), giver of the luminaries (Gen. 1:17), creator of the great reptiles, marine life, and flying creatures (Gen 1:21), maker of the land animals (Gen. 1:25), and creator of the first man and woman (Gen. 1:27). A single, omnipotent, creator God is taught in contradiction to the pagan polytheistic beliefs of the time.

The events of Chapter 2 (Gen. 2:5–25) may be viewed as occurring throughout a period of several years (not hundreds, thousands or millions of years). They reflect Adam's knowledge of creation. The language of Genesis 2:5, 6, 8, 9, and 15 suggests that God made the Garden of Eden before He created man. The planting of the garden (Gen. 2:8) and the growing of trees in the garden (Gen. 2:9) implies somewhat of a conventional process rather than a completely miraculous process. Logically, God would have prepared the garden before He created man, rather than having created man, realizing he had no place for him to live, and then hastily making the garden as an afterthought. God then formed animals and birds for the garden (Gen. 2:19). During a period of time, God brought these creatures to Adam for naming. Lastly, God built Eve from Adam's rib (Gen. 2:22) and joined them together in marriage.

In Genesis, God is identified as creator of the heavens and Earth and all therein. Other than the information given in Chapters 1 and 2, we know little about the scope, time, or sequence of God's creative actions. We must come to grips with the fact that the Bible does not reveal details about creative events prior to the forming of man. To a limited extent, scientific evidence can fill in missing historical knowledge about the heavens and Earth during this time.

Appendix: A

The *Exemplar* Translation – Genesis Chapters 1 and 2

The *exemplar* translation of Genesis Chapters 1 and 2 is a careful rendering of the Hebrew text. The translation of all significant words is supported by their use in the remainder of the Old Testament, with the King James Version as a primary reference. The unique translation of words applicable only to Genesis is forbidden. Not a single word, phrase, or verse is treated as mythological, metaphorical, or untrue.

Words in the *exemplar* translation of Genesis Chapters 1 and 2 are about two percent different from orthodox translations such as the English Standard Version (a conservative, word-for-word translation). The changes are quite subtle, yet permit a significantly different explanation of the creation story while respecting the clear language of the inspired text. *Exemplar* creation revolutionizes one's understanding of the creation account.

The words in italics in the following *exemplar* translation are not in the original Hebrew text and are added for grammatical and explanatory purposes, similar to the King James Version of the Bible.

Chapter 1 – *Undefined time in the past*
1. In the beginning, God created the heavens and the Earth.
2. And the Earth was vacant and empty *of life*. And darkness *was* over the surface of the deep *waters*. And the Spirit of God hovered over the surface of the waters.

Day one of the seven-day chronicle
3. And God said, "There is light, and light exists."
4. And God saw that the light *was* good. And God distinguished between the light and between the darkness.
5. And God called the light "day" and called the darkness "night." And evening was, and morning was—day one.

The second day
6. And God said, "There is an expanse in the middle of the water, and it exists to separate between water *above* from water *below*."
7. And God *is the one who* made the expanse and separated between the waters under the expanse and between the waters over the expanse. And *it* was so.
8. And God called the expanse "sky." And evening was, and morning was—second day.

The third day

9. And God said, "The waters under the sky wait in one place and the dry ground is seen." And *it* was so.

10. And God called the dry ground "land" and called the collection of waters "seas." And God saw that *it was* good.

11. And God said, "The land is sprouting sprouts: plants seeding seeds and the fruit trees making fruit—to which kind is in the seed—over the land." And *it* was so.

12. "And the land is growing sprouts: plants seeding seeds *according* to *their* kind, and the trees making fruit—in which seed is to kind." And God saw that *it was* good.

13. And evening was, and morning was—third day.

The fourth day

14. And God said, "There are luminaries in the expanse of the heavens to distinguish between the day and between the night, and *they* are for a sign for appointed times and for days and years."

15. "And luminaries exist in the expanse of the heavens to give light over the Earth." And *it* was so.

16. And God *is the one who* made two great luminaries: the greater luminary to rule the day and the smaller luminary to rule the night and the stars.

17. And God gave them in the expanse of the heavens to give light over the Earth.

18. And to rule in the day and in the night and to distinguish between the light and between the darkness. And God saw that *it was* good.

19. And evening was, and morning was—fourth day.

The fifth day

20. And God said, "The waters swarm *with* swarms of living creatures, and fliers flying over the land and over the surface of the expanse of the sky."

21. And God *is the one who* created the great reptiles and every moving living creature with which the waters swarm, *according* to *their* kinds, and every winged flier *according* to *its* kind. And God saw that *it was* good.

22. And God blessed them saying, "Be fruitful and multiply and fill the waters in the seas and multiply the fliers on the land."

23. And evening was, and morning was—fifth day.

The sixth day

24. And God said, "The land brings forth living creatures *according* to *their* kind: beasts and moving *things* and animals of the land, *according* to *their* kind." And *it* was so.

25. And God *is the one who* made the animals of the Earth *according* to *their* kind: the beasts *according* to *their* kind and every moving *thing* upon the ground *according* to *its* kind. And God saw that *it was* good.

26. And God said, "Man, made in our image *and* after our likeness, has dominion on

fish of the sea and on fliers in the sky and on beasts and on all the Earth and on all the moving *things* that move over the land."

27. And God *is the one who* created man in His image, in God's image created him, male and female *God* created them.

28. And God blessed them, and God said to them, "Be fruitful and multiply and fill the Earth and subdue it and have dominion on fish of the sea and on fliers in the sky and on all living *things* that move over the land."

29. And God said, "Behold, *I have* given to you every plant seeding seed which is over the surface of all the land, and every tree in which fruit is seeding seed. For you, *they* are for food."

30. "And to every animal of the land and to every flier in the sky and to every moving *thing* over the land, which is a living creature, *I have given* every green plant for food." And *it* was so.

31. And God saw all that *He had* done, and behold *it was* very good. And evening was, and morning was—the sixth day.

Chapter 2 – *The seventh day*

1. And the heavens and Earth *were* finished, and all their multitude *of miscellaneous things*.

2. And on the seventh day God finished His work that *He had* done, and rested on the seventh day from all His work that *He had* done.

3. And God blessed the seventh day and sanctified it, because on it *God* rested from all work that He created to do.

Introduction to Adam's historical account

4. These accounts *that follow are about* the heavens and the Earth at their creation—in the days Yahweh God did *the* Earth and heavens.

The Garden of Eden

5. And every bush of the field was not yet on the land, and every plant of the field *did* not yet grow, because Yahweh God had not caused rain over the land and there was no man to cultivate the ground *where the garden was to be.*

6. And mists rose up from the land and watered all the surface of the ground *where the garden was to be.*

7. And Yahweh God formed the man *of* dust from the ground and breathed in his nostrils the breath *of* life. And the man existed as a living creature.

8. And Yahweh God planted a garden from the east in Eden, and there *He* put the man whom *He had* formed.

9. And Yahweh God grew from the ground every tree *that was* desirable to the sight and good for food, and the tree of life in the middle of the garden and the tree of knowledge of good and evil.

10. And a river went out from Eden to water the garden and from there diverged and became four branches.
11. The name of the first is Pishon; it winds through all the land of Havilah, where there is gold.
12. And the gold of that land is good; bdellium and onyx stone *are* there.
13. And the name of the second river is the Gihon. It winds through all the land of Cush.
14. And the name of the third river is the Tigris; it goes east of Asshur. And the fourth river is the Euphrates.

Man in the garden
15. And Yahweh God took the man and put him in the Garden of Eden to cultivate and to keep it.
16. And Yahweh God commanded over the man saying, "From every tree of the garden, you *may* eat-eat."
17. "But from the tree of the knowledge of good and evil, *do* not eat from, because on the day you eat from it you *shall* die-die."
18. And Yahweh God said, "*It is* not good *for* the man to be alone. For him *I shall* make as his counterpart a helper."

Animals of the garden
19. And Yahweh God formed from the ground every animal of the field and every flier of the sky *that lived within the garden*. And *God* brought *them* to the man to see what he *would* call them and whatever the man called the living creature, that *was its* name.
20. And the man called names to all the beasts and to the fliers of the sky and to all animals of the field *that lived within the garden*. And for Adam *was* not found as his counterpart a helper.

Woman is created
21. And Yahweh God caused a deep sleep to fall over the man and *during* sleep took from one of his ribs and closed up under the flesh.
22. And Yahweh God built—which *He* took *of* the rib from the man—into a woman, and brought her to the man.

Marriage is established
23. And the man said, "This is now bone from my bones and flesh from my flesh; for this *shall* be called woman, because this *was* taken from man."
24. So over *this reason,* a man *will* leave his father and his mother and hold fast on his wife. And *they shall* be as one flesh.
25. And the two were naked, the man and *his* wife, and not ashamed.

Appendix: B

The Ten Key Verbs of Genesis Chapter 1

This appendix is an extension of Chapter 5 and gives an in-depth examination of the seven verses and ten key verbs identified in Table 5.4. These key verbs are traditionally assigned a jussive verb state and are considered "jussive/command" verbs. According to traditional interpretations, God speaks in these seven verses and commands things to occur. In contrast, the *exemplar* translation views Genesis 1:3, 6, 9, 11, 14, 20, and 24 as declarative statements.

The complete Hebrew *verb form* is a combination of its *verb state* and one of *seven verb stems.* Six Hebrew verb states typically identified are the perfect, imperfect, imperative, infinitive, participle, and jussive.[1] The seven verb stems for Hebrew strong verbs are qal, niphal, piel, pual, hiphil, hophal, and hithpael.

Verb form is determined primarily by spelling and secondarily by context. For verb forms with the same spelling, context is used exclusively to determine the verb state. For example, standard verb tables for strong Hebrew verbs show that some imperfect verbs have the same spelling as jussive verbs. Furthermore, some perfect verbs have the same spelling as imperative verbs.[2,3] When word spelling is identical, context must be used to determine the state of a verb.

When the context of a verse is neutral or unclear, classifying verb states, which have identical spelling, can be a judgment call. For example, spelling is identical for some strong verbs classified as imperfect or jussive, and other verbs classified as perfect or imperative. Selecting the verb state in instances such as this can be a judgment decision, which in turn can be driven by theology—a significant force behind orthodox translations of Genesis 1:3, 6, 9, 11, 14, 20, and 24. The primary driver for treating these verses as commands is traditional young-Earth creation theology, which has been the dominant interpretative position for more than twenty-two hundred years.

Although "jussive/command" verbs dominate the explanation of Genesis Chapter 1, their influence elsewhere is essentially irrelevant. The number of jussive verbs in the Old Testament identified by the *Old Testament Parsing Guide* is quite small. Outside Genesis Chapter 1, jussive verbs are essentially insignificant in the Bible. If the first chapter of Genesis did not exist, I doubt there would be a jussive verb classification.

As mentioned, two main uninspired works are the basis for current errant interpretations of the Genesis creation story. The first five books of the Septuagint (the Pentateuch) were translated from Hebrew into Greek around 275 BC by Jewish scribes. Traditional young-Earth creation theology was the dominant belief at the time and was embedded into the Old Testament though this translation. The ten key verbs identified in Table 5.4 of Chapter 5 and their accompanying seven verses were translated as commands in the Septuagint.[4,5] The Masoretic scribes added vocal marks (starting around 500 AD) to support the Septuagint explanation. These two uninspired works control present-day interpretations of the creation account.

Exemplar creation now challenges traditional translations of the Genesis story. In doing so, the Septuagint translation and Masoretic vocal marks are subjugated to the original Hebrew text, and the Bible becomes the sole basis of religious authority. In the following discussion, the ten verbs in Table 5.4 are discussed in detail.

Genesis 1:3, 6 and 14 – Hebrew verb (יהי) meaning "be" or "exist"

The Hebrew verb (יהי), meaning "be," occurs in Genesis 1:3, 6, and 14, and is one of many derivatives based on the root (היה). Verbs based on the root (היה), identified as Strong's 01961, occur approximately 3,482 times in the Old Testament as shown in Table B.1 of this appendix. The verb (יהי) is considered a shortened version (apocopation) of (היה) in speech and writing.[6]

The verb (יהי) occurs three times in Genesis 1:3, 6, and 14 as shown in Table 5.4 of Chapter 5, and is assigned a qal jussive verb form by the *Old Testament Parsing Guide*.[7]

Jussive verbs are considered command verbs. The *American Heritage College Dictionary* defines jussive as: "A word, mood, or form used to express a command."[8] Jussive verbs are used in commands as when a king orders his subject to perform a specific task. In Genesis 1:3, 6, and 14, God speaks and allegedly commands things to occur; the standard explanation given for jussive verbs.

The verb (יהי) occurs as a stand-alone word 50 times in 49 verses of the Old Testament. The *Old Testament Parsing Guide* classifies all 50 occurrences, listed in Table B.3, as qal jussive. The classification of all 50 occurrences of the verb (יהי) as jussive supports explaining Genesis 1:3, 6, and 14 as commands of God.

Based on the above, linguistic evidence for treating (יהי) as a jussive verb appears to be an open and shut case. And since Genesis 1:3, 6, and 14 are commands of God, then the remaining verses starting with the expression "And God said" in Genesis Chapter 1 must be commands. At this point, the typical theology student accepts what he has been taught, his worldview becomes solidified, and further analysis and investigation are halted.

However, a close examination of the 49 verses that contain (יהי) casts serious doubt on the above conclusion. Subtracting Genesis 1:3, 6, and 14 from the above (since they are under contention), leaves 46 verses to examine. Since (יהי) is the poster child for the "jussive/command" verb, the 46 verses outside Genesis Chapter 1 deserve an in-depth examination.

A cursory reading identifies only 3 verses out of 46 in the KJV that can remotely be considered commands. The first occurrence, Genesis 33:9, is a discussion between two brothers. Esau explains to Jacob how he has enough and does not need a gift. The older brother is not commanding the younger to do anything. Compare the KJV translation given below against the highly literal, word-for-word rendering of the Hebrew text by the *exemplar* translation. The English word translated from (יהי) is underlined and identified by its Strong's number.

> • Genesis 33:9 And Esau said, I have enough, my brother; keep that thou hast unto thyself. (KJV)

> • Genesis 33:9 And Esau said, there is for me *an* abundance my brother—for you be[01961] what *is* for you. (ET)

In the second occurrence, Exodus 10:10, traditional translations have Pharaoh commanding a blessing on Moses and the nation of Israel by use of the words "let be." When correctly translated, Pharaoh is acknowledging that God is with Moses. Pharaoh has just been humiliated by the first seven plagues. Moses has beaten all Pharaoh's magicians, and they have openly conceded their afflictions are due to the finger of God (Exodus 8:19). God has hardened Pharaoh's heart (Exodus 10:1). In Exodus 10:10, Pharaoh affirms that Yahweh is with Moses. The meaning of the first part of this verse in the Hebrew text is quite plain. Pharaoh is simply stating a fact rather than a issuing a command. Keep in mind that Pharaoh worshiped the Egyptian gods and it would have been totally out of character for him to command a blessing in the name of Moses' God.

> • Exodus 10:10 And he said unto them, Let the LORD be[01961] so with you, as I will let you go, and your little ones: look to it; for evil is before you. (KJV)

> • Exodus 10:10 And *Pharaoh* said to them, "Yahweh is[01961] with you so that you are bold in trying to gain release for your children. I see that you have some evil purpose in mind." (ET)

In the third occurrence, Ezekiel 45:10, just weights and measurements are described for a future kingdom of Israel. This verse must be viewed within the context of Chapters 40 through 48, where the prophet Ezekiel describes the future state of Israel. Among many things that will exist in this future state, are honest standards of commerce. Notice how Ezekiel 45:10 is structured in a passive sense (based on a word-for-word translation of the Hebrew text) and is simply a statement rather than a command.

> • Ezekiel 45:10 Ye shall have[01961] just balances, and a just ephah, and a just bath. (KJV)

> • Ezekiel 45:10 Honest balances and an honest ephah and an honest bath *will* be[01961] for you. (ET)

Table B.1 – Hebrew Verbs Based on the Root (היה) in the Old Testament (hâyâh, Strong's 01961)					
Hebrew Word	First Occurrence	No. Times Occurs	Hebrew Word	First Occurrence	No. Times Occurs
ויהי	Gen. 1:3	808	בהיות	Exod. 5:13	14
יהיה	Gen. 1:29	423	ואהי	Judg. 18:4	13
והיה	Gen. 2:10	408	נהיה	Gen. 38:23	13
היה	Gen. 3:1	274	הייתם	Gen. 22:21	12
היו	Gen. 6:4	173	ואהיה	Gen. 26:3	12
תהיה	Gen. 4:12	165	תהיין	Gen. 41:36	12
והיו	Gen. 1:14	120	היינו	Gen. 42:31	11
ויהיו	Gen. 2:25	117	מהיות	Ruth 1:12	8
היתה	Gen. 1:2	116	שהיה	Ps. 124:1	8
יהיו	Gen. 6:9	115	ותהיינה	Num. 36:11	8
ותהי	Gen. 10:10	101	נהיתה	Exod. 11:6	8
והיתה	Gen. 9:13	93	להית	Exod. 23:1	6
להיות	Gen. 10:8	67	והיינו	Gen. 34:16	5
יהי	Gen. 1:3	50	בהיותם	Gen. 4:8	5
הייתי	Gen. 31:40	49	שיהיה	Eccles. 1:9	5
אהיה	Exod. 3:12	43	בהיותו	Ps. 63:1	4
היית	Gen. 40:13	29	מהית	Exod. 9:28	3
והיית	Gen. 17:4	27	ונהי	Num. 13:33	3
תהי	Gen. 13:8	25	ונהיה	Gen. 47:19	3
תהיינה	Lev. 23:15	20	היותם	Exod. 10:6	3
והייתי	Gen. 4:14	18	בהיתו	1 Kgs. 12:6	3
תהיו	Gen. 34:15	17	ותהיין	Gen. 26:35	2
והייתם	Gen. 3:5	17	ונהיתה	Ezek. 21:12	2
היות	Gen. 2:18	16	היהיה	2 Kgs 7:2	2

Note: There are approximately 3,482 occurrences of words and terms based on the Hebrew root (היה) in the Old Testament identified by reference (1) which represent 73 derivatives.

References:
(1) van der Merwe, Christo, ed. (2004) The Lexham Hebrew-English Interlinear Bible.
(2) Brown, Francis and S. R. Driver, Charles A. Briggs, (1907). A Hebrew and English Lexicon of the Old Testament, pp224–227.

In examining the remaining 43 verses containing the verb (יהי), 2 verses are clearly requests based on context.

- Judges 6:39 And Gideon said unto God, Let not thine anger be hot against me, and I will speak but this once: let me prove, I pray thee, but this once with the fleece; let it now be[01961] dry only upon the fleece, and upon all the ground let there be dew. (KJV) [Gideon is requesting that the fleece be dry and the ground be wet as a sign from God.]

- 1 Kings 22:13 And the messenger that was gone to call Micaiah spake unto him, saying, Behold now, the words of the prophets declare good unto the king with one mouth: let thy word, I pray thee, be[01961] like the word of one of them, and speak that which is good. (KJV) [The messenger, an emissary from the King of Israel, spoke to Micaiah and requested that he agree with the other prophets.]

Of the remaining 41 verses containing the verb (יהי), 4 verses make various statements in regard to God. In each case, the speaker invokes a blessing on Yahweh God.

- 1 Kings 10:9 Blessed be[01961] the LORD thy God, which delighted in thee, to set thee on the throne of Israel: because the LORD loved Israel for ever, therefore made he thee king, to do judgment and justice. (KJV)

- 2 Chronicles 9:8 Blessed be[01961] the LORD thy God, which delighted in thee to set thee on his throne, to be king for the LORD thy God: because thy God loved Israel, to establish them for ever, therefore made he thee king over them, to do judgment and justice. (KJV)

- Psalm 113:2 Blessed be[01961] the name of the LORD from this time forth and for evermore. (KJV)

- Job 1:21 And said, Naked came I out of my mother's womb, and naked shall I return thither: the LORD gave, and the LORD hath taken away; blessed be[01961] the name of the LORD. (KJV)

Of the remaining 37 verses that contain the verb (יהי), 13 verses are simply statements rather than commands. Notice how (יהי) is used and translated as a stative, state-of-being verb.

- Genesis 30:34 And Laban said, Behold, I would it might be[01961] according to thy word. (KJV) [Jacob has just made a wage proposal to Laban, to which he agrees.]

- Genesis 49:17 Dan shall be[01961] a serpent by the way, an adder in the path, that biteth the horse heels, so that his rider shall fall backward. (KJV) [Before he died, Jacob told all of his sons, including Dan, what was to happen to them in the future. This verse is a prophecy of coming events, rather than a command .]

• Exodus 7:9 When Pharaoh shall speak unto you, saying, Shew a miracle for you: then thou shalt say unto Aaron, Take thy rod, and cast it before Pharaoh, and it shall become[01961] a serpent. (KJV) [God told Moses what would happen when he cast his rod before Pharaoh. Moses was commanded to cast down the rod, but the rod itself was not commanded.]

Table B.2 – Occurrences of the Hebrew Verb (היתה) in the Old Testament
(Strong's 01961, *hâyâh* a stative verb meaning "be" or "exist")

Hebrew Word	KJV Translation	Number of Occurrences	Verse Location
היתה	Was	41	Gen. 1:2, 3:20, 29:17, 36:12; Exod. 16:24, 36:7; Deut. 2:15; Josh. 11:20; Ruth 1:7; 1 Sam. 14:20; 2 Sam. 3:37, 10:9, 14:27; Judg. 2:15; 1 Kgs. 2:15, 12:15, 18:46; 2 Kings 8:18; 1 Chron. 19:10; 2 Chron. 1:11, 10:15, 22:3, 22:7, 22:11, 30:12; Ezra 8:31; Est. 2:20; Ps. 114:2; Isa. 11:16; Jer. 26:24; Ezek. 16:56; 26:17, 31:3, 33:22, 36:17, 37:1, 40:1; Jonah 3:3; Mal. 2:5, 2:6
היתה	There was	15	Gen. 38:21, 38:22; Exod. 8:15; Deut. 2:36, 3:4; Josh. 11:19; 1 Sam. 5:11; 1 Kgs. 14:30, 15:16, 15:32, 15:6, 15:7; 2 Chron. 13:2, 14:14, 15:19
היתה	Had, have or hath	12	Gen. 18:12; Lev. 21:3; Num. 14:24; Josh. 17:6, 17:8; 1 Kgs. 4:11; 2 Chron. 21:6; Est. 8:16; Ps. 119:56; Eccl. 6:3; Isa. 50:11; Ezek. 44:25
היתה	Is	10	Judg. 21:3; 1 Kgs. 11:11; 2 Sam. 17:9; Ps. 118:23; Prov. 31:14; Isa. 64:10; Jer. 12:8, 25:38; Lam. 1:17, 1:8
היתה	Been	9	1 Sam. 4:17, 14:38, 4:7; 2 Sam. 13:32; Ezra 9:2, 9:8; Ps. 42:3; Jer. 32:31; Mal. 1:9
היתה	Become	8	Ps. 118:22; Isa. 1:21; Jer. 50:23, 51:41; Lam. 1:1; Ezek. 36:35; Zeph. 2:15
היתה	Came or come	7	Judg. 21:5; 2 Kgs. 24:3, 24:20; 2 Chron. 15:1, 20:14; Isa. 14:24; Jer. 52:3
היתה	Became	4	Gen. 47:26; Exod. 9:24; Josh. 14:14; 1 Sam. 10:12
היתה	Be	2	Jer. 2:10; Ezek. 21:12
היתה	Pertaineth	2	2 Kgs. 24:7; 1 Sam. 27:6
היתה	Not translated	2	Exodus 16:13; Joel 2:3
היתה	Are	1	Ezek. 36:2
היתה	By reason	1	Ezek. 19:10
היתה	Lay	1	Ezek. 36:34
היתה	Went	1	1 Chron. 7:23

Note: According to reference (1), (היתה) occurs 116 times in 114 verses in the Old Testament.
References:
(1) van der Merwe, Christo, ed. (2004) *The Lexham Hebrew-English Interlinear Bible.*
(2) Holy Bible, King James Version (1981). New York: Cambridge University Press.

• Deuteronomy 32:38 Which did eat the fat of their sacrifices, and drank the wine of their drink offerings? Let them rise up and help you, and be[01961] your protection. (KJV) [This verse is part of a song in Deut. 32:1–44 that Moses sang to the people of Israel.]

• 1 Kings 8:57 The LORD our God be[01961] with us, as he was with our fathers: let him not leave us, nor forsake us. (KJV) [Solomon did not have the authority to command God to be with or bless the nation of Israel. He *asked* God to be with Israel.]

• Job 24:14 The murderer rising with the light killeth the poor and needy, and in the night is[01961] as a thief. (KJV)

• Job 27:7 Let mine enemy be[01961] as the wicked, and he that riseth up against me as the unrighteous. (KJV)

• Psalm 72:16 There shall be[01961] an handful of corn in the earth upon the top of the mountains; the fruit thereof shall shake like Lebanon: and they of the city shall flourish like grass of the earth. (KJV)

• Psalm 72:17 His name shall endure[01961] for ever: his name shall be continued as long as the sun: and men shall be blessed in him: all nations shall call him blessed. (KJV)

• Psalm 104:31 The glory of the LORD shall endure[01961] for ever: the LORD shall rejoice in his works. (KJV)

• Jeremiah 20:14 Cursed be the day wherein I was born: let not the day wherein my mother bare me be[01961] blessed. (KJV)

• Jeremiah 42:5 Then they said to Jeremiah, The LORD be[01961] a true and faithful witness between us, if we do not even according to all things for the which the LORD thy God shall send thee to us. (KJV) [The people declared, with Yahweh as their witness, they would obey God as He spoke through Jeremiah. This is not a command or wish.]

• Ezekiel 16:15 But thou didst trust in thine own beauty, and playedst the harlot because of thy renown, and pouredst out thy fornications on every one that passed by; his it was[01961]. (KJV)

Of the 46 verses examined, 3 are statements (mistakenly considered commands), 2 are requests, 4 invoke a blessing on God, and 13 make statements. The remaining 24 verses can be considered a mixture of wishes or statements depending on the language of the text. The significant issue is that none of the 46 verses are commands based on context. If we accept the classification of all 50 occurrences of (יהי) by the *Old Testament Parsing Guide* as jussive, then we are forced to question the previous dictionary definition of a jussive verb.

Some Hebrew grammar books state that jussive verbs are a shortened form of imperfect verbs. *Gesenius' Hebrew Grammar* states, "Along with the usual form of the imperfect, there exists also a lengthened form of it (the cohortative), and a shortened form (the jussive)."[9] *Biblical Hebrew* by Harrison agrees and says, "This is in speech a shortened form of the imperfect to express the quick reaction of the mind to a situation, generally in terms of a wish or a command."[10] So if we define a jussive verb as a shortened form of an imperfect verb in speech and writing, then (יהי) fits the description perfectly. However, five of the jussive verbs identified in Genesis 1:9, 11, 20, and 24 in Table 5.4 of Chapter 5 are not shortened versions of the root. Based on this definition, these five verbs are not categorized correctly.

Both Harrison and Pratico in their Hebrew grammar books say that a jussive verb indicates the *speaker's command or wish*.[11,12] There is a huge difference between a command and a wish. They are almost opposites. Any beggar can wish, but only the rich and powerful command. Since none of the 46 verses containing (יהי) are commands, they must be something else. In truth, an analysis of all 46 verses shows they are statements, requests, curses, blessings, desires, or wishes—definitely not commands.

The verb (יהיה) is not a "jussive/command" verb. As mentioned, (יהי) is considered an apocopation (a shortened version) of (יהיה) in holy scripture.[13] The verb (יהיה) occurs 423 times in the Old Testament as shown in Table B.1. Although

Table B.3 – Occurrences of the Hebrew Verb (יהי) in the Old Testament
(Strong's 01961, *hâyâh* a stative verb meaning "be" or "exist")

Hebrew Word	KJV Translation	Number of Occurrences	Verse Location
יהי	Be	18	Gen. 30:34, 49:17; Deut. 32:38; Ruth 2:19; 2 Sam. 14:17; 1 Kgs. 1:37, 8:57, 10:9; 2 Kgs. 2:10; 1 Chron. 22:11; 2 Chron 9:8; Ezra 1:3; Job 1:21, 18:12; Ps. 72:16, 113:2, 122:7; Jer. 42:5
יהי	Let be	15	Ex. 10:10; Deut. 33:24; Jud. 6:39; 1 Kgs. 22:13; 2 Chron. 19:7; Job 3:4, 3:7, 27:7; Ps. 33:22, 35:6, 109:13, 119:76, 119:80; Prov. 5:18; Jer. 20:14
יהי	Let there be	5	Genesis 1:3, 1:6, 1:14; Psalm 109:12 (twice)
יהי	Let	2	Psalm 69:25; Jeremiah 50:29
יהי	Shall endure	2	Psalm 72:17, 104:31
יהי	Have	2	Job 16:18; Ezekiel 45:10
יהי	Become	2	Exodus 7:9; Psalm 69:22
יהי	Is	2	Job 20:23; 24:14
יהי	Keep	1	Genesis 33:9
יהי	Was	1	Ezekiel 16:15

Note: The verb (יהי) occurs 50 times in 49 verses. In many instances, the Hebrew text must be examined to identify where the Hebrew verb is placed in a verse in order to determine its translation.
Reference:
(1) van der Merwe, Christo, ed. (2004) *The Lexham Hebrew-English Interlinear Bible*.
(2) Holy Bible, King James Version (1981). New York: Cambridge University Press.

not all 423 occurrences were examined, the first 100 instances between Genesis 1:29 and Leviticus 25:4 are assigned a qal imperfect verb form by the *Old Testament Parsing Guide*. None are assigned a jussive verb form.

In English, dynamic verbs are normally used in imperative (command) sentences. For example, we might say, "Run to the store and buy some bread." Both "run" and "buy" are dynamic verbs that indicate action. Commands do not normally use stative verbs such as "be." While it is possible to give the command, "You be good," this imperative is more of a state-of-being.

In summary: (1) The verb (יהיה), of which (יהי) is considered a shortened version, is never assigned a jussive state. (2) When Genesis 1:3, 6, and 14 are excluded, then (יהי) is not used as a command in any of the remaining 46 verses in the Old Testament. (3) The context of Genesis 1:3, 6, and 14 does not force (יהי) to be a "jussive/command" verb. (4) The verb (יהי) is translated into the English state-of-being verbs "be, have, is, and was" about 86% of the time in the KJV. (5) Dynamic rather than stative verbs are used in commands where action is desired. Therefore, we can view (יהי) in Genesis 1:3, 6, and 14 as a stative, state-of-being verb and classify it as having a Hebrew perfect state. We can reject dogmatic claims that (יהי) is a "jussive/command" verb in these verses.

Genesis 1:6 – Hebrew term (ויהי) meaning "and be" or "and exist"

The Hebrew term (ויהי), meaning "and be," occurs in Genesis 1:6 as shown in Table 5.4. The term (ויהי) comes from (יהי) discussed in the previous section, but with the vav (ו) prefix added. In this verse, the *Old Testament Parsing Guide* assigns (ויהי) a qal jussive verb form, which allegedly makes it a command verb.

The term (ויהי) occurs a total of 21 times in Genesis Chapters 1 and 2 as shown in Table B.4. In the 20 occurrences outside Genesis 1:6, the *Old Testament Parsing Guide* assigns a qal wci form (qal waw consecutive imperfect form) to this particular verb expression.

The term (ויהי) occurs approximately 808 times in the entire Old Testament as shown in Table B.1. Although not all occurrences were examined, a sampling of verses indicates that in the vast majority of instances (ויהי) is assigned a qal wci verb form by the *Old Testament Parsing Guide*. Of the first 50 occurrences in the Old Testament, only 3 instances in Genesis 1:6, 9:26, and 9:27 are assigned a qal jussive. All 47 remaining occurrences are assigned a qal wci verb form.

Vocal marks inserted into the Hebrew text in Genesis 1:6 by the Masoretic scribes make (ויהי) a jussive verb. For example, in Genesis 1:6, 9:26, and 9:27 the vocal marks assigned to (ויהי) make it a jussive verb in contrast to the identical term in Genesis 1:3, 5, and 7. Based on spelling and verse context, there is nothing that forces (ויהי) in Genesis 1:6, 9:26, and 9:27 to be a "jussive/command" verb.

In summary: (1) Vocal marks inserted by the Masoretes make (ויהי) a jussive verb in Genesis 1:6. (2) Vocal marks are not in the original Hebrew text of the Old Testament. (3) The Hebrew term (ויהי) is assigned a non-jussive state in the vast majority of occurrences in the Old Testament. (4) The context of Genesis 1:6 does not force (ויהי) to be a "jussive/command" verb. Therefore, we can view (ויהי) in Genesis 1:6 as a stative, state-of-being verb and classify it as having a Hebrew perfect state. We can reject claims that (ויהי) is a "jussive/command" verb in this verse.

Genesis 1:9 – Hebrew verb (יקוו) meaning "wait"

The exact Hebrew verb (יקו), meaning "wait," identified as Strong's 06960, occurs only in Genesis 1:9; Isaiah 51:5, and 60:9 as shown in Table 5.4 of Chapter 5. A similar term (קוו) occurs in Job 6:19; Psalm 56:6; 119:95; Lamentations 3:25, and Jeremiah 3:17 as shown in Table 5.1 of Chapter 5.

Table B.4 – Occurrences of the Term (ויהי) in Genesis Chapters 1 and 2 (Strong's 01961, *hâyâh* and a conjunction meaning "and be" or "and exist")				
Verse	Hebrew Term	Number of occurrences	KJV Translation	Assigned Verb Form[2]
Gen. 1:3	ויהי	1	and there was	Qal wci
Gen. 1:5	ויהי	2	and were[1]	Qal wci
Gen. 1:6	ויהי	1	let there be	Qal jussive
Gen. 1:7	ויהי	1	and was	Qal wci
Gen. 1:8	ויהי	2	and were[1]	Qal wci
Gen. 1:9	ויהי	1	and was	Qal wci
Gen. 1:11	ויהי	1	and was	Qal wci
Gen. 1:13	ויהי	2	and were[1]	Qal wci
Gen. 1:15	ויהי	1	and was	Qal wci
Gen. 1:19	ויהי	2	and were[1]	Qal wci
Gen. 1:23	ויהי	2	and were[1]	Qal wci
Gen. 1:24	ויהי	1	and was	Qal wci
Gen. 1:30	ויהי	1	and was	Qal wci
Gen. 1:31	ויהי	2	and were[1]	Qal wci
Gen. 2:7	ויהי	1	and became	Qal wci

Notes:
(1) The term (ויהי) is only translated once in these verses in the KJV, although it occurs two times in Genesis 1:5, 8, 13, 19, 23 and 31.
(2) Assigned verb form based on the *Old Testament Parsing Guide* by Beall, Banks and Smith.

The verb (יְקָּוּ) occurs in Genesis 1:9 and is assigned a niph *jusm* verb form (rather than niph *jussive* verb form) by the *Old Testament Parsing Guide*. The parsing guide points out that, based on spelling, this verb is not jussive. The "jussive/command" meaning assigned is because of theological influence.

The verb (יְקָּוּ) is based on the root (קָוָה). Of the 49 verbs based on this root in the Old Testament, Job 3:9 is the only one assigned a piel jussive form by the *Old Testament Parsing Guide*. All 48 remaining verbs listed in Table 5.1 of Chapter 5 are primarily a mixture of the piel imperfect, piel perfect, and qal participle verb forms based on their spelling and context.

In summary: (1) The *Old Testament Parsing Guide* does not classify (יְקָּוּ) as a jussive verb. (2) As shown by its spelling, (יְקָּוּ) is not a shortened version of the root (קָוָה). (3) All verbs based on the root (קָוָה) listed in Table 5.1 are assigned a non-jussive state except for one. (4) The context of Genesis 1:9 does not force (יְקָּוּ) to be a "jussive/command" verb. (5) A "jussive/command" interpretation of this verse forces (יְקָּוּ) to be mistranslated "let be gathered together" rather than correctly translated "wait." We can reject claims that (יְקָּוּ) is a "jussive/command" verb in Genesis 1:9.

Genesis 1:9 – Hebrew term (וְתֵרָאֶה) meaning "and see"

The Hebrew term (וְתֵרָאֶה), meaning "and see," identified as Strong's 07200, occurs in Genesis 1:9. The term (וְתֵרָאֶה) is the same as (תֵרָאֶה) but with the vav (ו) prefix added. The term (וְתֵרָאֶה) occurs in Genesis 1:9 and is assigned a niph *jusm* verb form (rather than niph *jussive* verb form) by the *Old Testament Parsing Guide*. Based on spelling, this verb is not jussive. The "jussive/command" meaning assigned is because of theological influence.

The Hebrew verb (תֵרָאֶה) occurs 39 times in the Old Testament as shown in Table B.5. Genesis 1:9 is the only instance where the *Old Testament Parsing Guide* assigns (תֵרָאֶה) a jusm state. All 38 remaining occurrences are non-jussive.

In summary: (1) The *Old Testament Parsing Guide* does not classify (וְתֵרָאֶה) as a jussive verb. (2) As shown by its spelling, (וְתֵרָאֶה) is not a shortened version of the root (רָאָה). (3) Genesis 1:9 is the only instance in the Old Testament where (תֵרָאֶה) is assigned a "jusm" state. (4) The context of Genesis 1:9 does not force (וְתֵרָאֶה) to be a "jussive/command" verb. We can reject claims that (וְתֵרָאֶה) is a "jussive/command" verb in Genesis 1:9.

Genesis 1:11 – Hebrew verb (תַדְשֵׁא) meaning "sprouting"

The word (תַדְשֵׁא), meaning "sprouting," occurs in Genesis 1:11 and is based on the root (דָשֵׁא). Hebrew nouns and verbs based on the root (דָשֵׁא) occur 16 times in the Old Testament. In 14 occurrences, (דשא) is considered a noun and identified as Strong's 01877. In 2 occurrences, (דשא) is considered a verb and identified as Strong's 01876.[14] The two verbs occur in Genesis 1:11 as (תדשא) and in Joel 2:22 as (דשאו) and are respectively assigned a hiphil jussive and qal perfect by the *Old Testament Parsing Guide*.

In summary: (1) As shown by its spelling, (תדשא) is not a shortened version of the root (דשא). (2) Genesis 1:11 is the only instance in the Old Testament where the verb (תדשא) is assigned a jussive state. (3) The context of Genesis 1:11 does not force (תדשא) to be a "jussive/command" verb. We can reject claims that (תדשא) must be a "jussive/command" verb in Genesis 1:11.

Genesis 1:20 – Hebrew verb (ישרצו) meaning "swarming"

The word (ישרצו), meaning "swarming," occurs in Genesis 1:20 and is based on the root (שרץ). Hebrew nouns and verbs based on the root (שרץ) occur 29 times in the Old Testament. In 15 occurrences, words based on the root (שרץ), identified as

Hebrew Term	Basic Translation	Hebrew Word	Assigned Verb Form[1]	Verse Location
ותראה	and (you/she) see	תראה	Niph jusm	Genesis 1:9
ותראה	and (you/she) see	תראה	Qal wci	Jeremiah 3:7
ותראהו	and (you/she) see he	תראה	Qal wci	Exodus 2:6
נתראה	(us) see	תראה	Hith cohm	2 Kings 14:8; 2 Chron. 25:17
תראה	(you/she) see	תראה	Hiph impf	Leviticus 13:57; Isaiah 47:3
תראה	(you/she) see	תראה	Qal impf	Exodus 6:1, 23:5; Lev.20:17; Num. 11:23, 23:13, 23:13; Deut. 3:28, 12:13, 22:1, 22:4, 28:34, 28:67, 32:52; 1 Sam. 1:11; 2 Sam. 3:13; 2 Kings 2:10; Job 10:4, 22:11, 33:28, 38:17, 38:22; Psalm 35:17, 37:34, 91:8; Ecc. 5:7; Isaiah 33:19, 58:7; Ezek. 8:6, 8:13, 8:15, 12:6; Dan. 1:13

Table B.5 – Occurrences of (תראה) in the Old Testament
(Strong's 07200, a verb meaning "see")

Notes:
(1) Assigned verb form based on the *Old Testament Parsing Guide* by Beall, Banks and Smith.
(2) The exact spelling of the Hebrew verb (תראה) from the root (ראה) occurs 39 times in 38 verses in the Old Testament.
(3) Derivatives based on the root (ראה) occur approximately 1,313 times in the Old Testament.
Ref.: van der Merwe, Christo, ed. (2004) *The Lexham Hebrew-English Interlinear Bible*.

Strong's 08318, are considered nouns. In 14 occurrences, words based on the root (שרץ), identified as Strong's 08317, are considered verbs.[15]

The 14 verbs based on the root (שרץ) occur in Gen. 1:20, 1:21, 7:21, 8:17, 9:7; Exodus 1:7, 7:28; Lev. 11:29, 11:41, 11:42, 11:43, 11:46; Psalm 105:30, and Ezek. 47:9. The specific verb (ישרצו) occurs in Genesis 1:20 and is assigned a qal *jusm* verb form (rather than a qal *jussive* verb form) by the *Old Testament Parsing Guide*. The parsing guide points out that, based on spelling, this verb is not jussive. The "jussive/command" meaning assigned is because of theological influence. All 13 remaining verbs based on the root (שרץ) are assigned a non-jussive state.

In summary: (1) The *Old Testament Parsing Guide* does not classify (ישרצו) as a jussive verb. (2) As shown by its spelling, (ישרצו) is not a shortened version of the root (שרץ). (3) Genesis 1:20 is the only instance in the Old Testament where a verb based on the root (שרץ) is assigned a "jusm" state. (4) The context of Genesis 1:20 does not require (ישרצו) to be a "jussive/command" verb. (5) A command interpretation of this verse has caused (ישרצו) to be mistranslated "let bring forth abundantly" rather than correctly translated "swarm." We can reject dogmatic claims that (ישרצו) is a "jussive/command" verb in Genesis 1:20.

Genesis 1:20 – Hebrew verb (יעופף) meaning "flying"

The word (יעופף), meaning "flying," occurs in Genesis 1:20 and is based on the root (עוף). There are approximately 118 nouns and verbs based on the root (עוף) identified by a Hebrew word search of the Old Testament.[16] Nouns are identified as Strong's 05775. About 30 verbs are identified as Strong's 05774.[17] Verbs based on the root (עוף) have several variations and a number of different spellings. The specific verb (יעופף) occurs in Genesis 1:20 and is assigned a polel *jusm* verb form (rather than a polel *jussive* verb form) by the *Old Testament Parsing Guide*. The parsing guide points out that, based on spelling, this verb is not jussive. The "jussive/command" meaning assigned is because of theological influence. All 29 remaining verbs based on the root (עוף) are assigned a non-jussive verb state.

In summary: (1) The *Old Testament Parsing Guide* does not classify (יעופף) as a jussive verb. (2) As shown by its spelling, (יעופף) is not a shortened version of the root (עוף). (3) Genesis 1:20 is the only instance in the Old Testament where a verb based on the root (עוף) is assigned a "jusm" state. (4) In this verse, context does not force (יעופף) to be a "jussive/command" verb. We can reject claims that (יעופף) is a "jussive/command" verb in Genesis 1:20.

Genesis 1:24 – Hebrew verb (תוצא) meaning "bring forth"

The Hebrew verb (תוצא), meaning "bring forth," occurs in Genesis 1:24 and is based on the root (יצא). Words based on this root occur 1,069 times in the Old Testament with a number of prefixes and suffixes.[18] Of the first 50 occurrences of verbs based on the root (יצא), Genesis 1:24 is the only instance assigned a jussive state by the *Old Testament Parsing Guide*.

The exact verb (תוצא) occurs only in the Old Testament in Genesis 1:24 and is assigned a hiph jussive verb form by the *Old Testament Parsing Guide*. A similar spelling occurs in Genesis 1:12 and Ruth 2:18 in the form of (ותוצא), and in both instances assigned a non-jussive verb state.

In summary: (1) As shown by its spelling, (תוצא) is not a shortened version of the root (יצא). (2) Essentially all verbs based on the root (יצא) are assigned a non-jussive state. (3) The context of Genesis 1:24 does not force (תוצא) to be a "jussive/command" verb. We can reject claims that (תוצא) must be a "jussive/command" verb in Genesis 1:24.

The Myth of the Jussive/Command Verb

The term "jussive" is normally associated with a command. English dictionaries often define jussive as: "A word, mood, or form used to express a command."[19] However, a Hebrew "jussive verb" is something quite different. Hebrew grammar books describe the jussive verb as follows:

• *Gesenius' Hebrew Grammar*: "Along with the usual form of the imperfect [verb], there exists also a lengthened form of it (the cohortative), and a shortened form (the jussive)."[20]

• *Gesenius' Hebrew Grammar*: "The general characteristic of the jussive form of the imperfect [verb] is rapidity of pronunciation, combined with a tendency to retract the tone from the final syllable, in order by that means to express the urgency of the command in the very first syllable."[21]

• *Gesenius' Hebrew Grammar*: "The meaning of the jussive [verb] is similar to that of the cohortative, except that in the jussive the command or wish is limited almost exclusively to the 2nd or 3rd person."[22]

• *Biblical Hebrew* by Harrison: "This is in speech a shortened form of the imperfect [verb] to express the quick reaction of the mind to a situation, generally in terms of a wish or a command. It coincides with the imperfect in form in all parts of the regular verb except the hiphil (or causative) but is used only in the second and third persons."[23]

• *Biblical Hebrew* by Harrison: A jussive verb indicates the speaker's command or wish.[24]

• *Basics of Biblical Hebrew Grammar* by Pratico and Van Pelt: "The next three conjugations (Imperative, Cohortative and Jussive) are volitional conjugations, meaning they are used to express some type of command, wish, or desire."[25]

• *Basics of Biblical Hebrew Grammar* by Pratico and Van Pelt: "The jussive conjugation is also used to express either some type of mild command or strong wish. Strictly speaking, it occurs only in the third person, singular and plural."[26]

• *Learn Biblical Hebrew* by Dobson: Jussive is "A form of the imperative [verb] with a prefixed (י) (he, they) or (ת) (you)."[27]

• *Learn Biblical Hebrew* by Dobson: In most instances jussive [verb] forms are the same as imperfective forms. So it is only from the context that we can tell whether a word is imperfective or jussive.[28]

• *Learn Biblical Hebrew* by Dobson: What someone wishes, longs, or prays for may be expressed using the imperfective or jussive [verb] state.[29]

From these four Hebrew grammar books, we can conclude that: (1) A jussive verb is a shortened form of an imperfect verb. The shortened form applies to both writing and speaking. (2) A jussive verb can be used to express a command or wish. (3) Context must be used to determine if a verb is jussive or imperfect.

We should notice what the above grammar books *do not say.* None of them say that a jussive verb must be a command verb. None of them say that use of a jussive verb forces the sentence in which they occur to be a command. We should keep in mind that comments in the above books are dominated by the theological interpretation of Genesis Chapter 1. For centuries, Genesis 1:3, 6, 9, 11, 14, 20, and 24 have been considered commands because of their "jussive/command" verbs, and the belief that God spoke the universe and all therein into existence during six days.

As we examine additional verses in the Old Testament, a clear picture emerges in regard to commands and the verbs used therein. The Hebrew expression, "And God said," occurs at the start of the seven key verses previously examined in Genesis. The same expression also occurs 16 other times where God is directly speaking. In 8 instances God issues a command, while the remaining 8 verses are statements. The command verses are Genesis 6:13, 17:9, 17:15, 17:19, 21:12, 35:1; Exodus 3:14, and Numbers 22:12. If jussive verbs are command verbs, then one would expect all eight of these verses to contain jussive verbs. However, none contain a single jussive verb according to the *Old Testament Parsing Guide.* In the eight verses given below, syntax and the use of dynamic verbs define these sentences as commands, rather than the use of "jussive/command" verbs.

• Genesis 6:13–14 And God said unto Noah, The end of all flesh is come before me; for the earth is filled with violence through them; and, behold, I will destroy them with the earth. Make thee an ark of gopher wood; rooms shalt thou make in the ark, and shalt pitch it within and without with pitch. (KJV) [God commands Noah to make an ark.]

• Genesis 17:9 And God said unto Abraham, Thou shalt keep my covenant therefore, thou, and thy seed after thee in their generations. (KJV) [God commands Abraham to keep the covenant.]

• Genesis 17:15 And God said unto Abraham, As for Sarai thy wife, thou shalt not call her name Sarai, but Sarah shall her name be. (KJV) [God commands a name change for Sarai.]

• Genesis 17:19 And God said, Sarah thy wife shall bear thee a son indeed; and thou shalt call his name Isaac: and I will establish my covenant with him for an everlasting covenant, and with his seed after him. (KJV) [God commands what the child's name is to be.]

• Genesis 21:12 And God said unto Abraham, Let it not be grievous in thy sight because of the lad, and because of thy bondwoman; in all that Sarah hath said unto thee, hearken unto her voice; for in Isaac shall thy seed be called. (KJV) [God commands Abraham to listen to Sarah.]

• Genesis 35:1 And God said unto Jacob, Arise, go up to Bethel, and dwell there: and make there an altar unto God, that appeared unto thee when thou fled-dest from the face of Esau thy brother. (KJV) [God commands Jacob to go to Bethel.]

• Exodus 3:14 And God said unto Moses, I AM THAT I AM: and he said, Thus shalt thou say unto the children of Israel, I AM hath sent me unto you. (KJV) [God tells Moses what he should say.]

• Numbers 22:12 And God said unto Balaam, Thou shalt not go with them; thou shalt not curse the people: for they are blessed. (KJV) [God tells Balaam the course of action to take.]

If jussive verbs are truly command verbs, then one would expect them to be found in other important commands in the Bible. For example, Exodus 20:3–17 and Deuteronomy 5:7–21 record when God gave the Ten Commandments to the nation of Israel. God directly commanded the Hebrew people regarding actions that were either forbidden to do or required to perform. However, none of the verbs in these thirty verses are identified as jussive by the *Old Testament Parsing Guide*.

In addition to the Ten Commandments, the Bible has numerous other passages where God gives miscellaneous commands to the nation of Israel. For example, Leviticus 16:3–34 details a list of commands for Aaron to follow regarding worship. Leviticus 18:8–22 enumerates fifteen commands to abstain from specific forms of sexual behavior. Leviticus 19:9–19 lists ten commands about business and personal relationships. None of these verses contain jussive verbs according to the *Old Testament Parsing Guide*. Of the many different commands given by God throughout Leviticus, essentially none contain jussive verbs.

In summary, in Genesis Chapter 1 ten key verbs (which represent eight different words) in seven verses are traditionally treated as "jussive/command" verbs. Four of these words (יקוו, ותראה, ישרצו, and יעופף) are not jussive verbs based on spelling (they are identified as "jusm"). The remaining four words (יהי, ויהי, תדשא, and תוצא) are identified as jussive verbs by the *Old Testament Parsing Guide*, but are seldom used in commands. Outside Genesis Chapter 1, more than 97% of the time these four verbs are used in other than a command context in the Old Testament.

If not for the influence of young-Earth creation theology, I doubt there would be a jussive verb classification. There would be perfect and imperfect verbs. There would be verbs used within imperative statements. There would be sentences with a jussive mood. There would be verbs representing a shortened version of the root. In that vein, it is interesting to note that Pratico and Van Pelt in *Basics of Biblical Hebrew* do not give jussive verbs as a category in their appendix verb tables.

The "jussive/command" verb is mainly due to theological influence and is not well supported by scripture. The link between jussive verbs and commands, based on context, is exceptionally weak. Therefore: (1) The belief that "jussive/command" verbs, identified in Genesis Chapter 1, force verses in which they occur to be commands is patently false. (2) Verbs identified in Genesis Chapter 1 as jussive are essentially never used in commands throughout the Old Testament. (3) Treating (יְהִי, וַיְהִי, תַּדְשֵׁא and תּוֹצֵא) in Genesis Chapter 1 as command verbs is not well-supported elsewhere in the Old Testament. The "jussive/command" verb is primarily myth.

Conclusion

Sound hermeneutics and exegesis of scripture lead to the conclusion that the ten key verbs identified in Table 5.4 of Chapter 5 are not "jussive/command" verbs. Nothing inherent within Genesis 1:3, 6, 9, 11, 14, 20, and 24 requires these seven verses to be commands. At best, treating these verses as commands was a bad judgment call. More realistically, scripture was deliberately embellished (although with good intentions) and countless generations have been misled. The "jussive/command" is a fabrication of biblical Hebrew grammar.

The Septuagint translators and Masoretic scribes have been eminently successful in promoting young-Earth creation theology through the guise of scripture. When we lay aside their work and appeal strictly to the language of the biblical text, their deception becomes readily visible.

We should be aware of the current state of biblical scholarship in regard to this discussion. All biblical Hebrew parsing guides and grammar books treat the ten key verbs listed in Table 5.4 as jussive or "jusm." All English Bible translations treat these ten verbs as "jussive/command" verbs through use of the word "let." All commentaries on the creation story treat Genesis 1:3, 6, 9, 11, 14, 20, and 24 as commands. All biblical Hebrew scholars, theologians, and their predecessors for countless generations have been taught these seven verses are commands.

Biblical scholarship in support of traditional young-Earth creation theology appears overwhelming. One would expect no less from a paradigm that has dominated biblical origins thinking for more than twenty-two hundred years. Theological influence has built a significant barrier to correctly understanding these ten key verbs.

Once a paradigm has been established, change is difficult. Even when error is clearly exposed, going against the flow of public opinion is not easy. Peer pressure can be crushing. Rock solid evidence is needed to counteract doctrinal inertia built up during hundreds of years. This evidence is now provided by (1) an appeal to the original God-inspired text of the Old Testament and (2) powerful support from general revelation.

When the Bible is carefully examined, we can confidently accept the verbs of Table 5.4 as non-jussive, with no requirement for a command. Ten verbs are used in seven declarative statements. In Genesis 1:3–31, when God spoke He was describing a mature creation that had existed for some time.

Comparing the *Exemplar* Translation with the ESV
Genesis Chapters 1 and 2
(all significant differences are highlighted in bold)

Exemplar Translation	English Standard Version
Chapter 1	Chapter 1

Undefined time in the past	*Undefined time in the past*
1. In the beginning, God created the heavens and the Earth.	1. In the beginning, God created the heavens and the earth.
2. And the Earth was **vacant and empty** *of life.* And darkness *was* over the surface of the **deep** *waters.* And the Spirit of God hovered over the surface of the waters.	2. The earth was **without form and void,** and darkness was over the face of the **deep.** And the Spirit of God was hovering over the face of the waters.
Day one of the seven-day chronicle	*Day one of the seven-day chronicle*
3. And God said, "**There is light, and light exists.**"	3. And God said, "**Let there be light,**" **and there was light.**
4. And God saw that the light *was* good. And God **distinguished** between the light and between the darkness.	4. And God saw that the light was good. And God **separated** the light from the darkness.
5. And God called the light "day" and called the darkness "night." And evening was, and morning was—**day one.**	5. God called the light Day, and the darkness he called Night. And there was evening and there was morning, **the first day.**
The second day	*The second day*
6. And God said, "**There is an expanse** in the middle of the water, **and it exists to separate** between water *above* from water *below.*"	6. And God said, "**Let there be an expanse** in the midst of the waters, **and let it separate** the waters from the waters."
7. And God *is the one who* made the expanse and separated between the waters under the expanse and between the waters over the expanse. And *it* was so.	7. And God made the expanse and separated the waters that were under the expanse from the waters that were above the expanse. And it was so.
8. And God called the expanse "**sky.**" And evening was, and morning was—second day.	8. And God called the expanse **Heaven.** And there was evening and there was morning, the second day.

The third day

9. And God said, "**The waters
under the sky wait** in one place
and **the dry ground is seen**." And *it*
was so.
10. And God called the dry ground
"land" and called the **collection** of waters "seas." And God saw that *it was*
good.
11. And God said, "**The land is sprouting sprouts**: plants seeding seeds and
the fruit trees making fruit—to which
kind is in the seed—over the land." And
it was so.
12. "**And the land is growing sprouts**:
plants seeding seeds *according* to *their*
kind, and the trees making fruit—in
which seed is to kind." And God saw
that *it was* good.
13. And evening was, and morning
was—third day.

The fourth day

14. And God said, "**There are luminaries** in the expanse of the heavens to **distinguish** between the day and between
the night, **and *they*** are for a sign for
appointed times and for days and
years."
15. "**And luminaries exist** in the expanse of the heavens to give light over
the Earth." And *it* was so.
16. And God *is the one who* made two
great luminaries: the greater luminary to
rule the day **and the smaller luminary
to rule the night and the stars.**
17. And **God gave** them in the expanse
of the heavens to give light over the
Earth.
18. And to rule in the day and in the
night and to **distinguish** between the
light and between the darkness. And
God saw that *it was* good.
19. And evening was, and morning
was—fourth day.

The third day

9. And God said, "**Let the waters under the heavens be gathered together**
into one place, and **let the dry land
appear**." And it was so.
10. God called the dry land Earth, and
the waters **that were gathered together**
he called Seas. And God saw that it was
good.
11. And God said, "**Let the earth
sprout vegetation,** plants yielding seed,
and fruit trees bearing fruit in which is
their seed, each according to its kind, on
the earth." And it was so.
12. **The earth brought forth vegetation**, plants yielding seed according to
their own kinds, and trees bearing fruit
in which is their seed, each according to
its kind. And God saw that it was good.
13. And there was evening and there
was morning, the third day.

The fourth day

14. And God said, "**Let there be lights**
in the expanse of the heavens to **separate** the day from the night. **And let
them be** for signs and for seasons, and
for days and years,
15. **and let them be lights** in the expanse of the heavens to give light upon
the earth." And it was so.
16. And God made the two great
lights—the greater light to rule the day
**and the lesser light to rule the night—
and the stars.**
17. And **God set** them in the expanse
of the heavens to give light on the
earth,
18. to rule over the day and over the
night, and to **separate** the light from the
darkness. And God saw that it was
good.
19. And there was evening and there
was morning, the fourth day.

The fifth day

20. And God said, "**The waters swarm** *with* swarms of living creatures, **and fliers flying** over the land and over the surface of the expanse of the sky."

21. **And** God *is the one who* created the **great reptiles** and every moving living creature with which the waters swarmed, *according* to *their* kinds, and every winged flier *according* to *its* kind. And God saw that *it was* good.

22. And God blessed them saying, "Be fruitful and multiply and fill the waters in the seas and multiply the fliers on the land."

23. And evening was, and morning was—fifth day.

The sixth day

24. And God said, "**The land brings forth** living creatures *according* to *their* kind: beasts and moving *things* and animals of the land, *according* to *their* kind." And *it* was so.

25. And God *is the one who* made the animals of the Earth *according* to *their* kind: the beasts *according* to *their* kind and every moving *thing* upon the ground *according* to *its* kind. And God saw that *it was* good.

26. And God said, "Man, made in our image *and* after our likeness, has dominion on fish of the sea and on fliers in the sky and on beasts and on all the Earth and on all the moving *things* that move over the **land**."

27. **And** God *is the one who* created man in His image, in God's image created him, male and female *God* created them.

28. And God blessed them, and God said to them, "Be fruitful and multiply and fill the Earth and subdue it and have dominion on fish of

The fifth day

20. And God said, "**Let the waters swarm** with swarms of living creatures, **and let birds fly** above the earth across the expanse of the heavens."

21. **So** God created the **great sea creatures** and every living creature that moves, with which the waters swarm, according to their kinds, and every winged bird according to its kind. And God saw that it was good.

22. And God blessed them, saying, "Be fruitful and multiply and fill the waters in the seas, and let birds multiply on the earth."

23. And there was evening and there was morning, the fifth day.

The sixth day

24. And God said, "**Let the earth bring forth** living creatures according to their kinds—livestock and creeping things and beasts of the earth according to their kinds." And it was so.

25. And God made the beasts of the earth according to their kinds and the livestock according to their kinds, and everything that creeps on the ground according to its kind. And God saw that it was good.

26. Then God said, "**Let us** make man in our image, after our likeness. **And let them** have dominion over the fish of the sea and over the birds of the heavens and over the livestock and over all the earth and over every creeping thing that creeps on the **earth**."

27. **So** God created man in his own image, in the image of God he created him; male and female he created them.

28. And God blessed them. And God said to them, "Be fruitful and multiply and fill the earth and subdue it and have dominion over the fish of the sea and

the sea and on fliers in the sky and on all living *things* that move over the land."

29. And God said, "Behold, *I have* given to you every plant seeding seed which is over the surface of all the land, and every tree in which fruit is seeding seed. For you, *they* are for food."

30. "And to every animal of the land and to every flier in the sky and to every moving *thing* over the land, which is a living creature, *I have given* every green plant for food." And *it* was so.

31. And God saw all that *He had* **done,** and behold *it was* very good. And evening was, and morning was—the sixth day.

---

over the birds of the heavens and over every living thing that moves on the earth."

29. And God said, "Behold, I have given you every plant yielding seed that is on the face of all the earth, and every tree with seed in its fruit. You shall have them for food.

30. And to every beast of the earth and to every bird of the heavens and to everything that creeps on the earth, everything that has the breath of life, I have given every green plant for food." And it was so.

31. And God saw everything that he had **made,** and behold, it was very good. And there was evening and there was morning, the sixth day.

Chapter 2

The seventh day

1. And the heavens and Earth *were* finished, and all their multitude *of miscellaneous things*.

2. And on the seventh day God finished His work that *He had* done, and rested on the seventh day from all His work that *He had* done.

3. And God blessed the seventh day and sanctified it, because on it *God* rested from all work **that He created to do.**

Chapter 2

The seventh day

1. Thus the heavens and the earth were finished, and all the host of them.

2. And on the seventh day God finished his work that he had done, and he rested on the seventh day from all his work that he had done.

3. So God blessed the seventh day and made it holy, because on it God rested from all his work that **he had done in creation.**

Introduction to Adam's historical account

4. These **accounts** *that follow are about* the heavens and the Earth **at their** creation—in the **days** Yahweh God **did** *the* Earth and heavens.

Introduction to Adam's historical account

4. **These are the generations** of the heavens and the earth **when they were** created, in the **day that the** LORD God **made** the earth and the heavens.

The Garden of Eden

5. And every bush of the field was not yet on the land, and every plant of the

---

The Garden of Eden

5. When no bush of the field was yet in the land and no small plant of the

field *did* not yet grow, because Yahweh God had not caused rain over the land and there was no man to cultivate the ground *where the garden was to be.*

6. And mists rose up from the land and watered all the surface of the ground *where the garden was to be.*

7. And Yahweh God formed the man *of* dust from the ground and breathed in his nostrils the breath *of* life. And the **man existed** as a living creature.

8. And Yahweh God planted a garden from the east in Eden, and there *He* put the man whom *He had* formed.

9. **And Yahweh God grew from the ground** every tree *that was* desirable to the sight and good for food, and the tree of life in the middle of the garden and the tree of knowledge of good and evil.

10. And a river went out from Eden to water the garden and from there diverged and became four branches.

11. The name of the first is Pishon; it winds through all the land of Havilah, where there is gold.

12. And the gold of that land is good; bdellium and onyx stone *are* there.

13. And the name of the second river is the Gihon. It winds through all the land of Cush.

14. And the name of the third river is the Tigris; it goes east of Asshur. And the fourth river is the Euphrates.

Man in the garden

15. And Yahweh God took the man and put him in the Garden of Eden to cultivate and to keep it.

16. And Yahweh God commanded over the man saying, "From every tree of the garden, you *may* **eat-eat.**"

17. "But from the tree of the knowledge of good and evil, *do* not eat from, be-

field had yet sprung up—for the LORD God had not caused it to rain on the land, and there was no man to work the ground,

6. and a mist was going up from the land and was watering the whole face of the ground—

7. then the LORD God formed the man of dust from the ground and breathed into his nostrils the breath of life, and the **man became** a living creature.

8. And the LORD God planted a garden in Eden, in the east, and there he put the man whom he had formed.

9. **And out of the ground the LORD God made to spring up** every tree that is pleasant to the sight and good for food. The tree of life was in the midst of the garden, and the tree of the knowledge of good and evil.

10. A river flowed out of Eden to water the garden, and there it divided and became four rivers.

11. The name of the first is the Pishon. It is the one that flowed around the whole land of Havilah, where there is gold.

12. And the gold of that land is good; bdellium and onyx stone are there.

13. The name of the second river is the Gihon. It is the one that flowed around the whole land of Cush.

14. And the name of the third river is the Tigris, which flows east of Assyria. And the fourth river is the Euphrates.

Man in the garden

15. The LORD God took the man and put him in the garden of Eden to work it and keep it.

16. And the LORD God commanded the man, saying, "You may **surely eat** of every tree of the garden,

17. but of the tree of the knowledge of good and evil you shall not eat, for in

cause on the day you eat from it you *shall* **die-die**.”

18. And Yahweh God said, “*It is* not good *for* the man to be alone. For him *I shall* **make as his counterpart a helper**.”

Animals of the garden

19. **And Yahweh God formed from the ground** every animal of the field and every flier of the sky *that lived within the garden.* And *God* brought *them* to the man to see what he *would* call them and whatever the man called the living creature, that *was its* name.

20. And the man called names to all the beasts and to the fliers of the sky and to all animals of the field *that lived within the garden.* And for Adam *was* not **found as his counterpart a helper.**

Woman is created

21. And Yahweh God caused a deep sleep to fall over the man and *during* sleep took from one of his ribs and closed up under the flesh.

22. And Yahweh God built—which *He* took *of* the rib from the man—into a woman, and brought her to the man.

Marriage is established

23. And the man said, “This is now bone from my bones and flesh from my flesh; for this *shall* be called woman, because this *was* taken from man.”

24. So over *this reason,* a man *will* leave his father and his mother and hold fast on his wife. And *they shall* be as one flesh.

25. And the two were naked, the man and *his* wife, and not ashamed.

the day that you eat of it you shall **surely die**.”

18. Then the LORD God said, “It is not good that the man should be alone; **I will make him a helper fit for him**.”

Animals of the garden

19. **Now out of the ground the LORD God had formed** every beast of the field and every bird of the heavens and brought them to the man to see what he would call them. And whatever the man called every living creature, that was its name.

20. The man gave names to all livestock and to the birds of the heavens and to every beast of the field. But for Adam there was not **found a helper fit for him.**

Woman is created

21. So the LORD God caused a deep sleep to fall upon the man, and while he slept took one of his ribs and closed up its place with flesh.

22. And the rib that the LORD God had taken from the man he made into a woman and brought her to the man.

Marriage is established

23. Then the man said, “This at last is bone of my bones and flesh of my flesh; she shall be called Woman, because she was taken out of Man.”

24. Therefore a man shall leave his father and his mother and hold fast to his wife, and they shall become one flesh.

25. And the man and his wife were both naked and were not ashamed.

Appendix: D

The Septuagint Translation – Genesis Chapters 1 and 2

The following English translation of the Septuagint is from *The Septuagint with Aprocrypha: Greek and English* by Sir Lancelot C. L. Brenton originally published in 1851 by Samuel Bagster & Sons Ltd., London, England. The Brenton translation can be compared with *A New English Translation of the Septuagint* by Albert Pietersma and Benjamin J. Wright published in 2007 or to the Orthodox Study Bible published in 2008 (all three English translations of the Septuagint are available on the Internet).

The first five books of the Septuagint, the Pentateuch, were translated from Hebrew to Greek around 275 BC by Hebrew scribes. This translation established the interpretative paradigm for the Genesis creation story, which has continued unchallenged until the present. The Septuagint translation has numerous errors as the following illustrates. Significant words that are mistranslated or poorly translated are underlined in the text below. Significant words added to the original text are highlighted in **bold**. Significant words that were left out and not translated in any manner have been added to the text and enclosed in [brackets].

Chapter 1
1. In the beginning God made the heaven and the earth.
2. But the earth was unsightly and unfurnished, and darkness was over [the surface] the deep, and the Spirit of God moved over [the surface] the water.
3. And God said, **Let** there be light, and there was light.
4. And God saw the light that it was good, and God divided between the light and [between] the darkness.
5. And God called the light Day, and the darkness he called Night, and there was evening and there was morning, the first day.
6. And God said, **Let** there be a firmament in the midst of the water, and **let** it be a division between water and water, **and it was so.**
7. And God made the firmament, and God divided between the water which was under the firmament and the water which was above the firmament. [And it was so.]
8. And God called the firmament Heaven, **and God saw that it was good**, and there was evening and there was morning, the second day.
9. And God said, **Let** the water which is under the heaven be collected into one place, and **let** the dry land appear, and it was so. **And the water which was under the heaven was collected into its places, and the dry land appeared.**

10. And God called the dry land Earth, and the gatherings of the waters he called Seas, and God saw that it was good.

11. And God said, **Let** the earth bring forth the herb of grass bearing seed **according to its kind and according to its likeness,** and the fruit-tree bearing fruit whose seed is in it, according to its kind on the earth, and it was so.

12. And the earth brought forth the herb of grass bearing seed according to its kind **and according to its likeness,** and the fruit tree bearing fruit whose seed is in it, according to its kind **on the earth,** and God saw that it was good.

13. And there was evening and there was morning, the third day.

14. And God said, **Let** there be lights in the firmament of the heaven to **give light upon the earth,** to divide between day and [between] night, and **let them** be for signs and for seasons and for days and for years.

15. And **let them** [luminaries] be for light in the firmament of the heaven, **so as to** shine upon the earth, and it was so.

16. And God made the two great lights, the greater light for regulating the day and the lesser light for regulating the night, the stars also.

17. And God placed them in the firmament of the heaven, **so as to** shine upon the earth,

18. and to regulate day and night, and to divide between the light and [between] the darkness. And God saw that it was good.

19. And there was evening and there was morning, the fourth day.

20. And God said, **Let** the waters bring forth reptiles having life, and **winged** creatures flying above the earth in the firmament of heaven, and it was so.

21. And God made great whales, and every living reptile, which the waters brought forth according to their kinds, and every **creature** that flies with wings according to its kind, and God saw that they were good.

22. And God blessed them saying, Increase and multiply and fill the waters in the seas, and **let** the creatures that fly be multiplied on the earth.

23. And there was evening and there was morning, the fifth day.

24. And God said, **Let** the earth bring forth the living creature according to its kind, quadrupeds and reptiles and wild beasts of the earth according to their kind, and it was so.

25. And God made the wild beasts of the earth according to their kind, and cattle according to their kind, and all the reptiles of the earth according to their kind, and God saw that they were good.

26. And God said, **Let us** make man according to our image and [our] likeness, and **let them** have dominion over the fish of the sea, and over the flying creatures of heaven, and over the cattle and all the earth, and over all the reptiles that creep on the earth.

27. And God made man, according to the image of God he made him, male and female he made them.

28. And God blessed them, [and God] saying, Increase and multiply, and fill the

earth and subdue it, and have dominion over the fish of the seas and flying **creatures** of heaven, **and all the cattle and all the earth**, and all the <u>reptiles</u> that creep on the earth.

29. And God said, Behold I have given to you every seed—bearing herb sowing seed which is upon [the surface of] all the earth, and every tree which has in itself the fruit of seed that is sown, to you it shall be for food.

30. And to all the <u>wild beasts</u> of the earth, and to all the flying <u>creatures</u> of heaven, and to every <u>reptile</u> creeping on the earth, which has in itself the breath of life, even every green plant for food; and it was so.

31. And God saw all the things that he had <u>made</u>, and, behold, they were very good. And there was evening and there was morning, the sixth day.

Chapter 2

1. And the heavens and the earth were finished, and the <u>whole world</u> of them.

2. And God finished on the <u>sixth</u> day his works which he <u>made</u>, and he ceased on the seventh day from all his works which he <u>made</u>.

3. And God blessed the seventh day and sanctified it, because in it he ceased from all his [creative] works which God **began to** do.

4. This is the book of the generation of heaven and earth, when they were <u>made</u>, in the day in which the Lord God <u>made</u> the <u>heaven and the earth</u>,

5. and every herb of the field before it was on the earth, and all the grass of the field before it sprang up, for [the Lord] God had not rained on the <u>earth</u>, and there was not a man to cultivate [the ground] it.

6. But there rose a fountain out of the earth, and watered the whole face of the <u>earth</u>.

7. And [the Lord] God formed the man of dust of the <u>earth</u>, and breathed upon his <u>face</u> the breath of life, and the man became a living soul.

8. And [the Lord] God planted a garden eastward in Edem, and placed there the man whom he had formed.

9. And [the Lord] God <u>made to spring up also</u> out of the <u>earth</u> every tree beautiful to the eye and good for food, and the tree of life in the midst of the garden, and the tree of **learning** the knowledge of good and evil.

10. And a river proceeds out of Edem to water the garden, thence it divides itself into four heads.

11. The name of the one, Phisom, this it is which encircles the whole land of Evilat, where there is gold.

12. And the gold of that land is good, there also is carbuncle and emerald.

13. And the name of the second river is Geon, this it is which encircles the whole land of Ethiopia.

14. And the third river is Tigris, this is that which flows forth over against the Assyrians. And the fourth river is Euphrates.

15. And the Lord God took the man **whom he had formed**, and placed him in the garden of Delight, to cultivate and keep it.

16. And the Lord God gave a charge to Adam, saying, Of every tree which is in the garden thou mayest freely eat,

17. but of the tree of the knowledge of good and evil—of it ye shall not eat, but in whatsoever day ye eat of it, ye shall surely die.

18. And the Lord God said, It is not good that the man should be alone, **let** us make for him a help <u>suitable to him</u>.

19. And [the Lord] God formed **yet farther** out of the <u>earth</u> all the <u>wild beasts</u> of the field, and all the <u>birds</u> of the sky, and he brought them to Adam, to see what he would call them, and whatever Adam called any living creature, that was the name of it.

20. And Adam gave names to all the <u>cattle</u> and to all the <u>birds</u> of the sky, and to all the <u>wild beasts</u> of the field, but for Adam there was not found a help like to himself.

21. And [the Lord] God brought a <u>trance</u> upon Adam, and he slept, and he took [from] one of his ribs, and <u>filled</u> up the flesh instead thereof.

22. And [the Lord] God <u>formed</u> the rib which he took from Adam into a woman, and brought her to Adam.

23. And Adam said, This now is bone of my bones, and flesh of my flesh; she shall be called woman, because she was taken out of <u>her husband</u>.

24. Therefore shall a man leave his father and his mother and shall cleave to his wife, and they **two** shall be one flesh.

3:1. (2:25) And the two were naked **both** Adam and his wife, and were not ashamed.

References

Chapter 1 – The Battle over Biblical Creation

1. Templeton, Charles (1999). *Farewell to God: My Reason for Rejecting the Christian Faith.* Toronto: McClelland & Steward Inc. p30.
2. Ibid. p31.
3. Morris, Henry (1976). *The Genesis Record.* Grand Rapids, MI: Baker Book House. p45.
4. Sarfati, Jonathan (2004). *Refuting Compromise.* Green Forest, AR: Master Books. pp120–137.
5. Batten, Don, ed. and Ken Ham, Jonathan Sarfati, Carl Wieland (1990). *The Revised & Expanded Answers Book*, 24th printing. Green Forest, AR: Master Books. p58.
6. Rhodes, Ron (2004). *The 10 Things You Should Know About the Creation vs. Evolution Debate.* Eugene, OR: Harvest House Publishers. p49.
7. Duncan, Samuel J., Chairman (2000). What is the Day-Age Interpretation? *Report of the Creation Study Committee. Presbyterian Church in America.* Retrieved on October 21, 2009 from http://www.pcahistory.org/creation/report.html
8. Eliyah.com (2009). Strong's Concordance – King James Version. Search on H3117. Retrieved on Oct. 20, 2009 from http://www.eliyah.com/lexicon.html
9. Collins, C. John (2006). *Genesis 1–4: A Linguistic, Literary, and Theological Commentary.* Phillipsburg, NJ: P & R Publishing Co. p124.
10. Ibid. p123.
11. Ibid. p78.
12. Ibid. p78.
13. Ibid. p126.
14. Borchert, Donald M., ed. (1996). *The Encyclopedia of Philosophy, Supplement.* New York: Simon and Schuster-Macmillan. p372.
15. Dembski, William A. (1996, Apr. 1). What Every Theologian Should Know About Creation, Evolution and Design. *The Princeton Theological Review.* Retrieved on May 20, 2008 from http://www.discovery.org/scripts/viewDB/index.php?command=view&id=122. p4.
16. Collins, Francis S. (2006). *The Language of God.* New York, NY: Free Press. p200.
17. Ibid. p193.
18. Center for Science and Culture, Discovery Institute (2009). *The Theory of Intelligent Design: A Briefing Packet for Educators.* Seattle, WA: Discovery Institute. p4.
19. Discovery Institute (2009). What is the Science behind Intelligent Design? Retrieved on October 21, 2009 from http://www.discovery.org/a/9761
20. White, J. Gene (2009). *Exemplar Creation: Credible Origins for the Next Millennium.* St. Louis, MO: Sunnybrooke Publications. p202.
21. Duncan, Samuel J., Chairman (2000).Introductory Statement. *Report of the Creation Study Committee. Presbyterian Church in America.* Retrieved on October 21, 2009 from http://www.pcahistory.org/creation/report.html
22. Ibid. Recommendations.
23. Blocher, Henri (1984). *In the Beginning: The Opening Chapters of Genesis*, (English translation by David G. Preston). Downers Grove, IL: Inter Varsity Press, pp213–231.
24. Baylor University Department of Biology (2010). Statement on Evolution. Retrieved on January 26, 2010 from http://www.baylor.edu/Biology/index.php?id=27622
25. Baylor University Department of Anthropology (2010). Evolution. Retrieved on January 29, 2010 from http://www.baylor.edu/afsa/anthropology/index.php?id=65416

Chapter 2 – *Exemplar* Creation: The Original Story

1. Castagno, Joseph M., ed. (2006). *The New Book of Popular Science*, vol. 2. Scholastic Library Publishing Inc. p14.
2. Hancock, Paul L. and Brian J. Skinner, eds. (2000). *The Oxford Companion to the Earth*. New York: Oxford University Press. p230.
3. Emsley, John (1998). *The Elements*, 3rd ed. Oxford: Clarendon Press. p289.
4. Dasch, E. Julius, ed. (1996). *Encyclopedia of Earth Sciences*, vol.1. New York: Simon & Schuster Macmillan. p134.
5. Hancock. *The Oxford Companion to the Earth*. p278.
6. Darling, David (2004). *The Universal Book of Astronomy*. Hoboken, NJ: John Wiley & Sons Inc. p340.
7. Angelo, Joseph A. Jr. (2006). *Encyclopedia of Space and Astronomy*. New York: Facts on File. p403.
8. National Aeronautics and Space Administration (1999, Apr.). NASA's Goddard Space Flight Center: The First Forty Years. *NASA Facts*, FS-1999 (01)-003GSFC. p4.
9. Faulkner, Danny (2004). *Universe by Design*. Green Forest, AR: Master Books. p126.
10. Johnston, Sarah Iles, ed. (2004). *Religions of the Ancient World: A Guide*. Cambridge, MA: Harvard University Press. p395.
11. Bergeron, Lou (1997, Aug. 30). Deep Waters. *New Scientist*, 155(2097):22–26.
12. Swenson, Herbert (2008). Why is the Ocean Salty? U.S. Geological Survey Publication. Retrieved on March 12, 2008 from http://www.palomar.edu/oceanography/salty_ocean.htm
13. Schneider, S. H. (1996). Water resources by P. H. Gleick. *Encyclopedia of Climate and Weather*, vol. 2. New York: Oxford University Press. pp817–823.
14. Dalrymple, G. Brent (1991). *Age of the Earth*. Stanford, CA: Stanford University Press. p207, 223.
15. Dasch. *Encyclopedia of Earth Sciences*. pp496–498.
16. Doniger, Wendy, ed. (1999). *Merriam-Webster's Encyclopedia of World Religions*. Springfield, MA: Merriam-Webster Inc. p910.
17. Ibid. p1095.
18. Ibid. p637.
19. MacArthur, John (2001). *Battle for the Beginning: Creation, Evolution and the Bible*. Nashville, TN: Thomas Nelson, Inc. p165.
20. Eliyah.com (2006). Strong's Concordance – King James Version. Search on "earth and heaven." Retrieved on May 20, 2006 from http://www.eliyah.com/lexicon.html
21. Emsley. *The Elements*.
22. McDowell, Josh and Don Stewart (1980). *Answers to Tough Questions Skeptics Ask About the Christian Faith*. Wheaton, IL: Tyndale House Publishers, Inc. pp205–241.

Chapter 3 – Roots of Deception

1. MacArthur, John (2001). *Battle for the Beginning: Creation, Evolution and the Bible*. Nashville, TN: W Publishing Group. p27.
2. Würthwein, Ernst (1988). *The Text of the Old Testament*, 5th ed. (translated by Erroll F. Rhodes and published in English in 1995) Grand Rapids, MI: William B. Eerdmans Publishing Co. pp107–122.
3. *Catholic Encyclopedia* (2009). Popes. Retrieved on October 23, 2009 from http://www.newadvent.org/cathen/12272b.htm
4. DeRose, Peter (1988). *Vicars of Christ: The Dark Side of the Papacy*. New York, NY: Crown Publishers, Inc. p15.
5. Ibid. p151.
6. Remembering the wives of Joseph Smith (2009). Retrieved on October 19, 2009 from http://www.wivesofjosephsmith.org/

7. Michael Davis Mormonism (2009). Retrieved on October 22, 2009 from http://www.leaderu.com/offices/michaeldavis/docs/mormonism/onlytrue.html
8. *Wikpedia, The Free Encyclopedia* (2009). Charles Taze Russell. Retrieved on October 23, 2009 from http://en.wikipedia.org/wiki/Charles_Taze_Russell
9. Christian Apologetics and Research Ministries (2009). Jehovah's Witnesses. Retrieved on October 23, 2009 from http://www.carm.org/religious-movements/jehovahs-witnesses
10. Magness, Jodi (2002). *The Archaeology of Qumran and the Dead Sea Scrolls*. Grand Rapids, MI: William B. Eerdmans Publishing Company. p42.
11. Freedman, David Noel (1992). *The Anchor Bible Dictionary*, vol. 5. New York: Doubleday. pp892−894.
12. Magness. *The Archaeology of Qumran and the Dead Sea Scrolls*. p42
13. Freedman. *The Anchor Bible Dictionary*, vol. 5. pp289−303.
14. Freedman. *The Anchor Bible Dictionary*, vol. 2. pp620−626.
15. Lubenow, Marvin L. (1992). *Bones of Contention: A Creationist Assessment of Human Fossils*. Grand Rapids, MI: Baker Books. p218.
16. Ussher, James (1658). *The Annals of the World*. (Ussher's timeline chart by Paul Hansen, published in *Creation*, Sept. 2005). Retrieved on March 3, 2006 from http://www.answersingenesis.org/creation/v27/i4/TimelineOfTheBible.pdf
17. Freedman. *The Anchor Bible Dictionary*, vol. 4. p599.
18. *Britannica, The New Encyclopedia*, vol. 7, 15th ed. (2005). Masoretic Text. Chicago, IL: Encyclopedia Britannica Inc. p914.
19. Würthwein. *The Text of the Old Testament*. p21.
20. Josephus, Flavius (1987). *The Works of Josephus: Complete and Unabridged*, 13th printing. (translated by William Whiston) Peabody, MA: Hendrickson Publishers. p29.
21. Philo (1993). *The Works of Philo: Complete and Unabridged*, 4th printing. (translated by C. D. Yonge) Peabody, MA: Hendrickson Publishers. p6.
22. Ibid. p7.
23. Ibid. p9.
24. Ibid. p10.
25. Fahlbusch, Erwin and Jan Lochman, John Mbiti, Jaroslav Pelikan, Lukas Vischer, eds. (2005). *The Encyclopedia of Christianity*, vol. 4. Grand Rapids, MI: William B. Eerdmans Publishing Co. p913.
26. Freedman. *The Anchor Bible Dictionary*, vol. 5. p1094.
27. Pietersma, Albert and Benjamin J. Wright (2007). *A New English Translation of the Septuagint*. New York, NY: Oxford University Press. Retrieved on May 20, 2008 from http://ccat.sas.upenn.edu/nets/edition/
28. Brenton, Lancelot C. L., trans. (1851). *The Septuagint with Apocrypha: Greek and English*. London: Samuel Bagster & Sons. Retrieved on May 20, 2008 from http://www.ccel.org/bible/brenton/
29. The Thompson Chain-Reference Bible, New International Version (1978). Grand Rapids, MI: Zondervan Bible Publishers. p1512.
30. Ibid. p1512.
31. Freedman, David Noel (1992). *The Anchor Bible Dictionary*, vol. 6. New York: Doubleday. pp819−823. A history of Bible translations only-no discussion of theological influence.
32. Hawkins, Craig S. (1998). *Witchcraft*. Grand Rapids, MI: Baker Book House, p140.
33. Fisher, Richard G. (July-Sept. 2000). *The Quarterly Journal*, vol. 20, no. 3. St. Louis, MO: Personal Freedom Outreach, p16.
34. Ibid. p16.
35. Ibid. p16.

Chapter 4 − Evidence of Age

1. Stobel, Nick (2005). Astronomy Notes. Retrieved on October 10, 2005 from http://www.astronomynotes.com/starprops/s1.html

2. European Space Agency (2008). The Hipparcos Space Astronomy Mission. Retrieved on May 27, 2008 from http://www.rssd.esa.int/index.php?project=HIPPARCOS
3. Angelo, Joseph A. Jr. (2006). *Encyclopedia of Space and Astronomy*. New York: Facts on File. p522.
4. Ribas, Ignasi and Carme Jordi, Francesc Vilardell, Edward L. Fitzpartick, Ron W. Hilditch, Edward F. Guinan (2005, Nov.). First Determination of the Distance and Fundamental Properties of an Eclipsing Binary in The Andromeda Galaxy. *Astrophysical Journal Letters*, 635 (2005) L37-L40.
5. Central Bureau for Astronomical Telegrams (2007). List of Recent Supernovae. Retrieved on May 7, 2007 from http://www.cfa.harvard.edu/iau/lists/RecentSupernovae.html
6. Batten, Don, ed. and Ken Ham, Jonathan Sarfati, Carl Wieland (1990). *The Revised & Expanded Answers Book*, 24th printing. Green Forest, AR: Master Books. p97.
7. Humphreys, D. Russell (2004). *Starlight and Time: Solving the Puzzle of Distant Starlight in a Young Universe*, 9th printing. Green Forest, AR: Master Books. p26.
8. Ibid. pp32–38.
9. Batten. *The Revised & Expanded Answers Book*. pp98–101.
10. Ibid. p97.
11. Morris, Henry (2003, June). The Uncertain Speed of Light, *Back to Genesis*, no. 174.
12. Dasch, E. Julius, ed. (1996). *Encyclopedia of Earth Sciences*, vol. 1. New York: Simon & Schuster Macmillan. p494.
13. Dalrymple, G. Brent (1991). *Age of the Earth*. Stanford, CA: Stanford University Press. p207, 223.
14. McDowell, Jonathan (2007, Mar. 30). A merge of NASA-RP-1097 (Anderson and Whitaker 1982) and USGS lunar crater data. Retrieved on April 26, 2007 from http://host.planet4589.org/astro/lunar/
15. Hines, Jason (2007, Feb. 16). Earth Impact Database, Planetary and Space Science Centre at the University of New Brunswick, Canada. Retrieved on April 23, 2007 from http://www.unb.ca/passc/ImpactDatabase/
16. Ussher, James (1658). *The Annals of the World*. (Ussher's timeline chart by Paul Hansen, published in *Creation*, Sept. 2005). Retrieved on March 3, 2006 from http://www.answersingenesis.org/creation/v27/i4/TimelineOfTheBible.pdf
17. Lorius, C. and L. Merlivat, J. Jouzel, M. Pourchet (1979). A 30,000 Year Isotope Climatic Record from Antarctic Ice. *Nature*, 280:644–648.
18. Petit, J. R. and J. Jouzel, D. Raynaud, N. I. Barkov, J-M. Barnola, I. Basile, et al (1999, June 3). Climate and Atmospheric History of the past 420,000 years from the Vostok ice core, Antarctica. *Nature*, vols. 399, 6735.
19. Stauffer, Bernhard and Jacqueline Flückiger, Eric Wolff, Piers Barnes (2004). The EPICA Deep Ice Cores: First Results and Perspectives, *Annals of Glaciology*, 39 2004.
20. Parrenin, F. and J. M. Barnola, J. Beer, T. Blunler, E. Castellano, J. Chappellaz, et al (2007, Mar. 12). The EDC3 Chronology for the EPICA Dome C Ice Core. *Climate of the Past*, 3, 575–606.
21. Cross, M., compiler (2003, Jan.). Greenland summit ice cores. Boulder, CO: National Snow and Ice Data Center in association with the World Data Center for Paleoclimatology at NOAA-NGDC and the Institute of Arctic and Alpine Research. CD-ROM.
22. Ibid.
23. Andersen, Katrine (2004). North Greenland Ice Core Project. Retrieved on January 1, 2007 from http://www.gfy.ku.dk/~www-glac/ngrip/index_eng.htm
24. Svensson, A. and S. W. Nielsen, S. Kipfstuhl, S. J. Johnsen, J. P. Steffensen, M. Bigler, U. Ruth, R. Röthlisberger (2005, Jan. 21). Visual Stratigraphy of North Greenland Ice Core Project (NorthGRIP) Ice Core During the Last Glacial Period. *Journal of Geophysical Research*, vol. 110, D02108.
25. White, James (2004, Aug 13). Greenland Ice Core Project Yields Probable Ancient Plant Remains. Retrieved on April 1, 2007 from http://www.eurekalert.org/pub_releases/2004-08/uoca gic081304.php

26. Oard, Michael J. (2005). *The Frozen Record*. El Cajon, CA: Institute for Creation Research. p73.
27. Oard, Michael J. (2007, Apr.-Jun.). Setting the Stage for an Ice Age, *Answers*, vol. 2, no. 2.
28. Oard. *The Frozen Record*. pp45–49.
29. *Antarctica* (1985). Surrey Hills, NSW: Reader's Digest Services Pty. Ltd. p175.
30. Ibid. p28.
31. Walton, D. W. H. (1987). *Antarctic Science*. New York: Cambridge University Press. p41, 186.
32. McKelvey, B. C. and N. C. N. Stephenson (1990). A Geological Reconnaissance of the Radok Lake Area, Amery Oasis, Prince Charles Mountains. *Geological Magazine*, vol. 134 and *Antarctic Science*, 1990.
33. Hammer, William R. and William J. Hickerson (1994, May 6). A Crested Theropod Dinosaur from Antarctica. *Science*, vol. 264, issue 5160, 828–830.
34. Lubick, Noami (2004, Mar. 8). Dinosaurs in the Cold, Dark Antarctic, *Geotimes*.
35. Roehler, Henry W. (1992). Information derived from Figure 11. Correlation, Composition, Areal Distribution, and Thickness of Eocene Stratigraphic Units, Greater Green River Basin, Wyoming, Utah, and Colorado. *U.S. Geological Survey Professional Paper 1506-E*. Washington, D.C.: United States Government Printing Office. pE20.
36. Bradley, Wilmot H. (1929). Varves and Climate of the Green River Epoch. *U.S. Geological Survey Professional Paper 158-E*. Washington, D.C.: United States Government Printing Office. p95.
37. Ibid. p107.
38. Ibid. p107.
39. Ibid. p101.
40. Buchheim, Paul H. and Robert Biaggi (1988). Laminae Counts Within a Synchronous Oil Shale Unit: A Challenge to the Varve Concept. *GSA Abstracts & Programs*, Article 18279, v. 20, no. 7, p317.
41. Buchheim, Paul (1994). Paleoenvironments, Lithofacies and Varves of the Fossil Butte Member of the Eocene Green River Formation, Southwestern Wyoming. *Contributions to Geology, University of Wyoming*, 30:1. p8.
42. Oard, Michael J. and John H. Whitmore (2006). The Green River Formation of the west-central United States: Flood or post-Flood? *Journal of Creation* 20(1), p48.
43. Roehler, Henry W. Information derived from Figure 11. *U.S. Geological Survey Professional Paper 1506-E*. pE20.
44. Roehler, Henry W. (1993). Figure 6. Eocene Climates, Depositional Environments, and Geography, Greater Green River Basin, Wyoming, Utah, and Colorado. *U.S. Geological Survey Professional Paper 1506-F*. Washington, D.C.: United States Government Printing Office. pF12.
45. Ibid. pF15.
46. Ibid. pF29–F30.
47. Dalrymple. *Age of the Earth*. p14.
48. Wiens, Roger C. (2005). Radiometric Dating - A Christian Perspective. American Scientific Affiliation. Retrieved on September 17, 2005 from http://www.asa3.org/ASA/resources/Wiens.html
49. Dasch. *Encyclopedia of Earth Sciences*, vol. 2, p767.
50. Dalrymple. *Age of the Earth*. p230.
51. Ibid. p239.
52. Ibid. p287.
53. Ibid. p305.
54. Ibid. p357.
55. Dean, John A. (1999). *Lange's Handbook of Chemistry*, 15th ed. New York: McGraw-Hill Inc. p7.124.
56. Taylor, R. E. (2007). Radiocarbon Dating. *McGraw-Hill Encyclopedia of Science & Tech-*

nology, vol. 15, 10th ed. New York: McGraw-Hill. p146.
57. Ibid. p151.
58. Suess, H. E. and T. W. Linick (1990). The [14]C Record in Bristlecone Pine Wood of the past 8000 Years Based on the Dendrochronology of the Late C. W. Ferguson. *Philosophical Transactions of the Royal Society of London. Series A, Mathematical and Physical Sciences,* vol. 330, issue 1615, pp. 403−412.
59. Reimer, P. J. and M. G. L. Baillie, E. Bard, A. Bayliss, J. W. Beck, C. J. H. Bertrand, P. G. Backwell, et al (2004). IntCal04 Terrestrial Radiocarbon Age Calibrations, 0-26ka BP. *Radiocarbon,* 46, 1029−1058.
60. Ibid. p1029−1058.
61. Fairbanks, Richard G. and Richard A. Mortlock, Tzu-Chien Chiu, Li Cao, Aley Kapan, Thomas P. Guilderson, et al (2005, Apr.). Radiocarbon Calibration Curve Spanning 0 to 50,000 Years BP Based on Paired ^{230}Th /^{234}U/^{238}U/ and [14]C Dates on Pristine Corals. *Quaternary Science Reviews* 24:1781−1796.
62. Kitagawa, H. and J. van der Plicht (1998, Feb. 20). Atmospheric Radiocarbon Calibration to 45,000 yr B.P.: Late Glacial Fluctuations and Cosmogenic Isotope Production. *Science,* vol. 279, 1187−1190.
63. Taylor. *McGraw-Hill Encyclopedia of Science & Technology.* p151.
64. Maslin, M. A. and Thomas, E. (2003, Apr.). Balancing the Deglacial Global Carbon Budget: The Hydrate Factor. *Quaternary Science Reviews,* 22:p1733.
65. Arens, Nan Crystal and A. Hope Jahren, Ronald Amundson (2000). Can C3 Plants Faithfully Record the Carbon Isotopic Composition of Atmospheric Carbon Dioxide? *Paleobiology* 26(1), p147.
66. Turney, C. S. M. and D. Wheeler, Allan R. Chivas (2006). Carbon Isotope Fractionation in Wood During Carbonization. *Geochimica et Cosmochimica Acta,* 70, p962.
67. Lowe, J. J. and M. J. C. Walker (1997). Chapter 5, Dating Methods. *Reconstructing Quaternary Environments.* Prentice Hall.
68. Higham, Tom (2002, May 16). Sample isotopic fractionation. Radiocarbon Laboratory, University of Waikato, New Zealand. Retrieved on February 24, 2007 from http://www.c14dating.com/frac.html
69. Taylor. *McGraw-Hill Encyclopedia of Science & Technology.* p151.
70. Batten, Don, ed. and Ken Ham, Jonathan Sarfati, Carl Wieland (1990). *The Revised & Expanded Answers Book,* 24th printing. Green Forest, AR: Master Books. pp75−79.
71. Ham, Ken, ed. (2006). *The New Answers Book.* Green Forest, AR: Master Books. pp77−84.
72. VanderKam, James and Peter Flint (2002). *The Meaning of the Dead Sea Scrolls.* San Francisco, CA: Harper Collins, p31.
73. Damon, P. E. and D. J. Donahue, B. H. Gore, A. L. Hatheway, A. J. T. Jull, et al. (Feb. 16, 1989). Radiocarbon Dating the Shroud of Turin, *Nature,* vol. 337, no. 6208. pp611−615. Retrieved on Nov. 4, 2009 from http://www.shroud.com/nature.htm
74. Batten, Don, ed. and Ken Ham, Jonathan Sarfati, Carl Wieland (1990). *The Revised & Expanded Answers Book,* 24th printing. Green Forest, AR: Master Books. p90.
75. Baillieul, Thomas A. (2009). Polonium Haloes Refuted. Retrieved on Nov. 18, 2009 from http://www.talkorigins.org/faqs/po-halos/gentry.html
76. Ibid.
77. Ibid.
78. Polonium Halos in Deep Earth Granite (2009). Picture of a five ring U-238 halo. Retrieved on Nov 18, 2009 from http://www.ichthus.info/Creation-Evidence/Polonium-Halos/intro.html
79. Gannon, Robert (Nov. 1979). How Old is It?-The Elegant Science of Dating Ancient Objects. *Popular Science.* Picture of a five ring U-238 halo.
80. *The New Encyclopedia Britannica,* vol. 5, 15th ed. (2005). Giza, Pyramids of. Chicago, IL: Encyclopedia Britannica Inc. p288.

Chapter 5 – Key Words in Genesis

1. Brown, Francis and S. R. Driver, Charles A. Briggs (1907). *A Hebrew and English Lexicon of the Old Testament,* 1978 printing. Oxford: Oxford Clarendon Press. p135.
2. Strong, James (1890). *Strong's Exhaustive Concordance of the Bible*, 31st printing. New York: Abingdon Press.
3. Brown. *A Hebrew and English Lexicon of the Old Testament*. p793.
4. Eliyah.com (2006). Strong's Concordance – King James Version. Retrieved on May 20, 2006 from http://www.eliyah.com/lexicon.html
5. Gesenius, Wilhelm (1846). *Hebrew and Chaldee Lexicon to the Old Testament Scriptures*, 1st ed. (translated by Samuel P. Tregelles) London: Samuel Bagster & Sons Ltd. Retrieved on May 20, 2008 from http://www.eliyah.com/lexicon.html
6. Brown. *A Hebrew and English Lexicon of the Old Testament*. p96.
7. Eliyah. Strong's Concordance – King James Version.
8. Brown. *A Hebrew and English Lexicon of the Old Testament*. p1062.
9. Eliyah. Strong's Concordance – King James Version.
10. Young, Robert (1898). Holy Bible, Young's Literal Translation. Retrieved on May 20, 2008 from http://www.blueletterBible.org/
11. Brown. *A Hebrew and English Lexicon of the Old Testament*. p1062.
12. Eliyah. Strong's Concordance – King James Version.
13. Darby, John N. (1890). Holy Bible, The Darby Translation. Retrieved on May 20, 2008 from http://www.blueletterBible.org/
14. Freedman, David Noel (1992). *The Anchor Bible Dictionary*, vol. 2. New York: Doubleday. p125.
15. Eliyah. Strong's Concordance – King James Version.
16. Crosswalk.com (2006). Word search for "sky" in the NIV using the online study Bible. Retrieved on May 20, 2008 from http://bible.crosswalk.com/
17. Eliyah. Strong's Concordance – King James Version.
18. Snoke, David (2006). *A Biblical Case for an Old Earth*. Grand Rapids, MI: Baker Books. p199–202.
19. Brown. *A Hebrew and English Lexicon of the Old Testament*. p874.
20. Gesenius, Wilhelm (1846). *Hebrew and Chaldee Lexicon to the Old Testament Scriptures*, 1st ed. (translated by Samuel P. Tregelles) London: Samuel Bagster & Sons Ltd. Retrieved on May 20, 2008 from http://www.eliyah.com/lexicon.html
21. Eliyah. Strong's Concordance – King James Version.
22. Ibid.
23. Ibid.
24. Ibid.
25. Ibid.
26. Ibid.
27. Pietersma, Albert and Benjamin J. Wright (2007). *A New English Translation of the Septuagint*. New York, NY: Oxford University Press. Retrieved on May 20, 2008 from http://ccat.sas.upenn.edu/nets/edition/
28. Webster, Noah (1833). Holy Bible, Noah Webster's Translation. Retrieved on May 20, 2008 from http://www.blueletterBible.org/
29. Brown. *A Hebrew and English Lexicon of the Old Testament*. p876.
30. Eliyah. Strong's Concordance – King James Version.
31. Gesenius. *Hebrew and Chaldee Lexicon to the Old Testament Scriptures*.
32. Brown. *A Hebrew and English Lexicon of the Old Testament*. p226.
33. Chalker, Sylvia and Edmund Weiner (1994). *The Oxford Dictionary of English Grammar*. Oxford: Clarendon Press. p128.
34. Ibid. p372.
35. *American Heritage College Dictionary,* 4th ed. (2004). Boston, MA: Houghton Mifflin Company. p122.

36. Ibid. p75.
37. Ibid. p489.
38. van der Merwe, Christo, ed. (2004). *The Lexham Hebrew-English Interlinear Bible*. (translated by the University of Stellenbosch, Stellenbosch, South Africa) Bellingham, WA: Logos Research Systems Inc. Based on a search of the Hebrew text for the root word (היה)
39. Strong. *Strong's Exhaustive Concordance of the Bible*.
40. van der Merwe. *The Lexham Hebrew-English Interlinear Bible*. Based on a search of the Hebrew text for the root word (היה)
41. Scofield, Cyrus I. (1917). Scofield notes for Genesis 1:2. Holy Bible, King James Version, Scofield Reference. Oxford University Press.
42. Batten, Don, ed. and Ken Ham, Jonathan Sarfati, Carl Wieland (1990). *The Revised & Expanded Answers Book*, 24th printing. Green Forest, AR: Master Books. p58.
43. Custance, Arthur C. (1970). *Without Form and Void*. Brookville, Canada: Pub. by Arthur C. Custance. pxi.
44. Harrison, R. K. (1955). *Biblical Hebrew*. Berkshire, England: Cox & Wyman Ltd. p90.
45. Dobson, John H. (2005). *Learn Biblical Hebrew*, 2nd ed. Grand Rapids, MI: Baker Publishing Group. pp157, 182, 194.
46. Pratico, Gary D. and Miles V. Van Pelt (2001). *Basics of Biblical Hebrew Grammar*. Grand Rapids, MI: Zondervan. p137.
47. Ibid. p137.
48. Dobson. *Learn Biblical Hebrew*. pp354–355.
49. Ibid. pp339, 354–355.
50. Harrison, R. K. (1955). *Biblical Hebrew*. Berkshire, England: Cox & Wyman Ltd. p160, 161.
51. Beall, Todd S. and William A. Banks, Colin Smith (2000). *Old Testament Parsing Guide, Revised and Updated Edition*. Nashville, TN: Broadman & Holman Publishers. pviii.
52. van der Merwe. *The Lexham Hebrew-English Interlinear Bible*. Count is based on a search of the Hebrew text for the exact expression "and God said" in Genesis 1:3.

Chapter 6 – Translating Genesis

1. Pratico, Gary D. and Miles V. Van Pelt (2001). *Basics of Biblical Hebrew Grammar*. Grand Rapids, MI: Zondervan. p129.
2. Ibid. p129–130.
3. van der Merwe, Christo, ed. (2004). *The Lexham Hebrew-English Interlinear Bible*. (translated by the University of Stellenbosch, Stellenbosch, South Africa) Bellingham, WA: Logos Research Systems Inc.
4. Brenton, Lancelot C. L., trans. (1851). *The Septuagint with Apocrypha: Greek and English*. London: Samuel Bagster & Sons. Retrieved on May 20, 2008 from http://www.ccel.org/bible/brenton/
5. Waltke, Bruce K. (2001). *Genesis: A Commentary*. Grand Rapids, MI: Zondervan. p58.
6. Morris, Henry M. (1976). *The Genesis Record*, 10th printing. Grand Rapids, MI: Baker Book House. p40.
7. Ibid. p41.
8. Ibid. p41.
9. Sailhamer, John H. (1996). *Genesis Unbound: A Provocative New Look at the Creation Account*. Sisters, OR: Multnomah Books. p38–40.
10. Eliyah.com (2006). Strong's Concordance – King James Version. Retrieved on May 20, 2006 from http://www.eliyah.com/lexicon.html
11. Ibid.
12. Brown, Francis and S. R. Driver, Charles A. Briggs (1907). *A Hebrew and English Lexicon of the Old Testament*, 1978 printing. Oxford: Oxford Clarendon Press. p912.
13. Eliyah. Strong's Concordance – King James Version.

14. Brenton. *The Septuagint with Apocrypha: Greek and English.*
15. Tyndale, William (1530). *William Tyndale's Five Books of Moses Called the Pentateuch.* (by Jacob Isidor Mombert, 1884, Anson D. F. Randolph & Co. New York). Retrieved on January 18, 2010 from http://wesley.nnu.edu/biblical_studies/tyndale/
16. Coverdale, Myles (1535). Myles Coverdale Bible. Retrieved on May 20, 2008 from http://www.studylight.org/
17. Waltke. *Genesis: A Commentary.* p59.
18. Ibid. p59.
19. Sailhamer. *Genesis Unbound: A Provocative New Look at the Creation Account.* p23.
20. Ibid. p23.
21. Ibid. p23.
22. Morris. *The Genesis Record.* p50.
23. Brenton. *The Septuagint with Apocrypha: Greek and English.*
24. Beall, Todd S. and William A. Banks, Colin Smith (2000). *Old Testament Parsing Guide: Revised and Updated Edition.* Nashville, TN: Broadman & Holman Publishers. p1.
25. Waltke. *Genesis: A Commentary.* p76.
26. van der Merwe. *The Lexham Hebrew-English Interlinear Bible.* Based on a word search of the Hebrew text.
27. Eliyah. Strong's Concordance – King James Version.
28. Ibid.
29. Gesenius, Wilhelm (1846). *Hebrew and Chaldee Lexicon to the Old Testament Scriptures,* 1st ed. (translated by Samuel P. Tregelles) London: Samuel Bagster & Sons. Retrieved on May 20, 2008 from http://www.eliyah.com/lexicon.html
30. Strong, James (1890). *Strong's Exhaustive Concordance of the Bible,* 31st printing. New York: Abingdon Press. p19.
31. Morris. *The Genesis Record.* p55.
32. Ibid. p41.
33. Pratico, *Basics of Biblical Hebrew Grammar.* p111.
34. Ibid. p111.
35. Eliyah. Strong's Concordance – King James Version.
36. Ibid.
37. Brenton. *The Septuagint with Apocrypha: Greek and English.*
38. Beall. *Old Testament Parsing Guide: Revised and Updated Edition.* p1.
39. Eliyah. Strong's Concordance – King James Version.
40. van der Merwe. *The Lexham Hebrew-English Interlinear Bible.* Based on a word search of the Hebrew text.
41. Pietersma, Albert and Benjamin J. Wright (2007). *A New English Translation of the Septuagint.* New York, NY: Oxford University Press. Retrieved on May 20, 2008 from http://ccat.sas.upenn.edu/nets/edition/
42. Beall. *Old Testament Parsing Guide: Revised and Updated Edition.* p1.
43. Eliyah. Strong's Concordance – King James Version.
44. Ibid.
45. Beall. *Old Testament Parsing Guide: Revised and Updated Edition.* p1.
46. Eliyah. Strong's Concordance – King James Version.
47. van der Merwe. *The Lexham Hebrew-English Interlinear Bible.* Based on a word search of the Hebrew text.
48. Eliyah. Strong's Concordance – King James Version.
49. Ibid.
50. Ibid.
51. Ibid.
52. Beall. *Old Testament Parsing Guide: Revised and Updated Edition.* p1.
53. Ibid. p1.
54. Pietersma. *A New English Translation of the Septuagint.*
55. Eliyah. Strong's Concordance – King James Version.

56. Ibid.
57. Pietersma. *A New English Translation of the Septuagint*.
58. Beall. *Old Testament Parsing Guide: Revised and Updated Edition*. p1.
59. Eliyah. Strong's Concordance – King James Version.
60. Ibid.
61. Ibid.
62. Ibid.
63. Ibid.
64. Ibid.
65. Ibid.
66. Ibid.
67. Ibid.
68. Ibid.
69. Pietersma. *A New English Translation of the Septuagint*.
70. Beall. *Old Testament Parsing Guide: Revised and Updated Edition*. p1.
71. van der Merwe. *The Lexham Hebrew-English Interlinear Bible*. Based on a combined search of (חית) and "animal."
72. van der Merwe. *The Lexham Hebrew-English Interlinear Bible*. Based on a word search of the Hebrew text.
73. Beall. *Old Testament Parsing Guide: Revised and Updated Edition*. Occurrences where *ramas* is translated as the verbs "creep" or "move."
74. van der Merwe. *The Lexham Hebrew-English Interlinear Bible*. Based on a word search of the Hebrew text.
75. Eliyah. Strong's Concordance – King James Version.
76. Ibid.
77. Brenton. *The Septuagint with Apocrypha: Greek and English*.
78. Eliyah. Strong's Concordance – King James Version.
79. Ibid.
80. Brenton. *The Septuagint with Apocrypha: Greek and English*.
81. van der Merwe. *The Lexham Hebrew-English Interlinear Bible*. Based on a word search of the Hebrew text.
82. Sarfati, Jonathan (2004). *Refuting Compromise*. Green Forest, AR: Master Books. p71–72.
83. Eliyah. Strong's Concordance – King James Version.
84. Ibid.
85. Ibid.
86. Collins, C. John (2006). *Genesis 1–4: A Linguistic, Literary, and Theological Commentary*. Phillipsburg, NJ: P & R Publishing Co. p137.
87. Ibid. p126.
88. Eliyah. Strong's Concordance – King James Version.
89. Ibid.
90. Ibid.
91. Pietersma. *A New English Translation of the Septuagint*.
92. Eliyah. Strong's Concordance – King James Version.
93. Ibid.
94. van der Merwe. *The Lexham Hebrew-English Interlinear Bible*. Based on a word search of the Hebrew text.
95. Young, Robert (1898). Holy Bible, Young's Literal Translation, 3rd ed. Retrieved on May 20, 2008 from http://www.blueletterBible.org/
96. Brown. *A Hebrew and English Lexicon of the Old Testament*. p617.
97. Ross, Allen P. (1988). *Creation and Blessing: A Guide to the Study and Exposition of the Book of Genesis*. Grand Rapids, MI: Baker Book House. p126.
98. Henry, Matthew (1706). *Matthew Henry's Commentary on the Whole Bible*, vol. 1. Fleming H. Revell Company. p20.

99. van der Merwe. *The Lexham Hebrew-English Interlinear Bible*. Based on a word search of the Hebrew text.

Chapter 7 – A New Paradigm of Biblical Origins

1. *The New Encyclopedia Britannica*, 15th ed., vol. 19 (2005). Geochronology. Chicago, IL: Encyclopedia Britannica Inc. pp773–774.
2. *The New Encyclopedia Britannica*, 15th ed., vol. 25 (2005). Oceans. Chicago, IL: Encyclopedia Britannica Inc. p140.
3. *The New Encyclopedia Britannica*, pp773–774.
4. Friedman, Harold L. (2007). Water. *McGraw-Hill Encyclopedia of Science and Technology*, 10th ed., vol. 19. New York, NY: McGraw-Hill Inc. p404.
5. Dean, John A. (1999). Water, Critical Properties. *Lange's Handbook of Chemistry*, 15th ed. New York, NY: McGraw-Hill Inc. p6.185.
6. Torrens, Hugh (1992, April 4). When did the dinosaur get its name? *New Scientist*: 40–44.
7. Ham, Ken, ed. (2006). *The New Answers Book*. Green Forest, AR: Master Books. p48.
8. Sarfati, Jonathan (2004). *Refuting Compromise*. Green Forest, AR: Master Books. p195.
9. Morris, Henry (1976). *The Genesis Record*. Grand Rapids, MI: Baker Book House. pp118–126.
10. Ham. *The New Answers Book*. pp204–205.
11. Morris. *The Genesis Record*. p118.
12. Sarfati. *Refuting Compromise*. p205, 211.
13. Ibid. p195.
14. Collins, C. John (2006). *Genesis 1–4: A Linguistic, Literary, and Theological Commentary*. Phillipsburg, NJ: P & R Publishing Co. p183.
15. Sarfati. *Refuting Compromise*. p212.
16. Snoke, David (2004, June). Why were Dangerous Animals Created? *Perspectives on Science and Christian Faith*, vol. 56, no. 2, p125.
17. Barna, George (Jan. 1999). OmniPoll. Ventura, CA: Barna Research Group
18. Castell, Alburey and Donald M. Borchert, Arthur Zucker (1994). *An Introduction to Modern Philosophy: Examining the Human Condition*, 6th ed. Englewood Cliffs, NJ: Macmillian College Publishing Company. p247.
19. Ibid. p564
20. Kushner, Harold S. (1989). *When Bad Things Happen to Good People*. New York, NY: Shocken Books. p16.
21. Ibid. p46.
22. Ibid. p58.
23. Ibid. p79.
24. Ibid. pp116–117.
25. Bridges, Jerry (1988). *Trusting God: Even When Life Hurts*. Colorado Springs, CO: Navpress. p25.
26. Ibid. p28.
27. Ibid. p38.
28. Ibid. pp29–31.
29. Ibid. p122.
30. Ibid. p125.
31. Boyd, Gregory A. (2003). *Is God to Blame? Beyond Pat Answers to the Problem of Suffering*. Downers Grove, IL: InterVarsity Press. p56.
32. Ibid. p16.
33. Ibid. p42.
34. Ibid. p113.
35. Ibid. pp115–121.
36. Ibid. p121.
37. Simons, Lewis M. (2006, January). Genocide and the Science of Proof, *National Geographic*.

38. National Academy of Sciences, Steering Committee on Science and Creationism (1999). *Science and Creationism: A View from the National Academy of Sciences*, 2nd ed. Washington, DC: National Academy Press. p6.

Appendix B – The Ten Key Verbs of Genesis Chapter One

1. Pratico, Gary D. and Miles V. Van Pelt (2001). *Basics of Biblical Hebrew Grammar*. Grand Rapids, MI: Zondervan. p137.
2. Dobson, John H. (2005). *Learn Biblical Hebrew*, 2nd ed. Grand Rapids, MI: Baker Publishing Group. pp339, 354–355.
3. Harrison, R. K. (1955). *Biblical Hebrew*. Berkshire, England: Cox & Wyman Ltd. pp158–161.
4. Brenton, Lancelot C. L., trans. (1851). *The Septuagint with Apocrypha: Greek and English*. London: Samuel Bagster & Sons. Retrieved on May 20, 2008 from http://www.ccel.org/bible/brenton/
5. Pietersma, Albert and Benjamin J. Wright (2007). *A New English Translation of the Septuagint*. New York, NY: Oxford University Press. Retrieved on May 20, 2008 from http://ccat.sas.upenn.edu/nets/edition/
6. Dobson. *Learn Biblical Hebrew*. p334.
7. Beall, Todd S. and William A. Banks, Colin Smith (2000). *Old Testament Parsing Guide*, Revised and Updated Edition. Nashville, TN: Broadman & Holman Publishers. p1.
8. *American Heritage College Dictionary*, 4th ed. (2004). Boston, MA: Houghton Mifflin Company. p753.
9. Kautzsch, E. (1909). *Gesenius' Hebrew Grammar*, 2nd ed. (translated by A. E. Cowley from the 28th German edition) Oxford: Clarendon Press. p129.
10. Harrison. *Biblical Hebrew*. p81.
11. Ibid. p81.
12. Pratico. *Basics of Biblical Hebrew Grammar*. p130.
13. Dobson. *Learn Biblical Hebrew*. p334.
14. Eliyah.com (2006). Strong's Concordance – King James Version. Retrieved on May 20, 2006 from http://www.eliyah.com/lexicon.html
15. Ibid.
16. van der Merwe, Christo, ed. (2004). *The Lexham Hebrew-English Interlinear Bible*. (translated by the University of Stellenbosch, Stellenbosch, South Africa) Bellingham, WA: Logos Research Systems Inc.
17. Eliyah. Strong's Concordance – King James Version.
18. van der Merwe. *The Lexham Hebrew-English Interlinear Bible*. Based on a word search of the Hebrew text.
19. *American Heritage College Dictionary*. p753.
20. Kautzsch. *Gesenius' Hebrew Grammar*. p129.
21. Ibid. p131.
22. Ibid. p131.
23. Harrison. *Biblical Hebrew*. p81.
24. Ibid. p81.
25. Pratico. *Basics of Biblical Hebrew Grammar*. p130.
26. Ibid. p130.
27. Dobson. *Learn Biblical Hebrew*. p338.
28. Ibid. p123.
29. Ibid. p213.

Index

CPSIA information can be obtained at www.ICGtesting.com
Printed in the USA
LVOW070146170413

329500LV00001B/1/P

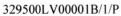

9 781467 568708